Penguin Education

Economics of Education 1

Edited by M. Blaug

Penguin Modern Economics Readings

General Editor

B. J. McCormick

Advisory Board

K. J. W. Alexander
R. W. Clower
G. R. Fisher
P. Robson
J. Spraos
H. Townsend

Economics of Education 1

Selected Readings

Edited by M. Blaug

Penguin Books

Penguin Books Ltd, Harmondsworth,
Middlesex, England
Penguin Books Inc., 7110 Ambassador Road,
Baltimore, Maryland 21207, U.S.A.
Penguin Books Australia Ltd,
Ringwood, Victoria, Australia

First published 1968
Reprinted 1971
This selection copyright © M. Blaug, 1968
Introduction and notes copyright © M. Blaug, 1968

Made and printed in Great Britain by
Richard Clay (The Chaucer Press) Ltd,
Bungay, Suffolk
Set in Monotype Times

Contents

Introduction

Ten years ago there was hardly such a subject as the economics of education. Today it is one of the most rapidly growing branches of economics. Together with health economics, it makes up the core of the economics of human resources, a field of inquiry which in the last few years has been silently revolutionizing such traditional subjects as growth economics, labour economics, international trade, and public finance. Ten years ago, economists made no apologies for talking about aggregate production functions and international factor endowments in terms of homogeneous units of labour and capital, for concentrating on current wages and salaries in their studies of the operations of a labour market, rather than expectations of lifetime earnings, and for confining their discussions of educational planning to sources and methods of finance. Today, all that would be regarded as rather old-fashioned. It is now realized that improvements in the quality of the labour force can have dramatic effects on economic growth; that labour market adjustments involve changing hiring standards and promotions within jobs and not merely variations in hourly wage rates and starting salaries; and that the planned expansion of collectively provided education should be related to specific economic targets and objectives. In short, the economics of education with its concept of human investment has rapidly transformed large areas of orthodox economics, to emerge in the 1960s as a full-blown discipline in its own right.

The sort of questions that are asked in the economic analysis of education are: how much should a country spend on education and how should the expenditure be financed? Is education mainly 'investment' or mainly 'consumption'? If investment, how large is its yield compared to other forms of investment in people and material equipment? If consumption, what are the determinants of the private demand for more or better education? What is the optimum combination of pupils' time, teachers, buildings, and equipment embodied in schooling? What is the optimum structure of 'the educational pyramid', that is, the number in the

7

different levels and channels of the educational system? What is the optimum mix of formal education within schools and colleges, and informal education outside them? Lastly, what contribution does education make to the overall development of human resources and how far can we accelerate economic growth, particularly in low-income countries, by controlling the expansion of educational systems? Consideration of questions such as these shows that the subject falls rather neatly into two classes: analyses of the economic value of education, on the one hand, and analyses of the economic aspects of educational systems, on the other. The first is concerned with the impact of schooling on labour productivity, occupational mobility, and the distribution of income. The second deals with the internal efficiency of schools and with the relations between the costs of education and methods of financing these costs.

This book of readings is almost solely confined to the first range of problems. The neglect of the second is only justified by lack of space; there is no suggestion that it is less important but simply that adequate coverage of it would require another volume. Much of the fascination of the economics of education derives from the peculiarities of education when it is conceived as an industry absorbing material and human resources like any other: in most countries, the whole of this industry is collectively provided and financed; although the inputs of the industry are typically bought in the market place, the output is not sold, at least directly; the production-cycle of the industry is longer than that of most other industries and it consumes a relatively large fraction of its own output; it is not engaged in profit-maximizing activity and, indeed, it is not self-evident that it is maximizing anything at all. All of these peculiarities make it difficult to appraise the efficiency with which resources are allocated in the education industry and raise the question whether the traditional apparatus of economists is, in fact, applicable to the operations of schools and colleges. Nevertheless, as the Further Reading list at the end of this volume shows, economists have made valuable contributions to the study of educational productivity. These contributions, however, are only hinted at in this book of readings.

We have not finished listing the peculiar characteristics of education as an economic activity: its chief function is to diffuse the existing stock of knowledge but it also serves to increase that stock; it both preserves and disseminates social values, sometimes fostering and sometimes impeding social mobility; its economic effects are so thoroughly intertwined with its cultural and political consequences that any notion of separating them can be made to seem absurd. For all these reasons, the economics of education shades almost imperceptibly into the sociology of education and into the general areas of psychology and political science. Again, there is little in the book about this no-man's land between the traditional disciplines of social science, although the readings in the concluding section on educational planning in low-income countries touch on some of these interdisciplinary issues.

Having said what is not in the book, it is time to summarize the material that is included. The readings, most of which are printed in full as originally published, survey the various methods that have been employed in recent years to evaluate the contribution of education to economic growth, with particular emphasis on what has sometimes been called 'the manpower-forecasting approach' and 'the rate-of-return approach'. They give the case for and against 'the human investment revolution in economic thought' and illustrate the application of the new thinking to the much-discussed question of labour training in industry. There is a full treatment of the problems in educational planning in both developed and developing countries and considerable attention is given in the last three or four readings to the difficulty of combining economic with specific social and political objectives for education. No book of readings in a fast-growing subject such as this one can do more than introduce the reader to the subject-matter of the discipline. A second volume of readings will cover some of the topics neglected in this one: productivity *in* rather than the productivity *of* schools and colleges; the use of mathematical models of the educational system; the finance of education and the budgetary implications of educational expansion; the particular problems of educational planning in low-income countries, and the like. There can be no doubt, however, that the average reader will be aware at the end of this first admittedly limited collection of readings why the economics of education has generated so much interest in recent years.

Part One The Concept of Human Capital

Rarely is it possible to trace the take-off point of a new subject or a new branch of an old subject to a particular book, much less to a particular article. The 'birth' of the economics of education, however, can be clearly dated from the presidential address of Theodore W. Schultz, Professor of Economics at the University of Chicago and a long-distinguished authority on agricultural economics, to the Annual Meeting of the American Economic Association in December 1960. This is not to say that nobody published in this field or even that nobody used the label 'economics of education' before 1960, but simply that most economists before 1960 were not aware of the fact that widely different observed economic phenomena could be rendered intelligible by the idea of human capital formation. The result was a sudden acceleration of research in this area and a sudden proliferation of publications concerned with the economic value of education – is this not what we mean by a 'take-off'?

Schultz's argument is restated with particular reference to the problems of development in poor countries by Harry G. Johnson, Professor of Economics at the London School of Economics. His essay provides a telling illustration of the new vistas opened up by the concept of human investment.

H. G. Shaffer, Associate Professor of Economics at the University of Kansas, vigorously restates the older Marshallian view that 'human capital' is a metaphor without substantive economic meaning. His brief essay is a veritable compendium of all the objections that have since been advanced against the idea that education as a form of investment can be usefully distinguished from education as a form of consumption. (See also Balogh and Streeten, 18.) In reply, Schultz upholds Irving Fisher's view that the absence of a capital market for human labour does not preclude examination of the services of human investment 'as if' they were capitalized and shows that valuable insights result from such a treatment. (See also Blaug, 11.)

1 T. W. Schultz

Investment in Human Capital

T. W. Schultz, 'Investment in human capital', *American Economic Review*, vol. 51, (1961), pp. 1–17.

Although it is obvious that people acquire useful skills and knowledge, it is not obvious that these skills and knowledge are a form of capital, that this capital is in substantial part a product of deliberate investment, that it has grown in Western societies at a much faster rate than conventional (nonhuman) capital, and that its growth may well be the most distinctive feature of the economic system. It has been widely observed that increases in national output have been large compared with the increases of land, man-hours, and physical reproducible capital. Investment in human capital is probably the major explanation for this difference.

Much of what we call consumption constitutes investment in human capital. Direct expenditures on education, health, and internal migration to take advantage of better job opportunities are clear examples. Earnings foregone by mature students attending school and by workers acquiring on-the-job training are equally clear examples. Yet nowhere do these enter into our national accounts. The use of leisure time to improve skills and knowledge is widespread and it too is unrecorded. In these and similar ways the *quality* of human effort can be greatly improved and its productivity enhanced. I shall contend that such investment in human capital accounts for most of the impressive rise in the real earnings per worker.

I shall comment, first, on the reasons why economists have shied away from the explicit analysis of investment in human capital, and then, on the capacity of such investment to explain many a puzzle about economic growth. Mainly, however, I shall concentrate on the scope and substance of human capital and its formation. In closing I shall consider some social and policy implications.

The Concept of Human Capital

I. Shying Away from Investment in Man

Economists have long known that people are an important part of the wealth of nations. Measured by what labor contributes to output, the productive capacity of human beings is now vastly larger than all other forms of wealth taken together. What economists have not stressed is the simple truth that people invest in themselves and that these investments are very large. Although economists are seldom timid in entering on abstract analysis and are often proud of being impractical, they have not been bold in coming to grips with this form of investment. Whenever they come even close, they proceed gingerly as if they were stepping into deep water. No doubt there are reasons for being wary. Deep-seated moral and philosophical issues are ever present. Free men are first and foremost the end to be served by economic endeavor; they are not property or marketable assets. And not least, it has been all too convenient in marginal productivity analysis to treat labor as if it were a unique bundle of innate abilities that are wholly free of capital.

The mere thought of investment in human beings is offensive to some among us.[1] Our values and beliefs inhibit us from looking upon human beings as capital goods, except in slavery, and this we abhor. We are not unaffected by the long struggle to rid society of indentured service and to evolve political and legal institutions to keep men free from bondage. These are achievements that we prize highly. Hence, to treat human beings as wealth that can be augmented by investment runs counter to deeply held values. It seems to reduce man once again to a mere material component, to something akin to property. And for man to look upon himself as a capital good, even if it did not impair his freedom, may seem to debase him. No less a person than J. S. Mill at one time insisted that the people of a country should not be looked upon as wealth because wealth existed only for the sake of people [15]. But surely Mill was wrong; there is nothing in the concept of human wealth contrary to his idea that it exists only for the advantage of people. By investing in themselves, people can enlarge the range of choice available to them. It is one way free men can enhance their welfare.

1. This paragraph draws on the introduction to my Teller Lecture [16].

Among the few who have looked upon human beings as capital, there are three distinguished names. The philosopher-economist Adam Smith boldly included all of the acquired and useful abilities of all of the inhabitants of a country as a part of capital. So did H. von Thünen, who then went on to argue that the concept of capital applied to man did not degrade him or impair his freedom and dignity, but on the contrary that the failure to apply the concept was especially pernicious in wars; '. . . for here . . . one will sacrifice in a battle a hundred human beings in the prime of their lives without a thought in order to save one gun'. The reason is that, '. . . the purchase of a cannon causes an outlay of public funds, whereas human beings are to be had for nothing by means of a mere conscription decree' [20]. Irving Fisher also clearly and cogently presented an all-inclusive concept of capital [6]. Yet the main stream of thought has held that it is neither appropriate nor practical to apply the concept of capital to human beings. Marshall [11], whose great prestige goes far to explain why this view was accepted, held that while human beings are incontestably capital from an abstract and mathematical point of view, it would be out of touch with the market place to treat them as capital in practical analyses. Investment in human beings has accordingly seldom been incorporated in the formal core of economics, even though many economists, including Marshall, have seen its relevance at one point or another in what they have written.

The failure to treat human resources explicitly as a form of capital, as a produced means of production, as the product of investment, has fostered the retention of the classical notion of labor as a capacity to do manual work requiring little knowledge and skill, a capacity with which, according to this notion, laborers are endowed about equally. This notion of labor was wrong in the classical period and it is patently wrong now. Counting individuals who can and want to work and treating such a count as a measure of the quantity of an economic factor is no more meaningful than it would be to count the number of all manner of machines to determine their economic importance either as a stock of capital or as a flow of productive services.

Laborers have become capitalists not from a diffusion of the ownership of corporation stocks, as folklore would have it, but

15

from the acquisition of knowledge and skill that have economic value [9]. This knowledge and skill are in great part the product of investment and, combined with other human investment, predominantly account for the productive superiority of the technically advanced countries. To omit them in studying economic growth is like trying to explain Soviet ideology without Marx.

II. Economic Growth from Human Capital

Many paradoxes and puzzles about our dynamic, growing economy can be resolved once human investment is taken into account. Let me begin by sketching some that are minor though not trivial.

When farm people take nonfarm jobs they earn substantially less than industrial workers of the same race, age, and sex. Similarly non-white urban males earn much less than white males after allowance is made for the effects of differences in unemployment, age, city size, and region [21]. Because these differentials in earnings correspond closely to corresponding differentials in education, they strongly suggest that the one is a consequence of the other. Negroes who operate farms, whether as tenants or as owners, earn much less than whites on comparable farms.[2] Fortunately, crops and livestock are not vulnerable to the blight of discrimination. The large differences in earnings seem rather to reflect mainly the differences in health and education. Workers in the South on the average earn appreciably less than in the North or West and they also have on the average less education. Most migratory farm workers earn very little indeed by comparison with other workers. Many of them have virtually no schooling, are in poor health, are unskilled, and have little ability to do useful work. To urge that the differences in the amount of human investment may explain these differences in earnings seems elementary. Of more recent vintage are observations showing younger workers at a competitive advantage; for example, young men entering the labor force are said to have an advantage over unemployed older workers in obtaining satisfactory jobs. Most of these young people possess twelve years of school, most of the

2. Based on unpublished preliminary results obtained by Joseph Willett in his Ph.D. research at the University of Chicago.

older workers six years or less. The observed advantage of these younger workers may therefore result not from inflexibilities in social security or in retirement programs, or from sociological preference of employers, but from real differences in productivity connected with one form of human investment, i.e. education. And yet another example, the curve relating income to age tends to be steeper for skilled than for unskilled persons. Investment in on-the-job training seems a likely explanation, as I shall note later.

Economic growth requires much internal migration of workers to adjust to changing job opportunities [10]. Young men and women move more readily than older workers. Surely this makes economic sense when one recognizes that the costs of such migration are a form of human investment. Young people have more years head of them than older workers during which they can realize on such an investment. Hence it takes less of a wage differential to make it economically advantageous for them to move, or, to put it differently, young people can expect a higher return on their investment in migration than older people. This differential may explain selective migration without requiring an appeal to sociological differences between young and old people.

The examples so far given are for investment in human beings that yield a return over a long period. This is true equally of investment in education, training, and migration of young people. Not all investments in human beings are of this kind; some are more nearly akin to current inputs as for example expenditures on food and shelter in some countries where work is mainly the application of brute human force, calling for energy and stamina, and where the intake of food is far from enough to do a full day's work. On the 'hungry' steppes and in the teeming valleys of Asia, millions of adult males have so meager a diet that they cannot do more than a few hours of hard work. To call them underemployed does not seem pertinent. Under such circumstances it is certainly meaningful to treat food partly as consumption and partly as a current 'producer good', as some Indian economists have done [3]. Let us not forget that Western economists during the early decades of industrialization and even in the time of Marshall and Pigou often connected additional food for workers with increases in labor productivity.

17

Let me now pass on to three major perplexing questions closely connected with the riddle of economic growth. First, consider the long-period behavior of the capital–income ratio. We were taught that a country which amassed more reproducible capital relative to its land and labor would employ such capital in greater 'depth' because of its growing abundance and cheapness. But apparently this is not what happens. On the contrary, the estimates now available show that less of such capital tends to be employed relative to income as economic growth proceeds. Are we to infer that the ratio of capital to income has no relevance in explaining either poverty or opulence? Or that a rise of this ratio is not a prerequisite to economic growth? These questions raise fundamental issues bearing on motives and preferences for holding wealth as well as on the motives for particular investments and the stock of capital thereby accumulated. For my purpose all that needs to be said is that these estimates of capital–income ratios refer to only a part of all capital. They exclude in particular, and most unfortunately, any human capital. Yet human capital has surely been increasing at a rate substantially greater than reproducible (nonhuman) capital. We cannot, therefore, infer from these estimates that the stock of *all* capital has been decreasing relative to income. On the contrary, if we accept the not implausible assumption that the motives and preferences of people, the technical opportunities open to them, and the uncertainty associated with economic growth during particular periods were leading people to maintain roughly a constant ratio between *all* capital and income, the decline in the estimated capital–income ratio[3] is simply a signal that human capital has been increasing relatively not only to conventional capital but also to income.

The bumper crop of estimates that show national income increasing faster than national resources raises a second and not unrelated puzzle. The income of the United States has been increasing at a much higher rate than the combined amount of

3. I leave aside here the difficulties inherent in identifying and measuring both the nonhuman capital and the income entering into estimates of this ratio. There are index number and aggregation problems aplenty, and not all improvements in the quality of this capital have been accounted for, as I shall note later.

land, man-hours worked, and the stock of reproducible capital used to produce the income. Moreover, the discrepancy between the two rates has become larger from one business cycle to the next during recent decades [5]. To call this discrepancy a measure of 'resource productivity' gives a name to our ignorance but does not dispel it. If we accept these estimates, the connections between national resources and national income have become loose and tenuous over time. Unless this discrepancy can be resolved, received theory of production applied to inputs and outputs as currently measured is a toy and not a tool for studying economic growth.

Two sets of forces probably account for the discrepancy, if we neglect entirely the index number and aggregation problems that bedevil all estimates of such global aggregates as total output and total input. One is returns to scale; the second, the large improvements in the quality of inputs that have occurred but have been omitted from the input estimates. Our economy has undoubtedly been experiencing increasing returns to scale at some points offset by decreasing returns at others. If we can succeed in identifying and measuring the net gains, they may turn out to have been substantial. The improvements in the quality of inputs that have not been adequately allowed for are no doubt partly in material (nonhuman) capital. My own conception, however, is that both this defect and the omission of economies of scale are minor sources of discrepancy between the rates of growth of inputs and outputs compared to the improvements in human capacity that have been omitted.

A small step takes us from these two puzzles raised by existing estimates to a third which brings us to the heart of the matter, namely the essentially unexplained large increase in real earnings of workers. Can this be a windfall? Or a quasirent pending the adjustment in the supply of labor? Or, a pure rent reflecting the fixed amount of labor? It seems far more reasonable that it represents rather a return to the investment that has been made in human beings. The observed growth in productivity per unit of labor is simply a consequence of holding the unit of labor constant over time although in fact this unit of labor has been increasing as a result of a steadily growing amount of human capital per worker. As I read our record, the human capital component has become very large as a consequence of human investment.

Another aspect of the same basic question, which admits of the same resolution, is the rapid postwar recovery of countries that had suffered severe destruction of plant and equipment during the war. The toll from bombing was all too visible in the factories laid flat, the railroad yards, bridges, and harbors wrecked, and the cities in ruin. Structures, equipment, and inventories were all heaps of rubble. Not so visible, yet large, was the toll from the wartime depletion of the physical plant that escaped destruction by bombs. Economists were called upon to assess the implications of these wartime losses for recovery. In retrospect, it is clear that they overestimated the prospective retarding effects of these losses. Having had a small hand in this effort, I have had a special reason for looking back and wondering why the judgment that we formed soon after the war proved to be so far from the mark. The explanation that now is clear is that we gave altogether too much weight to nonhuman capital in making these assessments. We fell into this error, I am convinced, because we did not have a concept of *all* capital and, therefore, failed to take account of human capital and the important part that it plays in production in a modern economy.

Let me close this section with a comment on poor countries, for which there are virtually no solid estimates. I have been impressed by repeatedly expressed judgments, especially by those who have a responsibility in making capital available to poor countries, about the low rate at which these countries can absorb additional capital. New capital from outside can be put to good use, it is said, only when it is added 'slowly and gradually'. But this experience is at variance with the widely held impression that countries are poor fundamentally because they are starved for capital and that additional capital is truly the key to their more rapid economic growth. The reconciliation is again, I believe, to be found in emphasis on particular forms of capital. The new capital available to these countries from outside as a rule goes into the formation of structures, equipment, and sometimes also into inventories. But it is generally not available for additional investment in man. Consequently, human capabilities do not stay abreast of physical capital, and they do become limiting factors in economic growth. It should come as no surprise, therefore, that the absorption rate of capital to augment only particular non-human resources is necessarily low. The Horvat [8] formulation of the optimum rate of investment which treats knowledge and skill as a critical investment variable in determining the rate of economic growth is both relevant and important.

III. Scope and Substance of These Investments

What are human investments? Can they be distinguished from consumption? Is it at all feasible to identify and measure them? What do they contribute to income? Granted that they seem amorphous compared to brick and mortar, and hard to get at compared to the investment accounts of corporations, they assuredly are not a fragment; they are rather like the contents of Pandora's box, full of difficulties and hope.

Human resources obviously have both quantitative and qualitative dimensions. The number of people, the proportion who enter upon useful work, and hours worked are essentially quantitative characteristics. To make my task tolerably manageable, I shall neglect these and consider only such quality components as skill, knowledge, and similar attributes that affect particular human capabilities to do productive work. In so far as expenditures to enhance such capabilities also increase the value productivity of human effort (labor), they will yield a positive rate of return.[4]

How can we estimate the magnitude of human investment? The practice followed in connection with physical capital goods is to estimate the magnitude of capital formation by expenditures made to produce the capital goods. This practice would suffice also for the formation of human capital. However, for human capital there is an additional problem that is less pressing for physical capital goods; how to distinguish between expenditures for consumption and for investment. This distinction bristles with both conceptual and practical difficulties. We can think of

4. Even so, our *observed* return can be either negative, zero, or positive because our observations are drawn from a world where there is uncertainty and imperfect knowledge and where there are windfall gains and losses and mistakes aplenty.

three classes of expenditures: expenditures that satisfy consumer preferences and in no way enhance the capabilities under discussion – these represent pure consumption; expenditures that enhance capabilities and do not satisfy any preferences underlying consumption – these represent pure investment; and expenditures that have both effects. Most relevant activities clearly are in the third class, partly consumption and partly investment, which is why the task of identifying each component is so formidable and why the measurement of capital formation by expenditures is less useful for human investment than for investment in physical goods. In principle there is an alternative method for estimating human investment, namely by its yield rather than by its cost. While any capability produced by human investment becomes a part of the human agent and hence cannot be sold, it is nevertheless 'in touch with the market place' by affecting the wages and salaries the human agent can earn. The resulting increase in earnings is the yield on the investment.[5]

Despite the difficulty of exact measurement at this stage of our understanding of human investment, many insights can be gained by examining some of the more important activities that improve human capabilities. I shall concentrate on five major categories: (1) health facilities and services, broadly conceived to include all expenditures that affect the life expectancy, strength and stamina, and the vigor and vitality of a people; (2) on-the-job training, including old-style apprenticeship organized by firms; (3) formally organized education at the elementary, secondary, and higher levels; (4) study programs for adults that are not organized by firms, including extension programs notably in agriculture; (5) migration of individuals and families to adjust to changing job opportunities. Except for education, not much is known about these activities that is germane here. I shall refrain from commenting on study programs for adults, although in agriculture the extension services of the several states play an important role in transmitting new knowledge and in developing skills of farmers [17]. Nor shall I elaborate further on internal migration related to economic growth.

5. In principle, the value of the investment can be determined by discounting the additional future earnings it yields just as the value of a physical capital good can be determined by discounting its income stream.

Health activities have both quantity and quality implications. Such speculations as economists have engaged in about the effects of improvements in health,[6] has been predominantly in connection with population growth, which is to say with quantity. But surely health measures also enhance the quality of human resources. So also may additional food and better shelter, especially in underdeveloped countries.

The change in the role of food as people become richer sheds light on one of the conceptual problems already referred to. I have pointed out that extra food in some poor countries has the attribute of a 'producer good'. This attribute of food, however, diminishes as the consumption of food rises, and there comes a point at which any further increase in food becomes pure consumption.[7] Clothing, housing, and perhaps medical services may be similar.

My comment about on-the-job training will consist of a conjecture on the amount of such training, a note on the decline of apprenticeship, and then a useful economic theorem on who bears the costs of such training. Surprisingly little is known about on-the-job training in modern industry. About all that can be said is that the expansion of education has not eliminated it. It seems likely, however, that some of the training formerly undertaken by firms has been discontinued and other training programs have been instituted to adjust both to the rise in the education of workers and to changes in the demands for new skills. The amount invested annually in such training can only be a guess. H. F. Clark places it near to the amount spent on formal education.[8] Even if it were only one-half as large, it would represent currently an annual gross investment of about $15 billion.

6. Health economics is in its infancy; there are two medical journals with 'economics' in their titles, two bureaus for economic research in private associations (one in the American Medical and the other in the American Dental Association), and not a few studies and papers by outside scholars. Selma Mushkin's survey is very useful with its pertinent economic insights though she may have underestimated somewhat the influence of the economic behavior of people in striving for health [14].

7. For instance, the income elasticity of the demand for food continues to be positive even after the point is reached where additional food no longer has the attribute of a 'producer good'.

8. Based on comments made by Harold F. Clark at the Merrill Center for Economics, summer 1959; also, see [4].

Elsewhere, too, it is thought to be important. For example, some observers have been impressed by the amount of such training under way in plants in the Soviet Union.[9] Meanwhile, apprenticeship has all but disappeared, partly because it is now inefficient and partly because schools now perform many of its functions. Its disappearance has been hastened no doubt by the difficulty of enforcing apprenticeship agreements. Legally they have come to smack of indentured service. The underlying economic factors and behavior are clear enough. The apprentice is prepared to serve during the initial period when his productivity is less than the cost of his keep and of his training. Later, however, unless he is legally restrained, he will seek other employment when his productivity begins to exceed the cost of keep and training, which is the period during which a master would expect to recoup on his earlier outlay.

To study on-the-job training Gary Becker [1] advances the theorem that in competitive markets employees pay all the costs of their training and none of these costs are ultimately borne by the firm.[10] Becker points out several implications. The notion that expenditures on training by a firm generate external economies for other firms is not consistent with this theorem. The theorem also indicates one force favoring the transfer from on-the-job training to attending school. Since on-the-job training reduces the net earnings of workers at the beginning and raises them later on, this theorem also provides an explanation for the 'steeper slope of the curve relating income to age', for skilled than unskilled workers, referred to earlier.[11] What all this adds up to is that the stage is set to undertake meaningful economic studies of on-the-job training.

Happily we reach firmer ground in regard to education. Investment in education has risen at a rapid rate and by itself may well account for a substantial part of the otherwise unexplained rise in earnings. I shall do no more than summarize some

9. Based on observations made by a team of U.S. economists of which I was a member, see *Saturday Rev.*, 21 January 1961.

10. [See Reading 9.]

11. Becker has also noted still another implication arising out of the fact that the income and capital investment aspects of on-the-job training are tied together, which gives rise to 'permanent' and 'transitory' income effects that may have substantial explanatory value.

preliminary results about the total costs of education including income foregone by students, the apparent relation of these costs to consumer income and to alternative investments, the rise of the stock of education in the labor force, returns to education, and the contribution that the increase in the stock of education may have made to earnings and to national income.

It is not difficult to estimate the conventional costs of education consisting of the costs of the services of teachers, librarians, administrators, of maintaining and operating the educational plant, and interest on the capital embodied in the educational plant. It is far more difficult to estimate another component of total cost, the income foregone by students. Yet this component should be included and it is far from negligible. In the United States, for example, well over half of the costs of higher education consists of income foregone by students. As early as 1900, this income foregone accounted for about one-fourth of the total costs of elementary, secondary, and higher education. By 1956, it represented over two-fifths of all costs. The rising significance of foregone income has been a major factor in the marked upward trend in the total real costs of education which, measured in current prices, increased from $400 million in 1900 to $28·7 billion in 1956 [18]. The percentage rise in educational costs was about three and a half times as large as in consumer income, which would imply a high income elasticity of the demand for education, if education were regarded as pure consumption.[12] Educational costs also rose about three and a half times as rapidly as did the gross formation of physical capital in dollars. If we were to treat education as pure investment this result would suggest that the returns to education were relatively more attractive than those to nonhuman capital.[13]

Much schooling is acquired by persons who are not treated as income earners in most economic analysis, particularly, of course, women. To analyze the effect of growth in schooling on earnings,

12. Had other things stayed constant this suggests an income elasticity of 3·5. Among the things that did change, the prices of educational services rose relative to other consumer prices, perhaps offset in part by improvements in the quality of educational services.

13. This of course assumes among other things that the relationship between gross and net have not changed or have changed in the same proportion. Estimates are from my essay, 'Education and economic growth' [19].

it is therefore necessary to distinguish between the stock of education in the population and the amount in the labor force. Years of school completed are far from satisfactory as a measure because of the marked increases that have taken place in the number of days of school attendance of enrolled students and because much more of the education of workers consists of high school and higher education than formerly. My preliminary estimates suggest that the stock of education in the labor force rose about eight and a half times between 1900 and 1956, whereas the stock of reproducible capital rose four and a half times, both in 1956 prices. These estimates are, of course, subject to many qualifications.[14] Nevertheless, both the magnitude and the rate of increase of this form of human capital have been such that they could be an important key to the riddle of economic growth.[15]

The exciting work under way is on the return to education. In spite of the flood of high school and college graduates, the return has not become trivial. Even the lower limits of the estimates show that the return to such education has been in the neighborhood of the return to nonhuman capital. This is what most of these estimates show when they treat as costs all of the public and private expenditures on education and also the income foregone while attending school, and when they treat all of these costs as investment, allocating none to consumption.[16] But surely a part

14. From [19, sec. 4]. These estimates of the stock of education are tentative and incomplete. They are incomplete in that they do not take into account fully the increases in the average life of this form of human capital arising out of the fact that relatively more of this education is held by younger people in the labor force than was true in earlier years; and, they are incomplete because no adjustment has been made for the improvements in education over time, increasing the quality of a year of school in ways other than those related to changes in the proportions represented by elementary, high school and higher education. Even so the stock of this form of human capital rose 8·5 times between 1900 and 1956 while the stock of reproducible nonhuman capital increased only 4·5 times, both in constant 1956 prices.

15. In value terms this stock of education was only 22 per cent as large as the stock of reproducible physical capital in 1900, whereas in 1956 it already had become 42 per cent as large.

16. Several comments are called for here. (1) The return to high school education appears to have declined substantially between the late thirties and early fifties and since then has leveled off, perhaps even risen somewhat, indicating a rate of return toward the end of the fifties about as high as that to higher education. (2) The return to college education seems to have risen

of these costs is consumption in the sense that education creates a form of consumer capital[17] which has the attribute of improving the taste and the quality of consumption of students throughout the rest of their lives. If one were to allocate a substantial fraction of the total costs of this education to consumption, say one-half, this would, of course, double the observed rate of return to what would then become the investment component in education that enhances the productivity of man.

Fortunately, the problem of allocating the costs of education in the labor force between consumption and investment does not arise to plague us when we turn to the contribution that education makes to earnings and to national income because a change in allocation only alters the rate of return, not the total return. I noted at the outset that the unexplained increases in U.S. national income have been especially large in recent decades. On one set of assumptions, the unexplained part amounts to nearly

---

somewhat since the late thirties in spite of the rapid influx of college-trained individuals into the labor force. (3) Becker's estimates based on the difference in income between high school and college graduates based on urban males adjusted for ability, race, unemployment and mortality show a return of 9 per cent to total college costs including both earnings foregone and conventional college costs, public and private and with none of these costs allocated to consumption (see his paper given at the American Economic Association meeting, December 1959 [2]). (4) The returns to this education in the case of nonwhite urban males, of rural males, and of females in the labor force may have been somewhat lower (see Becker [2]). (5) My own estimates, admittedly less complete than those of Becker and thus subject to additional qualifications, based mainly on lifetime income estimates of Herman P. Miller [12], lead to a return of about 11 per cent to both high school and college education as of 1958. See [19, sec. 5].

Whether the consumption component in education will ultimately dominate, in the sense that the investment component in education will diminish as these expenditures increase and a point will be reached where additional expenditures for education will be pure consumption (a zero return on however small a part one might treat as an investment), is an interesting speculation. This may come to pass, as it has in the case of food and shelter, but that eventuality appears very remote presently in view of the prevailing investment value of education and the new demands for knowledge and skill inherent in the nature of our technical and economic progress.

17. The returns on this consumer capital will not appear in the wages and salaries that people earn.

three-fifths of the total increase between 1929 and 1956.[18] How much of this unexplained increase in income represents a return to education in the labor force? A lower limit suggests that about three-tenths of it, and an upper limit does not rule out that more than one-half of it came from this source.[19] These estimates also imply that between 36 and 70 per cent of the hitherto unexplained rise in the earnings of labor is explained by returns to the additional education of workers.

IV. A Concluding Note on Policy

One proceeds at his own peril in discussing social implications and policy. The conventional hedge is to camouflage one's values and to wear the mantle of academic innocence. Let me proceed unprotected!

1. Our tax laws everywhere discriminate against human capital. Although the stock of such capital has become large and even though it is obvious that human capital, like other forms of reproducible capital, depreciates, becomes obsolete, and entails maintenance, our tax laws are all but blind on these matters.

2. Human capital deteriorates when it is idle because unemployment impairs the skills that workers have acquired. Losses in earnings can be cushioned by appropriate payments but these do not keep idleness from taking its toll from human capital.

3. There are many hindrances to the free choice of professions. Racial discrimination and religious discrimination are still widespread. Professional associations and governmental bodies also hinder entry; for example, into medicine. Such purposeful interference keeps the investment in this form of human capital substantially below its optimum [7].

4. It is indeed elementary to stress the greater imperfections of

18. Real income doubled, rising from $150 to $302 billion in 1956 prices. Eighty-nine billions of the increase in real income is taken to be unexplained, or about 59 per cent of the total increase. The stock of education in the labor force rose by $355 billion of which $69 billion is here allocated to the growth in the labor force to keep the per-worker stcck of education constant, and $286 billion represents the increase in the level of this stock. See [19, sec. 6] for an elaboration of the method and the relevant estimates.

19. In per cent, the lower estimate came out to 29 per cent and the upper estimate to 56 per cent.

the capital market in providing funds for investment in human beings than for investment in physical goods. Much could be done to reduce these imperfections by reforms in tax and banking laws and by changes in banking practices. Long-term private and public loans to students are warranted.

5. Internal migration, notably the movement of farm people into industry, made necessary by the dynamics of our economic progress, requires substantial investments. In general, families in which the husbands and wives are already in the late thirties cannot afford to make these investments because the remaining payoff period for them is too short. Yet society would gain if more of them would pull stakes and move because, in addition to the increase in productivity currently, the children of these families would be better located for employment when they were ready to enter the labor market. The case for making some of these investments on public account is by no means weak. Our farm programs have failed miserably these many years in not coming to grips with the costs and returns from off-farm migration.

6. The low earnings of particular people have long been a matter of public concern. Policy all too frequently concentrates only on the effects, ignoring the causes. No small part of the low earnings of many Negroes, Puerto Ricans, Mexican nationals, indigenous migratory farm workers, poor farm people, and some of our older workers, reflects the failure to have invested in their health and education. Past mistakes are, of course, bygones, but for the sake of the next generation we can ill afford to continue making the same mistakes over again.

7. Is there a substantial underinvestment in human beings other than in these depressed groups? [2] This is an important question for economists. The evidence at hand is fragmentary. Nor will the answer be easily won. There undoubtedly have been over-investments in some skills, for example, too many locomotive firemen and engineers, too many people trained to be farmers, and too many agricultural economists! Our schools are not free of loafers and some students lack the necessary talents. Nevertheless, underinvestment in knowledge and skill, relative to the amounts invested in nonhuman capital would appear to be the rule and not the exception for a number of reasons. The strong and increasing demands for this knowledge and skill in laborers

are of fairly recent origin and it takes time to respond to them. In responding to these demands, we are heavily dependent upon cultural and political processes, and these are slow and the lags are long compared to the behavior of markets serving the formation of nonhuman capital. Where the capital market does serve human investments, it is subject to more imperfections than in financing physical capital. I have already stressed the fact that our tax laws discriminate in favor of nonhuman capital. Then, too, many individuals face serious uncertainty in assessing their innate talents when it comes to investing in themselves, especially through higher education. Nor is it easy either for public decisions or private behavior to untangle and properly assess the consumption and the investment components. The fact that the return to high school and to higher education has been about as large as the return to conventional forms of capital when all of the costs of such education including income foregone by students are allocated to the investment component, creates a strong presumption that there has been underinvestment since, surely, much education is cultural and in that sense it is consumption. It is no wonder, in view of these circumstances, that there should be substantial underinvestment in human beings, even though we take pride, and properly so, in the support that we have given to education and to other activities that contribute to such investments.

8. Should the returns from public investment in human capital accrue to the individuals in whom it is made?[20] The policy issues implicit in this question run deep and they are full of perplexities pertaining both to resource allocation and to welfare. Physical capital that is formed by public investment is not transferred as a rule to particular individuals as a gift. It would greatly simplify the allocative process if public investment in human capital were placed on the same footing. What then is the logical basis for treating public investment in human capital differently? Presumably it turns on ideas about welfare. A strong welfare goal of our community is to reduce the unequal distribution of personal income among individuals and families. Our community has

20. I am indebted to Milton Friedman for bringing this issue to the fore in his comments on an early draft of this paper. See preface of [7] and also Jacob Mincer's pioneering paper [13].

relied heavily on progressive income and inheritance taxation. Given public revenue from these sources, it may well be true that public investment in human capital, notably that entering into general education, is an effective and efficient set of expenditures for attaining this goal. Let me stress, however, that the state of knowledge about these issues is woefully meager.

9. My last policy comment is on assistance to underdeveloped countries to help them achieve economic growth. Here, even more than in domestic affairs, investment in human beings is likely to be underrated and neglected. It is inherent in the intellectual climate in which leaders and spokesmen of many of these countries find themselves. Our export of growth doctrines has contributed. These typically assign the stellar role to the formation of nonhuman capital, and take as an obvious fact the superabundance of human resources. Steel mills are the real symbol of industrialization. After all, the early industrialization of England did not depend on investments in the labor force. New funds and agencies are being authorized to transfer capital for physical goods to these countries. The World Bank and our Export–Import Bank have already had much experience. Then, too, measures have been taken to pave the way for the investment of more private (nonhuman) capital abroad. This one-sided effort is under way in spite of the fact that the knowledge and skills required to take on and use efficiently the super techniques of production, the most valuable resource that we could make available to them, is in very short supply in these underdeveloped countries. Some growth of course can be had from the increase in more conventional capital even though the labor that is available is lacking both in skill and knowledge. But the rate of growth will be seriously limited. It simply is not possible to have the fruits of modern agriculture and the abundance of modern industry without making large investments in human beings.

Truly, the most distinctive feature of our economic system is the growth in human capital. Without it there would be only hard, manual work and poverty except for those who have income from property. There is an early morning scene in Faulkner's *Intruder in the Dust*, of a poor, solitary cultivator at work in a field. Let me paraphrase that line, 'The man without skills and knowledge leaning terrifically against nothing.'

References

1. BECKER, G. S. (1960) preliminary draft of study undertaken for Nat. Bur. Econ. Research. New York. Now published under the title of *Human capital. A theoretical and empirical analysis, with special reference to education*, Princeton University Press (1964).
2. BECKER, G. S. 'Underinvestment in college education?', *Proc., Amer. Econ. Rev.*, May 1960, **50**, 346–54.
3. BRAHMANAND, P. R., and VAKIL, C. N. (1956) *Planning for an expanding economy*. Bombay.
4. CLARK, H. F. (1959) 'Potentialities of educational establishments outside the conventional structure of higher education', *Financing higher education, 1960–70*, D. M. Keezer (ed.), New York.
5. FABRICANT, SOLOMON (1959) *Basic facts on productivity change*, Nat. Bur. Econ. Research, Occas. Paper 63. New York. Table 5.
6. FISHER, IRVING (1906) *The nature of capital and income*. New York.
7. FRIEDMAN, MILTON, and KUZNETS, SIMON (1945) *Income from independent professional practice*, Nat. Bur. Econ. Research. New York.
8. HORVAT, B. (December 1958) 'The optimum rate of investment', *Econ. Jour.*, **68**, 747–67.
9. JOHNSON, H. G. (November 1960) 'The political economy of opulence', *Can. Jour. Econ. and Pol. Sci.*, **26**, 552–64.
10. KUZNETS, SIMON (1952) *Income and wealth in the United States*. Cambridge, England. Sec. IV, Distribution by industrial origin.
11. MARSHALL, ALFRED (1930) *Principles of economics*, 8th edn. London. App. E, pp. 787–88.
12. MILLER, H. P. (December 1960) 'Annual and lifetime income in relation to education: 1939–1959', *Amer. Econ. Rev.*, **50**, 962–86.
13. MINCER, JACOB (August 1958) 'Investment in human capital and personal income distribution', *Jour. Pol. Econ.*, **66**, 291–302.
14. MUSHKIN, S. J. (September 1958) 'Toward a definition of health economics', *Public health reports*, U.S. Dept. of Health, Educ. and Welfare, **73**, 785–93.
15. NICHOLSON, J. S. (March 1891) 'The living capital of the United Kingdom', *Econ. Jour.*, **1**, 95; see J. S. Mill, *Principles of political economy*, (ed.) W. J. Ashley, London, (1909), p. 8.
16. SCHULTZ, T. W. (June 1959) 'Investment in man: an economist's view', *Soc. Serv. Rev.*, **33**, 109–17.
17. SCHULTZ, T. W. (1956) 'Agriculture and the application of knowledge', *A look to the future*, W. K. Kellogg Foundation, Battle Creek, 54–78.
18. SCHULTZ, T. W. (December 1960) 'Capital formation by education', *Jour. Pol. Econ.*, **68**, Tables 3–7.
19. SCHULTZ, T. W. (1961) 'Education and economic growth', *Social forces influencing American education*, H. G. Richey (ed.), Chicago.

20. THÜNEN, H. VON (1875) *Der isolierte Staat*, 3rd edn, vol. 2, pt. 2, transl. by B. F. Hoselitz, reproduced by the Comp. Educ. Center, Univ. Chicago, pp. 140–52.
21. ZEMAN, MORTON, (1955) *A quantitative analysis of white–nonwhite income differentials in the United States.* Unpublished doctoral dissertation, Univ. of Chicago.

2 H. G. Johnson

Towards a Generalized Capital Accumulation Approach to Economic Development

H. G. Johnson, 'Towards a generalized capital accumulation approach to economic development', *Residual factors and economic growth*, Paris, O.E.C.D. (1964), pp. 219–25.

I. The Importance of Human Capital

The contemporary interest in the economics of education, and more broadly in the economics of all processes connected with the augmentation and application of knowledge, represents a confluence of interests derived from concerns with widely divergent problems. These problems include such matters as the economic value of education, the contribution of education to past economic development in advanced countries, and the role of education and expenditure on increased education in the planned development of underdeveloped countries.[1]

The title of this conference (The residual factor and economic development) gives primary weight to one avenue of approach to concern with the economics of education, the potency of the amount of educational capital and knowledge embodied in the human population as a variable to explain that part of measured economic growth in the advanced countries – specifically the United States, where the bulk of the empirical research has been performed – that cannot be accounted for by increases in the inputs of labour and capital as conventionally measured. Concern with education, human capital, or the 'quality' of labour inputs as an important determinant of the residual element of economic growth dovetails neatly with the apparent lessons of some fifteen years of experience with the planning of accelerated economic growth. This experience has strongly suggested that the early postwar emphasis on investment in material capital in

1. Cf. T. W. Schultz, editor, 'Reflections on investment in man', *Journal of Political Economy, Supplement*, vol. 70, no. 5, part 2, October 1962, pp. 1–8.

the methodology of economic planning was seriously mistaken, and that economic development depends vitally on the creation of a labour force both equipped with the necessary technical skills for modern industrial production and imbued with a philosophy conducive to the acceptance and promotion of economic and technical change.

The formulation of concern with the economics of education (in a broad sense) in these particular terms, while appropriate to the current state of economic research and thinking, is for this very reason both restrictive in its implications and likely to appear before much more time has passed as a transient stage in the evolution towards a more comprehensive formulation of economic development problems in terms of a broadly conceived concept of capital accumulation. For one thing, progress in economics, and especially in those parts of economics of most direct relevance to policy-making, tends to proceed in a series of alternating phases of exaggerated concentration on one aspect of a problem to the denigration of others, the ascendancy of one approach eventually evoking insistence on the importance of factors neglected in that approach. Thus, in the general field of economic growth, concentration on the role of material capital and the shortcomings of this approach have led to a contrasting emphasis on the role of people, conceptualized in terms of an alternative type of capital, human capital.

Concentration on the role of human capital has already proceeded far enough to generate the beginnings of a counter-revolution. The general outlines of the counter-revolution are indeed already apparent. On the one hand, the recent emphasis on human capital formation in growth accountancy is based on the recognition that conventional measures of labour input fail to take account of improvements in the quality of labour and aims primarily at more accurate measurement of labour inputs. Application of the same criteria to inputs of capital suggests that the contribution of capital may also have been grossly underestimated, as a result both of understatement of the flow of capital services into production by the conventional equation of service flow with the depreciated value of capital stock and of failure to measure accurately improvements in the performance characteristics ('quality') of capital equipment.[2] On the other hand, the evidence on rates of return to educational investment in the United States does not suggest that there has been serious general underinvestment in education there, while both casual empirical observation of underdeveloped countries and some detailed research on the relative returns to investments in education and material capital in them[3] suggest that at least in some cases the proportion of resources devoted to human capital formation may be too high rather than too low.[4] A rehabilitation of investment in material capital as a potent source of economic growth may therefore be in prospect. What is more important, while the process of increasing economic knowledge proceeds in phases of exaggerated concentration on one or another aspect of a problem, both the effect and the intent are to arrive at a unified and more powerful synthesis of explanations of economic phenomena. The contemporary phase, in which the concepts of human capital and of investment in it figure as corrections of emphasis in a system of economic ideas dominated by material capital, is bound to merge into one in which human and non-human capital are treated as alternative forms of capital in general. The desirability of achieving such a synthesis is not merely a matter of scientific economy and elegance, it is also a pre-requisite for rational discussion and formulation of policy for economic growth in both advanced and underdeveloped countries. The purpose of this paper, accordingly, is to sketch the outlines of such a synthesis, in the form of a generalized capital accumulation approach to

2. Cf. Zvi Griliches, 'The sources of measured productivity growth: U.S. agriculture, 1940–1960', *Journal of Political Economy*, vol. 74 no. 4, August 1960.

3. Cf. Arnold C. Harberger, *Investment in man versus investment in machines: The case of India*, a paper prepared for the Conference on Education and Economic Development, University of Chicago, 4–6 April 1963. [*Education and economic development*, (eds.) C. A. Anderson and M. J. Bowman. Aldine Publishing Co., 1966.] Harberger finds the rate of return on real investment in India to be substantially higher than the rate of return on investment in education.

4. This proposition becomes almost a truism if the concept of investment in human capital formation is extended to include expenditures on improved health, whose effects on the rate of population increase constitute one of the major economic problems of underdeveloped countries.

economic development, and to discuss some of its implications for social and economic policy.

II. A General Approach to Economic Development

The essential elements of a generalized capital accumulation approach to economic development are already present in the literature of economics, and at least some applications of the approach (for example, the explanation of wage differentials) have been familiar to economists ever since economics became established as a separate subject of study. The foundations of it were explicitly laid in Irving Fisher's classic work on capital and income, and carried forward by F. H. Knight's work on the theory of capital; and the approach is exemplified, and its potency demonstrated, in the recent research of T. W. Schultz, Gary Becker, and others on human capital.[5] The essence of it is to regard 'capital' as including anything that yields a stream of income over time, and income as the product of capital. From this point of view, as Fisher pointed out, all categories of income describe yields on various forms of capital, and can be expressed as rates of interest or return on the corresponding items of capital. Alternatively, all forms of income-yielding assets can be given an equivalent capital value by capitalizing the income they yield at an appropriate rate of interest. By extension, the growth of income that defines economic development is necessarily the result of the accumulation of capital, or of 'investment'; but 'investment' in this context must be defined to include such diverse activities as adding to material capital, increasing the health, discipline, skill, and education of the human population, moving labour into more productive occupations and locations, and applying existing knowledge or discovering and applying new knowledge to increase the efficiency of productive processes. All such activities involve incurring costs, in the form of use of current resources, and investment in them is socially worth while if the rate of return over cost exceeds the general rate of interest, or the capital value of the additional income they yield exceeds the cost of obtaining it. From the somewhat different perspective of planning economic development, efficient development involves

5. See T. W. Schultz, op. cit.

allocation of investment resources according to priorities set by the relative rates of return on alternative investments.

The conception of economic growth as a process of accumulating capital, in all the manifold forms that the broad Fisherian concept of capital allows, is a potent simplification of the analytical problem of growth, and one which facilitates the discussion of problems of growth policy by emphasizing the relative returns from alternative investments of currently available resources. The Fisherian concept of capital, however, and the approach to the analysis of production and distribution problems associated with it, are not as yet characteristic of the work and philosophical approach of the majority of economists, and to some the implications of the approach for policy with respect to human beings appear to be positively repugnant. Must economists instead employ a narrower concept of capital that identifies capital with material capital goods and equipment used in the production process, and distinguishes it sharply from labour?

This approach to the theory of production derives from English classical economics, which developed in response to the early stages of the industrial revolution, when a sharp distinction between capital goods and raw labour power made more sense than it does under modern industrial conditions, and when moreover the distinction between wages, profit, and rent corresponded to a meaningful division of society into politico-economic classes. With the progress of technology, the replacement of brute human strength by mechanical power, and the increasing importance of skill and scientific knowledge on the part of the labour force, the traditional distinction between labour as an original factor and capital as a produced factor has become increasingly unrealistic, while these developments together with the declining importance of rent consequent on technical progress in agriculture and the alteration of the relationship of property ownership to economic control consequent on the development of corporate enterprise have increasingly deprived the functional distribution of income of socio-political content. Nevertheless, the English neo-classical tradition continues to dominate the theory and policy of economic growth. Indeed, this tradition has been powerfully reinforced by the impact of Keynes' *General Theory*, with its emphasis on fixed capital investment as the key variable in the economic system and its assumption of a homogeneous labour force of a given quality, and by the subsequent conversion of the Keynesian short-run equilibrium model into the Harrod growth model.

As already mentioned, the limitations of accumulation of material capital as an explanation of a prescription for growth have prompted the contemporary interest in human capital formation, and suggest a generalization of the concept of capital accumulation to include investment in all types of capital formation. An important obstacle to such a generalization is that the treatment of human beings as a form of capital, even if only conceptually, seems offensive to some economists as being contrary to democratic political philosophy. This reaction, however, involves a confusion of analytical approach and normative recommendations unfortunately only too common in discussions of economic problems with policy connotations. To recognize that important areas of socio-economic policy involve decisions analytically identical with decisions about investing in machines is not at all to imply that people should be regarded as no different from machines; on the contrary, refusal to recognize the investment character of a problem because people are involved may result in people receiving worse treatment than machines. One might, indeed, hazard the generalization that democratic free-enterprise economies tend to make wasteful use of their human resources, precisely because people are not sufficiently regarded as socially productive assets.

Conception of economic growth as a generalized process of capital accumulation provides a unifying principle for the statistical explanation of past growth and the formulation of policy for future growth or plans for economic development. It does not, however – and cannot be expected to – dispose of any real problems, though it does clarify understanding of them. Instead, it transforms these problems into problems of the special characteristics of particular types of capital, or of the specification of efficient investment programmes.

III. Classifying Types of Capital

From the point of view of economically relevant differentiations, items of capital can be classified in a variety of ways. One fundamental distinction to be drawn relates to the nature of the yield or contribution to economic welfare – the distinction between consumption capital, which yields a flow of services enjoyed directly and therefore contributing to utility, and production capital, which yields a flow of goods the consumption of which yields utility. The returns from production capital are directly observable, and therefore more amenable to measurement than the returns on consumption capital.

Another fundamental distinction relates to the form in which capital is embodied – here it seems necessary not only to distinguish capital embodied in human beings from capital embodied in non-human material forms, but also to distinguish between capital embodied in both human and non-human physical forms and capital embodied in neither, the latter category comprising both the state of the arts (the intellectual production capital of society) and the state of culture (the intellectual consumption capital of society). The significance of this distinction is closely related to a third distinction – one which is particularly relevant to policy problems – between types of capital according to whether the returns to investment in capital accumulation accrue to the investor or to others. Here it seems necessary to distinguish: (a) capital goods which render specific services to production or consumption by the owner; (b) human capital, the distinguishing characteristic of which is that, both inherently and by legal tradition, control over the use of the capital is vested in the individual embodying the capital, regardless of the source of finance of the investment in it; (c) social capital or collective capital, the distinguishing characteristic of which is that for reasons of inherent necessity or administrative convenience its services to production or consumption are not charged to individual users but are paid for by taxation of the community at large; (d) intellectual capital or knowledge, the distinguishing characteristic of which is that, once created it is a free good, in the sense that use of it by one individual does not diminish its availability to others.

All forms of capital other than capital goods rendering specific services to production or consumption raise serious problems for economic analysis measurement and policy formation. The fusion of human capital with the personality of its owner raises among other things the problem of how far expenditure on the creation of human capital should be accounted as investment, and how far it should be classed as consumption; while the vesting of control over the use of the capital invested in the individual, given the imperfection of markets for personal credit, poses the problem of how far education should be provided at public expense. The divergence of private and social costs and benefits inherent in free or subsidized education raises some particularly difficult policy problems in conjunction with the fact that educated people are especially mobile interregionally and internationally, so that resources devoted to education in poor countries may run substantially to waste in unilateral transfers of human capital to richer countries.[6] Social capital investment involves a similar separation of costs of investment from benefits, and a similar mixture of equity and efficiency considerations. Investment in knowledge raises the thorniest of all problems, since the zero marginal cost of knowledge to additional users implies that no system of recouping the cost of investment in knowledge-creation by charging for its use can be economically efficient. (The patent and copyright laws, as is well known, constitute a very inefficient compromise between encouraging investment in knowledge by rewarding the inventor and encouraging the use of knowledge by making it freely available; in general, the more far-reaching an advance in knowledge the more does its creator have

6. Brinley Thomas has emphasized the economic absurdity of the contemporary migration pattern between advanced and underdeveloped countries, in which the advanced countries cream off the professional talent of the underdeveloped countries by immigration and attempt to replace it by their own experts supplied at great expense as part of development aid. See Brinley Thomas, 'International factor movements and unequal rates of growth', *The Manchester School of Economic and Social Studies*, vol. 29, no, 1, January 1961. The ease of migration of educated people from underdeveloped countries, especially those in which English is the language of instruction, to advanced countries is a serious limitation on the potentialities of achieving economic development by educational investment and suggests the social desirability of devising means of obliging either the emigrants themselves or the countries receiving them to repay the social capital invested in them to their countries of origin.

[For subsequent analysis and rather different conclusions on 'brain drain' by this author, see H. G. Johnson, 'The economics of the "brain drain": The Canadian case', *Minerva*, vol. 3 (1965) no. 3. Reprinted in M. Blaug (Ed.), *Economics of Education 2*.]

to be satisfied with the non-material rewards of intellectual accomplishment.)

The distinctions discussed above do not include a distinction between natural resources (natural capital) and man-made capital. For most economic purposes, such a distinction is unnecessary – natural resources, like capital goods, can be appropriated, transferred, and invested in. Natural resources do, however, raise two sorts of special problems. First, property rights in some ranges of natural resources are typically vested in society or the state; this poses the problem of ensuring efficient exploitation of these resources through appropriate accounting and charging for the use of the state's natural capital, a problem particularly important at the time when resources are first brought into use. Secondly, some kinds of natural resources, which are likely to be of particular importance to developing countries, are non-renewable, and pose the problems of efficient depletion and exhaustion – of efficient capital decumulation, rather than accumulation. The problems of achieving economic development through the exploitation of depleting natural resources become particularly acute and politically highly charged when such exploitation is dependent on the participation of foreign capital and enterprise.

IV. Investment Criteria

Conception of economic development as a generalized process of capital accumulation, in conjunction with recognition of economically significant differences between various types of capital, has important implications for the efficient programming of investment of economic development. These implications centre on the relationships of complementarity and substitutability in both production and consumption that may exist between types of capital provided by different investment processes, and the consequent desirability of aiming at both balanced investment in the production of complementary types of capital and the selection of the most efficient combinations of types of capital in the light of the relative costs of different kinds of investment. The complementarity between modern equipment and technology, a skilled labour force, and social overhead capital in the transportation and distribution systems is by now sufficiently recognized for development planning to aim at producing integrated investment programmes comprising investment in education and vocational training (manpower programmes) as well as investment in industrial capital and social overheads. For such comprehensive development investment programmes to maximize the contribution of investment to economic growth, however, recognition of complementarity must be allied with recognition of substitutability and analysis of rates of return on the total investment of capital in alternative programmes involving investment in capital goods, human capital, social capital, and the acquisition of new knowledge.

Much of the literature on economic development assumes far too easily that low-wage labour is necessarily cheap industrial labour, ignoring the magnitude of the investments in human and social capital that may have to be made to convert rural workers into skilled industrial labour, and the possibility that investment of the same capital in agricultural improvement might yield far higher returns. On the other hand, there is a strong possibility, exemplified by the successful development of exports of some technologically fairly advanced products from otherwise underdeveloped countries, that the greatest comparative advantage for such countries lies in skilled-labour-intensive products, for the reason that a generally low wage level makes the cost of investment in human capital low (especially forgone earnings and the cost of instruction and educational structures) by comparison with comparable costs in advanced countries. In addition, such countries may be able to catch up with the advanced countries far more rapidly in the accumulation of knowledge than in the accumulation of material capital.

Apart from its implications for planning for economic growth, a generalized capital accumulation approach to economic development points to the potential fruitfulness of research into and analysis of the efficiency of a wide range of processes and policies that involve the allocation of capital but are not usually thought of as concerned with investment. It has, for example, been amply demonstrated by empirical research that rates of return on investment in education vary widely between different levels of the education system; and there is good reason for doubting that existing educational systems are very efficient when considered as an industry producing extremely long-lived capital assets. The field of public health and medical care, viewed as an industry concerned with the repair and maintenance of human capital, also offers scope for economic analyses of rates of return on alternative investments. Institutional arrangements for supporting and rewarding fundamental and applied research, considered as an industry producing intellectual capital, provide an even greater challenge to economists. Within the traditional scope of economics, labour mobility, unemployment policy, and policy respecting the location of industry all demand the application of capital theory. Perhaps the most important area requiring rationalization in terms of a broadened concept of capital accumulation, however, is the theory and practice of public finance. Not only do income tax systems typically make a very poor adjustment for the capital investment element in personal income, but the necessity of recouping by income and profits taxation the costs of investments in human capital customarily provided free or at a subsidized price to the people invested in creates disincentives to the efficient use and accumulation of capital of all kinds.

3 H. G. Shaffer

A Critique of the Concept of Human Capital

H. G. Shaffer, 'Investment in human capital: comment', *American Economic Review*, vol. 52 (1961), no. 4, pp. 1026–35.

The treatment of currently or potentially productive human beings as capital and/or wealth has a long history in economic literature.[1] But during the first half of the twentieth century, certainly the overwhelming majority of economists, following Alfred Marshall [8, pp. 71–2], have shown a tendency to use the concept of capital as applicable only to that portion of the non-human, material, man-made stock of wealth which is utilized directly in further production.

In spite of 'majority opinion' the application of the capital concept to man has not disappeared from economic literature[2] and the past few years especially have witnessed a revival of the idea in U.S. economic journals. In the forefront of scholarly efforts in this direction stands the work of Theodore W. Schultz [13–17].

I shall grant unequivocally that theoretical models, incontestable from an abstract or mathematical point of view, can be built on the basis of the application of the capital concept to man. Yet, I shall contend that it is generally inadvisable to treat man as human capital.

Schultz believes that the main reason for the opposition to the human capital concept is based on a somewhat irrational fear that to accept the concept would be morally wrong and degrading to free man [13, p. 572; 16, p. 2; 17, p. 110]. This, however, is not the reason for my opposition. It is my contention that, mainly for three reasons, economics has little to gain and much

1. See, for instance, [11; 19, pp. 265–6; 5, p. 13; 4, p. 65].
2. See [21, n. p. 255] for a short bibliography of articles in British, German, French, and Italian journals during the first three decades of the twentieth century.

to lose by the universal application of the capital concept to man.

First, 'investment in man' is essentially different from investment in nonhuman capital. The difference arises largely from the fact that, as a general rule, at least a part of any one direct expenditure for the improvement of man is not investment as the term is usually used, i.e. it is undertaken for reasons other than the expectation of a monetary return, it has not traceable effects on future output and it satisfies wants directly. To the extent to which any part of such an expenditure is investment in this sense it is rarely if ever 'rational' investment based on a careful comparison of alternate investment opportunities, with the anticipated monetary return and the degree of safety as guiding rods. Furthermore, any such part is inseparable from other parts which, not being classified as investment, are then conveniently referred to as consumption expenditure.

Secondly, where it is possible to separate consumption expenditure from investment in man it would still remain a virtual impossibility to allocate a *specific* return to a *specific* investment in man (though aggregate expenditures for the improvement of man's skill, abilities, and productive capacities certainly have a positive influence of indeterminable magnitude on man's efficiency as a productive agent and, hence, on his output).

Finally, if consumption expenditure could be separated from investment in man, and if it were possible to compute the part of man's income that results from a given investment-in-man expenditure, it would in most instances still be ill-advised – from the point of view of social and economic welfare – to utilize the information thus obtained as the exclusive or even the primary basis for policy formation, public or private.[3]

I shall attempt to illustrate how these three arguments are

3. Joan Robinson sees the main difference between investment in acquiring earning power and investment in income-yielding property in the fact that in a capitalist society the earning power is not a saleable commodity in the sense in which the income-yielding property is – a point not stressed in this paper. From this, she reaches the conclusion that 'the present capital value of future personal earning has a metaphorical, not an actual financial meaning'. While this seems a valid comment, her view that 'from the point of view of the economy as a whole, the similarity is more important than the difference,' is one contested in this paper [12, pp. 11–12].

applicable to expenditures on education. I shall then indicate briefly that the same arguments are applicable to direct expenditures on man for purposes other than his education.

I. Education: Consumption Expenditure or Investment?

Few U.S. social scientists today will argue with the basic spirit of Marshall's statement that: 'There is no greater extravagance more prejudicial to the growth of national wealth than that wasteful negligence which allows genius that happens to be born of lowly parentage to expend itself in lowly work' [8, p. 212]. But Marshall did not utilize this realization to treat expenditures for education as 'investment in man' and neither should we.

Up to a certain age, public school attendance is compulsory and any private expenditures connected therewith (such as expenditures for notebooks, gym clothes, etc.) are taken out of the area of private decision-making (except for whatever influence the parent may have as a voter or vote-getter). Some parents decide to incur additional expenses, beyond those required by law, for their children's education. They may send their children to 'better' private schools or to parochial schools, they may provide them with private dancing or piano lessons, they may employ the services of a French governess. But such expenditures, more often than not, are at least in part consumption expenditures as far as both the economic motivation of the investor and the economic effects on the individual and on society are concerned. Due to the inseparability of the consumption and the investment part of such expenditures (and for other reasons discussed below) the return on any incremental expenditure to either the individual or society is not computable.

When we turn from legally required minumum education to voluntary private expenditures for education at the high-school and the college level it still seems quite impossible to explain human behavior in terms of capital investment (as we have been using the term). Many a parent who would not think of spending thousands of dollars to establish his son in business or who would at least require a partnership in such a business, does not hesitate to spend an equal amount on his son's education without expecting any monetary return for himself (and with higher anticipated life income for his son often at best one of several motivating factors). The young college student who finances his own education will probably enroll in many courses and read many books that would bear only a remote relation, if any, to future expected or realized income. Although some of these may be required for graduation and therefore may be of indirect economic value, it is in all probability still a fair evaluation of human motivation that 'the prospects of achieving more subtle satisfactions from mastering a higher education are more compelling to many people than the prospects of greater financial success' [6, p. 308]. Any attempt to show that rational individuals tend to undertake expenditure on education up to the point where the marginal productivity of the human capital produced by the process of education equals the rate of interest – a point at which the marginal expenditure on education yields a return equal to the return on marginal expenditure for any other factor of production – would be a mockery of economic theory.

At best, we can go along with Schultz's contention that '... *some* individuals and families make decisions to invest in *some* kinds of education, either in themselves or in their children, with an eye to the earnings that they expect to see forthcoming from such expenditures on education'.[4] And Schultz has to admit that in the case of expenditures on human beings, those for consumption and those for the purpose of increasing income are quite interwoven, 'which is why the task of identifying each component is so formidable and why the measurement of capital formation by expenditures is less useful for human investment than for investment in physical goods' [16, p. 8]. He therefore proposes yield (measured in increased earnings) as an alternate method for estimating human investment.

II. Education and Income

Studies showing a close correlation between schooling (measured in numbers of years of attendance and/or type of school attended) and success (measured in terms of social position and/or annual or

4. [13, pp. 572–3], Emphasis mine.

life earnings) antedate the turn of the century.[5] Some recent studies attempt to measure the financial return to 'investment' in education. The value of a college education in the late 1950s, for instance, has been estimated anywhere from $100,000 to almost $180,000 [2, p. 180; 7, p. 28; 9, p. 981]. However, the present value of a lifetime income differential of nearly $106,000 between a high school and a college graduate amounts to a mere $3,305 when figured after taxes and when discounted at 8 per cent [7, p. 28] – not an unreasonable rate of discount if one considers the risk involved in 'investing' in a college education.

To obtain valid figures for lifetime incomes (on the basis of present actuarial tables), to correlate such figures with years of schooling, to compute the cost of such schooling in terms of private expenditures, public expenditures, and opportunity costs (*without* any attempt to segregate 'consumption' from 'investment in education' expenditures), to compute the rate of discount which will equate the expenditures with lifetime income differentials, and, finally, to compare this rate with the rate of return on investment in nonhuman capital – all these do not present insurmountable difficulties. But to establish a cause–effect relationship, to prove, in other words, that the income differential is the result of the additional education is quite a different matter. To do so, one would have to assume that the more educated individual does not differ from the less educated in any characteristic (other than education) that could explain part or all of the income differential. Such an assumption would be highly unrealistic as it is evident that there is a close correlation between intelligence and years of schooling (especially at the higher levels). There are also good indications of at least some correlation between the financial standing of parents and the years of schooling of their children. Finally, there is the possibility, if not the strong probability, that other factors such as connections, residence (urban *vs* rural, North *vs* South, etc.), occupational and cultural level of parents, health, etc., have some influence on years of school attendance. And surely all these factors have a direct bearing on income, independent of years of preparation.

5. See [3] for a discussion of many of these early studies and a bibliography of more than 125 books and journal articles on the subject published between 1898 and 1917.

In the early forties, Elbridge Sibley studied the case records of 2,158 Pennsylvania students and discovered that, at the below-college level, intelligence had a greater influence on years of education than parental status. However, as to the probability of spending at least one year in an institution of higher learning, 'while the most intelligent boys have only a 4 to 1 advantage over the least intelligent, the sons of men in the highest occupational category enjoy an advantage of more than 10 to 1 over those from the lowest occupational level' [18, p. 330].[6] In his study of the relationship between income (annual and lifetime) and education for the years 1939–59, Herman P. Miller noted that at least part of the higher income of those with more education could probably be accounted for by differences in intelligence, home environment, family connections and other factors [9, p. 964; 6, p. 312]. D. S. Bridgman points to evidence that 'unearned' (property) income of college graduates is higher than that of noncollege-trained individuals and he expresses the view that factors such as ability and property income have been given insufficient recognition in the past as causal agents of higher income of the more educated [2].

In 1958, Jacob Mincer constructed a model to account for personal income distribution in terms of differential 'investment' in education [10]. He started out with many admittedly oversimplified assumptions, one of which was the assumption of identical abilities. But when he relaxed this unrealistic assumption, the plausibility of a positive correlation between ability traits and amount of education (with the obvious effect on income distribution) became apparent [10, p. 286]. To this he added that 'when incomes rather than earnings are considered, the positive association of property incomes with occupational level . . . magnifies income differences' (thus accentuating whatever effects the training factor *per se* might have) [10, p. 302]. Therefore, he could not and did not claim that a quantitative estimate of the effect of training on personal income distribution could be derived using his model.

6. Sibley's study was published in 1942. Since then (in the United States, at least) increased numbers of scholarships and public subsidization of education have certainly diminished the dependence of schooling upon parental status.

J. R. Walsh, in his early (1935) study of the applicability of the capital concept to man explained that in order to isolate the effect of education he would have to eliminate all other influences (such as ability, age, occupation, health, etc.) but that he had attempted no such elimination as he considered it impossible [21, p. 272]. Indeed, it is so completely impossible to eliminate all other influences [7] that one has to agree with Houthakker that '. . . we cannot even be sure that the apparent effect of education on income is not completely explicable in terms of intelligence and parents' income, so that the *specific* effect of education would be zero or even negative' [7, p. 28].

There is another factor that enhances the difficulty of determining the return on 'investment in education'. This factor I shall call 'maintenance costs'.

Certainly, whenever the financial return on any investment in nonhuman capital is computed, maintenance costs of the capital good are considered. But, to the best of my knowledge, such maintenance costs have been utterly neglected in the case of human capital by all economists who have advocated the application of the capital concept to man. These maintenance costs first arise during the investment period. The tuxedo, the evening dress, the more frequent haircuts may not be absolutely necessary for the increase in subsequent earning capacity but they are *de facto* expenses connected with higher education (and they might be indirectly necessary for the intended investment goals lest the anxiety and the loss of tranquility caused by their absence interfere with scholastic accomplishments). But maintenance costs by no means end with the completion of the investment period. A part of these continuous maintenance costs (such as the more expensive car, the more luxuriously dressed wife, and the more lavishly furnished home of the 'organization man', or the more frequently washed shirt and the more frequently dry-cleaned suit of the white collar worker) are almost unavoidably connected

7. Theoretically it would not be necessary to eliminate all other influences, as partial (or multiple) correlation methods could be employed to allow for the effects of some other variables. However, amount of education is at least partly a matter of personal choice. As long as this is true, no matter how many factors have been considered, one can never be certain that there are not some unanalyzed variables influencing this choice which in themselves are responsible for the income differential attributed to education.

with the retention of the position which yields the higher income to the more educated.

Another part of these maintenance costs, perhaps less compulsive but still widely prevalent, relates to increased qualitative (and to some extent also quantitative) consumption demands resulting from higher education, higher income, or both.[8] To the extent to which increased consumption expenditure results from increased income *per se* (which it will whenever the marginal propensity to consume is more than zero) it is independent of the cause of the increase in income. To the extent, however, to which increased consumption expenditure results from the educational development of greater cultural, aesthetic, and discriminating tastes (which is not a separable part but rather a result of the aggregate education process), it reflects an increased expenditure directly and uniquely attributable to the specific type of investment (in education).[9] In time, these education-created expenditures will probably tend to become essential for the former student's efficient performance as a producer and, thus, part of the maintenance costs of the education-created human capital.[10]

III. Public Policy in Relation to Expenditure on Education

At present, the investment-in-human-capital concept appears to be gaining in favor among 'liberals' who apparently intend to utilize it as a rationalization of federal aid to education (and, secondarily, other government investment-in-man expenditures). Walter Heller, Chairman of the Council of Economic Advisers to the President, for instance, refers to the human mind as America's greatest resource and points to the 'vast implications

8. Other causes of increased consumption, if any, are disregarded as irrelevant to the main argument.

9. That there is *some* education-created increase in consumption (and not just substitution of one kind of consumption for another) appears evident from observation.

10. Schultz does not count such education-created consumption expenditures as maintenance costs. On the contrary, while acknowledging their existence, he suggests that the part of the cost of education that induces them be classified as consumption expenditure. By so decreasing the cost base for investment in education Schultz arrives at a higher rate of return on the investment than he would otherwise [16, pp. 12–13].

for public policy' embodied in the development of the investment-in-human-capital concept [20]. But nothing is more
dangerous to the very position of the liberals, I fear, than to
attempt to defend government expenditures for education as a
type of collective business investment which will yield economic
returns attractive to the investing society in term of maximum
increase in GNP over and above costs. To cite just one example
of the untenable position to which such argumentation could
lead: Schultz sees a direct correlation between the lower incomes
of Negroes in the United States (as compared with whites) and
their relatively lower productivity resulting from inadequate
educational preparation [16, pp. 3–4; 17, p. 109] and he considers
an 'investment' in their education as financially sound. But more
specific studies clearly show that due to greater vocational
opportunities, the income differential correlated with additional
education is considerably higher for whites than for Negroes.[11]
Were we to agree that the government should treat expenditures
for education as investment, could not a good case be made for
the decrease, if not the discontinuation, of governmental subsidization of nonwhite students and a consequently higher
subsidization of the financially more remunerative white
students?

By the same token, should society discourage advanced studies
by women unless they can give some reasonable assurance that
their 'human capital' will be used even after they are married?
Or should we – COULD WE??? – compute the indirect, long-
range value of such women to society in terms of increased
future productivity of their children whom they would perhaps
rear more efficiently? The education of many young men and
women who choose to prepare themselves for professions which
they expect will yield them comparatively low monetary but
comparatively high psychic incomes (such as teaching) might be
of great value to society. But if we were to take return on investment as the guiding rod, how would we proceed? A teacher's *im-*

11. In 1949, for instance, the difference in income between nonwhite
college graduates and nonwhite males with one to three years in college
(for the 45–54-year age group) was about $500 for the year while the
corresponding differential for white males was about twice as great [6, p.
309].

mediate, direct contribution to GNP (equal to his gross income) would not be a true reflection of his value to society, and his *indirect, long-run* effect (expressed in terms of his influence on the income of others) is not measurable. Marshall proclaimed that: 'All that is spent during many years in opening the means of higher education to the masses would be well paid for if it called out one more Newton or Darwin, Shakespeare or Beethoven' [8, p. 216]. Was Marshall wrong? I do not think he was. Yet, how would one obtain empirical evidence that such investment would be 'well paid for'? How would one go about computing a significance rate of return on such an investment?

Indeed the advocate of more governmental aid to education who attempts to defend his proposal exclusively on an 'it's sound investment policy' basis stands on shaky ground, for he would logically have to advise expenditures on education up to the point where the marginal productivity of the human capital created equaled the marginal productivity of other nonhuman capital, as well as the rate of interest. And what would this advocate of more government aid to education do if he were confronted with a study such as Becker's which reaches the conclusion that '. . . it would appear that direct returns alone cannot justify a large increase in expenditures on college education relative to expenditures on business capital' [1, p. 349]? He could find support in arguments such as Schultz's that Becker failed to take into consideration that a part of the expenditure on education is always for education as a pure consumer's good, that Becker therefore underestimated the return on investment in education, and that it is reasonable to assume that there has been underinvestment in education [16, p. 15]. But, on the other hand, our advocate of more government aid to education might also have to cope with the argument that Becker, perhaps, overestimated the return on investment in education, as no allowance was made in Becker's study for such parts of total returns as may have been attributable to factors other than education (as discussed in section II above) or offset by increased 'maintenance costs'. And once the advocate of increased government aid to education reaches the conclusion that it is impossible to compute a scientifically unassailable rate of return for such investment, he loses even his theoretical basis for *any* government 'investment' in education, forcing him once more to utilize arguments other than 'it's sound investment policy' to defend his proposals.

IV. Expenditures on Human Beings Other Than for Education

For essentially the same reasons as presented in sections I and II above, it seems for most purposes impractical, inconvenient, and of relatively little use to attempt the explanation of direct expenditures on man, other than for his education, in terms of the investment in human capital concept. And for essentially the same reasons as those presented in section III above, it seems ill-advised to base governmental policy on such a concept.

Whether we deal with outlays on food, improved medical care, housing, recreational facilities, or other 'investments in man', we once again are faced with the impossibility of separating consumption from investment in any of those areas and with the impossibility of computing scientifically valid marginal returns on any of these expenditures. And once again it might prove detrimental to the best interests of society (measured in terms other than aggregate economic returns on investment) to have governmental policy determined (or even substantially influenced) by an investor's point of view. Governmental programs, for instance, providing for medical care or financial assistance to individuals beyond the retirement age (individuals thus fully depreciated as human capital) would be difficult to defend from the point of view of profitable investment *per se* (except, perhaps, in terms of the greater tranquility and therefore productivity of those still serviceable as human capital); and slum clearance projects might be considered poor investments as compared with the improvement of golf courses that would aid in steadying the nerves of more productive human capital.

V. Conclusions

Whether productive human beings should be treated as capital and whether some direct expenditures intended for or resulting in an increase in their productive capacities should be treated as investment in human capital are not questions of principle. There is no 'right' or 'wrong' way, because what constitutes *capital* and what constitutes *investment* is a matter of definition. Should one decide to include under 'investment in human capital' everything that tends to increase man's productivity, the overwhelming part of all expenditures to which we usually refer as consumption expenditures would have to be considered investments. A substantial part of all expenditures for food, shelter, and clothing, many expenditures for recreation, entertainment, and travel, and even some expenditures for mere conveniences and luxuries would certainly need to be reclassified as investments to the extent to which they contribute, directly or indirectly, to the enhancement of a person's productivity.

While it is undeniable that the sum total of countless sensible expenditures on man (including expenditures for his education, health, proper nourishment, etc.) will tend, on the average, to have a beneficial impact upon his productivity, present and future, each of these expenditures individually and all of them in the aggregate consist of inseparable and indistinguishable parts of consumption and investment expenditures. The spender's motivation is essentially different from that of the investor in non-human capital. The return on the investment cannot be computed satisfactorily as both the amount of pure 'investment' and the return to be allocated thereto are conjectural. And in society's allocation of productive resources for the advancement of economic and noneconomic welfare, the question of the financial wisdom of any direct expenditure on man must be reduced to one of secondary importance. We have come to accept as axioms that health is preferable to illness, knowledge preferable to ignorance, freedom (whatever the term may mean) preferable to slavery, peace preferable to war, etc. Governmental expenditures directed towards the realization of these preferences bear no necessary relation to their economic profitability as investments.

This paper's opposition to the application of the capital concept to man, then, is not based on any argument that such application is 'wrong' but only that, more often than not, it would confuse more than elucidate, it would create more problems than it would solve, and – as a basis for public policy – it would be of questionable value.

References

1. BECKER, G. S. (1960) 'Underinvestment in college education', *Amer. Econ. Rev.* Proc., vol. 50, pp. 346–54.
2. BRIDGMAN, D. S. (1960) 'Problems in estimating the monetary value of college education', *Rev. Econ. Stat.*, Suppl., vol. 42, pp. 180–4.
3. CASWELL, ELLIS A. (1917) 'The money value of education', Dept. of the Interior, *Bureau of Education, Bull.*, 1917, No. 22, Washington.
4. FISHER, IRVING (1906) *The nature of capital and income*. New York.
5. FISHER, IRVING (1930) *The theory of interest*. New York.
6. GLICK, P. C., and MILLER, H. P. (1956) 'Educational level and potential income', *Amer. Soc. Rev.*, vol. 21, pp. 307–12.
7. HOUTHAKKER, H. S. (1959) 'Education and income', *Rev. Econ. Stat.*, vol. 41, pp. 24–8.
8. MARSHALL, ALFRED (1946) *Principles of economics*, 8th edn. London.
9. MILLER, H. P. (1960) 'Annual and lifetime income in relation to education: 1939–1959', *Amer. Econ. Rev.*, vol. 50, pp. 962–86.
10. MINCER, JACOB (1958) 'Investment in human capital and personal distribution of income', *Jour. Pol. Econ.*, vol. 66, pp. 281–302.
11. PETTY, SIR WILLIAM (1899) 'Political arithmetic' (first published in 1676), *The economic writings of Sir William Petty*, Charles Henry Hull (ed.), Cambridge vol. I, pp. 233–313.
12. ROBINSON, JOAN (1956) *The accumulation of capital.* Homewood, Ill.
13. SCHULTZ, T. W. (1960) 'Capital formation by education', *Jour. Pol. Econ.*, vol. 68, pp. 571–83.
14. SCHULTZ, T. W. (1961) 'Education and economic growth', in *Social forces influencing American education*, H. G. Richey (ed.), Chicago.
15. SCHULTZ, T. W. 'Human capital: A growing asset', *Sat. Rev.*, 21 January 1961, pp. 37–9.
16. SCHULTZ, T. W. (1961) 'Investment in human capital', *Amer. Econ. Rev.*, vol. 51, pp. 1–17.
17. SCHULTZ, T. W. (1959) 'Investment in man: An economist's view', *Soc. Service Rev.*, vol. 33, pp. 109–17.
18. SIBLEY, ELBRIDGE (1942) 'Some demographic clues to stratification', *Amer. Soc. Rev.*, vol. 7, pp. 322–30.
19. SMITH, ADAM (1937) *The wealth of nations,* Modern Lib. edn, New York, pp. 265–6.
20. *Time magazine*, March 1961, p. 22.
21. WALSH, J. R. (1935) 'Capital concept applied to man', *Quart. Jour. Econ.*, vol. 49, pp. 255–85.

4 T. W. Schultz

The Concept of Human Capital: Reply

T. W. Schultz, 'Investment in human capital: reply', *American Economic Review*, vol. 52 (1961), no. 4, pp. 1035–9.

I am surprised and pleased that under the restraints of a presidential address to the American Economic Association, enough could be said to warrant so careful and valuable a comment. Harry G. Shaffer discusses some of the minor difficulties that arise in practice in distinguishing between consumption and investment expenditures in the formation of human capital and then examines in considerable detail, and in my judgment correctly, some major difficulties in identifying and measuring the earnings (return) that are associated with a particular investment in man. Shaffer does not object to the concepts of investment in man and human capital; on the contrary, he explicitly accepts the underlying theory. He is, also, careful to disassociate himself from those who believe that it is morally wrong to apply the concepts of investment and capital to people. However, if any new knowledge were attainable by the use of these concepts, despite the empirical difficulties, Shaffer appears to believe that such knowledge would be grossly misused – by implication, more so than other economic knowledge – in making policy decisions. This view of the relation between economic analysis and policy seems unreal and irrelevant.

Shaffer's first point is addressed to the question: When are educational expenditures consumption and when are they investment? This question deserves careful investigation because so much depends upon the correctness of the answer. To follow the conventional procedure of treating all such costs as serving only current consumption will not do. But to allocate all of these costs to investment in future earnings, is fully as extreme and unwarranted. Although the economic logic for allocating the costs of education is clear and compelling, no one has as yet developed a wholly satisfactory empirical procedure for identifying and measuring the particular resources that enter into each of these components. Faced with this difficulty, any allocation that one makes, based on such clues as seem relevant, must in all honesty be labeled 'arbitrary'. There is little intellectual comfort in the fact that a similar brand of arbitrariness characterizes other areas of analysis, for example, in the way expenditures for electricity and for automobiles used by farmers are divided and distributed between household and farm expenses, or the way a part of the costs of some private residences used for offices, libraries, or studies are treated as business expenses.

In discussing the central question of allocating resources between consumption and investment, Shaffer emphasizes two facts, namely that most students attend public schools, and that up to a certain age school attendance is compulsory. But neither of these facts is relevant to a logical basis for distinguishing between consumption and investments. If education were altogether free, a person would presumably consume of it until he were satiated and 'invest' in it until it would no longer increase his future earnings. If a part of the education expenditures were borne on public account, the direct private costs of education would of course be less than the total costs of education, and to the extent that such education increased the future earnings of the student, his private rate of return to what he spent on education would be higher than the rate of return to total educational expenditures entering into this part of his education. Thus, private incentives to consume and to invest in education are affected by public educational expenditures, but the fact that there are such public expenditures has no bearing on the question whether education is consumption or investment. The fact that some schooling is compulsory is also irrelevant to the question at hand. To argue that it applies is analogous to saying that a city ordinance which requires private owners of houses to install plumbing and sewage disposal facilities is a factor in determining whether such facilities are a consumer or producer durable. Clearly, the compulsory city ordinance does not provide a logical basis for distinguishing between these two types of durables.

Although Shaffer is clear in seeing the positive effects of education upon the future earnings of students, he believes that the economic motivations of students and parents to invest in education is weak or even nonexistent. They are, in Shaffer's view, strongly motivated as consumers of education but only weakly or not motivated at all as investors in education. Such a dichotomy with respect to economic motivations is far from convincing. It is undoubtedly true, as Shaffer points out, that some education is wholly for consumption, and obviously in that case there would be no investment opportunity, hence no bases for an investment motivation. But are there no economic motivations in the case of students who attend our medical schools, schools for dentists, lawyers, and engineers to invest in each of these particular skills with an eye to increases in future earnings? I am sure that the prospects of larger future earnings play a strong motivating role in these situations. Let me observe again, however, that private incentives either to consume education or to invest in it are affected by the amount and the nature of public expenditures for education. It is of course true that any attempt to explain total behavior with regard to the allocation of all public and private resources entering into education, takes one beyond the scope of the conventional private economic calculus of people. In studying the responses of private individuals to whatever investment opportunities education affords, it should be borne in mind: (a) that where the capital market does serve human investment it is subject to more imperfections than in financing physical capital; (b) that most investment in people, notably in the case of education, is in a long-period capacity, for it has a relatively long life and it is thus subject to the additional uncertainties which this implies; (c) that many individuals face serious uncertainty in assessing their innate talents when it comes to investing in themselves; and (d) that our laws discriminate against human investments [3]. These factors affect the observed responses, and their adverse effects may be confused with the real economic response, other things equal, to a given rate of return which is then thought to be weak or nonexistent.

Let me do no more than restate the effects of education upon consumption and earnings. The consumption component of education is either for current consumption, satisfying consumer well-being in the present, like food, or for future consumption, like houses. Education can also improve the capabilities of people and thus enhance their future earnings. The investment formed by education is, therefore, of two parts: a future consumption component and a future earnings component.

In 'Education and economic growth' [4], in examining education for consumption, I emphasized the current consumption component. It is now clear to me that most education that satisfies consumer preferences is for future consumption and that this component has substantial durability and it is, therefore, to the extent that it serves consumption, mainly an *enduring* consumer component, even more so than other consumer durables. As an enduring consumer component, it is the source of future utilities (and thus this component, also, contributes to future real income) which in no way enters into *measured* national income.[1] This component accordingly is like investment in houses, automobiles, refrigerators, and the like. Thus we have the following: (a) education for current consumption (which, it seems to me, is of minor importance); (b) education for long-period future consumption, making it an investment in an enduring consumer component, which is undoubtedly of considerable importance; and (c) education for skills and knowledge useful in economic endeavor and, thus, an investment in future earnings [5].

Shaffer's second point, which presents a number of the real difficulties that arise when one attempts to identify and measure the increase in earnings that are associated with education, is well founded. Differences in innate abilities, race, employment, mortality, and family connections all enter and must be faced. It should not detract from the merits of his presentation to observe that these several difficulties are very much in the forefront in the work of economists who to my knowledge are engaged in studying this set of problems. The forthcoming study by Becker [1] will be a landmark on this score as well as on other relevant theoretical and empirical issues. A major new study by Denison [2] is both bold and original in bringing aggregate analysis to bear on the *sources* of economic growth in the United States. He finds

---

1. Immediately following my presidential address, 'Investment in human capital', Abba Lerner pointed out to me in conversation the role of future utilities from education and that this part of education also represented an investment. His logical and precise mind helped to clarify my thinking on this point and I am much indebted to him.

education to be one of the major sources of economic growth after adjusting for differences in innate abilities and associated characteristics that affect earnings independently of education. Shaffer introduces a concept which he calls 'maintenance costs' which in terms of the studies available to him has been neglected. But Weisbrod [6] in his paper 'The valuation of human capital', builds on 'the proposition that the value of a person to others is measured by any excess of his contribution to production over what he consumes from production – this difference being the amount by which everyone else benefits from his productivity'. Weisbrod then proceeds to estimate the relevant consumption, or if you please, 'maintenance costs' thus conceived, and subtracts such costs from gross earnings to obtain net earnings to be capitalized.

I am reluctant to tread upon the boulders Shaffer has collected in his comments on policy. I suspect, however, from what he says about them that they are conglomerates of compressed sand and at best weak materials for his conclusions. To have started off by lecturing 'liberals' on their rationalization of federal aid to education, is not conducive to a calm and reasoned discussion of the policy implications of expenditures for education. If the argument were that the knowledge now available about the increases in earnings from education is still too fragmentary to be of any use whatsoever in making policy decisions, it would deserve careful consideration. If the argument were that knowledge about the effects of education upon future earnings will be misused by people and therefore any efforts to acquire such knowledge should be very much discouraged, this conclusion from such an argument would be patently false.

The principal source of Shaffer's confusion in discussing policy arises from his belief that, if it were to become known that particular forms of education pay in terms of increases in future earnings, policy decision which took this fact into account would necessarily no longer take into account any of the other important contributions of education. People, including those who make policy decisions, are simply not that monolithic in their evaluation of education. Shaffer's implied apprehension that society will proceed to deny advanced education to women merely because most of them do not enter the labor market is a pure illusion. If Shaffer only means that knowledge about economic returns accruing from investment in human capital, in terms of future earnings, *should not* be the exclusive basis for public policy decisions in making expenditures for education, we are in full agreement. My view on this issue can be stated very simply: It is altogether proper that people should prize highly the cultural contributions of education and they will continue to do exactly that; but it is very short-sighted of us not to see its economic contributions. Education has become a major source of economic growth [5] in winning the abundance that is to be had by developing a modern agriculture and industry. It simply would not be possible to have this abundance if our people were predominantly illiterate and unskilled. Education, therefore, in addition to having high cultural values, is presently also an investment in people to the extent that it improves their capabilities and thereby increases the future earnings of people.

Shaffer says that there are specific studies which 'clearly show . . . the income differential correlated with additional education is considerably higher for whites than for Negroes' and suggests the inference that less rather than more should therefore be spent on education for Negroes, provided this were the sole criterion. The specific studies in this case are based on national averages, making no adjustments for the effects of city size, different rates of unemployment, regions, and the quality of education. Nor is any account taken of the differences in the cost of education, including income foregone by the students, which is fully half of the total cost of college education. Furthermore, should there still remain a differential, as is to be expected because of discrimination the relevant figure is not this income differential but the absolute difference between the Negro who has, let us say, a college education and one who had only a high school education. The increase in earnings represented by this absolute difference is the reward to which one would turn in estimating the return on this investment. Zeman's [7] study, it seems to me, strongly supports the inference that differences in education are the major explanatory variable for the very large white–nonwhite income differentials in the United States.

Despite my serious misgivings about Shaffer's attempt to relate economic analysis and policy, I am, as I said at the outset, grateful to him for his most valuable comment.

References

1. BECKER, G. S. has a major study on investment in education virtually completed for the Nat. Bur. Econ. Research, New York. [Now published under the title of *Human capital*, op. cit.]
2. DENISON, E. F. (1962) *The sources of economic growth in the United States and the alternatives before us*, a study by the Committee for Economic Development. New York.
3. SCHULTZ, T. W. (1961) 'Investment in human capital', *American Economic Review*, vol. 51, pp. 14–15.
4. SCHULTZ, T. W. (1961) 'Education and economic growth', *Social forces influencing American education*, N. B. Henry (ed.), Chicago.
5. SCHULTZ, T. W. 'Education as a source of economic growth', Paper no. 61–5, 14 August, 1961, Dept. of Econ., University of Chicago.
6. WEISBROD, B. A. (1961) 'The valuation of human capital', *Jour. Pol. Econ.*, vol. 69, pp. 425–36.
7. ZEMAN, M. *A quantitative analysis of white–nonwhite income differentials in the United States*, unpublished doctoral dissertation, Univ. of Chicago, 1955.

Part Two Surveys of the Literature

In 1962 when William G. Bowen, Professor of Economics at
Princeton University, wrote his now classic survey of the literature
on the economics of education he did not hesitate to focus his
review on efforts to measure the contribution of education to
economic growth. Much of the work in the subject since 1962 still
falls within that purview. Nevertheless, the internal dynamics of
educational systems has received increasing attention since then, and
the economics of education is now conceived by economists to mean
more than the analysis of the economic value of education.
Mary Jean Bowman, Associate Professor in the Department of
Economics and the Comparative Education Center at the
University of Chicago, in her review of recent work in the area ranges
far and wide, touching on almost every issue taken up by Bowen but
many more besides. In particular, her closing pages deal with
econometric models of educational systems, a subject which, if one
may prophesy, will come to dominate the economics of education in
the 1970s.

5 W. G. Bowen

Assessing the Economic Contribution of Education

W. G. Bowen, 'Assessing the economic contribution of education: an appraisal of alternative approaches', *Higher Education. Report of the Committee under the Chairmanship of Lord Robbins 1961–63*, London, H.M.S.O., 1963, Appendix IV, pp. 73–96. Comnd 2154–4.

Of late, economists have been spending considerable time attempting to assess the economic contribution of education, and one of the hallmarks of the burgeoning literature is the variety of approaches that have been employed. The variety of tacks taken can, I suppose, be regarded as a tribute to the inventiveness of the profession, as an index of the complexity of the problem(s), or as an indicator of the fact that we simply don't know as yet how best to proceed.

The preparation of this paper has been based on the premise that at this stage it might be helpful to have a critical appraisal of the main approaches that have been tried. It is hoped that this exercise may be of some use to persons trying to interpret the results of the research that has been carried out thus far and perhaps also to persons contemplating new research.

The reader should know that I myself have not contributed to the body of literature under discussion and that I therefore write somewhat in the capacity of an outsider – a role which has some fairly obvious advantages and disadvantages. It should also be said that most of the ideas expressed in this paper are the common property of economists. I make no special claim to originality.

The following discussion is couched mainly in analytical terms, although references to data problems and to actual findings are interspersed throughout. The focus is on major approaches, not on individual studies.[1]

1. For a more broadly-gauged and comprehensive survey of work in the area of the economics of education, see Alice Rivlin's paper in *Economics of higher education*, (ed.) Selma J. Mushkin (U.S. Dept. of Health, Education, and Welfare, Office of Education, 1962); Seymour Harris' study, *Higher education, resources, and finance, 1962*, (McGraw-Hill) includes a wealth of material and references germane to the problems of planning and

Four main approaches (each having a number of variants) can be distinguished: (I) the simple correlation approach; (II) the residual approach; (III) the returns-to-education approach; and (IV) the forecasting-manpower-needs approach. In this paper each of these methods of analysis is discussed in turn, but considerably more space is devoted to the returns-to-education approach than to any of the others.

I. The Simple Correlation Approach

In the generic sense, this approach consists of correlating some overall index of educational activity with some index of the level of economic activity.

Inter-country comparisons (cross-sectional)

Inter-country correlations at a fixed point in time constitute one well-known member of this group. Svennilson, Edding, and Elvin, for example, have correlated enrolment ratios and GNP *per capita*, and have found that there is indeed a positive relationship, although there is also considerable dispersion, particularly among the countries falling in the middle range.[2]

Comparisons of this kind serve a number of useful purposes. For one thing, they enable countries to see their own educational efforts in the perspective of what is being done elsewhere, and thus can serve to disturb complacency. Comparisons between countries in similar economic circumstances may also provide at least a rough idea of what is possible, with 'possible' defined in terms of actual educational outlays in countries having an approximately equal GNP *per capita*. Comparisons between countries at different stages of economic development may provide the less-advanced countries with a rough notion of what general level of educational activity is associated with a more advanced stage of economic development – so long as one remembers that standards

financing higher education. John Vaizey's recent book, *The economics of education*, Faber and Faber, 1962, contains discussions of many of the topics treated below.

2. *Targets for education in Europe in 1970*, paper prepared for Washington Conference of the O.E.C.D., 1961, p. 75.

in this respect, as in so many others, have a habit of changing rapidly.

The construction of meaningful inter-country comparisons is, of course, beset by many practical problems. We can leave aside the problem of obtaining comparable GNP figures – provided we realize that we are leaving aside a subject to which a whole segment of professional literature has been devoted. Finding comparable indices of educational activity (or attainment) is no less difficult, given the pronounced inter-country variations in educational systems.[3] If expenditure data are used, it is essential that cognizance be taken of the opportunity costs (foregone output) involved in having students attend school rather than work.[4] It is also necessary to recognize that equal resource expenditures in two countries imply equal educational output only if resources are used with the same degree of efficiency in both countries – and we know astonishingly little about how efficiency is to be defined and measured, in spite of a recent upsurge of interest in the subject.

The practical problems of constructing indices can no doubt be solved to a tolerably satisfactory extent, and emphasis ought not to be placed here. It is the more basic question of what cause and effect relationship is bound up in education – GNP correlations[5]

3. The debate in the British House of Commons on the Government's policies toward university education illustrates beautifully the way in which different measures of educational activity can lead to radically different conclusions. Mr Gaitskell, leading off for the Opposition, cited estimates of total university students as a proportion of the total population in various countries to show how far Britain was lagging behind other countries. Mr Henry Brooke, replying for the Government, cited percentages of the relevant age group *graduating* from universities to show that in fact Britain was doing better than many of the same Western European countries mentioned by Mr Gaitskell. (See *Hansard*, v. 657, no. 91 (5 April 1962) pp. 719 ff., and especially pp. 726, 734–6.)

4. In the case of the United States, T. W. Schultz ('Capital formation by education', *Journal of Political Economy*, December 1960, p. 582) has estimated that opportunity costs were equal to about three-fifths of the total costs of high school and college education in 1956.

5. From here on, all general references to correlations between education and GNP should be interpreted to mean correlations between *relative* measures of educational activity (e.g. proportions of the total population in school or fractions of the total GNP spent on education) and GNP *per capita*.

that deserves emphasis. A positive correlation can be viewed as evidence in support of the proposition that spending money on education is an important way of raising a country's GNP. But the same correlation can also be viewed as evidence in support of the proposition that education is an important consumer good on which countries elect to spend more as their GNP rises.[6]

The trouble is that these propositions are almost certainly both true *to some extent* – and, in the absence of other information, we have no way of disentangling the two relationships. The inescapable conclusion is that simple education – GNP correlations, in and of themselves, cannot tell us anything about the quantitative dimensions of the contribution that education makes to economic growth.[7]

Inter-temporal correlations

A second basic variant of the simple correlation approach consists of correlating education and GNP within a given country over time. Schultz has recently made a correlation of this type for the U.S. over the period 1900 to 1956, and, treating education solely as a consumer good, he found that the income-elasticity of demand for education was 3.5.[8] But treating education solely as a consumer good begs the question of course (as Schultz is the first to admit), and one must conclude that here again the two-way causation problem makes it impossible to give a satisfactory interpretation to the figures.

Attempts at inter-temporal correlations also highlight the time-

6. This assumes that the income-elasticity of demand for education is greater than unity and that any negative substitution effect, arising as a consequence of the (likely) possibility that the price of education will go up relative to other prices, will be swamped by the positive income effect. These assumptions seem reasonable.

7. There are, of course, many other considerations in addition to the two-way causation problem that make it difficult to interpret cross-sectional correlations between education and GNP. Apart from the universal problem of holding other things constant, there are time-lag and external economies problems, both of which will be discussed below in other contexts.

8. T. W. Schultz, 'Education and economic growth', in *Yearbook of the National Society for the Study of Education*, 1961, p. 60; Seymour Harris, in *The market for college graduates*, Harvard University Press, 1949, pp. 160–72, has also made correlations of this kind.

lag problem that plagues many approaches. Education is a long-lived asset, in that an educated man presumably contributes more on account of his education, not just one year after his graduation, but for much of the rest of his life. If a country doubled its expenditure on education in year t, the positive economic effects ought not to be looked for in year t's GNP figures (which actually will be lower because students who would have worked are now in school), but in the figures for all the years from, say, $t + 4$ on.[9]

Inter-industry and inter-firm correlations

Just as countries differ in the relative emphasis placed on education, so do industries and firms within industries. While it is difficult to find an entirely satisfactory way of measuring an industry's emphasis on 'education', we can perhaps think in terms of such measures as the proportion of the work force that has had training beyond the secondary school level or the percentage of gross receipts spent on research and development activities. Correlations can then be made between one of these indices of educational emphasis and the profitability of the industry or firm. Comparisons of this type can, of course, be made on a cross-sectional basis within a single country, over time, or on an inter-country basis. The rest of this discussion will deal only with the one-country, cross-sectional case, although many of the comments will also be applicable to inter-temporal and inter-country comparisons.

The first thing to be said is that we should certainly not expect to find all of the industries (or firms) under investigation using the same combination of inputs. Differences in the technological possibilities open to firms engaged in different lines of business,

9. The best way of surmounting this problem is by measuring the total *stock* of education at different points in time, not just the current level of educational activity. (For a recent attempt at this, see Schultz's paper in the 1961 *Education and economic growth* volume, pp. 64 ff. Note, however, that in some of his work Schultz suggests the desirability of calculating a kind of present value of the stock by weighting younger persons more heavily than older persons; this makes good sense if one wants to know what the economic worth of the stock is, but not if one just wants to relate current educational attainments to current economic output.) Stock measurements are also better than flow measurements, in the case of cross-sectional inter-country comparisons, for exactly the same reasons.

and differences in the relative scarcity of various inputs in the geographical areas where the firms happen to be located would both tend to produce differences in the relative emphasis placed on 'educationally-heavy' inputs. It is this line of reasoning that has led Jewkes to object to the argument that the industries spending comparatively little on research and development should try to raise themselves to the standards of expenditure characteristic of other industries.[10]

The usual profit-maximization model of firm behaviour does indeed suggest the likelihood that firms in different circumstances will employ different combinations of inputs, but the model does *not* suggest that there should be any systematic difference between profit levels in industries using an exceptionally large amount of any particular input (trained manpower in this case) and industries using relatively small amounts of the input. And this is why inter-industry correlations between emphasis on educational inputs and profitability may prove to be of real interest. If a pronounced positive correlation were to be found, there would indeed be something to be explained.

This kind of inter-industry or inter-firm correlation has a real advantage over the more aggregative kinds of education-GNP correlations, in that the two-way causation problem is not so serious. We do not usually think of firms 'consuming' education simply because they 'like it' in the way that we think of individual persons partaking of education for its own sake. Even if we concede that modern-day firms have a certain element of the consumer mentality in their make-up (and thus may simply enjoy, for status or other reasons, having some high-powered scientists about), this element is surely not as pronounced as in the household sector of the economy. Consequently, a positive correlation here would at the very least suggest the possibility that differences in expenditures on educationally-heavy inputs have helped to create profit differences; that a dis-equilibrium situation still persists, and that a shift of resources toward the educationally-heavy inputs would be justified purely on the private profitability criterion.[11]

10. John Jewkes, 'How much science?', *Economic Journal*, March 1960, pp. 9–10.

11. It should be recognized that the shift of resources could take one of two forms: first, there might simply be an increase in expenditure on trained

Mention should be made of one serious pitfall in making inter-industry correlations of this kind. It may be that industries which place a relatively heavy emphasis on educational inputs also happen to be industries which enjoy an above-average degree of market power, and that the apparent relation between relatively high profits and educational inputs is better interpreted as a reflection of the profitability of market power than as a reflection of the profitability of emphasizing educational inputs. Actually, for reasons advanced by Schumpeter and others, expenditures on trained manpower (a key ingredient in the process of innovation) and degree of market power may be inextricably bound up in many instances. This cross-relationship would certainly have to be studied carefully by anyone intent on carrying out a serious inquiry into correlations between profitability and educational inputs.[12]

Inter-industry correlations will most certainly not answer many of the crucial questions involved in assessing the economic contribution of education – for instance, the importance of external economies will not be reflected. Research along these general lines does appear to offer at least a modest promise of being helpful, however, and deserves to be encouraged.

II. The Residual Approach

In general terms, this approach consists of taking the total increase in economic output of a country over a given period of time, identifying as much of the total increase as possible with

---

manpower by the firms and industries that had lagged behind in this respect; second, there might be a shift of resources away from industries in which the nature of activities did not justify spending more money on trained manpower, and toward those industries where the emphasis on trained manpower was already comparatively great.

12. Another type of objection that can be raised against this sort of inquiry is that, if industry would gain by devoting a larger part of its collective resources to educationally-oriented inputs, it would automatically do so. But this line of argument overlooks the very real possibility that ignorance of rewards is particularly likely to exist in this nebulous area, and that imperfections in capital markets may prevent the raising of new capital and the interchange of capital between industries both of which are necessary for an equilibrium situation to obtain.

measurable inputs (capital and labour being the two measurable inputs usually chosen) and then saying that the residual is attributable to the unspecified inputs. It is because education and advances in knowledge are usually regarded as the most important of the unspecified inputs that this approach deserves to be discussed in the context of the contribution-of-education question.

When it comes to actually implementing the residual approach, there are a number of alternative techniques that can be adopted, only a few of which will be mentioned here. First, it is possible to proceed by calculating an input series for the labour input (based, for instance, on hours worked), a separate, constant-price input series for the capital input, and then combining these two input series into an overall arithmetic index of inputs (using the relative shares of labour and capital in the total GNP as weights). Next the rate of increase in this aggregate input series is compared with the rate of increase in an aggregate output series (also expressed in constant prices); and by simply subtracting it is possible to obtain a measure of the contribution of the 'residual' or 'third factor'.

Kendrick of the National Bureau of Economic Research has followed this general procedure, and he has found that for the U.S. economy, over the period between 1889 and 1957, the combined input index increased at an average rate of 1.9 per cent per annum and the output index increased about 3.5 per cent per annum, leaving a 'residual' increase of about 1.6 per cent per annum (called by Kendrick the increase in 'total factor productivity').[13] Thus, 46 per cent of the increase in total output is ascribed to the residual. The contribution of the residual can also be expressed as a percentage of the increase in output per unit of labour input, rather than as a percentage of the increase in total output. Following this procedure (and working with a figure of 2.0 per cent per year as the average rate of increase in output per unit of labour input)[14] it is possible to attribute roughly 80 per

13. John W. Kendrick, *Productivity trends in the United States*, Princeton University Press for the National Bureau of Economic Research, 1961. The figures given in the text are from Table 6, p. 79.

14. Actually, the 2·0 per cent figure (taken from Table 1, p. 60 of Kendrick's study) is not strictly comparable with the figures given above in that it is for only the private sector of the economy, whereas the earlier figures were for the national economy as a whole. However, over long periods, the differences involved in these two types of measures are slight.

cent of the increased output per unit of labour input to the residual, with only about 20 per cent being attributed to increases in the stock of physical capital.

Solow and others have followed a somewhat different procedure, the basic difference being that Solow *et al.* have made explicit assumptions about the nature of the underlying production function. Dealing with a linear, homogeneous production function, and assuming that technical change is 'neutral' (i.e. in and of itself does not alter the rate of substitution between capital and labour), the residual has been found to equal roughly 90 per cent of the increase in output per man-hour in the U.S. economy between 1915 and 1955.[15]

In some respects the recent study by Edward F. Denison of the sources of U.S. economic growth[16] constitutes a third variant of the residual approach, in that Denison estimates the effect of *advances in knowledge* by simply subtracting the rate of growth attributable to all the other inputs he identifies from the total rate of growth. Denison ends up with a residual that is very much smaller than any of the figures given above, but this is because he has made separate estimates of the contributions of factors such as formal education and economies of scale, which have been included in the residual category by most other authors. And, in making his estimate of the contribution of formal education, Denison has employed the direct returns-to-education approach, which is discussed in considerable detail in the next section of this paper.

Before moving on to this topic, however, a few general

15. The 90 per cent figure has been taken from a paper by B. F. Massell: 'Capital formation and technological change in United States manufacturing', *Review of Economics and Statistics*, May 1960, pp. 182–8. Massell adopts the theoretical approach originally used by Solow 'Technical change and the aggregate production function', *Review of Economics and Statistics*, August 1957, pp. 312–20, but deals with somewhat different data and makes slightly different adjustments for factors such as idle capital. Actually Solow ended up with a figure of 87 per cent and so the results are really very similar. Evsey Domar presents a lucid discussion of Solow's work and of the work of others in his recent paper: 'On the measurement of technological change', *Economic Journal*, December 1961, pp. 709–29.

16. *The sources of economic growth in the United States and the alternative before us*, Supplementary Paper No. 13, published by the Committee for Economic Development (New York, 1962).

comments concerning the residual approach are in order. Viewed from the standpoint of a desire to know something about the economic contribution of education, the residual approach has two main defects.

Taking the more technical of the two problems first, neither the National Bureau of Economic Research work nor the production function procedure takes adequate account of the interplay between capital inputs and the advancing knowledge component of the residual. As Domar put it in commenting on Solow's work, capital in this context 'does not serve as the instrument for the introduction of technical change into the production process . . . (It is simply) wooden ploughs piled up on the top of existing wooden ploughs'.[17]

Another way of making essentially the same point (or at least a very closely-related point) is by noting that available indices of capital inputs generally fail to reflect improvements in the quality, or 'productivity', of capital. Anderson[18] has shown that the apparent historical decline in the constant-price capital–output ratio is misleading for this very reason. The source of the problem is that, while the deflation of money measures of national income to a constant-price basis is done by using prices per unit of *output* (thus catching improvements in output per unit of input), money measures of capital are deflated on an elements-of-cost basis which cannot reflect improvements in the productivity of the capital equipment itself. (If a constant amount of labour and materials goes into two capital assets produced in different years, the deflated values will be equal, even though the newer capital asset may produce much more than did the older capital asset.) Consequently, the 'true' contribution of physical capital is likely to have been somewhat greater than the figures cited earlier suggest, and the 'true' size of the residual correspondingly smaller.

The more general difficulty is, of course, the 'residual' nature of the 'residual'. For reasons noted above, the residual, as usually measured, no doubt embodies the results of some secular improvement in the quality of capital assets; it also encompasses changes in output attributable to economies of scale, to improve-

17. Domar, *Economic Journal*, December 1961, p. 712.
18. Paul S. Anderson, 'The apparent decline in the capital output ratios', *Quarterly Journal of Economics*, November 1961, pp. 615–34.

ments in the health of the labour force, to informal as well as formal education, to changes in the product mix, to reorganizations of the economic order, and to who knows what else. Moses Abramovitz has called it a 'measure of our ignorance'.[19] The heterogeneity of the elements that go to make up the residual means, of course, that a large residual cannot safely be interpreted as a mandate for more spending on any particular project, whether it be a massive research and development effort or better school lunches.

However, the size of the residual certainly does serve as a mandate to explore in detail the economic effects of activities often neglected. It seems clear that the simple accumulation of physical capital, in and of itself, has not played the dominant role in economic growth sometimes ascribed to it.

III. The Direct Returns-to-Education Approach

An obvious way of studying the economic consequences of education is by contrasting the lifetime earnings of people who have had 'more' education with the lifetime earnings of people who have had 'less' education. The difference in lifetime earnings can then be expressed as an annual percentage rate of return on the costs involved in obtaining the education.[20] Actually, as the following discussion is likely to make painfully clear, this approach, like so many others, is deceptively simple.

At the outset it is useful to distinguish two ways of looking at direct returns to education: (a) the personal profit orientation; (b) the national productivity orientation.

The 'personal profit orientation' consists of looking at

19. *Resources and output trends in the United States since 1870*, Occasional Paper 52, New York, National Bureau of Economic Research, 1956, p. 11. It is to the great credit of the authors of the estimates of the residual that without exception they have repeatedly emphasized this aspect of its character.

20. For references to some early studies of this kind, see J. R. Walsh, 'The capital concept applied to man', *Quarterly Journal of Economics*, February 1935, p. 235. Among the more recent studies, Gary Becker's work has received by far the most attention from professional economists, although only a preliminary report on his research has been published so far ('Underinvestment in college education?' *American Economic Review*, May 1960, pp. 346–54.)

differences in the net earnings of people with varying amounts of education as evidence of the amount of personal financial gain that can be associated with the attainment of a given level of education. This is, of course, the relevant orientation for the individual trying to make private calculations (in a country where students pay a substantial share of educational costs), and it can also be argued that evidence of this kind is germane to a country's decision as to what fraction of the costs of education should be borne by the students themselves.

The 'national productivity orientation' consists of looking at education-related earnings differentials as partial evidence of the effects of education on the output of the country, and is based on the premise that in a market economy differences in earnings reflect differences in productivity. This orientation is relevant to the question of whether society as a whole is investing the right share of its resources in education.

From the standpoint of procedures and problems, these two ways of looking at direct returns to education are sufficiently similar to allow us to discuss them together, although there are also differences which will require comment from time to time. Right here it is worth noting that in calculating rates of return the relevant concept of educational cost depends on the investigator's orientation (only private costs, including opportunity costs, are relevant to an assessment of the private rate of return, whereas all costs, including public subsidies, are relevant to the measurement of direct social returns) as does the relevant concept of earnings (after tax in the private returns case, before tax in the social returns case). Other differences will be touched on in due course.

So far we have spoken of two groups of persons: a group having 'more' education and a group having 'less' education. When it comes to calculating actual rates of return, however, this vague dichotomy will not do, and many of the recent studies have calculated separate rates of return for each stage of the educational process. While there is obviously much to be said for dividing education into stages, the results can be misleading if looked at in isolation from one another. Calculating the rate of return on primary education by comparing the net earnings of persons who have completed just the primary grades with the net earnings of persons who have not had even this much education is bound to produce an erroneously low result in that no account is taken of the fact that primary education is a stepping stone to secondary and college education. The value of the option to continue one's education ought to be included in the rate of return on both primary and secondary education, and the value of this option obviously depends on the rate of return to be had from the higher levels of education and on the probability that the option will be exercised. Education must be viewed as a series of related steps. Weisbrod has made this point quite clearly, and, to illustrate the order of magnitude involved, has shown that recognizing the value of the option to obtain additional education raises the expected 1939 rate of return on grade school education from a previous estimate of 35 per cent to 52 per cent.[21]

Separate rates of return can also be calculated for males and females, for persons of different races, and so on. One of Becker's most interesting (and disturbing) findings is that whereas the rate of return on the cost of college education was 9 per cent for urban white males in the United States as of 1950, the comparable rate of return for non-whites was about two percentage points lower than this – presumably because of greater job discrimination against college-educated non-whites than against other non-whites.[22]

The rate-of-return approach has many attractions, not the least of which is that educational benefits are related to educational costs in a way that holds out the hope of providing useful information concerning the adequacy of the overall level of investment in education and the extent to which economic benefits accrue directly to private individuals. But, the implementation of this approach is also subject to many difficulties, which must be examined in some detail if we are to minimize the risk of misinterpreting results.

The 'holding other things constant' problem

Unfortunately for purposes of analysis, groups with differing amounts of education tend to differ systematically in terms of other attributes which are also likely to influence relative

21. Burton A. Weisbrod, 'Education and investment in human capital', *The Journal of Political Economy*, October 1962, pp. 106–23. [See Reading 8.]

22. Becker, op. cit., pp. 347–8.

earnings. An oft-quoted (and justifiable) criticism of many studies purporting to show that a person could add 'X' thousand dollars to his lifetime income by going to college is that they attribute results to education which were caused, *in part*, by differences in intelligence, ambition, family connections, and so on. At the same time, it must be emphasized that this problem has been recognized by the investigators themselves and that attempts have been made to adjust for differences in factors such as ability and family background.[23]

No one would claim that the efforts to date have been entirely satisfactory, and one of the reasons is the difficulty of obtaining satisfactory measures of such elusive variables as ability and motivation. (It is much easier to adjust for differences in mortality rates and unemployment experience.) We also need to know more than we do at present about the relationship between different *levels* of ability and differences in earnings associated with varying amounts of formal education. The results of a questionnaire study reported by Bridgman suggest that differences in earnings (between college graduates and 'comparable' high school graduates) were greatest for those of highest ability.[24] The relation between levels of intellectual ability and the likelihood that one will profit economically from higher education deserves much more study, particularly in the context of discussions concerning the extension of higher education to a larger proportion of a given population.

23. Becker has standardized his data for differences in ability on the basis of test score information, and for differences in unemployment and mortality as well. He reports (op. cit. p. 349) that adjusting for differential ability reduces the rate of return on a college education by about two percentage points (from 11 to 9 per cent). Results of detailed case-study type inquiries into the education–ability-earning relationship have been reported by Wolfle and Bridgman in the volume of papers edited by Seymour Harris, *Higher Education in the United States; the economic problems*, Harvard University Press, 1960, pp. 178–9 and pp. 180–4. Denison, in his C.E.D. study of the sources of economic growth, has reduced actual earnings differentials by one-third in order to take account of the effects of characteristics correlated with education (especially ability), but he acknowledges in a very forthright fashion that this adjustment represents nothing more than a rough guess on his part as to the quantitative importance of differences in ability and in other associated factors. (op. cit., pp. 69–70.)

24. op. cit., p. 178.

Do earnings measure productivity?

The question of whether differences in relative earnings reflect differences in productivity does not arise so long as one looks at returns to education solely from the personal profit point of view. But, if we wish to interpret rates of return on education as indicative of over- or under-investment in education from the national productivity point of view, then this question becomes very important indeed.

In general, in an economy where relative earnings are subject to the push and pull of market forces, we should certainly expect to find relatively high earnings accruing to persons possessing special skills which enable them to make a greater economic contribution than the average person. However, there are also reasons for thinking that earnings differentials may not always be an accurate reflection of differences in marginal productivities, and the likely effects of these other considerations on rates of return figures must be examined carefully.

'Conspicuous production' and 'tradition-bound' wage structures

The link between relative wages and marginal productivities will be weakened to the extent that employers do not set wages so as to maximize their profits. The phrase 'conspicuous production' refers to the possibility that some employers may choose to hire college graduates (and pay them 'college graduate' salaries) for jobs which do not really require college training. Instances of this type can no doubt be found in a country such as the United States, but I suspect that we tend to exaggerate the frequency with which bosses insist on paying extra for unnecessary qualifications.[25]

25. It may well be that as a higher proportion of the people in a country receive a college education, employers, in order to recruit people possessing a certain level of ability, will find themselves forced to recruit college graduates – even though college training may be unnecessary for the job. However, this situation ought not to be confused with the 'conspicuous production' case. To the extent that these people are paid higher salaries solely because of their basic ability, employers cannot be accused of non-profit-maximizing behaviour. Actually this kind of situation affords an excellent illustration of the need to avoid attributing higher salaries due to ability differentials to education (as discussed above), but it is quite different from a situation in which an employer pays more to a college graduate holding a particular job just because he is a college graduate.

The phrase 'tradition-bound wage structures' refers to what may well be a more important variant of non-profit-maximizing behaviour. Persons who have studied the so-called 'under-developed countries' have noted a tendency to continue paying relatively high salaries to educated persons in, for example, the Government service, when such a salary policy is no longer necessary from a recruitment standpoint.[26] In countries where the salary structure is rigid because of status overtones, calculations of monetary returns to education can be very misleading as a guide to educational policy.

The non-monetary attractions of jobs open to graduates

All occupations have their non-monetary plusses and minuses, and the wage structure presumably adjusts accordingly – occupations which are dirty, hard, or unpleasant in any respect will be characterized by higher earnings than those which require the same kinds of qualifications but which are cleaner, easier, more interesting, have a higher status appeal, and so on. There would be no need to dwell on the existence of these non-monetary attractions if they were of roughly the same order of importance in the case of jobs open to highly-educated persons and jobs open to persons with less education. In actual fact, however, it seems clear that non-monetary attractions are much greater in the case of the usual jobs filled by college graduates; hence, non-monetary considerations cannot be dismissed as a neutral factor.[27]

It may also be mentioned in passing that there is likely to be an income effect at work here, and that the higher the real income of

26. See, for example, the paper prepared by F. H. Harbison for the O.E.C.D. Conference on Education held in Washington in the fall of 1961.

27. I grant that attitudes toward the non-monetary attractions of certain jobs vary significantly from one person to the next; and I also grant that my own preferences no doubt influence my judgement on this point. But it still seems safe to say that, if salaries were the same and if qualifications were not a constraint, most people would prefer the kinds of jobs that are in fact open only (or mainly) to holders of degrees. Studies that have been made of popular attitudes towards various vocations support this position. (A poll conducted for the President's Commission on Higher Education and cited by Harris [*The market for college graduates*, 1949, p. 7] showed that, with regard to prestige, virtually all occupations ranked in the top twenty-five by a cross-section of Americans would normally require a college education but most others would not.)

a society, the greater the weight that the society as a whole is likely to put on the non-monetary side of occupational choice. The President of an American University remarked not long ago that as real income continues to rise we may well see the day when a garbage collector is paid more than a full professor.

The important question is: how (if at all) should one adjust rates of return to take account of differences in non-monetary advantages? This is a very troublesome question at the conceptual level, as well as at the empirical level, and part of the explanation is that the answer depends on whether one is looking at returns to education from the personal profit or national productivity point of view.

From the standpoint of the individual gain from education (personal profit), it seems clear that we ought to add in a sum approximating the dollar equivalent of the non-monetary advantages. Non-monetary advantages certainly do accrue to the individuals concerned and increase their welfare. At the moment, quantitative estimates are lacking, but my guess is that taking account of this consideration would increase the calculated rate of return on higher education (and especially on graduate education) to a very marked extent.

From the national productivity standpoint, one might think at first that a similar upward adjustment is required.[28] But, to the extent that the non-monetary aspects of employment are purely a supply-side phenomenon (that is, affect only the willingness of individuals to take jobs at alternative rates of pay and not the costs incurred by employers in hiring additional men), this is not so. The greater the non-monetary attractions of any occupation, the greater the number of people who will be willing to enter the occupation at a given wage and thus the greater the ability of the employer to hire a given number of people at a lower rate of pay. The extent of non-monetary attractions determines the position of the supply curve of labour, but this does not alter the fact that the employer will still pay that money wage which will equal the

28. This seems to be Villard's position (see his criticism of Becker's work in the *American Economic Review*, May 1960, p. 376). Many other writers have said essentially the same thing, and I should add that at one point I too shared this position. As the rest of this discussion indicates, I have now revised my views; I have Ralph Turvey to thank for forcing me to think this problem through more fully.

value of the marginal product produced by the last man hired. If there were suddenly a sharp increase in the non-monetary attractions of a particular occupation, the result would be a south-easterly shift of the supply schedule (more people willing to enter the occupation at each possible wage) and a movement along the demand (marginal revenue productivity) schedule to a new equilibrium characterized by a lower relative wage and a larger number of people engaged in the occupation. To put the matter another way, if we compare two occupations for which there are identical marginal revenue productivity schedules but which differ in their non-monetary attractions, we should expect to find a lower wage and a larger number of persons engaged in the more attractive of the two occupations – and the discrepancy in relative wages would measure the difference in *marginal* productivities.[29]

The above line of argument holds only to the extent that non-monetary attractions are truly 'non-monetary' and do not cost the employer anything. This is generally true of such attractions as prestige, but it may not be true of attractions such as subsidized housing, subsidized travel, and long, paid vacations. Allowances for 'fringe benefits' of this type should be added to the basic wage, and it may be that fringes of this kind are more common in occupations filled by relatively well-educated people. An upward adjustment in the rate of return on education should be made to take account of any such discrepancies that can be shown to exist.

29. The reason for going through this much detail (and presenting what will appear to professional economists to be a very elementary exposition) is that there have been some misunderstandings, most of which no doubt stem from mixing together the personal profit and national productivity orientations. A major source of confusion to many persons not trained as professional economists is the fact that the 'productivity' of an occupation cannot be thought of as a fixed magnitude but must be expected to vary according to the number of persons engaged in the occupation – and it is the productivity of the last person employed (the marginal productivity) which is relevant for most purposes. The fact that in equilibrium (at the level of employment where it will not pay the employer either to add or lay off one more man) the marginal revenue product (and thus the wage) in occupation 'A' may be lower than in occupation 'B' does not mean that at other levels of employment this same relationship between the marginal productivities would necessarily hold; nor does it mean that if the same number of persons were employed in each occupation the marginal productivity in occupation 'A' would still be lower than in occupation 'B' – it might or it might not.

There is one final point – the argument presented here is based on the assumption that persons interested in rates of return on education, from what we have called the 'national productivity' standpoint, are concerned solely with the effects of education on the nation's G N P. If one wishes to work from a broader national frame of reference and look at the effects of education on the total 'welfare' of the citizenry, then once again, as in the case of the personal profit orientation, a full adjustment for non-monetary attractions is in order since such attractions most certainly do contribute to the aggregate welfare of the populace.

External economies, indirect benefits, or social benefits

Anyone using direct returns to education as a guide to the proper level of spending must recognize that rates of return based on the relative earnings of groups of individuals will never reflect the external economies (or indirect benefits, or social benefits, depending on one's terminological preferences) generated by education. By definition, external economies consist of those benefits which are not confined to individual economic units – and thus do not show up in the relative earnings of identifiable groups – but which 'spill-over' to the economy as a whole, raising the level of real income and welfare generally.

While external effects are by no means confined to education, education is probably more likely to generate indirect benefits than any other single activity of comparable scope. Without pretending to present anything resembling a complete catalogue, it may be useful to mention a few of the main kinds of external effects.

As everyone knows, the educational process is intimately related to advances in knowledge, and it is equally clear that advances in knowledge can have important economic effects. Yet, because new ideas are not used up by being understood, and because the results of basic research are rapidly disseminated free of charge (over the entire world in many cases), the economic contribution of basic research will not be fully reflected in the relative earnings of the producers of this new knowledge.[30] Nor is

30. W. Leontief presents a lucid discussion of the underlying reasons why advances in knowledge have the attributes of indirect benefits in his preface to Leonard Silk's *The research revolution*, McGraw-Hill, 1960.

it just research in natural science that has important economic consequences – it would be interesting to know the magnitude of the increase in real incomes that has stemmed from our improved understanding of how to prevent large-scale unemployment.

There are also, of course, important social and political benefits of education which accrue to the populace as a whole – a better informed electorate, more culturally alive neighbourhoods, a healthier and less crime-prone population, and so on. What is not always recognized is that these social and political consequences may in turn have significant economic effects – the efficiency with which goods are exchanged is obviously enhanced by general literacy. To the extent that education reduces crime (even if only by keeping children off the streets during the day) the country can shift resources that would have had to be used for the police function to other ends, and so on.

While education could conceivably entail social costs as well as social benefits (for instance by producing a class of unemployed, unproductive, frustrated, and socially-destructive intellectuals), there is no doubt that on balance the positive benefits are paramount. However, it is one thing to be able to say that external benefits are obviously very important and quite another to know what order of magnitude to attach to the word 'very'. I think that most people who have worked actively on the problem of estimating national returns to education are agreed that this is the biggest unsolved riddle of all. At the present time all we know is that estimates of direct returns ought to be adjusted upward to take account of external economies – we do not know how much of an adjustment to make or even how to go about finding out how much of an adjustment to make.[31]

Collective power

Finally, it is worth noting that the existence of collective power in certain sectors may influence relative earnings. It has been argued,

31. Some progress can be reported, however. Weisbrod, in his recent *Journal of Political Economy* paper (October 1962, pp. 106–23), has suggested ways of estimating the value of savings in terms of certain 'avoidance costs' (i.e. costs that, were it not for education, we would have had to incur for, say, added police protection). Others have attempted direct assessments of the economic value of various kinds of basic research. But all would agree that there is room for much more work on this problem.

for example, that some part of the relatively high earnings enjoyed by doctors in the United States should be attributed directly to the effectiveness of the American Medical Association in limiting entry and keeping fees high.[32]

In interpreting the implications for educational policy of an 'artificially' high rate of return of this kind, it is necessary to be very careful indeed. While the wage will be higher than under competitive conditions, so will marginal productivity (because of a smaller active labour input), and therefore an increased investment in this particular type of activity would be called for. The fact that in cases of this type relatively high rates of return have been caused in part by organized power groups (rather than solely by ignorance, underestimates of returns by policy makers, or imperfections in the capital market) makes no difference at all to the basic conclusion – that the relatively high rates of return imply under-investment and a mis-allocation of resources. But, the cause of the relatively high rate of return has, of course, important implications for the selection of the most appropriate remedial policy measure – a relatively high rate of return attributable to the exercise of market power may be best treated by trying to eliminate the source of the market imperfection.[33]

The consumption versus *investment problem*

Critics of the direct returns to education approach have repeatedly emphasized that such calculations ignore the so-called 'consumption' or 'cultural' contributions of education. The point is that education presumably has purposes besides that of increasing a person's potential economic productivity – yet it is only his economic productivity (and in fact only that part of his economic productivity which passes through the market mechanism)[34] that enters into the measurement of returns to education.

32. The classic is by M. Friedman and S. S. Kuznets *Income from independent professional practice*, National Bureau of Economic Research, 1946.

33. I am indebted to Thomas Ribich for helpful comments on the subject-matter of this paragraph.

34. The importance of non-market production furthered by education is illustrated by Weisbrod's estimate that the annual value of services performed by persons who fill out their own income tax returns has amounted to about 66 million dollars, which is almost 1 per cent of elementary school

Thus, no account is taken of the value of the current consumption enjoyed by the student who may say that his college years were 'the best years of his life'. (True, there may be some students who regard education as a painful process to be endured for the sake of future gain, but such students would no doubt turn out to be in the minority, especially if forced to contrast the net attractions of being a student with the net attractions of what in fact they would be doing if they were not students rather than with the attractions of what they would like to be doing.) In the case of primary education, parents no doubt derive immediate pleasure from having the children in school rather than at home, apart from that felt by the children.

It is also generally agreed that education confers long and lasting benefits of a consumption variety by extending the range of activities which a person is able to enjoy during his leisure hours. For many people, education has no doubt awakened interests which have been a source of pleasure over an entire lifetime. In this sense, education can be thought of as conferring a durable consumer good of great value.

The important question is not whether education is a source of present and future pleasure – unquestionably it is, quite apart from its effects on one's ability to obtain a satisfying and productive job – but how, if at all, estimates of the direct monetary returns to education should be adjusted to take account of such considerations.

Certainly the individual trying to decide whether or not to continue his education will want to add his own estimate of 'consumption' values to his estimate of job-related values in coming to a decision.

To calculate a national rate of return figure, Schultz has argued that the way to proceed is by first identifying the consumption component of educational costs, and then subtracting this amount from total educational costs in order to arrive at the base level of costs which can properly be used (in conjunction with earnings data) to calculate the rate of return on the investment

---

costs. Were this service provided through the market it would, of course, be priced and included in the national income. (This estimate comes from the paper by Weisbrod cited in footnote 31.)

portion of educational expenditures. If we suppose, for example, that half of all educational costs can be regarded as consumption outlays, then it would follow that the rate of return on educational investment was twice as high as the figure suggested by a simple comparison of differential earnings with total educational costs – Becker's 9 per cent rate of return would be raised to 18 per cent.[35]

The above approach suffers from two related limitations. First of all, it is exceedingly difficult to estimate the so-called consumption component of educational costs. As Schultz himself has emphasized, to a large degree the consumption and investment components of a person's education are inextricably bound up. In our better educational systems, pure enjoyment (present and future) is in the nature of the case obtained simultaneously with the training necessary for a future career. Distinctions based on 'general' or 'liberal arts' courses *versus* 'vocational' courses fail to appreciate both that general courses can make a great contribution to one's ability to do many kinds of work well and that the so-called vocational courses can often be highly stimulating and enjoyable. In short, we must recognize that here we are dealing with a joint cost problem in which essentially the same inputs are transmuted simultaneously into two end-products (professional preparation and pleasure).

In the second place, even if we somehow succeed in isolating a pure consumption element, subtracting this portion of costs from total educational costs is a valid procedure only if we are prepared to assume that society values this 'educational consumption' as highly as it values all alternative kinds of consumption – ranging from cars to public parks. This implicit assumption must be made explicit and defended. The problem is, of course, complicated by the fact that the consumption and investment aspects noted above are complementary – society does not really have the option of ceasing to make expenditures on the consumption aspect of education (assuming for the sake of argument that a higher value was attached to public parks) without simultaneously curtailing expenditures on the investment aspect.

Given this situation, the logical way to proceed is to make an

35. See T. W. Schultz, 'Investment in human capital', *American Economic Review* March 1961, pp. 12–13. [See Reading 1.]

explicit evaluation of the worth of the consumption contributions of education to society (expressed in dollar terms), next add this sum to the monetary returns from education, and then compare the total benefits to the total costs in order to see if the undertaking as a whole is sufficiently worthwhile to merit devoting more resources to it. The evaluation of the consumption component depends, of course, on society's preferences and cannot be deduced in a mechanical way from any known set of figures. This is also true of parks and many other things, and the difficulties involved in making this kind of evaluation certainly do not justify the easy escape of ignoring the value of the consumption benefits altogether.[36]

The discount rate (or 'other' rate of return) problem

Since the monetary benefits of education accrue over time, it is necessary to use some discount factor to take account of the fact that a dollar earned tomorrow is less valuable than a dollar earned today, and computations of the present value of the future stream of benefits to be expected from education are, of course, very sensitive to the discount factor used. Houthakker has made some calculations (based on 1950 census data for the U.S.) which indicate that the capital value (present value) at age 14 of before-tax lifetime income associated with four or more years of college, ranged from a figure of $280,989 if a zero discount rate is used to $106,269 at a 3 per cent rate of discount, to $47,546 at 6 per cent and to $30,085 at 8 per cent.[37] Unfortunately, there is no simple answer to the question of what is the right discount factor, and this question has in fact been the subject of considerable debate.

Before going any further, it must be emphasized that this same question has, of course, to be faced by the investigator who prefers to express his results in terms of an internal rate of return rather than in terms of a present value figure. True enough, the internal rate of return figure is obtained simply by finding that rate which makes the estimated future gain in earnings equal to

36. It may be noted in passing that the existence of a significant *personal* consumption component in the educational benefit stream also raises some nice questions germane to the issue of who should pay for education.

37. H. S. Houthakker, 'Education and income', *Review of Economics and Statistics*, February 1959, Table 2, p. 26.

the present cost of obtaining the education, and no discount factor enters into this calculation. But, once one has obtained the internal rate of return on education, it is then necessary to decide which other rate of return is to be compared with the rate of return on education in order to determine whether this is relatively high or low. Thus, the 'other' rate of return used for comparative purposes serves the same function that the discount factor serves in the case of present value calculations.

Some authors have used 4 per cent as the discount factor (or the other rate of return) on the ground that this is roughly the long-term rate of interest and represents the cost that the government itself must incur in borrowing money. To the extent that one is prepared to assume that in fact it is going to be the government that will be providing any additional funds for education, there is much to be said for using a figure of this kind.

However, if we assume that individual students (or their families) are the ones contemplating investing in education, then a higher rate is surely appropriate, partly to take account of the greater risk involved in financing a single (typical) individual than in financing a large group. An individual would find it simply impossible to borrow educational funds on the private market at anything like 4 per cent interest.[38]

Becker[39] has made use of a comparative rate of return in the neighbourhood of 9–10 per cent, on the ground that this is roughly the average rate of return on private investment in the United States – businesses would certainly be reluctant to undertake any project that did not promise to yield at least this high a rate of return. The argument is, of course, that if we can earn 9–10 per cent on alternative investments, a purely economic case for investing relatively more in education would have to be based on at least as high a rate of return on education.

From the standpoint of the large private investor, the logic of

38. It is true that individual universities, charitable groups, and some governments will make loans at lower rates of interest. The individual with access to such sources should, of course, calculate accordingly. However, since special terms of this sort do not reflect current market demands for loanable funds, they are of limited use as a guide to social policy (they in fact already reflect social policy).

39. op. cit., pp. 348–9.

this argument is unassailable, provided that there are no appreciable differences in the degree of risk involved (and whether this proviso holds I do not know). But, whether this is the appropriate rate for the purposes of government policy can be questioned on the ground that, for a host of primarily political reasons (and this does not mean they are bad reasons), the actual alternative investment opportunities open to the government may not be nearly so lucrative. (In the U.S. economy at any rate, there is a strong presumption that public funds will not be invested in such commercially profitable fields as chemicals, applied electronics, soft drink production and the like but rather, in such activities as running the post office and supporting agricultural prices, as well as in research and development and education.)

A rather different approach to this 'other rate of return' question has been taken by Denison. His argument is that even if Becker were right in concluding that the rate of return on college education was about the same as the rate of return on private investment, 'college education for more students could fail to make a net contribution to economic growth only if it replaced investment in capital goods by an amount equal to its full cost (including the value of the work not performed by the additional college students).[40] Denison goes on to argue that in fact the great bulk of expenditures on higher education comes from what would have been consumption expenditures rather than from the savings-investment stream. Thus, he concludes that 'additional college enrolments would make a net contribution to growth even if the rate of return on a college education were only a small fraction of that on capital investment in other "things".'[41]

This approach (which really amounts to combining a calculation of the rate of return on private investment with a calculation of the amount of private investment that would be displaced by more spending on education) makes perfect sense if one is interested exclusively in economic growth as the objective of public policy. These days many people would no doubt agree that for political as well as economic reasons growth deserves more emphasis as a policy objective and that the U.S. should be devoting a larger share of total resources to investments of *all* types. There is also a strong case, on welfare grounds, for recognizing that

40. op. cit., p. 78.   41. loc. cit.

postponing present consumption in favour of future consumption entails sacrifices, and that an appropriate discount factor must be used to allow for such sacrifices.

Danger of extrapolating the past

The rates of return that I have been discussing are, of course, *average* rates of return for *past* periods, and so the question naturally arises: are there any particular cautions that must be borne in mind when using such rates of return as a guide to future actions?

The first answer to this question is that we should, of course, prefer to have a *marginal* rate of return figure rather than an average figure, since we are especially interested in the consequences of marginal changes in educational expenditures. Unfortunately, no direct way of estimating a marginal rate of return has as yet been found, and so we are forced to address ourselves to the question of whether we might expect the marginal figure to differ from the average figure in any systematic way. If we make the usual assumption that the conditions of a competitive market equilibrium obtained at the time the earnings and cost measurements were taken, then it follows that the average value can be regarded as equal to the marginal value, and this problem of the relationship between average and marginal values can be disposed of accordingly. Actually, this is taking too easy a way out in that the profit-maximization considerations which push industries to the equilibrium level of output are presumably less operative in the education field. Nonetheless, for want of a better assumption, we must act as if the past average rate of return were equal to the marginal rate of return.

Moving now to the question of how accurate a guide to future rates of return is afforded by the average rates computed for past periods, it has been argued by Renshaw that the (marginal) rate of return applicable to additional investments is apt to be below the calculated average rates by virtue of the law of diminishing returns and because of 'the likelihood that any general increase in educational attainment will be accompanied by a decrease in the average level of ability'.[42]

Renshaw himself admits that 'dynamic factors . . . might act to

42. *Review of economics and statistics*, August 1960, pp. 321–2.

maintain a *constant* marginal rate of return over time in the face of increases in the average level of educational attainment',[43] and others, reasoning on the grounds that we are now entering a period in which knowledge and education will be of unparalleled importance have suggested that rapid increases in the demand for skilled manpower could quite conceivably *raise* the marginal rate of return over time. Evidence of past trends in earnings differentials associated with various levels of education is of some relevance in this context. Miller has found that in the United States over the years since 1939, contrary to the expectations of some analysts, the economic advantages associated with the completion of additional years of schooling have *not* diminished, in spite of the fact that an ever-increasing proportion of the population has been educated.[44]

Predicting the future rates of return that will be associated with possible expansions in education is likely to be more difficult than making similar predictions for other activities, for three main reasons: (a) so much depends on the quality of the additional students, a factor which is variable and hard to judge – when one is considering whether or not to produce more shoes, it can be safely assumed that the extra shoes produced will be much like their predecessors, but in education the extra student may turn out to be an academic failure or an Einstein; (b) the future educational requirements of a country will depend to a substantial degree on future discoveries and advancements in knowledge – which are almost impossible to foresee; (c) education is such a long process, and education once acquired is such a long-lived asset, that educational decisions must be based on an unusually long time-horizon.

In any case there is no avoiding the necessity of predictions – and past experience, modified by our understanding of trends and new developments, is likely to provide a better basis for decisions than implicit guesses predicated on unstated assumptions.

It is hoped that the above discussion has helped to clarify some of the reasons why various users of the direct returns approach

43. loc. cit. (my italics).
44. 'Income in relation to education', *American Economic Review*, December 1960, p. 965. Becker (op. cit., pp. 347–8) has also reported roughly constant rates of return for the two years of 1940 and 1950.

have drawn somewhat different conclusions from their work. Procedural choices and decisions have to be made at many steps in the analysis, and personal judgments and value preferences inevitably enter in.

None the less, the results obtained for the U.S. economy offer rather consistent (some might say surprisingly consistent) support for the notion that education, on the average, has paid significant financial as well as non-financial rewards. The evidence is quite strong that individuals with the requisite ability have been well advised to continue their education through university level – and there is no reason to think that this pattern will not continue.

The difficulties involved in identifying earnings differentials with productivity differentials force one to be somewhat more cautious in drawing sweeping conclusions as to the effects of education on national output. However, here too the burden of proof is surely on those who would play down the economic importance of education. The likely existence of obscured relationships between ability and earnings constitutes the main reason for supposing that rate of return figures have an upward bias, and even after allowing (as best he could) for this cross-relation, Becker still obtained a 9 per cent per annum figure. When we then recognize that on top of this 9 per cent one surely must make some allowance for external benefits, and for the non-pecuniary contributions of education (if one wishes to think in terms of total welfare and not just in terms of GNP figures), the grounds for thinking that past investments in education have paid handsome returns to the nation as a whole are quite impressive.

It would be utter folly to pretend that the rate-of-return approach is free of troublesome difficulties or that it can be relied on to prove conclusively to a staunch unbeliever that investing resources in education makes good economic sense. But this approach does have three rather important appeals: (a) it enables us to obtain results in a form which permits comparisons of costs with benefits; (b) it permits us, in making calculations, to examine the quantitative effect on our results of alternative assumptions about such things as the proper discount rate and the effect of ability differentials on earnings differentials; and (c) as I hope the above discussion and the references to work in progress have shown, this approach is susceptible to further refinement and holds out the possibility that further research will remedy some of the present difficulties.

My own conclusion is that we have learned a great deal from the work that has already been done and that additional research along these lines – including more investigations into the external economies problem – ought certainly to be encouraged.

IV. The Forecasting-Manpower-Needs Approach

This paper would be incomplete if it did not include at least a brief commentary on the 'forecasting-manpower-needs' approach to educational planning. No more than a brief commentary will be attempted here, however, partly because this approach falls a bit outside the scope of the present paper, in that this approach is not really directed at assessing the economic contribution of education, and partly because I am simply not sufficiently familiar with the important work in this field that has been done in France and in certain of the so-called underdeveloped countries.[45]

The objective of all 'forecasts' (or 'projections', the two terms will be used interchangeably here) of manpower needs is, of course, to provide the persons responsible for educational planning with information as to the likely future needs of the economy for persons with various kinds of training. Such forecasts can be expressed in terms of broad aggregates of people (e.g., all those completing a course of secondary or higher education), or in terms of much more specific occupational categories (e.g. botanists and teachers of mathematics).

45. The reader interested in delving into the manpower projection literature would do well to look at the papers prepared for the Washington O.E.C.D. Conference (fall of 1961), at a general summary paper by Mills, which will appear shortly in the U.S. Office of Education volume mentioned earlier, at the various reports published in the United Kingdom by the Committee on Scientific Manpower (the Zuckerman Committee), at Payne's excellent summary of British experience in this field (*Britain's scientific and technological manpower*, Stanford University Press, 1960), and at the commentary and references contained in Vaizey's *Economics of education*. The continuing controversy in both the United States and the United Kingdom over the alleged 'shortage' of scientific manpower is also relevant – see, for example, the article by Lee Hansen in the *Review of Economics and Statistics*, August 1961, pp. 251–6, and the paper by Jewkes in *Economic Journal*, March 1960, pp. 1–16. [See also readings in part 4.]

A variety of methods has been used in arriving at manpower projections: (a) employers have been asked to specify how many persons with certain kinds of qualifications they will need, a given number of years in the future, and the responses have then been aggregated; (b) present ratios of trained manpower to total employment have been projected into the future on the basis of demographic information and, in some cases, assumptions about likely shifts in the relative importance of different industry groups; (c) the above method has been refined to take account of past *trends* in the utilization of manpower; (d) in projecting the manpower needs of the newly developing countries, recourse has been had to present ratios between skilled manpower and the total work force in countries at more advanced stages of economic development.

The great appeal of this general line of approach is that it offers definite guide lines framed in the terms in which decisions must actually be made. Whereas the returns-to-education approach hopes to tell us only whether, at a point in time, it is likely that we are spending too much or too little on education, manpower studies often culminate in recommendations that 'X' number of new student places in field 'Y' should be created by year 'Z'. This type of advice is obviously much more useful to the practical policy maker (or much more embarrassing, if he does not happen to agree with it).[46]

On the negative side of the ledger, a criticism of many manpower projections made to date is that they have been disproved rather speedily by the march of events. While I know of no really ambitious study that has compared a large number of manpower projections with actual happenings, I suspect that such a study would reveal a rather systematic tendency for projections to understate the true future demand for trained manpower.

Reasons why manpower projections may be considerably off target are not hard to find. A major problem is that neither

46. It should be noted, however, that simply creating a given number of additional student places in a particular subject will not lead to a concomitant increase in the number of graduates unless labour market incentives are strong enough to entice suitable candidates to accept the places. Labour market policy and educational policy can be pursued independently of one another only at the risk of producing anomalous results.

individual employers nor professional investigators are able to foresee the implications of new scientific developments. A second problem is that the manpower projections I know about have not succeeded in taking account of the elasticity of substitution between capital and labour and between highly-trained manpower and less-highly-trained manpower. There are few, if any, products that can be produced by only one specific combination of manpower, materials, and machinery, and as the relative scarcity of the various factors changes one would expect adjustments in factor proportions to follow.

These projection difficulties are particularly pronounced in the case of persons whose training is general, and it is for this reason that many manpower studies have dealt only with groups such as engineers – and, of course engineers can upset supply and demand forecasts by taking managerial posts which are not 'just' engineering jobs. At the other end of the spectrum, projecting the demand for very specific occupations is also fraught with risks in that advancements in knowledge (or miscalculations of any kind) can lead to a very large proportionate error; the reason for concern about the possibility of such errors is not just that national plans may have to be modified, but that students making irrevocable career choices may have been misled. (The great potential influence of manpower projections on career choices is, for this very reason, a cause of real concern to a number of people.)

Manpower projections as a guide to policy are also subject to a still more fundamental criticism, which is implicit in my earlier comment, to the effect that this approach is not really directed at assessing the economic contribution of education. The point is that estimates of the future number of people with a given kind of training who are 'needed' or 'wanted' are rather devoid of meaning unless one also has a good idea of the relation between the benefits to be obtained by having this number of trained persons *and the costs involved in having them*. To the basic question of whether a country is well advised to devote more of its resources to training manpower, estimates of future 'needs', unless based on a balancing of costs and benefits, do not really provide much guidance.

The conclusion to draw from this is that manpower projections ought not to be viewed as an alternative method of approach, but as a way of obtaining information that can usefully be incorporated into broader-gauged analyses. Many manpower studies are already being carried out in the context of some kind of more general economic exercise, and all one can hope is that this trend will continue. At a more specific level, it would seem that future research along the manpower-projection line might fruitfully concentrate on the elasticity-of-substitution question and on the costs of inducing more people to move into various occupations.

A Final Comment

The reactions of persons interested in the relations between educational policy and economic policy to the kinds of analyses discussed in this paper are bound to depend on what they expected to find.

Two kinds of people, in particular, will be disappointed at the progress made to date in assessing the economic contribution of education. The first group consists of those who have already reached a firm conclusion as to what ought to be done about educational spending, and who are looking for conclusive 'proof' to support their point of view. The second group consists of those who have an entirely open mind on the subject and are looking for purely 'scientific' evidence that will settle the matter one way or another.

The work done thus far will evoke a happier response from those who want, and will use, as much help as can be obtained from careful analysis, but who are also prepared to invest their own efforts in interpreting the results in the context of the limitations of the methods employed and with reference to their own values.

It must also be said that the kinds of research described in this paper will positively displease some people – especially those who feel that educational policy discussions ought not to be 'contaminated' by references to costs and economic consequences. But surely one can feel strongly about the non-economic objectives of education and still acknowledge the importance of *also* weighing likely economic effects in arriving at policy decisions. A good case can be made (at least to economists) that this is a field in which economic issues are inevitably involved and that therefore economists must do what they can to clarify the consequences of alternative courses of action. As more and more money is spent on education, the old undocumented assertions that 'we know', or 'we believe' that 'education pays', will prove less and less satisfactory to the private and public groups who have to pay the mounting bills. Surely the issue is not whether attempts should be made to apply the techniques of economic analysis to education, but how best to do so.

Almost without exception, the persons who have actually done the kinds of research described above have been commendably modest in describing their success – and well they should be, for there is certainly much that is unknown. The mark of how far we still have to go is that economists who have strong personal opinions about the proper course of educational policy are not likely to have their opinions shaken by the results of their own research. It is becoming more and more difficult to reconcile any conclusion with the evidence, and this is the mark of progress.

6 M. J. Bowman

The Human Investment Revolution in Economic Thought

M. J. Bowman, 'The human investment revolution in economic thought', *Sociology of Education*, vol. 39 (1966), pp. 111–38.

In his selective annotated bibliography of work in *The economics of education*, published in 1964, Mark Blaug listed 420 items (excluding other bibliographies).[1] Education in the earlier history of economic thought was deliberately omitted, so that this is in fact a list of twentieth-century items, published in English. Although a few selections in relatively conventional educational finance are included, the bulk of the citations deal with relations between education and income distribution, effects of education on productivity, the spread of education and economic growth, schooling *versus* on-the-job training as human-resource formation, concepts and measures of human capital, social benefit–cost analysis, and educational policy – and also (less fully indexed) the literature on manpower requirements forecasting and manpower planning along with that (still very limited) on the economics of educational planning.

Of these 420 items, I found on a rough count that 14 had appeared before 1940, 6 appeared in the decade of the 1940s, and 19 in the years 1950 through 1954. The remaining 381 items, constituting 91 per cent of the total, appeared within the decade 1955–64 (or were in press in 1964); 283 of these 381 appeared in 1960 or later. The revised bibliography, to come out in 1966, will contain a thousand items, most of the added ones being post-1960 contributions. Even allowing for a selection bias against earlier work, the pace at which social scientists (and pseudo-social scientists) are adding to the printed pages on the economics of education is stunning.

1. Mark Blaug, *A selected annotated bibliography in the economics of education*, University of London, Institute of Education, 1964. [Subsequently revised as *Economics of education: A selected annotated bibliography*. Pergamon Press, 1966. The new version listed nearly 800 items.]

This florescence of a new specialty in economics is closely allied to a shift of economic theory toward emphasis on *creative* man. The economics of information, communication, transfer of knowledge and know-how is growing on all fronts, including study of how innovations come about and their effects upon every aspect of economic life. In fact the 1965 meeting of the American Economic Association was built around the key themes of innovation, knowledge, and education. Among the titles of papers directly concerned with education were: 'Education and the personal distribution of income', 'Investment in the education of the poor: A pessimistic report', 'Measurement of the quality of schooling', 'Investment in humans, technological diffusion, and economic growth', 'The tax treatment of individual expenditures for research and education', 'The effect of education on labor force participation', 'Skill, earnings and the growth of wage supplements', 'A planning model for the efficient allocation of resources in education', 'A linear programming model for educational planning in an underdeveloped economy', 'Labor skills and comparative advantage', 'International flows of human capital', The last paper of the sessions was entitled 'Trends, cycles, and fads in economic writing'!

The Investment Orientation

A year or two ago it was still possible to give a reasonably adequate picture of what was happening in 'the economics of education' by classifying work under a few main headings,[2] ignoring odd items scattered here and there. However, this will no longer suffice. Furthermore, with the building up of empirical–analytical work close to the cores of theoretical economic systems, the economics of education itself takes off from such cores. Or re-

2. The usual categorization is that used by William Bowen: (1) cross-country comparisons of income and education indices; (2) longitudinal 'aggregate input-output' studies of national income growth (most of which had no education in them, however); (3) the so-called 'rate-of-return' and Bowen's analysis still constitutes an excellent starting point. See his 'Assessing the contribution of education' in *Economic aspects of higher education, Paris* O.E.C.D. (1964) or in his book of three essays carrying the title *Economic aspects of education*, Industrial Relations Section, Princeton University, 1964. [See Reading 5 in this volume.]

stating the same point, the economics of education is genuinely economics, rather than a collection of techniques of estimation and special isolated investigations, only to the extent to which it is geared into a systematic body of economic thought.

With these considerations in mind, I have elected to focus this paper around a core concept that has come as something of a revolution in economic thought, that of investment in human beings. For as soon as such an approach is taken really seriously and followed through into its important ramifications, the economics of education begins (as it has begun) an infiltration into economics generally.

In an investment orientation to education we are concerned above all with the relations between the resources utilized to form human competencies (resource costs of education – whether in school, on the job, or elsewhere) and the increments to productivity that result. That is, an investment view of education entails cost–benefit assessments, sometimes from an individual decision-maker's point of view, sometimes from a school principal's point of view, and sometimes from the point of view of a government or of a society as a whole. But this is resource allocation; how can there be anything *new* about this? Hasn't the idea of investment in human beings been lying around for a long time? It may help to take a quick look at a few high points in the history of economic thought.

Evidently the mercantilists had some sort of appreciation of the investment in man idea, for they laid great stress on the importance of 'art and ingenuity', or skilled manpower, as a key to growth in national wealth, and William Petty even attempted to measure 'human capital'. But the mercantilists were not human investment men, for they did not follow through with their observations concerning human skills and productivity to analyze costs and returns. They had as yet no system of economic thought, no analytical framework for doing this. Adam Smith reversed the mercantilist view, concerning himself with efficiency in the 'education industry', but primarily as an industry producing consumer services. In fact Smith believed that economic progress was based on division of labor and that it would reduce rather than raise supplies of human skills and demands for them. Both Smith and Malthus were concerned with education for the betterment of man, not for the creation of human resources. Malthusianism does indeed bring education back into the economics of growth, but walking backwards as it were, education would contribute to population control and hence raise or maintain national income by *reducing* the numbers in the labor force. There would seem to be nothing at all closely related to contemporary human investment concepts in all this. However, turning the pages of the *Wealth of nations* we come to Smith's analogies between men and machines, where acquisition of skills is viewed specifically as an investment – an unambiguous anticipation of recent work. Through the middle years of the nineteenth century the neo-classicists often considered education in its relations to social stratification and social mobility and the segmentalization of labor markets, but this again was not an investment approach as such. Alfred Marshall went further, including discussion of the socio-economics of 'talent wastage'. These sections of his work probably come the closest of all, prior to the twentieth century, to many modern discussions of investment in human beings. But Marshall stopped short when he discarded the notion of 'human capital'. It was Irving Fisher, in his highly abstract capital theory, who brought the human component of capital fully into the fold. Fisher was not particularly interested in education, however. What he did was to place the emphasis in dealing with capital where it logically must be. Capital is something (a stock) that yields a flow of services over time. Whether the physical entity in which the capital stock is embodied can be bought and sold is a matter of degree (in modern terminology, degree of 'liquidity'), and is not a defining criterion. But resources put into schooling are (among other things) investments in the acquisition of potential future income streams, whether looked at from the individual or from the societal points of view. This is a kind of capital formation. It is the formation of human capital in that the stock that will yield the future income stream is embodied in human beings.

As the reader will be aware, the view of education as an investment in the creation of future income streams is a special view of education. It says nothing about education as a pleasurable (or painful) 'consumer' experience while in school. It says nothing about education for citizenship or political ends generally. What it says about education as either a private or a societal investment in the acquisition of a future income stream depends upon how we define 'income' and, in applied economics, on what elements of income get measured – directly or indirectly. In practice what is most easily measured is money income, but there is also the 'real income' potential of the capacity to 'do it yourself', whether this is home carpentry or filling out your own income-tax form. Where income in kind is an important part of total real income, as in subsistence farming, incorporation of such earnings in income estimates becomes essential; this is an important consideration in attempts to compare income positions or assess economic returns to schooling in less developed countries. Along with income in kind there is also the problem of returns to education that enter the future income stream, in a broad definition of income, as psychic satisfactions – whether as enjoyment of leisure or as non-monetary satisfactions associated with the kinds of jobs to which more education may give access. Clues as to the likely importance of the latter may sometimes be derived indirectly, from observation of large cost–benefit discrepancies working persistently against highly educated people in some occupations. However, the main concern of the investment orientation to education is with the formation of human capital that will yield flows of services that are *transferable* and could thus be measured in 'rental' or 'hire' terms (whether or not a man in fact works for himself or rents his services to others).

More difficult than the treatment of individual incomes in kind, though equally or more important, is the assessment of *indirect* economic returns to education from a societal point of view. Just adding up the observed returns to individuals may not give the right answer; in fact it would give a truly right answer only by accident. This is the pervasive problem of 'external' effects, economies of scale, and shifts in production functions, that plagues all study of economic growth. There is nothing in this that is peculiar to education, although the untutored wayfarer in the literature might easily be led to believe that education was especially 'difficult'. Exactly the same problems arise in attempts to assess societal effects of any sort of investment, whether in physical capital in the private sectors of the economy, in physical infra-structure, such as roads and dams, or in the formation of human competencies at school and on the job. In fact, there is ferment today on all of these fronts, and treatment of physical capital is being drastically overhauled as part of the modern effort to analyze factor substitutions and complementarities and the processes of economic growth and development in a dynamic world.

Finally, whether we look from an individual or a societal perspective, it should be noted that expressing income in money terms is simply a way of measuring a mix of goods and services; as such it is essential for useful analysis of the most basic questions. Money is of course a necessity for the operation of a complex economy, as the Russians discovered, whether or not overt prices are the proper weights or measures to use in assessing costs and benefits or talking about 'national income'. Where observed prices are clearly inappropriate measures, economists substitute for them what has come to be termed 'shadow prices' – estimates of more nearly 'correct' value measures. The analysis of relations between education of various levels and kinds and occupational roles is exceedingly important, and much of this work has been done without regard to earnings. However, in an investment view, occupations are intervening variables between human competencies, however acquired, and the incomes these human resources yield (their 'productivity'). Similarly, the acquisition of competencies or gains in achievement scores in school are intervening variables between inputs of teacher and student time and the future earnings of graduates.

It is convenient to distinguish four main foci of the economics of education viewed as an investment in human beings. These are: (1) global or aggregative measurements of the magnitude of human capital formation and of its contribution to national income growth; (2) applications of micro-decision theory to analysis of demands for schooling and supplies of educated people, career choices, factors that determine the nature and extent of on-the-job training, income and opportunity distribution, and constraints on mobility and freedom of choice; (3) contemporary and a few historical investigations into determinants of demands for educated or trained people, changes in those demands with economic development, and dynamic interactions between human-resource demands and supplies; (4) methodological research in the development and application of systematized procedures and criteria for educational planning. Cutting across these, sometimes merely as stated and unstated assumptions but sometimes of major direct concern, are technical parameters involved in the use of resources (including student time) to form human competencies and those involved in the combining of human skills with other resources in productive activity. Expressed in terms of substitutions and complementarities among resources in their employment for various purposes (e.g. various combinations of inputs of teacher time, student time, and library facilities to produce 'learning') these technical alternatives are called 'production functions'. Many of the most impassioned arguments among those economists who have become involved in discussions of social decision models and planning, go back to differences in (unproven) beliefs about production functions in human learning and in human resource use.

In the Aggregate

The global or aggregative measurement of relations between human resource development and national income is discussed in every article on contemporary work in the economics of education, even though aggregative input–output analysis has by no means a monopoly of the economics of education and its beginnings had nothing to do with education at all. The explanation is that it has probably done more to convince economists of the importance of studying education than has any other single academic endeavor. That impact tells us something about the sociology of the growth of knowledge rather than evidencing any intrinsic merits in aggregate production function analysis. But if we judge it by the scope and importance of innovative research in all directions that it has stimulated, the naïve discovery of our ignorance – now called 'the residual' – must go down as a major event. Given the mixed scientific, econometric, and polemical character of aggregate input–output history, perhaps I may be forgiven if I sum it up in a dialectical sequence. For it did more than anything else to set the stage for the 'human investment revolution' of the 1950s, so ably fostered by the innovative entrepreneurial genius of T. W. Schultz.

That revolution, like all well-behaved revolutions, can claim its historical thesis and antithesis. Thesis in this case was the labor theory of value, according to which men were most assuredly 'capital' in Fisher's definition, Marxism to the contrary notwithstanding.[3] Furthermore, the formation of physical capital in Austrian economics depended upon a 'subsistence fund' to maintain workers while they devoted their time to constructing implements of further production instead of goods for immediate consumption.[4]

Both the labor theory of value in its original sense and the Austrian 'roundaboutness' theory of capital had largely disappeared from the main stream of economics by the 1930s, even though a few modern economists like to count in 'labor efficiency units' and Marx has contributed more to modern economics than is commonly recognized. With the formalization of value theory 'factors of production' had become abstractions and Man had become a purified indifference surface, addicted to geometry and calculus. But Man and his labor were still on a par with other agents of production.

Antithesis came with Keynes' *General theory*. For all the variants of Keynesianism shared in a trait that is significant for the present discussion (as in many other contexts). They shifted the emphasis of a whole generation of economists from viewing labor as an active agent of production to viewing labor as a passive agent that would find employment only if there were a high enough rate of 'investment' and, most especially, of investment in the production of physical producer capital. Furthermore, out of Keynes' great but ambiguous polemic, written initially to deal with economic fluctuations and persistent unemployment, came some quite remarkable progeny – long-term 'growth' theories in which virtually everything was explained by the amount of physical capital and its rate of increase.

So it was that economists set themselves up for a series of pragmatic–political and theoretical–econometric shocks. For it was

3. Note, however, that the original labor theory of value was modified in Soviet practice, where a training and crude manpower and materials planning view took hold, reminiscent more of the mercantilists than of Ricardo.

4. For a quick picture of where everyday man has stood in the history of economics see my 'The consumer in the history of economic doctrine', *American Economic Review*, vol. 41 (1951), no. 2, pp. 1–18.

obvious after World War II that physical capital worked its miracles only in lands where there were many qualified men who knew how to use it (the Marshall Plan countries and Japan). And the econometricians discovered that their old aggregate capital–output ratios weren't behaving properly. Nor did undifferentiated 'labor' combined with capital inputs do any better. By conventional measures econometricians were accounting for economic growth only when there was very little growth to explain. For the period from the late 1920s to the 1950s in Western Europe and Japan they were doing very badly indeed, explaining half or less of national income growth.

Reactions to the large residuals were almost as various as the economists who looked at them, but even those who strove hardest to rehabilitate theories of investment in physical capital as the chief key to growth had to draw implicitly upon learning and creative man. This is least evident in Solow's 'vintage capital' articles.[5] Having labeled the residual 'technical change' he argued that such change could take place only as it was embodied in new physical capital; hence even after correcting for price level changes, a dollar spent on physical capital in 1965 should count as more than a dollar so spent in 1964 or 1963. In fact Solow constructed a 'vintage' model of physical capital inputs that did the job *too* successfully. Among other things, it left all quality improvements in labor *un*embodied, a neglect that might have passed before but could hardly get by once the monolithic capital–output models had been challenged on 'quality' grounds. Furthermore, what is the process whereby technological change takes place and gets itself embodied? Another reaction to the residual has been to step up research on investments-in-research by industry, government, and other agencies. This gets a little closer to investment in man. Meanwhile Eric Lundberg, in Sweden, came up with the 'Horndal effect' – steady growth in productivity in a firm with little or no change in its physical capital. What did this have to say about human learning and productivity? By contrast, Kenneth Arrow would probably be more inclined to count his article on 'Learning by doing'[6] in the

5. In particular, see R. M. Solow, 'Technical progress, capital formation, and economic growth', *American Economic Review*, vol. 52 (1962), no. 2.

6. In the *Review of Economic Studies*, vol. 29 (1962), no. 2.

physical capital than in the educational investment camp, though I would plant it quite firmly in both at once. He argued (1) that people learn by being challenged with new experiences, (2) gross investment in physical capital (before depreciation) is the best index of rate of exposure to learning situations, and hence (3) the best measure of capital inputs into aggregate production is gross physical-capital formation, and the use of net values has underestimated the role of physical capital in economic growth. Looked at in another way, which was not Arrow's, his thesis could be turned around to read: (1) increases in skill and knowledge are the main key to growth, (2) exposure to new situations speeds learning, and hence (3) rapid replacement of obsolescent equipment is a sound investment in man and through man in economic growth. Neither statement is more correct, or incorrect, than the other.

Two other scholars who have recently concerned themselves with aggregate input–output analysis introduced schooling of the labor force explicitly. One is Zvi Griliches, who started out with a study of social returns to investment in research on hybrid corn. Subsequently, in connection with his very interesting (and sophisticated) work on aggregate production functions and technological progress in selected sectors of the American economy, he found that rising levels of education have made a significant contribution to productivity in both agriculture and manufacturing industries.[7] Meanwhile, Edward Denison has given us *The sources of economic growth in the United States and the alternatives before us*.[8] This book attempts to measure every sort of input Denison could identify, including educational attainments of the labor force. Every measured input is assumed to yield constant returns per unit, so that, for example, the fourth year of secondary school embodied in a male member of the labor force will make the same additional contribution to national income in 1956 as in 1929. The education parts of Denison's study were presented in fuller form as the first (and most discussed) major paper in a 1964

7. Zvi Griliches, 'The sources of measured productivity growth in U.S. agriculture, 1940–60', *Journal of Political Economy*, vol. 71 (1963) no. 4; 'Research expenditures, education and the agricultural production function', *American Economic Review*, vol. 54 (1964), no. 6; 'Production functions in manufacturing, some preliminary results', mimeo., October 1965.

8. Supplementary Paper No. 13, Committee for Economic Development, New York, January 1962.

conference of the O.E.C.D. Study Group in the Economics of Education.[9] Given his assumptions, Denison attributed to education 23 per cent of the growth in total national income and 42 per cent of the growth in *per capita* income in the United States over the period 1929–57. In fact, though he did not say so, Denison included in his measure of education's contributions the net contributions of on-the-job training as well as of schooling embodied in the labor force. For this reason among many others, it would be quite unjustified to draw any general conclusions from his estimates, for what schooling contributes depends upon the factors with which human skills are combined in production and the opportunities for on-the-job learning and training, which are in turn functions of the pace of change.

T. W. Schultz is unique among those who have analyzed empirical aggregrate input–output series in that he explicitly linked his analysis with the theme of investment in human beings. This led him, among other things, to measure the value of student time as a labor input into the educational process.[10] On conservative assumptions he showed that earnings foregone (the measure of student inputs) accounted for over half of the total costs of secondary and higher education in the United States. Also, he estimated that over the period from 1900 to 1956 total investments in 'human capital formation' in schools rose from 9 to 34 per cent of total investments in physical capital formation. But the significance of his book, *The economic value of education*,[11] and the numerous closely related articles that he has written on this subject is not in the least dependent upon his rather vulnerable methods of estimating education's contributions, or even on his more valid empirical estimates of the magnitude of human capital formation measured in cost terms. Rather, it is in the combination of detail and sweeping vision with which he argues the human investment revolution.[12]

9. 'Measuring the contribution of education to economic growth' in *The residual factor and economic growth*, Paris, O.E.C.D., 1964.

10. His fullest presentation of these estimates and their interpretation is in his 'Capital formation by education', *Journal of Political Economy*, December 1960, pp. 571–84.

11. Columbia University Press, 1963.

12. See also his remarkable little book, *Transforming traditional agriculture*, Yale University Press, 1964.

Investments in Human Beings and Micro-Decision Theory

The second major focus of work on the economics of education as an investment centers on decision theories framed as testable behavioral hypotheses, and the analysis of major institutional influences and constraints upon private investment choices with respect to schooling and on-the-job training. Decision theory in this context is micro cost–benefit analysis. I have already indicated that it has a wide range of potential uses in the study of economic structure and processes, although taken by itself it also has severe limitations and should not be casually introduced in analysis of economic growth or used without other supplementary analytical tools as a guide in making large-scale educational decisions. The decision units on which such analysis focuses are either individuals (or their parents) or business firms; the decisions concern what people invest in themselves (in school and also, indirectly, on the job) and what firms put into the training of employees. It must be stressed, however, that the economist is not concerned, as is the psychologist, with explaining individual behavior *per se*. If people behave *as if* they were economically rational, that is quite enough, provided we are dealing with multiple decision units.

In applying economic decision theory to analysis of education as self-investment, the first question is then: do individuals behave in an economically rational manner with respect to investment in the acquisition of future potential earnings streams via schooling? The first economist to pose this question explicitly, and to test it in cost–benefit terms was Ray Walsh (1935).[13] He asked: did doctors, lawyers, engineers get back more or less than they put into qualifying themselves, taking into account the delays in their earnings and the lifetime paths of their income streams? What about men who invested in college training instead of entering the labor market when they completed secondary school? Walsh's method of taking into account the timing of earnings was to discount income streams at an 'external rate' of 4 per cent to get their 'present values' for comparison with what the education cost. The 'present' in this context is the date at

13. J. R. Walsh, 'Capital concept applied to man', *Quarterly Journal of Economics*, February 1935.

which the decision to continue in college or in post-college education is made. If Walsh had used a higher (lower) rate as the implied basis for comparison with alternative investments, his present value estimates would of course have been lower (higher). Although he did not discuss foregone earnings as a cost, his method in fact took them into account when he set up his earnings streams. The earnings of college graduates start four years later than for high school graduates, and foregone earnings are there in the income streams of the high school graduates with which the college streams are compared.[14] Unfortunately, Walsh's pioneer effort went virtually unnoticed until after World War II; the time was not yet ripe.

A much more elaborate study, of incomes of doctors and dentists in independent professional practice, was published by Milton Friedman and Simon Kuznets in 1946.[15] Again using an 'external' 4 per cent discount rate, they found doctors to do much better than dentists, and they asked a series of questions as to why this should be the case. How far might income differences be explained by differences in ability, or by differential non-monetary preferences or satisfactions unfavourable to doctors (which seemed on the face of it unlikely)? Or again, what evidence was there of monopolistic constraints on entry into training for the higher paying professions? Although this work has been sharply attacked, it too was undeniably a pioneer study, and demonstrated something of what could be done with such an approach. At the same time it gave explicit attention to many of the problems that must be solved in adjusting observed education–income relationships to take account of variables such as ability and parental status. It set the stage also for a number of subsequent studies of the economics of investment in training for the professions.

The empirical study of investment in education that evoked really widespread reactions was first reported on in 1960 in a preliminary article by Gary Becker. He asked: 'is there under-investment

14. Walsh made the mistake of also introducing a cost of subsistence estimate into his cost figures, thereby biasing his findings downward with respect to benefit–cost ratios. Subsistence clearly is not a cost of education; it is a cost of remaining alive.

15. *Income from independent professional practice*, New York: National Bureau of Economic Research, 1946.

in college education?'[16] There were evidently two reasons why this drew so much attention. First, Schultz had paved the way with his writing concerning education as an investment in economic growth, even though there was no 'growth' in Becker's analysis. Second, as soon as a man talks about too much or too little he is talking societal effects and normative economics; even if measurements of social costs and benefits could be unambiguously pinpointed (which they clearly cannot) there will always be plenty of men to rise to such bait. Starting from the private side, in essence Becker's analysis was essentially like Walsh's, except for one thing. Instead of taking an arbitrary external rate of return with which to discount earning streams and estimate 'present values', Becker asked the question: what is the rate of return that the average man investing in a college education will make on that investment? If that rate, termed an 'internal rate', is higher than the returns he could get in alternative investments (and higher than his own subjective time preference), then it is evidently a good investment. In figuring private costs the public subsidy to schooling is of course ignored, and the increments to income streams are adjusted to deduct associated increments in income taxes. But Becker then asked the more nearly social question: Including public subsidies to schooling in the cost measures, and measuring returns by pre-tax increments to income streams, what is the social or 'total' internal rate of return on investment in a college education? His conclusion was that it was about in line with alternatives, that there was neither significant under- nor over-investment in college education. His internal rate of return estimates were attacked as too high because he ignored ability, too low because he ignored indirect returns, fallacious because incomes are (it was asserted) poor measures of productivity, and so on. For several years most educational and manpower planners who had heard about this and the other U.S. rate-of-return studies that followed either ignored or attacked the work; a few complained that this was all very well in the United States, where we had census tabulations on incomes by age and educational attainment, but that it was impractical elsewhere.[17]

16. In an article by that title, *American Economic Review*, vol. 50 (1960), no. 2, pp. 346–54.

17. The leadership of American economists in the development and

Meanwhile Gary Becker went on to construct a theoretical model that incorporated business decisions and on-the-job training in the same broad framework – supported by Jacob Mincer as his empirical mind and conscience.[18] But before taking a look at that tour-de-force, let us see what has been going on even without on-the-job refinements.

First, what has been happening in other countries? Using either external or internal rate of return techniques (or both) estimates of direct private and social cost–benefit relationships have been made in at least the following: Canada, England, India (two studies), Israel, Japan, Mexico, Nigeria, Venezuela, and even (a confidential report) the U.S.S.R. In two cases, Mexico and Nigeria, the authors gathered their own data, demonstrating that meaningful information could be obtained for this purpose more, not less, readily than for the heretofore more popular and common 'manpower' studies. For Nigeria and in a second small non-representative study (not yet completed) in England,[19] the analysis is differentiated by types of secondary and higher education as well as level of schooling. Findings in these studies are varied, but indicate consistent patterns in relation to other known characteristics of social status structures and constraints associated with educational structures and selection

empirical testing of models for analysis of investment in education rests firmly upon the imaginative and yet unwitting contributions of sociologists, demographers, and very practical market analysts in private business. It is these people who persuaded the U.S. Census to put earnings and educational attainments into the 1940 census, along with breaks by sex, age, race, and region. These data were improved in the 1950 and especially the 1960 census, and will be even better in 1970. They are the envy of economists in other lands concerned with human resource problems.

18. See their articles, and others in the special October 1962 Supplement of the *Journal of Political Economy*, on *Investment in human beings*. (Schultz's introduction is well worth reading even by those who will find some of the other papers too technical.)

19. The findings of a pilot study of eight firms in electrical engineering, together with interesting background analysis and rate of return estimates, are reported in Mark Blaug, M. H. Peston, and A. Ziderman, *The utilization of educated manpower in industry* (mimeo, London School of Economics, January 1966). [Now published under that title by Oliver & Boyd (1967).] See also Mark Blaug, 'The rate of return on investment in education in Great Britain', *Manchester School*, September 1965. [See Reading 11].

policies. Thus far there is no evidence that there actually is, in less developed countries, the relative shortage of men with secondary level education that has been so often asserted in the literature – a fact that suggests on the one hand a need for more intensive examination of distortions in labor market structures and processes that determine how men's skills are used, and on the other hand, a serious reconsideration of just what the evidence is with respect to the economics of the education mix in countries at lower and middle stages of development. For at least Mexico, Nigeria, and apparently (taking cruder evidence) most of East Africa, the returns to later years of primary schooling are especially high, as they are also in the United States. The limited available information with respect to technical schools in Nigeria[20] supports findings by Foster, Callaway,[21] and others that in West Africa these schools are poor private and public investments, at least as they stand at the present time and in existing labor market settings.

It should be noted that only the Mexican study among those outside of the United States includes adjustments of any kind to correct for ability or for parental status. Martin Carnoy[22] found that among urban males in Mexico standardizing for parental occupation had little effect; it actually raised, instead of lowering, estimated returns to university education. There is some evidence to suggest that in Japan and the United States ability factors play an especially significant part in the observed income differentials as between the lowest and next-lowest educational attainment groups; men with less than eight years of schooling are becoming

20. Included in a linear programming study by Samuel Bowles. I will come back to this later.

21. Philip Foster, *Education and social change in Ghana*, University of Chicago Press, 1966. See also his 'The vocational school fallacy' in C. A. Anderson and M. J. Bowman (eds.), *Education and economic development*, Aldine Publishing Co., 1965. Archibald Callaway, 'Unemployment among African school leavers', *Journal of Modern African Studies*, vol. 1 (1963), no. 3, pp. 351–7. Reprinted in [*Economics of education 2*], and 'Nigeria's indigenous education; the apprentice system' in *ODU* (University of Ife Journal of African Studies) vol. 1 (1964), no. 1.

22. *Cost and return to schooling in Mexico*, Chicago Ph.D. dissertation, September 1964 (multilith). [Now published as 'R tes of return to schooling in Latin America', *Journal of Human Resources*, vol. 2, no. 1, summer 1967, pp. 359–74.]

such a small group in those countries as to be clearly selected out for defective ability and (in the United States) exceptional cultural deprivation.

In the United States, both private and 'total' rate-of-return and present-value studies have multiplied. In some cases the empirical analysis concentrates primarily upon sorting out the returns or benefits side, without explicit comparisons of returns with costs. Most of the work on relations between educational attainments and incomes in agriculture, using small area or state data, has this focus on the linkage between schooling and incomes. Finis Welch[23] has gone further. Using a number of sources, including state reports and the one-in-a-thousand tapes from the 1960 U.S. Census, he has attempted to identify characteristics of schools that may be associated with interstate differences in agricultural income of men with any given number of years of schooling (after controlling for other inputs into agriculture). His best predictors were teacher salaries and school size, both of which are of course correlated with degree of rural ' urbanization'.

The first study of which I am aware in which data from the 1940 or 1950 censuses were used to analyze regional and racial differences in relations between educational attainments and incomes was C. A. Anderson's 'Regional and racial differences in relations between income and education' (1955).[24] Though costs of schooling were not estimated, the relative gross returns to schooling were discussed in incentive terms. Morton Zeman included schooling (along with region) in his analysis of 1939 earnings differentials between urban whites and Negroes.[25] Gary Becker analyzed rates of return to whites and to non-whites separately. Also, in his *Human capital* (1965)[26] he attempted some adjustments of the income differentials associated with college education to allow for differences in ability. The most refined analysis of income differentials by race and region is in Giora

23. Part of this work is summarized in his paper on ' Measurement of the quality of schooling', *American Economic Review*, May 1966; the full dissertation (winter 1966) is *Determinants of the return to schooling in rural farm areas* (1959).

24. *School Review*, January 1955, pp. 38–45.

25. Chicago dissertation, *Quantitative analysis of white–non-white income differentials in the United States*, 1958.

26. Princeton University Press, 1965.

Hanoch's Chicago dissertation.[27] Using the one-in-a-thousand sample tapes he was able to make a number of important adjustments in the income figures and to try out a large number of control variables. Comparing Hanoch's findings with the internal rates of return computed earlier by Hansen,[28] from unadjusted income data, the most notable modification is in raising the estimated white male rate of return to investment in some college (without college completion) from around 5 to 7 per cent in the North and 9 per cent in the South, while at the same time reducing the rates of return to investment in the last two years of college from about 15 to 12 per cent in the North and 11 per cent in the South. Taking into account the fact that even with all his adjustments Hanoch did not have scores on intelligence or achievement tests,[29] this substantially modifies the previous unfavorable investment image for junior colleges, even though it hardly points to them as a priority investment. The evident priority is in getting genetically normal people at the educational bottom effectively into the main stream. But this brings us also to the problem of market discrimination against some groups, especially Negroes.

Among Hanoch's most striking findings are that the private internal rate of return to two years of college among northern non-white men was negative and that among northern non-whites the life-income patterns of those who had completed college ran close to the life incomes of those who were only high-school graduates.

On the whole Hanoch's findings are consistent with the education–income patterns delineated in my 'Human inequalities and

27. *Personal earnings and investment in schooling*, 1965. [Now published as 'An economic analysis of earnings and schooling', *Journal of Human Resources*, vol. 2, no. 3, summer 1967, pp. 310–30.]

28. W. Lee Hansen, 'Total and private rates of return to investment in schooling', *Journal of Political Economy*, April 1963, pp. 128–41. [See Reading 7.]

29. Concerning potentials for interdisciplinary effort that relates to rate-of-return analysis, see my 'Converging concerns of economists and educators', *Comparative Education Review*, October 1962. That article points also to the limitations and potentials of rate-of-return analysis. For a more critical view of rate-of-return work, see Chapter 3 in John Vaizey's *Economics of education* (1962). He has written extensively on many aspects of the economics of education.

Southern underdevelopment',[30] which shows median and upper and lower quartile earnings of white and of non-white males by educational attainments for two age groups, 25–34 and 45–54, in 1939, 1949, and 1959. Income gradients by schooling were consistently steeper for whites than for non-whites and steeper in the South than in the North. Furthermore, these patterns were remarkably stable over time. This study, like Anderson's earlier work, pointed especially to the Southern drag at the bottom combined with convergence into the national economy at the top, both in proportions of the adult population who had completed high school or better and in the incomes of college graduates.

Thus far no one has estimated returns to increments of schooling received in the South by men moving into the North (whether white or non-white). One of the major difficulties is evident: how far can years of schooling (at lower costs) in the South prepare a man for the jobs open to a northerner with the same number of years of schooling?[31] Nevertheless, micro-decision theory has been applied to analysis of both intra- and inter-national migration of human capital. Sjaastad has analyzed migration within the United States as a private investment.[32] Grubel and Scott are applying private decision theory to analysis of international migration in selected professions, especially between the United States and Canada,[33] and a doctoral candidate in Comparative Education at the University of Chicago (Robert Myers) is pressing further with some aspects of this problem. Both the Grubel and Scott study and that by Myers are concerned also with social

30. In James W. McKie (ed.), *Education and the Southern economy*, Supplement to the *Southern Economic Journal*, vol. 32 (1965), no. 1, part 2.

31. It was this problem of differences in school 'quality', defined in terms of the economic productivity potential acquired by students, to which Welch was directing his efforts in his aforementioned study.

32. Larry A. Sjaastad, 'The costs and returns of human migration', in *Investment in human beings*, Supplement to the *Journal of Political Economy*, vol. 70 (1962), no. 5, part 2.

33. The main study is in final stages of revision. However, a stimulating and thought-provoking paper that challenges many of the recent 'brain drain' arguments was presented at the 1965 meeting of the American Economic Association, and will appear in the Proceedings (May 1966). H. G. Grubel and A. D. Scott, 'The international flow of human capital'. [Now published in *American Economic Review*, vol. 56 (1966), no. 2, pp. 268–75. Also in *Economics of education 2*.]

benefit–cost theory in application to international migration and, in Myers' case, to study abroad. Meanwhile, of special interest in the context of American debates over Federal and local roles in financing education, Burton Weisbrod treated a 'community' as an abstracted economic decision-unit to build up an educational investment cost–benefit analysis that takes into account migration into and out of the community. He applied this to illustrative cases.[34]

'Far out', though not necessarily unimportant on that account, are attempts to build indirect or vicarious individual satisfactions into decision models and analysis of voting behavior with respect to public investments in education. The most formalized (and hence the most likely to be ignored or unjustifiably ridiculed by economists as well as sociologists) is W. C. Stubblebine's abstract analysis of preference functions, voting behavior, and the private–public mix in educational expenditure (1965).[35] It is my prediction that his paper will prove important to quite pragmatically oriented researchers in this field, appearances to the contrary notwithstanding.

Very different and much less formal treatments of the rationale of incorporating indirect individual satisfactions in a socio-economic analysis of public investments may be found in work by A. D. Scott on parks and fisheries[36] and in my treatments of vicarious and related satisfactions as returns to social investments in Appalachia.[37] This brings up, incidentally, a whole range of work that I have had to neglect here, the growing research on causes of school drop-outs and effects of training and retraining programs. Some of the best work on these problems is of course being done by sociologists, but the interesting thing is that some of their work fits very tidily into the economist's investment-

34. Burton A. Weisbrod, *External benefits of public education*, Industrial Relations Section, Princeton University, 1964.

35. See his article, under the somewhat misleading title 'Institutional elements in the financing of education', in James W. McKie, op. cit.

36. In his 'The valuation of game resources: some theoretical aspects' (ditto, November 1964).

37. See Chapter 12 of M. J. Bowman and W. W. Haynes, *Resources and people in East Kentucky*, Johns Hopkins University Press, 1963. Also, a brief but more formal statement of the same idea is included in C. A. Anderson and M. J. Bowman, 'Interdisciplinary aspects of the theory of regional development', forthcoming in a symposium edited by James G. Maddox.

decision framework. A striking example is Beverly Duncan's article on relations between unemployment and school drop-out rates.[38]

Finally, let us come back into the heart of micro-decision theory in its applications to human investment, to look at the Becker–Mincer treatment of on-the-job training.[39] They make no distinction between 'training' and 'learning', but tie their analysis to the opportunity–cost concept.

All costs are opportunity costs. In other words, what something 'costs' is what must be given up to get it. Though this concept is at the heart of economics, it has all too often been either ignored or inappropriately applied (and attacked).[40] Next to his vital role as leader in the revolution of thought concerning the importance of human resources in economic growth, Schultz's most important contribution was the great stress that he placed upon one element of opportunity costs, the earnings students forego while attending school.[41]

In essence, what Becker did was to carry Schultz's student foregone incomes the next step, to income a man may forego now

38. 'Dropouts and the unemployed', *Journal of Political Economy*, vol. 73 (1965), no. 2. There is of course an extensive literature in economics on 'structural unemployment' *versus* deficiency of aggregate demand which is highly relevant in assessing the economics of public investments in youth and adult training programs, along with empirical research on the early results of particular programs. And economists must be as interested as sociologists in the new monograph, *Big city drop-outs* by R. A. Dentler and M. E. Warshauer, Columbia University Press, 1965.

39. Gary S. Becker, 'Investment in human capital: A theoretical analysis', and Jacob Mincer, 'On-the-job training: Costs, returns, and some implications', both in the *Journal of Political Economy*, vol. 70 (1962), no. 5, part 2, a Supplement on *Investment in human beings*. Becker's article is incorporated with minor changes in his book, *Human capital*, loc. cit.

40. For a discussion of this concept in its multiple dimensions and applications, see my 'Costing of human resource development' and comments on that paper in the proceedings of the 1963 conference of the International Economics Association, on *The economics of education*, London, Macmillan, 1966. The last section of this paper includes also a theoretical contrast of the Mincer model and an alternative one.

41. Notice that teacher salaries are indicators of costs from a societal point of view only to the extent to which they measure what teachers would produce in other activities – the best alternative 'opportunity'. On the other hand, to the school principal a teacher's salary is a direct measure of what he could buy for the school if he didn't hire the teacher, and hence from his point of view it is a very exact measure of 'opportunity cost'.

in order to take a job in which he will learn more (whether through formal training or by more informal experience).[42] So long as what he learns is transferable from one firm to another and he is free to move, the difference between his current take-home pay and what he could earn measures the extent of his on-the-job investment in his own human–capital formation. This is Becker's 'general' skills case,[43] and it is the assumption upon which Mincer based estimates of the extent of on-the-job training associated with various levels of education in schools in the United States in 1939, 1949, and 1958. Mincer's findings indicated very substantial investments in on-the-job training and learning in the United States, and a substantial increase in those investments. Valued in cost terms, the aggregate of investments in human beings on the job has consistently exceeded investments in learning in schools.

All that Mincer needed to make these estimates was the data used in analyses of internal rates of return to schooling – that is, direct schooling costs and life-income streams. In fact one of the things that Becker's analysis showed up very clearly was that computed internal rates of return to investment in schooling were in fact average rates to investments in schooling and complementary on-the-job training. This is an exceedingly important fact to keep in mind, and it is not dependent for its validity upon any restrictive assumptions. Actually Mincer had to make assumptions much more restrictive than Becker's theory to get his empirical on-the-job training estimates – the most critical was the assumption that the average rate of return to schooling and on-the-job training jointly was also the marginal rate to each successive on-the-job investment in one's self.

It is as easy to attack the Becker–Mincer work as to attack the theory of pure competition, which certainly does not dispose of

42. Fritz Machlup also makes effective use of opportunity cost estimations for important components of his measures of *The production and distribution of knowledge in the United States*, Princeton University Press, 1962.

43. For a further discussion of Becker's and other categorizations of skills, as these may be pertinent to analysis of on-the-job training, see my 'From guilds to infant training industries', in C. A. Anderson and M. J. Bowman (eds.), *Education and economic development*, Aldine Publishing Co., 1965.

it. Even when their assumptions are not satisfied, the analytical tools they provide form an extremely important point of departure for other future studies, using other assumptions and testing the validity of those assumptions in diverse institutional settings.

Human Resource Demands, Supplies, and Development

None of the kinds of studies thus far discussed has focused attention upon determinants of demands for human skills and how those demands change. In their first approximations, which is where most of them have stopped, the rate-of-return studies have treated the census cross-section income–education data for a given year as though the age patterns in that year represented the income path that would be traced out through real time (or had been so traced) by any cohort of men with the indicated schooling. Projection of such patterns into the future assumes that demands for the better educated will rise with increases in their relative numbers in such a way as to maintain the same real incomes (correcting for inflation). A similar assumption underlies the aggregative approach to assessing education's contribution to growth as applied by both Denison and Schultz. Unfortunately, to go at the problem the other way and attempt to assess determinants of demand change and to measure such change is fraught with difficulties.

Most of the attempts to examine demand changes have been associated with 'manpower planning'. Since it ignores costs of human resource development it is only at a half-way point toward an investment orientation to economic analysis of education, and I shall therefore be brief. European economists and planners have devoted the major part of their efforts in 'the economics of education' to such work, and some Americans have also been very active in these endeavors.[44] In many instances manpower

44. At one time or another, most of the major manpower planning endeavors have been at least summarized in O.E.C.D. publications, which are the best place to start to get an international view, at least for the more developed parts of the world. Elsewhere the manpower planning work has frequently been tied in with the work of UNESCO. For a relatively sophisticated and yet eminently readable introduction to this field, and its relations to educational planning, see Herbert S. Parnes, *Forecasting educational needs for social and economic development*, O.E.C.D., 1962.

planning has been no more than naïve projections of past trends, though in some cases the work has been technically intricate and very ingenious. The underlying assumptions are very different from those that have usually characterized 'aggregate production function' studies or attempts to extend rate-of-return analysis to social planning.[45] For the manpower planners assume very rigid demand structures at any given national income level, even though those structures may shift drastically through time. So far projection has not been very successful, though the attempts have constituted a valuable learning experience for those involved. Manpower planning has forced also a closer inspection of the links between schooling and job skills, including quite elaborate technical (non-economic) analysis of these relationships.[46] However, manpower planning does not incorporate in its models any analysis of inter-active processes between human resource demands and supplies.

Both historical studies and those cross-national comparisons that go analytically beyond the level of searching for coefficients to plug into manpower projections must and do look at inter-active development processes. There are more historical materials on these problems, and with more modern relevance, than is commonly assumed, and these are slowly being explored. I cannot summarize the historical work here, partly because what I know of it is so scattered and diverse. It must suffice to note that the investment view of human resources is beginning to make itself felt in this sort of work too. There is much to be done in painstaking historical investigation of relationships between evolving

45. For a sharp summing up of the extremes in the rationale of rate-of-return versus manpower planning views of the economics of education and the markets for human skills, see Mark Blaug, 'An economic interpretation of the private demand for education', *Economica*, May 1966.

46. An outstanding contribution in this area is R. S. Eckaus, 'Criteria for education and training', *Review of economics and statistics*. See also Bruce W. Wilkinson, *Some economic aspects of education in Canada*, Ph.D. dissertation, Massachusetts Institute of Technology, May 1964. This dissertation includes, among other things, a sample survey of employers' perceptions of training requirements (Chapter 5) and a 'present value' analysis from a special run of income–age–education data in the Canadian Census (Chapter 6). [Now published as *Studies in the economics of education*. Economics and Research Branch, Department of Labour, Canada, Occasional Papers, no. 4. Ottawa, Queen's Printer, 1966.]

institutional characteristics of a society and the evolving loci and extent of private and public investment in human resource development.[47]

So far as I am aware, the first cross-national comparison that went beyond simple cross-tabulations of literacy rates against *per capita* incomes was a small essay by C. A. Anderson and the writer.[48] Controlling for 'energy potential' and the proportion of the population engaged in agriculture, that study examined world regions separately. The most striking conclusions were (1) an apparent threshold effect of something like 40 per cent adult literacy, as a necessary but not sufficient condition of economic emergence, (2) negligible income effects of proportions of the adult population with secondary schooling once those with primary schooling were taken into account (excepting countries with over 90 per cent literate), and (3) that income positions in the 1930s explained enrolment rates in the 1950s better than schooling in the 1930s explained income in the 1950s. Already some of these relationships are changing among countries in the lower and middle income ranges; the world-wide emphasis upon education both as an instrument variable in public policy oriented to growth and as a national prestige symbol is producing a situation in which schooling must almost inevitably lead economic development rather than following upon it. Partly we have of course the chicken-and-the-egg, but the relationship is not quite so closed a circle as that.

In 1964, Harbison and Myers published their book, *Education, manpower and economic growth*.[49] This book is two things. It is an enlightening and perceptive discussion of situations the authors have observed in many countries. It is also a set of cross-tabulations of and simple correlations among indexes of human resource development (school enrolments by levels and by types of curricula within higher education, expenditures on education), proportions of the population in selected occupations, and national income. They construct a composite education index by

47. Some initial explorations are included in C. A. Anderson and M. J. Bowman (eds.), *Education and economic development*, loc. cit.

48. M. J. Bowman and C. A. Anderson, 'Concerning the role of education in development', in C. Geertz (ed.), *Old societies and new states*, The Free Press, 1963.

49. New York, McGraw-Hill.

which they classify countries. In their recommendations the authors lay stress, and with good reason, on the important role of informal education and training and learning on the job. Unfortunately, however, their statistical evidence does not support the inferences they try to draw with respect to emphasis upon secondary schooling and especially vocational and technical education.

The latest and technically most sophisticated of the cross-national studies is that by Walter Galenson and Graham Pyatt, prepared for the International Labor Office.[50] This work might equally well have been classified with the aggregate production function studies discussed earlier. It is an investigation into determinants of growth in labor productivity over the years 1951–61 in 52 nations. The capital–input figures are adjusted to allow for improvements by 'vintages' but indexes of labor quality are also used. Unfortunately, the education variables, as with Harbison and Myers, were enrolment data. Evidently school enrolments *reflect* income; they cannot explain it except as they are proxies (which they may well be) for the educational attainments of the adult labor force. We must still wait for such a study using educational characteristics of the labor force itself (not available in most countries), or introducing lead education variables from enrolment rates of a previous period. It should be added that the physical–capital investment ratio taken by itself accounted for only 9 per cent of the variation in growth of labor productivity for all countries together, the percentage being highest in the wealthy nations (20 per cent) and lowest in the poor ones (5 per cent). Given rate of growth in labor productivity as the dependent variable and taking physical capital investment ratio, calories consumed per head, and enrolments in higher education as the independent variables gave an overall coefficient of determination (R^2) of 0·47.

The Economics of Educational Planning

Even a smattering of historical awareness is enough to demonstrate that educational planning is not new. Neither is par-

50. *The quality of labour and economic development in certain countries*, Geneva, 1964.

ticipation of economists in such planning (witness, for example, Nassau Senior in nineteenth-century England). We can go further. The tensions between centralized control of education and planning strategies that give greater scope to local and private decision-making in education is at least a hundred if not several hundred years old, both in practice and in papers in 'political economy'. And 'economic' considerations in educational planning have always been multiple; they have not been confined to the 'cost-saving' that was so often the lay image only a decade ago. It would be difficult to find a more clearcut example of a 'manpower' orientation to educational policy than that of Peter the Great. And if 'manpower' is a little less obvious in the Morrill Act which established the land-grant college system in the United States, this is only because a frontier democratic rebellion against classical education joined social–political pressures with economic pragmatism. If we are to look for the most deliberative and all-inclusive human-development planning we probably must turn to Japan, beginning from the early Meiji period; for then, as now, the Japanese have taken an integrated view of the learning process in schools and on the job, and policies have been developed accordingly.

What, then, has changed? For one thing, the last of the bastions of the sacredness of education have been shaken. Even in the holiest of ivory towers and elitist cultures it is becoming respectable to say out loud that one of the most important things schooling can do is to raise human productive capacities, capacities to do work that puts ever increasing demands upon men's minds. Economics, like sex, is becoming almost respectable parlor conversation! But this is only part of the story. The rest may be summed up by saying that educational planning has become Educational Planning, and in a world community. For the first time, it has become methodologically self-conscious, and it is generating 'experts' (with or without expertise).

Methodological self-consciousness has both its advantages and its disadvantages. So far as formalized solutions are concerned, there is an evident bias toward consideration of the more easily measured variables and criteria of evaluation – hence, typically, toward the economic. On the other hand, as the most recent efforts attest, the non-economic variables that enter as

127

constraints can easily dominate the solutions. Under such circumstances the economic aspect of educational planning comes to be a posting of what the non-economic constraints are costing a society. But turning things around again, methodological self-consciousness without methodological sophistication holds the ever present danger of reifying invalid assumptions and by rigidifying policy making those assumptions self-fulfilling. And technical virtuosity misapplied can aggravate future adjustment problems quite as readily as more sophisticated and subtle planning may ease or prevent them. My concern in this brief final section is not with the pros and cons, the potentials and the limitations or dangers of planning, however.[51] Rather, in line with the main theme of this paper, I would ask what use planning models have made of the human-investment concept, and what have attempts at such planning contributed to our understanding of how the various components of the educational system may combine and change through time in a reasonably efficient interaction with economic development.

Up to about 1963, economists who participated actively in human-resource development planning were concerned almost exclusively with manpower planning, and this meant projections of manpower requirements geared in varying degrees into general economic planning. However, there was in fact little integration between manpower and educational plans.

The first steps toward a formal integration of manpower with educational planning was taken by Jan Tinbergen and some of his associates.[52] They started at first with an extremely simplified model that resembled manpower planning in that it assumed fixed coefficients in the relation between growth of each type or level of manpower and growth of national income. However, the Tin-

51. Many of these matters are discussed in C. A. Anderson and M. J. Bowman, 'Theoretical considerations in educational planning', in Don Adams (ed.), *Educational planning*, Syracuse University Press, 1965. [See Reading 17.]

52. Jan Tinbergen and Hector Correa, 'Quantitative adaptation of education to accelerated growth', *Kyklos*, vol. 15 (1962); Jan Tinbergen and H. C. Bos, 'A planning model for the educational requirements of economic development' in *The residual and economic growth*, O.E.C.D., 1964; Jan Tinbergen, H. C. Bos, and others, *Econometric models of education*, O.E.C.D., 1965. Reprinted in [*Economics of education 2.*]

bergen models defined their manpower categories by educational attainments, thus jumping the hurdle of linking skills to schooling. Furthermore, they used three manpower (educational) categories only. This had the advantage of admitting flexibility of skill combinations within the broad categories even though not between them. It had the parallel disadvantage, however, that the practical problems of deciding which types of schools and curricula to expand or contract were untouched. Moreover, except that they included importation of high-level manpower as a possibility, the Tinbergen models matched the manpower ones in ignoring costs. They were not properly speaking social decision models at all. What, then, did they contribute, and why have they received so much attention?

The second part of this question is easily answered: Tinbergen's approach was close enough to the thinking of the manpower planners to get a hearing, and his model incorporated only variables for which empirical data were readily available in most O.E.C.D. countries. As I see them, his main contributions were three: First, he demonstrated the difficulties of rapid transitions, the internal inconsistencies inherent in many manpower goals that disregarded intervening processes of educational adaptation between the planning and the target dates. This laid the groundwork for development of programming models that would take into account the intricate interdependencies involved in educational expansion. Second, his models stimulated empirical research in a series of countries that has resulted in a relatively orderly process of revision of both the models themselves and perceptions of the range of alternatives in patterns of adjustment between economic and educational development. Finally, in introducing choice between importing more qualified manpower and producing it at home, Tinbergen stepped toward cost–benefit analysis; this was a partial or limited 'optimization' problem, and as such constituted a critical departure from the conventions of prior manpower analysis.

Meanwhile there had been a running battle between the manpower planners and those who argued that internal rate-of-return analysis (or present-value–cost comparisons derived from education–age–income data) could provide useful guidelines for social investment planning. Or perhaps it would be more accurate to say that a few economists were conducting this battle on the sidelines, while most of those engaged actively in manpower planning went their way undisturbed. (So, for that matter, did most of the 'rate-of-returners'.) However, at least a partial joining of these approaches seems now to be on the way. There are three recent efforts to apply systems analysis (in these cases linear programming) to educational planning, and all use at least some elements of both cost–benefit and manpower planning methods. These are a study in French by Jean Benard,[53] not yet applied in practice, a study by Irma Adelman[54] using Argentine data, and a study of Northern Nigeria by Samuel Bowles.[55]

The Benard and Adelman models apply to the total economy, though working out the education sector in special detail. Bowles' model is for the education sector only, taking inputs into that sector from elsewhere as exogenous variables or constraints. None treat on-the-job training explicitly, though I understand that Bowles has done the preliminary work for its inclusion. Benard and Bowles take experience into account whereas Adelman does not. All three distinguish technical or vocational from other types of schools.

Since the Benard model has not yet been applied empirically, I shall say only a word or two about it. The model is set up to solve for maximization of national income. Working in an environment in which neo-classical economics and rate-of-return analysis is automatically suspect, special care is taken in developing the argument for measuring inputs and outputs in money terms, for considering life age–income patterns, and for discounting. In

53. Jean Benard, 'Analyse des relations entre production, travail et éducation á l'aide d'un modèle dynamique d'optimation' (mimeo.), CEPREL, Arcueil 1965. [Now published as 'General optimization model for the economy and education', *Mathematical models in Educational Planning*, O.E.C.D., Paris, 1967, pp. 267–344.]

54. Irma Adelman, 'A linear programming model of educational planning – A case study of Argentina'. [Now published in I. Adelman and E. Thorbecke (eds.), *The theory and design of economic development*, The Johns Hopkins Press, Baltimore, 1966, pp. 385–412.]

55. Samuel Bowles, 'A planning model for the efficient allocation of resources in education', (mimeo.). Also his Harvard doctoral dissertation: *Efficiency in the allocation of resources in education; a planning model with application to Northern Nigeria*, 1965. [Now published in the *Quarterly Journal of Economics*, May 1967, pp. 189–219. *Economics of education 2.*]

some other respects he incorporates manpower-planning assumptions, however, placing his model somewhere between the Adelman model (closest to manpower) and the Bowles model (closest to the rate-of-return orientation).

The Adelman model is worked out for each of three objective functions: (1) maximization of the discounted sum of GNP (using a 5 per cent discount rate); (2) maximization of growth of the GNP from the base year to a designated future target year; (3) minimization of the discounted sum of net foreign capital inflows. As in manpower planning, this model generates its demands upon the educational system from the production (the non-education) side of the economy. It measures human resources in 'labor efficiency units' which are in principle based upon observed education–income data *within* each of three manpower categories. However, like conventional manpower studies, it allows no substitution among these categories and it assumes fixed ratios of labor-efficiency units to outputs. Also, the proportion of men with each educational attainment who enter any given manpower category is predetermined. The industry mix and hence the overall manpower category mix can vary. Thus the model allows for interaction between the demand and supply sides of human resource development.[56] It is in the cost–benefit family in that it compares the marginal social benefit of each type of education (what it adds at the margin to GNP) with its marginal social cost, or 'opportunity cost', given the cultural, political, or other constraints imposed on the model. As with the Benard, Bowles, and other linear programming models, it is possible also to measure the marginal social economic cost of adhering to particular non-economic constraints.

Adelman introduces her findings with many caveats. One in particular should be noted: in the absence of education–income data for Argentina her measures of labor-efficiency units were inevitably crude. Also, she used a simple variant of her model that required that all manpower must be home produced. Bearing these facts and other cautions in mind, it is interesting nevertheless

56. The model includes behavioral balance of payments constraints, constraints defining the maximum rate at which new investment can be absorbed, specification of an income-savings function, as well as its specifications more directly related to manpower and education.

to look at some of her results. First, her solution gave top priority to university education, and to such an extent that the rest of the educational program hung upon it. However, her findings suggested that the removal of constraints (or assumptions) inhibiting expansion of junior colleges relative to universities might raise total output of the economy substantially. Unfortunately, her findings for both university education and the university drop-out group were highly sensitive to the ratios estimated for her labor-efficiency units. The firmest of her findings, quite insensitive to any plausible changes in labor efficiency units and unaffected by constraints on the model, concerned vocational-technical schools. They simply washed out; what they contributed could not match their costs.

The Bowles model concentrates upon the education sector. Treating inputs into that sector from the rest of the economy as exogenously determined, he sets up as his objective function the maximization of the excess of total economic benefits over costs of education. The problem is one of resource allocation within education, studied in sequence over an 8-year time period. He included the choice between importation of qualified manpower and its home production in his problem, however. Furthermore, he tested for choices among alternative 'educational technologies', like team teaching. Like Tinbergen (and unlike Adelman) he classified labor directly by educational attainments, without introducing any intervening specifications of occupations or skills between his educational categories and associated incomes.[57] Like both Schultz and Denison, he assumes unchanging prices or rental values of men of given age and educational attainments (again implying either high substitutability in production or, more plausibly, changes in demands that match changes in supplies to maintain human resource prices unchanged). Boundary conditions that set limits on his solutions include, for example, socially or politically conditioned minima with respect to numbers of students in secondary school and feasibility limits on the pace of expansion of facilities. Solutions were derived for

57. Bowles obtained these data directly, by field work. He points out that this can be done much more easily and at less expense than is entailed in getting the kinds of data used by manpower planners, at least in developing nations.

several paces of change in the quality mix of teachers in primary schools.

The first thing Bowles demonstrates, unambiguously, is that existing educational plans for Northern Nigeria were simply impossible of realization. As a matter of simple arithmetic, in the immediate future Northern Nigeria could not simultaneously upgrade teachers, maintain teacher–pupil ratios and expand primary enrolments as specified in government plans. But to arrive at this conclusion did not require a linear programming model. More interesting was the fact that in all his solutions there was an initial lag in primary education because of the teacher problem but thereafter it took over, and together with higher education dominated the secondary level. Secondary school leavers directly entering the labor force were a very low priority. Technical and vocational secondary schools were again washed out; they are too expensive. To sum up, when costs are taken into account the allocation of resources within education that have been advocated by manpower planners were virtually reversed, even when the unemployment adjustments were deliberately biased against those entering the labor force from primary schools. Furthermore, test runs showed that in the Northern Nigerian context the solutions were insensitive to a wide range of variations in ratios of incomes of various educational groups as one or another increased. On the other hand, the solutions were highly sensitive to some of the constraints set up by existing regulations and institutional practice.

As Bowles himself has remarked, 'there is nothing in all this that you couldn't do on the back of an envelope – if you had enough envelopes'. But the 'if' is important; it refers to the extreme complexity of the web of interdependencies, even in a simplified programming model. On the other hand, such models cannot give out theoretical formulations of relationships that are not put into them in the first place. Their main contribution to positive science (as against public decisions) is indirect. It is in their capacity to identify which constraints are important, which are not – and so to point to problems that may be especially worthy of research, and of innovative *search*. Bowles' work is especially interesting from this point of view because he presses further into educational systems than has any other economist model-builder. This brings us to where educators and educational administrators in particular might well take over.

Although I have heard it rumored that a graduate student in California is currently attempting to apply systems analysis to intra-educational decisions at a sub-national level,[58] there is only one man of whom I have any direct knowledge who has been opening up this field in anything like a balanced way. I refer to Alan Thomas, in educational administration at the University of Chicago. His *Productivity in education*[59] delineates a framework for applying systems analysis to the educational decision process in a multi-stage input–output scheme. Productivity is *value added*, whether measured by performance on tests (for example) or, ultimately, by increments to earning capacity. His methods are very similar to Bowles', but with much more complex sets of input–output matrices. This is cost–benefit analysis of a subtle and complicated kind. In empirical application it entails among other things the identification of sets of intra-education production functions, building in part on prior empirical research in educational psychology and educational administration but requiring in the main the design of new empirical studies. Thomas is stimulating just such endeavors, especially in that ambiguous territory where economist, sociologist, and educator must converge. The multiplier process is indeed at work, and none of us need pause for lack of a new challenge and a new opportunity!

58. [The student in question is Dr L. P. Nordell, whose dissertation on an imput–output model of the Californian educational system was submitted to the University of California, Berkeley, 1967.]

59. This book is at present in manuscript and is being revised for publication. As partial background, see H. T. James, J. Alan Thomas, and Harold J. Dyck, *Wealth, expenditure, and decision-making for education*, in U.S. Department of Health, Education and Welfare, Cooperative Research Project No. 1241, Stanford (School of Education), 1963.

Part Three
Cost–Benefit Analysis of Educational Expenditures

What we here call 'cost–benefit analysis' is what Bowen (Reading 5) calls 'the direct returns-to-education approach'. His phrase is less than satisfactory as there is nothing about the approach that inhibits the addition of the indirect to the direct returns to education. The difficulty is that of quantifying the indirect returns. For that reason, Lee Hansen, Professor of Economics at the University of Wisconsin, confines himself to the direct returns in estimating both the private and the social rate of return to years of schooling in the United States in 1949. His essay discusses the many statistical and conceptual problems that arise in making such calculations and, in particular, compares rate-of-return analysis of educational expenditures with the more conventional additional-lifetime-income or present-value-of-additional-lifetime-income methods. It is only fitting that an article by Lee Hansen should be followed by one by Burton A. Weisbrod, also Professor of Economics at Wisconsin University; the two have worked together for years. Weisbrod's paper deals concretely with the indirect returns to or 'external effects' of education and shows how some of these can be measured on a piecemeal basis. His contribution raises the hope that we may soon be able to attach numbers to the broader economic benefits of educational expenditures.

Gary S. Becker, Professor of Economics at Columbia University, examines the economics of on-the-job training with surprising results: under perfect competition, it is workers rather than employers that pay the costs of certain kinds of training. In a brief note, Richard S. Eckaus, Professor of Economics at the Massachusetts Institute of Technology, takes exceptions to Becker's conclusions. Whatever the student may think of this controversy, Becker's analysis is virtually the first serious discussion of on-the-job training in 200 years of economics and it has already left its mark on the debate about labour training that is now going on in almost all advanced countries.

Mark Blaug, Professor of Economics of Education at the University of London Institute of Education, sums up the criticisms of cost–benefit analysis applied to education in terms of six basic objections, which he then attempts to meet in turn. The final section of his paper on the manpower-forecasting approach looks ahead to our next group of readings (see also Anderson and Bowman, Reading 17).

7 W. Lee Hansen

Rates of Return to Investment in Schooling in the
United States

W. Lee Hansen, 'Total and private rates of return to investment in school-ing', *Journal of Political Economy*, vol. 81 (1963), no. 2, pp. 128–41.

The costs of schooling and the money returns resulting from in-vestment in schooling are currently receiving more and more attention by economists, not only because of their possible im-plications for economic growth, but also because they may help individuals to determine how much they should invest in the development of their own human capital. This note provides some further evidence on these two topics; it presents estimates of internal rates of return based on both total and private resource costs for various amounts of schooling, from elementary school through college.

The fragmentary treatment of both the costs of schooling and the money returns to schooling found in much of the recent literature provided the stimulus for preparing these internal rate-of-return estimates. For example, Miller calculates lifetime in-come values by level of schooling,[1] Houthakker estimates, on the basis of alternative discount rates, the present value of income streams associated with different levels of schooling,[2] Schultz provides estimates of total resource costs of education by broad level of schooling,[3] and Becker and Schultz calculate for several levels of education the expected rates of return, sometimes on a total resource cost basis and at other times on a private resource cost basis.[4] Given this diversity of treatment, it is difficult to

1. Herman P. Miller, 'Annual and lifetime income in relation to educa-tion: 1929–59', *American Economic Review*, vol. 50 (1960), pp. 962–86.

2. H. S. Houthakker, 'Education and income', *Review of Economics and Statistics*, vol. 41 (1959), pp. 24–8.

3. Theodore W. Schultz, 'Capital formation by education', *Journal of Political Economy*, vol. 68 (1960), pp. 571–83.

4. Gary S. Becker, 'Underinvestment in college education?' *American Economic Review*, vol. 50 (May 1960), pp. 346–54; and Theodore W. Schultz,

obtain an overall picture of the relationship among rates of return to different amounts of schooling or to see the nature of the differences between the rates of return as viewed by society and those viewed by individuals. Moreover, the relationship among the various methods of contrasting the economic gains from education – the lifetime income, the present value, and the rate of return comparisons – has been obscured.

It becomes important to understand what some of these relationships are when society and individuals allocate such a large portion of their resources to schooling. At the societal level, for example, we might be interested in determining whether to allocate more funds to reduce the number of dropouts from high school or to stimulate an increased flow of college graduates. As individuals, we would more likely be concerned with deciding whether to continue or to terminate our schooling, on the basis of the relative costs that will be incurred and the benefits that will accrue. To this end, the comprehensive sets of internal rates of return developed here should be useful as a first approximation in seeking answers to questions of this kind.

At the outset, it should be made clear that the measured rates of return are money rates of return; any other costs and benefits associated with schooling are excluded from consideration. In addition, there are problems of measurement, many of which have not been resolved, that make the estimation of even direct money rates of return difficult. Some of these difficulties are discussed in Section I, which outlines the methods and data employed. Section II presents evidence on rates of return to total and to private resource investment in schooling. Section III contrasts three different methods of measuring the economic gains to schooling, while Section IV offers some concluding comments.

'Education as a source of economic growth', Economics of Education Research Paper, 15 August 1961 (Mimeographed), and 'Education and economic growth', *Social forces influencing American education*, (ed.) H. G. Richey, Chicago, 1961. It should be noted that Schultz uses a short-cut method to derive his rate of return estimates.

I. Estimation Procedures

To estimate internal rates of return to investments in schooling, we require data on costs – total resource costs and private resource costs – for various levels of schooling as well as data on age–income patterns by each level of schooling. From these, life-cycle cost–income streams can be established that show for each level of schooling the flows of costs incurred during schooling and the subsequent flows of additional income that can be attributed to that schooling. The internal rate of return is then estimated by finding that rate of discount that equates the present value of the cost outlays with the present value of the additional income flows.

The basic source of income data is the *1950 Census of Population*,[5] which provides distributions of income for males by age and level of schooling in 1949. From these, average income figures can be calculated for each age-schooling category, as shown in Table 1. Although Houthakker had previously presented such figures, his method of estimation produces a rather peculiar bias.[6] In addition, Houthakker's data show mean incomes of all males over age fourteen, whether they were receiving income or not. But to the extent that only income recipients are represented in the data shown here in Table 1, most of the males outside the labor force, either because of school attendance (younger males) or retirement (older males), are probably excluded. Exclusion of these groups seems likely to provide better estimates of the age–income profiles, particularly at their extremities.

In order to make the task of estimating the rates of return

5. United States Bureau of the Census, *1950 Census of Population, Special Report*, P.E. No. 5B, *Education*, Table 12.

6. The mean income figures used in this study were estimated by weighting the mid-values of each income size class by the numbers of income recipients in each size class, for each age-level-of-schooling category. A value of $20,000 was used for the mid-value of the open-ended class. Houthakker used a 'representative' income in his weighting, in order to take account of the skewness. However, such a procedure superimposes the skewness of the entire distribution upon each age-level-of-schooling category; this leads to serious problems, particularly at the younger age levels, where the resulting mean income values will substantially overstate the 'correct' values.

more manageable, the age–income profiles were assumed to commence at the 'average' age of completion of each level of schooling.[7] For those with one to four years of schooling, the average amount of school completed was taken as two years; hence the age–income profile for this group was assumed to begin at age eight. For the next group, those with five to seven years of school,

Table 1

Average Income by Age and Years of School Completed, Males, United States, 1949

| | Years of school completed | | | | | | | |
| | Elementary school | | | | High school | | College | |
Age	0	1–4	5–7	8	1–3	4	1–3	4+
14–15	$ 610	$ 350	$ 365	$ 406				
16–17	526	472	514	534	$ 429			
18–19	684	713	885	1,069	941	$ 955		
20–21	944	1,009	1,216	1,535	1,652	1,744	$1,066	
22–24	1,093	1,227	1,562	1,931	2,191	2,363	1,784	$1,926
25–34	1,337	1,603	2,027	2,540	2,837	3,246	3,444	4,122
35–44	1,605	1,842	2,457	3,029	3,449	4,055	5,014	7,085
45–54	1,812	2,073	2,650	3,247	3,725	4,689	5,639	8,116
55–64	2,000	2,045	2,478	3,010	3,496	4,548	5,162	7,655
65 or more	1,140	1,189	1,560	1,898	2,379	3,155	3,435	5,421

Source: See notes 5 and 6.

six years of schooling were assumed, so that its age–income profile begins at age twelve. The other level of education groups and the ages at which their age–income profiles were assumed to begin are as follows: eight years, age fourteen; one to three years of high school, age sixteen; four years of high school, age eighteen; one to three years of college, age twenty; and four years of college, age twenty-two. In fact, however, for age groups under fourteen the age–income profiles take values of zero, because no income data are collected for these groups.[8]

7. This is an oversimplification, but it did not seem worthwhile to deal with this in a more detailed fashion.

8. It is unfortunate that such data are not collected since the earnings of male workers below age fourteen are assuredly not zero. Thus opportunity costs are understated to some extent.

Two major cost variants are used in the calculations – one for total resource costs and the other for private resource costs. The rationale and procedures for estimating total resource costs have been set forth by Schultz.[9] Total resource costs include (1) school costs incurred by society, that is, teachers' salaries, supplies, interest and depreciation on capital, (2) opportunity costs incurred by individuals, namely, income foregone during school attendance, and (3) incidental school-related costs incurred by individuals, for example, books and travel. Private resource costs include the same three components except that in (1) above, tuition and fees paid by individuals are substituted for society's costs which are normally defrayed through taxation.

In developing the cost figures used in these estimates, whether on a total or a private resource basis, the opportunity costs were taken directly from the age–income profiles of the alternative level of schooling being used in the calculations. For example, at age eighteen the opportunity cost for the person undertaking four years of college is the income that the high-school graduate would obtain from ages eighteen to twenty-one. This procedure made it unnecessary to rely upon indirectly estimated opportunity cost figures and yielded at the same time a more detailed set of opportunity costs by age and level of schooling.[10] In completing the estimates of per student total resource cost, school costs paid by society and school-related expenditures incurred by individuals were derived from Schultz's results.[11] In completing the estimates of private resource costs, the amount of tuition and fees paid per student was obtained from already available estimates.[12] Again, the school-related costs from Schultz's work were used. While the latter costs have an arbitrary quality to

9. 'Capital formation by education', op. cit.

10. These opportunity cost figures tend to be slightly lower, on a per student basis, than those of Schultz, which average $583 for high school and $1,369 for college, on an annual basis.

11. ibid.

12. Average college tuition and fees amounted to $245 in 1949 (see Ernest V. Hollis, 'Trends in tuition charges and fees', *Higher education*, vol. 12, 1956, p. 70). Actually, a figure of $245 was used; this figure was estimated from data on tuition and fees collected, reported for 1949–50 in *Biennial survey of education, 1955–6*, Washington, Government Printing Office (1957), ch. 4. See sources to Table 2.

them, they seem to be reasonable.[13] The cost figures, exclusive of opportunity costs, by age and grade are summarized in Table 2.

Lifetime cost–income streams were then constructed for each level of schooling with the help of the appropriate age–income profiles and the age–cost estimates. This was done by taking the difference between the cost–income profile for a given level of schooling and the income profile for the particular base level of schooling used in the comparison. For example, in the case of investment in four years of college, the income profile for the base group, high-school graduates, begins at age eighteen. The cost–income profile for the person who completes four years of college also begins at age eighteen; during the four years to age twenty-one it reflects both school and school-related costs and thereafter the somewhat higher income profile of the college graduate. The cost–income stream, the *difference* between these two profiles, reflects at ages eighteen to twenty-one both school and school-related costs as well as opportunity costs; at ages beyond twenty-one the difference reflects the net income stream resulting from four years of college. An additional adjustment is required to reflect the incidence of mortality; this involves adjusting the net cost–income stream downward to reflect the probabilities that at each age the costs or returns will not be incurred or received, respectively.[14] Finally, the internal rates of return must be estimated by finding that rate of discount which sets the present value of the cost stream equal to the present value of the net return stream.

When considering private rates of return, it is important to show them on both a before- and after-tax basis. Not only will all rates of return be lower after tax, but also the relative declines in

13. Schultz simply assumed that these costs were 5 per cent of income foregone at the high-school level and 10 per cent of income foregone at the college level. The absolute figures derived from Schultz's work were used in these calculations even though the income foregone figures differed somewhat.

14. Calculated from United States Department of Health, Education, and Welfare, National Office of Vital Statistics, *United States life tables, 1949–51* (Special Reports, vol. 41, no. 1, Washington, 1954). No attempt was made, however, to adjust for the incidence of unemployment, largely because of the difficulty of disentangling unemployment from non-labor-force status in the data, which show all males classified by the receipt or non-receipt of income rather than by labor-force status.

the rates will differ, given the progressivity of tax rates and the positive association between income and educational levels. The differences among the before-tax and after-tax rates could be of

Table 2
Average Annual per Student Costs, Exclusive of Opportunity Costs, by Age and Grade, United States, 1949 *

		Total resource costs			Private resource costs		
Age	School level (1)	School Costs (2)	Other costs (3)	Total (4)	Tuition and fees (5)	Other costs (6)	Total (7)
6–13	Elementary	$201		$201			
14–17	High school	354	31	385		31	31
18–21	College	801	142	943	245	142	387

* Though these cost data are indicated as being for 1950 in Schultz, 'Capital formation by education', op. cit., they actually apply to the 1949–50 school year. Thus these data may overstate somewhat the costs of schooling relative to the income derived from that schooling.

Source: col. (2), *elementary school:* Schultz, 'Capital formation by education', op. cit., Table 3, col. 11, 1950 figure divided by number of elementary-school students in 1950, from *Statistical abstract*, 1955, Table 152; *high school:* Schultz, 'Capital formation by education', op. cit., Table 5, 1950, col 4 divided by col. 1; *college:* ibid., Table 6, 1950, col. 4 divided by col. 1.

Col. 3, *elementary school:* assumed to be zero; *high school:* ibid.; Table 5, 1950, col 5 divided by col. 1; *college:* ibid., Table 6, 1950, col. 4 divided by col. 1.

Col. 4, sum of cols 2 and 3.

Col. 5, *elementary school* and *high school:* assumed to be zeros *college:* based on average tuition and fee charges, derived from *Biennial survey of education, 1955–6*, chaps. 1 and 4, after adjusting veteran charges for non-tuition items (see note 13).

Col. 6, same as col. 3.

Col. 7, sum of cols. 5 and 6.

considerable importance to individuals in the determination of their own investment planning.

To estimate the after-tax incomes and rates of return, the original income data in Table 1 were adjusted for federal income tax payments; while it probably would have been desirable to adjust for all types of taxes, this could not be done in view of the paucity of data. Subsequently, the rates of return were calculated in the same way as described for the before-tax data. The actual after-tax income figures were obtained by multiplying each income figure by the appropriate ratio of after- to before-tax income, derived from Houthakker.[15] These ratios prove to be almost identical to those that would have resulted had the marginal tax rates been applied to the distributions of income recipients in calculating after-tax income.[16]

As in most empirical studies the available data prove to be somewhat unlike those that we require, and so the rate of return estimates do not provide a full picture of the profitability of schoolings.[17] Therefore, several features of the data and the nature of their effects on age–income profiles, and hence on rates of return, deserve mention before the results are discussed. First, since only income rather than earnings data are available, the income profiles used reflect in part receipts from other assets. On the assumption that the relative income from other assets is a positive function of the level of earnings itself, the impact of this would presumably be to raise the age–income profiles of the higher level of schooling groups. Second, certain problems of 'mix' exist within the data. For example, among those with little schooling there may be heavy concentrations of certain minority groups, such as Negroes and Puerto Ricans. If they are effectively discriminated against, then the age–income profiles of the lower level of schooling groups would be depressed below their expected level. On the other hand, at higher levels of schooling the

15. Houthakker, op. cit., calculated from Tables 1 and 2, pp. 25–6.

16. Several of the education–age categories were adjusted for taxes by applying the average effective tax liability by size of income group to the midpoint of the size group to determine the mean tax paid. In general, the average effective tax rate derived for an education–age category was almost identical with that calculated by Houthakker.

Admittedly, the use of the average tax liability ignores the effects of age differences, family size, and so on, but it did not seem worthwhile to adjust for these factors, even to the limited extent that such adjustments could be attempted.

17. The main criticisms of this whole approach have been expressed most fully and forcefully by Edward F. Renshaw, 'Estimating the returns to education', *Review of Economics and Statistics*, vol. 42 (1960), pp. 318–24.

age–income profiles may be raised somewhat by reverse discrimination that favors sons, relatives, and others of higher social–economic status. Third, since those people who complete more schooling ordinarily possess greater intelligence, as measured by intelligence scores, some part of the differential income received might have accrued to them anyway. Although our present knowledge makes it difficult to separate the impact of intelligence and schooling, the observed income differences among the lower and higher levels of schooling undoubtedly overstate, and by increasing amounts, the differentials attributable to schooling.[18] Fourth, all cost elements were considered as investment even though some portions might better be regarded as consumption. To the extent that any of the cost is considered as consumption, the investment costs are overstated.[19] Fifth, all estimates rest on cross-section cost–income relationships and thereby ignore future shifts in the relationships of the cost–income streams. And finally, any number of other factors may impinge on the observed income differentials, in the form of education at home, on-the-job-training, and so forth.

While some would suggest that the presence of such problems seriously limits any conclusions concerning the empirical relationships between income and schooling, it nevertheless seems worthwhile to set forth the rate of return estimates in their crude form.[20] From them some preliminary conclusions about resource allocation can be drawn.

II. Internal Rate of Return Estimates

A. The return to total resource investment

Internal rates of return to total resource investment in schooling appear in Table 3. The boxed figures in the diagonal to the right show the rates of return to each successive increment of schooling

18. Becker, op. cit., has made some adjustments for differences in ability, but his method of doing so is not yet available. Differences in intelligence at different levels of schooling are given in Dael Wolfle, *America's resources of specialized talent*, Harper and Bros., 1954, pp. 142–9.

19. This point is discussed in T. W. Schultz, 'Investment in human capital', *American Economic Review*, vol. 51 (1961), pp. 1–17. [See Reading 1.]

20. For another dissenting note, see John Vaizey, *The economics of education*, Faber and Faber, 1962, ch. 3.

and can be interpreted as 'marginal' rates of return. For example, the rate of return to the first two years of elementary school is 8.9 per cent, to the next four years of elementary school 14.5 per cent, and so on to the last two years of college 15.6 per cent. Although the marginals provide all of the necessary information,

Table 3
Internal Rates of Return to Total Resource Investment in Schooling, United States, Males, 1949 *

From:			(1)	(2)	(3)	(4)	(5)	(6)	(7)
To:	Age		6	8	12	14	16	18	20
		Grade	1	3	7	9	11	13	15
(1)	7	2	8.9						
(2)	11	6	12.0	14.5					
(3)	13	8	15.0	18.5	29.2				
(4)	15	10	13.7	15.9	16.3	9.5			
(5)	17	12	13.6	15.4	15.3	11.4	13.7		
(6)	19	14	11.3	12.1	11.1	8.2	8.2	5.4	
(7)	21	16	12.1	12.7	12.1	10.5	10.9	10.2	15.6

* All rate-of-return figures are subject to some error, since the estimation to one decimal place was made by interpolation between whole percentage figures.

average rates of return to successively more years of schooling can be derived from the marginals; since the average rates are of some interest, they are also shown in the columns. For example, in column 1 we see that at age six the expected rate of return to investment in two years of elementary schooling is 8.9 per cent; the rate of return to investment in six years of elementary schooling (the weighted average of the two marginals) is 12.0 per cent, and so on to the investment in sixteen years of schooling, which yields a 12.1 per cent rate of return.

Several features of the configuration of rates of return deserve comment. First, the marginal rates rise over the first few years of schooling, reaching a peak with the completion of elementary schooling. This clearly suggests that rapidly increasing returns to schooling prevail over the early years and that a small initial amount of schooling, the first two years, has relatively little impact on earning power. Second, the trend in the rates is down-ward thereafter, though it is not smooth by any means. While the rate of return to the first two years of high school drops dra-matically, it rises somewhat with the completion of high school. The rate drops once again for the first two years of college, and it then displays a significant rise with the completion of four years of college. At this point one can only speculate as to the reasons underlying these declines.

Evidence such as this on the marginal or incremental rates of return is ordinarily used in discussing resource allocation. If on the basis of these rates of return a given amount of resources were to be spent on schooling, the ranking of the marginals from high to low is as follows: Grades 7–8, 15–16, 3–6, 11–12, 9–10, 0–2, and 13–14.[21] At an alternative rate of return to society of, say, 10 per cent, investment in all grade levels except the last three would be justified. Were the alternative rate, say, 7 per cent, only the last level would be excluded.

Viewing the matter in this fashion would be quite satisfactory if the rates of return declined steadily as we moved to successively higher increments of schooling, but because the marginal rates fluctuate some averaging is required. If we look at marginal rates for broader increments of schooling, for example, eight years of elementary school, four years of high school, and four years of college, then the rates of return to additional investment quite clearly decline, as shown by the respective figures: 15.0 per cent (col. 1, row 3), 11.4 per cent (col. 4, row 5), and 10.2 per cent (col. 6, row 7). At an alternative rate of return of 10 per cent, investment in all levels of schooling becomes profitable. But were the original rates considered independently of each other and an alternative rate of return of 10 per cent prevailed, it would not pay to permit any new enrolments, the schooling of those people in elementary school would be terminated at Grade 8, and of those people already in high school and college, only students in their last two years of each would be allowed to graduate. To allocate investment in schooling this way would obviously reflect a very short-run view of the implied economic opportunities.

However, it might be desirable to consider some longer term

21. It is interesting to note that most states require compulsory school attendance at least to age fourteen (in effect, to the end of Grade 8).

horizon instead, particularly if the alternative rate of return were expected to remain reasonably constant over time. Given an alternative rate of return of, say, 10 per cent, investment through the completion of college could easily be justified for each age group currently enrolled, since every rate of return figure in the bottom row (row 7) of Table 3 exceeds 10 per cent. Understandably, this result is no different than that obtained earlier.

On the basis of even longer-run considerations only the rate of return to investment in the schooling of new school entrants may be relevant, especially if schooling is thought of as a good to be purchased in large, indivisible quantities, for example, schooling from Grade 1 through college, or schooling from Grade 1 through high school. In this case the rates of return shown in column 1 indicate yields of 13.6 and 12.1 per cent, respectively, and suggest the obvious advantages of seeing to it that everyone completes college or high school, as the case may be. In fact, this averaging of the marginal rates makes such investment attractive at an alternative rate as high as 12 per cent.

B. The return to private resource investment

Internal rates of return to total resource costs of schooling are of undeniable importance in assessing the efficiency with which an economy's resources are allocated, but for individuals and/or their parents the relevant rates of return are those based upon private resource costs. These private rates of return both before and after tax are shown in Tables 4 and 5, respectively; the tables are to be read in the same fashion as Table 3.

For all levels of schooling under eight years, private rates of return have no real meaning (they are infinitely large) since opportunity costs are assumed to be zero, school-related costs are negligible, and tuition and fees are not charged. Above Grade 8, however, all private rates of return before tax are higher than the total rates of return shown in Table 3, with the greatest disparities appearing at the younger ages and lower levels of schooling, where individuals pay smaller proportions of total resource costs; private rates of return after tax are also higher than total rates of return with but two exceptions. Otherwise, the general configuration in both the columns and the diagonals appears to be about the same for both total and private rates, whether before or after tax, though the levels do differ.

When individuals and/or their parents plan an investment program in schooling, the private rates of return justify securing more schooling than do the rates of return on total resource investment. For example, the marginal rates of return to ele-

Table 4

Internal Rates of Return to Private Resource Investment in Schooling, before Tax, United States, Males, 1949 *

From:			(1)	(2)	(3)	(4)	(5)	(6)	(7)
To:	Age		6	8	12	14	16	18	20
		Grade	1	3	7	9	11	13	15
(1)	7	2	†						
(2)	11	6	†	†					
(3)	13	8	†	†	†				
(4)	15	10	28.3	34.6	25.9	12.7			
(5)	17	12	25.6	29.4	23.3	15.3	18.6		
(6)	19	14	18.1	18.7	14.8	10.4	9.5	6.2	
(7)	21	16	18.2	18.7	16.2	12.9	13.0	11.6	18.7

* All rate-of-return figures are subject to some error, since the estimation to one decimal place had to be made by interpolation between whole percentage figures.

† This indicates an infinite rate-of-return, given the assumption that education is costless to the individual to the completion of eighth grade.

mentary, high-school, and college schooling are infinite (col 1, row 3), 15.3 per cent (col. 4, row 5), and 11.6 per cent (col. 6, row 7), respectively. Thus, investment in schooling through college is still profitable even if the private alternative rate is as high as 11.5 per cent. But, on an after-tax basis, the alternative rate of 10 per cent just permits private investment at the college level (Table 5, col. 6, row 7).

When schooling is viewed in large blocks, a somewhat different picture emerges. If the decision-making age is fourteen and the objective is to complete schooling through college, the alternative rate of return would have to exceed 12.9 per cent (col. 4, row 7) on a before-tax basis and 11.5 per cent on an after-tax basis for the investment to be unprofitable. If the decision-making age is six and the objective is to complete schooling through college, the alternative rate would have to exceed 18.2 per cent (col. 1, row 7) on a before-tax basis and 17.2 per cent on an after-tax basis, for the investment to be unprofitable.

Table 5

Internal Rates of Return to Private Resource Investment in Schooling, after Tax, United States, Males, 1949 *

From:			(1)	(2)	(3)	(4)	(5)	(6)	(7)
To:	Age		6	8	12	14	16	18	20
		Grade	1	3	7	9	11	13	15
(1)	7	2	†						
(2)	11	6	†	†					
(3)	13	8	†	†	†				
(4)	15	10	27.9	33.0	24.8	12.3			
(5)	17	12	25.2	28.2	22.2	14.5	17.5		
(6)	19	14	17.2	17.5	13.7	9.4	8.5	5.1	
(7)	21	16	17.2	17.3	14.4	11.5	1.4	10.1	16.7

* All rate-of-return figures are subject to some error, since the estimation to one decimal place had to be made by interpolation between whole percentage figures.

† This indicates an infinite rate of return, given the assumption of costless education to the individual through the completion of eighth grade.

A comparison of the total rates of return with the private rates of return after tax is of interest in suggesting the extent to which distortions in the private rates caused by federal income taxes are offset by the counter-distortion of subsidized schooling. An examination of the results in Tables 3 and 5 indicates that even though income taxes do substantially reduce the levels of private rates of return, public subsidization of schooling makes the private rates of return net of tax considerably more attractive than the rate of return earned on total resource investment. Only two exceptions appear (col. 6); these suggest that the student pays more than his own way in securing schooling at the college level.

This might indicate the need for a re-study of the assessment of the costs of college against the individual, unless the possible underinvestment in college training that would be produced is regarded as acceptable in some broader sense. But these exceptions aside, the fact that private rates of return after taxes exceed the total rates of return would, in the absence of restraints on sources of private financing, probably give rise to overinvestment in schooling by individuals. However, a fuller treatment of the effects of other forms of taxation and methods of financing schooling would be required before any definitive judgment could be reached.

III. Alternative Measures of Private Economic Returns from Schooling

The economic returns to individuals from schooling can be observed from three different points of view: (1) the value of lifetime income as set forth by Miller,[22] (2) the present value of lifetime income as set forth by Houthakker,[23] and (3) the rate of return on investment in schooling as set forth here. While the lifetime income and present value of lifetime income methods, particularly the former, are rather widely used, they are not relevant to ranking the direct economic returns to schooling when schooling is treated as a type of investment expenditure. Both of these methods completely ignore the costs of schooling, while the lifetime income approach suffers from the further defect of ignoring the time shape of the returns. Because the rankings of the economic returns differ so substantially, it seems desirable to present all three measures of the returns and to discuss them briefly. To make the comparisons more manageable, we shall deal only with the additional returns to different amounts of schooling as seen at age fourteen. The before- and after-tax results appear in the upper and lower halves, respectively, of Table 6.

The value of additional lifetime income associated with higher levels of schooling is frequently cited as a justification for investment in schooling by the individual. Clearly, the values of additional lifetime income resulting from successively greater amounts

22. op. cit.   23. op. cit.

of schooling (col. 1), indicate that more schooling pays substantially larger dollar returns than less schooling.[24] But, since a portion of the costs of schooling is excluded from consideration,[25]

Table 6

Alternative Methods of Comparing Value of Private Economic Returns to Investment in Schooling, as Viewed at Age Fourteen, United States, Males, 1949

Schooling from completion of Grade 8 to completion of:	Additional lifetime income (1)	Present value of additional income at				Internal rate of return (%) (6)
		3% (2)	6% (3)	8% (4)	10% (5)	
Before tax						
2 years high school	$ 16,802	$ 7,756	$ 2,301	$1,190	$ 545	12.7
4 years high school	46,038	18,156	6,488	3,601	1,949	15.3
2 years college	66,763	23,800	7,352	3,215	996	10.4
4 years college	141,468	49,429	17,252	8,722	4,135	12.9
After tax						
2 years high school	$ 14,143	$ 5,081	$ 1,956	$ 996	$ 436	12.3
4 years high school	38,287	13,580	5,362	2,929	1,547	14.5
2 years college	52,485	17,000	5,364	2,084	336	9.4
4 years college	109,993	36,575	12,824	6,170	2,611	11.5

the full extent to which these returns offset the costs of schooling is not at all clear. Even more important, the fact that the time flows of these returns also differ remains hidden in the calculation of the lifetime income values. By virtue of these omissions, the

24. The differences shown here differ somewhat from those that are derived from Miller and Houthakker because of differences in the assumed shapes and levels of the age–income profiles.

25. Opportunity costs are reflected in the figures showing 'additional' lifetime income inasmuch as the income of the person in school is set at zero while his income-earning counterpart receives a positive income; the difference appears in the cost-return stream and measures opportunity costs. However, the other private costs of schooling are omitted in this calculation.

impression emerges that any and all amounts of schooling are worth obtaining.

Another method of measuring the economic returns to schooling involves comparing the present values of additional lifetime income, at various discount rates, to successively greater amounts of schooling. The values, at discount rates of 3, 6, 8, and 10 per cent appear in columns 2, 3, 4, and 5, respectively.[26] Again, schooling pays at any or all of the discount rates used, though the rankings do shift about as the discount rate is varied. For example, at 3 and 6 per cent the rankings coincide with those shown by the value of additional lifetime income, but at an 8 per cent discount rate schooling to the first two years of college becomes absolutely less attractive financially than schooling to high school, whether before or after tax. And at a 10 per cent discount rate the after-tax return to schooling to the first two years of college falls below that to the first two years of high school. Even though the present-value figures are quite sensitive to the discount rate used, once again all schooling pays. But the basic flaw in this method of calculation is the omission of some of the costs of education from the calculation; specifically, the method fails to subtract the present value of the non-opportunity costs from the present value of the additional income. Doing so would undoubtedly cause some additional changes in the rankings, particularly at the higher discount rates.

Finally, the rate-of-return approach remedies the defects inherent in the other two methods. The relevant data on internal rates of return from Tables 4 and 5 (see Table 6, col. 6), reveal a much different ranking of the returns to schooling. On a before-tax basis, investment in schooling to completion of high school, with a 15.3 rate of return, yields by far the most attractive return, followed by schooling to college with 12.9 per cent, and schooling to the first two years of high school with 12.7 per cent; schooling to the first two years of college, with a 10.4 per cent return, lags far behind.

When we shift to rates of return on an after-tax basis, the rankings of the return on schooling to the completion of college

26. The differences shown here differ somewhat from those derived from Houthakker because of differences in the assumed shapes and levels of the age–income profiles.

and to the completion of the first two years of high school change. Since the marginal tax rates are a function of the amount of the income differential, the effect of the tax on the college rate of return is decidedly greater than its effect on the rate of return to the first two years of high school, for example. Given the fact that the original rates of return were almost identical, the after-tax return to completion of college now drops considerably below that to completion of two years of high school.

In conclusion, it appears that ranking of the returns to investment in schooling by the rate-of-return method is clearly superior to the methods employed in the work of both Miller and Houthakker. Whether the more general rate-of-return rule is in fact superior to the present-value rule (when properly used) still remains an unsettled issue that will not be discussed here.[27]

IV. Conclusion

Estimates of the internal money rates of return to both total and private resource investment in schooling have been presented to provide a more complete picture of the costs of and returns to schooling. While the rates of return to private resource investment obviously exceed those to total resource investment, we find that the rates of return to the various increments of schooling also differ and have somewhat different implications for resource allocation at both the societal and individual level. Basically, the marginal rates of return rise with more schooling up to the completion of Grade 8 and then gradually fall off to the completion of college. We also find that private rates of return after tax almost invariably exceed the total rates of return, a situation that could presumably induce private overinvestment in schooling. Finally, the rate of return provides a superior method of ranking the economic returns to investment in schooling than do the more conventional additional lifetime income or present value of additional lifetime income methods currently used.

Thus, one might conclude that the high rates of return to investment in schooling go a long way toward explaining, or justi-

27. For a fuller treatment of this point see J. Hirshleifer, 'On the theory of optimal investment decision', *Journal of Political Economy*, vol. 66 (1958), pp. 329–52.

fying, this society's traditional faith in education, as well as the desire of individuals to take advantage of as much schooling as they can. But clearly we need to know much more about the relationship between income and ability, the importance of on-the-job training, the significance of education in the home, and so forth. My own suspicion is that full adjustment for these factors would have the effect of reducing the relative rates of return, especially at the higher levels of schooling.

In addition, we have barely begun to consider the possible disparity between the rate of return to total resource investment and the 'social' rate of return to investment in schooling that takes additional account of those returns that are produced indirectly. Intuition as well as the little evidence available suggests that these returns may be considerable, but a full accounting of the economic value of schooling will have to await further work.[28]

28. For an excellent analysis of some of the conceptual differences between private and social returns, see Mary Jean Bowman, 'Social returns to education', *International Social Sciences Journal*, vol. 14 (1962), no. 4, and Burton Weisbrod, 'Education and investment in human capital', *Journal of Political Economy: Supplement*, vol. 70 (1962), pp. 106–23. (See Reading 8).

8 B. A. Weisbrod

External Effects of Investment in Education

B. A. Weisbrod, 'Education and investment in human capital', *Journal of Political Economy*, vol. 70 (1962), no. 5, part 2 (Supplement), pp. 106–23. (Appendix omitted.)

I

As technological developments have altered production techniques, types of mechanical equipment, and varieties of outputs, society has begun to recognize that economic progress involves not only changes in machinery but also in men – not only expenditures on equipment but also on people. Investment in people makes it possible to take advantage of technical progress as well as to continue that progress. Improvements in health make investment in education more rewarding by extending life expectancy. Investment in education expands and extends knowledge, leading to advances which raise productivity and improve health. With investment in human capital and non-human capital both contributing to economic growth and welfare and in what is probably an interdependent manner, more attention should be paid to the adequacy of the level of expenditures on people.

The principal forms of direct investment in the productivity and well-being of people are: health, learning (both in school and on the job), and location (migration). Formal education and health constitute two large components of public and private spending in the United States. Private expenditures alone for hospital and physician services were over $18 billion in 1959, having risen from $8.6 billion in 1950.[1] Public education expenditures rose to $19.3 billion in 1960 from $7.3 billion at the turn of the decade.[2] Priced at cost, gross investment in education in the

1. United States Department of Health, Education and Welfare, *Health, education and welfare trends, 1961*, Washington, Government Printing Office, 1961, p. 23.

2. ibid., p. 53.

United States has risen from 9 per cent of gross physical investment in 1900 to 34 per cent in 1956.[3]

Investment in future productivity is occurring increasingly outside the private market and in intangible forms. Our traditional conception of investment as a private market phenomenon and only as tangible plant, machinery and equipment must give way to a broader concept which allows not only for government investment but also for intangible investment in the quality of human capital.

Most economic analysis of return from education has focused on the contribution of education to earning capacity (and, presumably, to production capacity). While this has been valuable, it is only part of the picture, and perhaps not even a large part. Even aside from market imperfections, which create inequalities between wage rates and marginal productivity, earnings are an incomplete measure of the productivity of education to the extent that production occurs outside the market. In addition, emphasis on incremental earnings attributable to education disregards external effects. Schooling benefits many persons other than the student. It benefits the student's future children, who will receive informal education in the home; and it benefits neighbors, who may be affected favorably by the social values developed in children by the schools and even by the quietness of the neighborhood while the schools are in session. Schooling benefits employers seeking a trained labor force; and it benefits the society at large by developing the basis for an informed electorate. Compulsory school attendance and public (rather than private) support for education in the United States both suggest that external economies from either the production or consumption of education are believed to be important.[4]

From the vantage point of one interested in Pareto's optimal resource allocation, it is essential to consider all benefits from some action (as well as all costs). Whether the benefits (or costs) involve explicit financial payments, or whether they

3. T. W. Schultz, 'Capital formation by education', *Journal of Political Economy*, December 1960, p. 583.

4. Similarly, but perhaps more clearly, compulsory smallpox vaccination together with public provision of vaccine reflects external economies of 'consumption' of the vaccine.

are internal to, or external from, a particular decision-maker is irrelevant.

In the private sector of the economy, private benefits from goods and services are reflected in consumer demand; assuming economic rationality, competition, and the absence of external effects, private producers will meet the demand in a socially optimum manner. But when goods and services either have significant external effects or are indivisible (in the sense that consumption by one person does not reduce consumption opportunities for others – as, for example, national defense), the private market is inadequate. If the public sector attempts to provide the service, and if consumer sovereignty is to reign, the extent of consumer demand must be judged. Thus arises the need for benefit–cost analysis.

Within the benefit–cost framework this paper focuses principal attention on the ways by which a society benefits from formal education, discussing much more briefly some of the ways by which it incurs costs in providing education. It is worth emphasizing that analyzing benefits (or costs) does not preclude specifying which people reap the returns (or incur the costs). We shall attempt to identify the benefits of education by recognizing the beneficiaries of the education process.

In the discussion which follows, a 'benefit' of education will refer to anything that pushes outward the utility possibility function for the society. Included would be (1) anything which increases production possibilities, such as increased labor productivity; (2) anything which reduces costs and thereby makes resources available for more productive uses, such as increased employment opportunities, which may release resources from law enforcement by cutting crime rates; and (3) anything which increases welfare possibilities directly, such as development of public-spiritedness or social consciousness of one's neighbor. Anything which merely alters relative prices without affecting total utility opportunities for the group under consideration will not be deemed a social benefit (or loss). For example, if expanded education reduces the number of household servants, so that the wage rates of those remaining rise, this rise would not constitute either a benefit or loss from education but rather a financial transfer. Without making interpersonal utility comparisons we cannot say more. Of course, the increased productivity of those with the additional education is a benefit of type 1.

In addition to an analysis of the forms of education benefits and the nature of the beneficiaries, I shall investigate opportunities for quantifying these returns and some implications of the benefits analysis for the financing of education.[5] In section II, I shall consider benefits which the individual receives in the form of market opportunities – including additional earnings resulting from increased productivity and benefits which the individual receives in ways other than earnings. In section III, I shall consider benefits which the individual does not capture but which accrue to other persons. Benefits from elementary, secondary, and higher education will receive attention.

II

In this section we examine those benefits of education (or returns from education) which are realized directly by the student. One form of such benefits is the 'financial return' accompanying additional education. A second form is the 'financial option' return. Previously unconsidered, this benefit involves the value of the opportunity to obtain still further education. Third are the non-monetary 'opportunity options', involving the broadened individual employment choices which education permits; fourth are the opportunities for 'hedging' against the vicissitudes of technological change. And fifth are the non-market benefits.

Direct financial return

Census Bureau data relating level of earnings to level of educational attainment show an unmistakable positive correlation. A number of investigators have estimated the percentage return from investment in education by attributing these observed

5. While I shall refer throughout this paper to the research of others I should like to mention particularly the excellent survey recently completed by Alice M. Rivlin; see her 'Research in the economics of higher education: Progress and problems', in Selma J. Mushkin (ed.), *Economics of higher education* (hereinafter cited as '*Higher education*'), Washington, United States Department of Health, Education, and Welfare (1962).

earnings differentials to education.[6] Some have attempted to adjust for or, at least, to recognize factors other than education which affect earnings and which are positively correlated with level of education. These include intelligence, ambition, informal education in the home, number of hours worked, family wealth, and social mobility. One factor which I believe has not been considered is that a positive correlation of educational attainment with family wealth suggests that those with more education may live longer and consequently tend to receive greater lifetime incomes, education aside, although it is true that longer life is not synonymous with longer working life. We are led to the presumption that, in general, persons who have obtained more education would have greater earnings than persons with less education, even without the additional schooling.[7] At the same time, at least one study has attempted to isolate some of the non-education variables affecting earnings, with the finding that median salaries rose with additional amounts of post-high-school education, even after adjustments were made for (1) level of high-school class rank, (2) intelligence-test scores, and (3) father's occupation.[8] Apparently at least part of the additional earnings of the more educated population are the results of their education.

Although earning differentials attributable to education may be of considerable significance to the recipients, the social significance depends upon the relationship between earnings and

6. On the relation between educational attainment and earnings, see G. Becker, 'Underinvestment in college education?' *American Economic Review, Proceedings*, May 1960, pp. 346–54; H. S. Houthakker, 'Education and income', *Review of Economics and Statistics*, February 1959, pp. 24–8; H. P. Miller, 'Annual and lifetime income in relation to education', *American Economic Review*, December 1960, pp. 962–86; E. F. Renshaw, 'Estimating the returns to education', *Review of Economics and Statistics*, August 1960, pp. 318–24.

7. See D. S. Bridgman, 'Problems in estimating the monetary value of college education', *Review of Economics and Statistics, Supplement*, August 1960, p. 181.

8. Dael Wolfle, 'Economics and educational values', *Review of Economics and Statistics, Supplement*, August 1960, pp. 178–9. See also his *America's resources of specialized talent*, New York, Harper and Bros., 1954; and Wolfle and Joseph G. Smith, 'The occupational value of education for superior high school graduates', *Journal of Higher Education* (1956), pp. 201–13.

marginal productivities. However, we know that market imperfections may make earnings a poor measure of one's contribution to output and that in a growing economy cross-section age–earnings data will understate future earnings. Mary Jean Bowman has suggested that older workers may receive more than their marginal productivity because status and seniority rules may maintain income although their productivity is falling.[9] But even assuming that earnings equal current marginal productivity, estimation of lifetime productivity from cross-section earnings data tends to understate future productivity of today's young men; this is true because in a growing society each new cohort of people into the labor force comes with better education and knowledge. These two examples suggest that the observed current earnings of men are less than fully satisfactory as reflections of future marginal productivity. Much work remains before we can feel confident of our ability to measure adequately the productivity return to education. Perhaps more serious, because apparently it has not been recognized, is a methodological limitation to previous estimates of the financial return to education.

Financial option return

Given our interest in resource allocation, we should like to know what financial return from additional education a person can expect. I suggested above that earnings differentials associated with education-attainment differentials would have to be adjusted for differences in ability, ambition, and other variables before we could isolate the education effects; and that an adjustment for systematic differences between earnings and productivity would also be required. Let us assume that these adjustments have been made and that we have computed the present values of expected future earnings of an average person with J and with K years of education, *ceteris paribus*; it is my contention that this would be an erroneously low estimate of the gross return which may be expected from the additional education. The value of the additional education may be thought of as having two components: (a) the additional earnings resulting from completion of a given level of education (properly discounted to the present, of

9. 'Human capital: concepts and measures', in Mushkin (ed.), *Higher education.*

course) and (b) the value of the 'option' to obtain still further education and the rewards accompanying it. It is (b) which I wish to elaborate upon here.

In formula (1) below, the first term represents the rate of return over cost for education unit j, as computed in the usual manner; it is the difference between the present value of expected future earnings of a person who has attained, but not exceeded, level j, and the present value of expected future earnings of a person without education j, as a percentage of the additional cost of obtaining j. This is the rate of return as computed heretofore.

Subsequent terms in the formula measure the option value of completing j and should be understood as follows: each of the R^* are rates of return on incremental education α, computed in the manner described in the paragraph above. $\bar{R}$ is the opportunity cost of expenditure on education in terms of the percentage return obtainable from the next best investment opportunity, so that $R_\alpha^* - \bar{R}$ indicates any 'supernormal' percentage return. C_α = the marginal social cost of obtaining the incremental education α (where each cost ratio, C_α/C_j, is a weighting factor, permitting the percentage returns on the costs of various levels of education to be added), and P_α is the probability that a person who has attained level j will go on to various higher levels.

$$R_j = R_j^* + (R_k^* - \bar{R}) \frac{C_k}{C_j} \cdot P_k$$

$$+ (R_l^* - \bar{R}) \frac{C_l}{C_j} \cdot P_l + \ldots + (R_z^* - \bar{R}) \frac{C_z}{C_j} \cdot P_z \quad (1)$$

$$= R_j^* + \sum_{\alpha = k}^{z} (R_\alpha^* - \bar{R}) \frac{C_\alpha}{C_j} \cdot P_\alpha.$$

Thus, for example, a decision to obtain a high-school education involves not only the likelihood of obtaining the additional earnings typically realized by a high-school graduate but also involves the value of the opportunity to pursue a college education.[10] The value of the option to obtain additional education

10. Research by Jacob Mincer suggests that additional schooling also provides opportunities to obtain additional on-the-job training (see his

will tend to be greater the more elementary the education. For the 'highest' level of formal education, the value of the option is clearly zero,[11] except insofar as the education provides the option to pursue independent work.

The option–value approach attributes to investment in one level of schooling a portion of the additional return over cost which can be obtained from further education – specifically, that portion which is in excess of the opportunity cost rate of return. Although part of the return from college education is indeed attributed to high-school education, there is no double-counting involved. In fact, the procedure is the same as that involved in the valuation of any asset, where the decision to retain or discard it may be made at various times in the life of the asset. Consider the following case: a machine is offered for sale. The seller, anxious to make the sale, offers an inducement to the buyer in the form of a discount on the purchase of a replacement machine when the present one wears out. Analyzing the prospective buyer's current decision, we see that he is being offered a combination of (a) a machine now, and (b) a discount (or option) 'ticket' for possible future use. Both may have value, and both should be considered by the prospective buyer.

Let us assume that the machine has been purchased and used, and the owner is now deciding whether he should buy a replacement. Needless to say, the rate of return expected from the prospective machine will be a function of its cost net of the discount. The profit-maximizing buyer will compare the rate of return on the net cost and compare it with the opportunity cost of capital. Thus, in a real sense, the discount ticket has entered into two decisions: to buy the original machine and to buy the

---

'On-the-job training: Costs, returns, and some implications', Table 1, *Journal of Political Economy*, vol. 70 (1962), part 2, supplement. The value of this opportunity should be included in the financial option approach developed here.

11. Thus, for estimating the return from college or graduate education, omission of the value of the option may not be quantitatively significant. At the same time, since the return from higher education as previously estimated seems to be close to the return on business investments, recognition of the value of the option might tip the balance.

replacement. But this is not equivalent to any erroneous double-counting.

The machine discount-ticket analogy also makes clear the point that the value of the option (or discount) cannot be negative. If a greater rate of return (or discount) is available elsewhere, the value of the option merely becomes zero, as long as it need not be used. Thus, as long as a high-school graduate need not go on to college the value of the option to go on cannot be negative. It is formally conceivable, however, that a positive option value of elementary-school education could consist of a negative value for the high-school component and a larger, positive value for the college component.

Formula (1) indicates that the value of the option to pursue additional schooling depends upon (a) the probability of its being exercised and (b) the expected value if exercised. Without further information, factor (a) may be estimated by the proportion of persons completing a particular level of education who go on to a higher level. The expected value of the option if exercised, factor (b), is any excess of the return on that increment of education over the return obtainable on the best comparable alternative investment, where the latter may be assumed to equal, say, 5 per cent. Actually, the 'excess' returns should be discounted back to the decision date from the time the higher education level would begin, but to illustrate the point simply I shall disregard this, at least to begin with.

According to some recent estimates reported elsewhere, the return to the individual on total high-school costs (including foregone earnings) for white urban males in 1939[12] was approximately 14 per cent and the return on college costs for those who graduated was estimated at 9 per cent.[13] We might assume the return to be somewhat lower – say, 8 per cent – for those who did

12. T. W. Schultz, 'Education and economic growth', *Social forces influencing American education* (hereinafter cited as 'Economic growth'), Chicago, National Society for the Study of Education, 1961, ch. 3, referring to G. S. Becker's work. H. H. Villard has seriously disagreed with these estimates. See his 'Discussion' of Becker's 'Underinvestment in college education?' in *American Economic Review, Proceedings*, May 1960, pp. 375–8. See also W. L. Hansen, 'Rate of return on human versus non-human investment' (draft paper), October 1960.

13. Schultz, 'Economic growth', p. 78.

not complete their college training.[14] Then with approximately 44 per cent of high-school male graduates beginning college and 24 per cent graduating,[15] the a priori expected return on a social investment in high-school education in 1939 was, substituting in equation (1) above, 17.4 per cent, as shown in equation (2).

$$\underset{\substack{\text{High-school}\\\text{graduates}}}{14} + \underset{\text{College graduates}}{(9\text{--}5)\,(2.70)\,(0.24)} + \underset{\substack{\text{Some college}\\\text{(Assumed} = 2\text{ years)}}}{(8\text{--}5)\,(1.35)\,(0.20)}$$

$$= 14 + 2.6 + 0.8 = 17.4 \text{ per cent} \quad (2)$$

To reiterate, the first term, 14, is the estimated percentage return to high-school education. In subsequent terms, the first element is an estimate of the return in excess of alternatives, obtainable on additional education; the second element is the total cost of the additional education as a proportion of the cost of high-school education;[16] the third element is the proportion of high-school graduates who obtain the additional education. If the returns to college education were discounted back four years to the date at which high-school education was initiated, at a 5 per cent discount rate the expected return to high-school education would drop to $14 + 2.1 + 0.7 = 16.8$, instead of 17.4 per cent.

In the example above it was assumed that a decision to complete high school would be realized with certainty. Other assumptions could be fitted easily into the framework. And if knowledge existed regarding the prospective high-school student's college plans, then *average* probabilities of his continuation should not be used.

If the option value of education has been overlooked by

14. While this paper deals with education benefits, quantitative comparison of benefits with costs are made to help assess the relative magnitudes of benefits. In doing this I do not intend to imply complete satisfaction with the cost estimates. The appendix of this paper [not reprinted here] presents some of the issues involved in defining and measuring social costs.

15. Computed from 1960 data for males of ages 25–29, in United States Bureau of the Census, *Current population reports: Population characteristics, projections of educational attainments in the United States, 1960–80* (hereinafter cited as '*Educational attainments*') (Series P-20, No. 91, 12 January 1959, p. 8, Table 2).

16. Computed from data in Schultz, 'Economic growth', p. 79.

parents as it has been by economists there would be a tendency toward underinvestment in education. If time horizons are short so that, for example, a prospective high-school student and his parents sometimes fail to consider that a few years later the child may wish he could be going on to college, there will be a systematic downward bias to the valuation of education by individuals. Even disregarding graduate education, the option value of high-school education increased the rate of return on high-school costs from 14 to 17 per cent, considering only the 'monetary' returns. For grade-school education, recognition of the value of the option to obtain additional education increases the expected 1939 return even more substantially above the previous estimate of 35 per cent.[17]

$$\underset{\substack{\text{Grade-school}\\\text{graduates}}}{35} + \underset{\text{High-school graduates}}{(14-5)\ (2.3)\ (0.67)} + \underset{\text{College graduates}}{(9-5)\ (6.3)\ (0.16)}$$

$$+ \underset{\substack{\text{Some college}\\\text{(assumed} = 2\text{ years)}}}{(8-5)\ (3.1)\ (0.13)}$$

$$= 35 + 13.9 + 3.8 + 1.2 = 53.9 \text{ per cent (3)}$$

The option turns out to be quite valuable indeed, increasing the return on elementary education from 35 to 54 per cent. It could be argued in this case that whether the return is 35 or 54 per cent[18] is relatively immaterial for policy purposes, both being

17. Again, disregarding the discounting, the 35 per cent estimate is from Schultz, 'Economic growth', p. 81. Relative costs were estimated from the same source (p. 79), except that Schultz's elementary-school cost figure was doubled, since it applied to only four years of school. The proportions of children continuing on to higher education were estimated from *Educational attainments*, p. 8.

In this paper I do not discuss any option value for college education; however, there may be a positive option value related to opportunities for graduate study and additional on-the-job training.

18. Previous estimates of rates of return represented a discounting of costs and returns back to the beginning of that particular level of schooling; since our time bench mark is the beginning of grade school, the values of the high-school and college options should be discounted back to the beginning of grade school. Doing so, at a discount rate of 5 per cent, reduces the 54 per cent return to $35 + 9.5 + 2.1 + 0.7 = 47.3$ per cent. The return would amost certainly be larger if persons obtaining only some high-school education were considered.

considerably greater than available alternatives. However, given the state of our confidence in the previously computed rates of return, it is comforting to see the estimates moved further from the decision-making margin. Of course, in addition to these returns, assuming they are attributable solely to education, are the non-market returns to education, including the direct consumption value of learning and the opportunity to lead the 'full life'.

Non-financial options

The words 'option' and 'opportunity' have appeared in the discussion above a number of times. Indeed, it seems that in many respects the value of education is a function of the additional options which became available to a person having it – job options, income-leisure-security options, additional-schooling options, on-the-job learning options, way-of-life options.

Recognizing the existence of such options suggests a possible means of estimating the monetary equivalent value of non-monetary returns from education. Thus, the college graduate who chooses to go to graduate school and then enter academic life may be assumed to obtain a total (not merely monetary) return on his graduate education costs at least equal to what he could have obtained from a comparable alternative investment. In general, added education permits widened job choices, and to some extent people with more education will choose employment which provides non-monetary rewards (for example, greater security) at the expense of monetary rewards. To the extent that this is correct and that knowledge of alternatives exists, previous estimates of the individual returns to education, utilizing incremental earnings figures for people with two different levels of education, have had a downward bias. If monetary returns from, say, graduate education turn out to be less than comparable alternative returns, the difference would be a minimum measure of non-monetary returns, though not necessarily of the employment-associated return alone.

'Hedging' option

There is another respect in which education provides a person with options: the increased ability to adjust to changing job

167

opportunities. With a rapid pace of technological change, adaptability (which may be a noteworthy output of additional education) becomes important. Education may be viewed as a type of private (and social) hedge against technological displacement of skills. New technology often requires new skills and knowledge,[19] and those persons having more education are likely to be in a position to adjust more easily than those with less education, and to reap the returns from education which the new technology has made possible. This line of reasoning suggests that a more general academic curriculum is desirable since it permits greater flexibility than a curriculum which requires earlier specialization.

Insofar as the return resulting from greater flexibility is realized in the form of earnings, it will be reflected directly in the estimated monetary value of education. The hedging option has additional value, however, to the extent that people have a preference for greater security and stability of earnings.

The hypothesis that added schooling develops added labor-force flexibility and thereby facilitates adjustments to changing skill requirements suggests the following implication: the greater the level of an individual's formal education attainment, the more he can benefit from additional on-the-job training, and, therefore, the more on-the-job training he will obtain. Jacob Mincer's data support this view,[20] that through time, investment in learning on the job is increasingly being concentrated on persons with education beyond elementary school. He estimates that in all three years, 1939, 1949, and 1958, on-the-job training costs per person were positively correlated with the level of education. Moreover, a trend is observable – in 1939, on-the-job training costs per person with elementary education were 38 per cent of

19. This view seems to be shared by H. Coombs, who states that 'there will be many unpredictable shifts in the proportions needed of specific categories of . . . manpower. Thus, it will be important . . . to enlarge the total supply of high ability manpower available for all purposes' ('Some economic aspects of educational development', in International Association of Universities, *Some economic aspects of educational development in Europe*, Paris, International Universities Bureau, 1961, p. 78).

20. op. cit., Tables 1 and 2. But E. F. Renshaw predicts that the principal educational requirements of the 1960s, with respect to the labor force, will be directed toward trade schools and apprenticeship programs ('Investment in human capital' unpublished manuscript, 1960, p. 13).

costs per college-educated person; in 1949 they were 30 per cent; and by 1958, 28 per cent. Over the twenty-year period, training costs *per capita* for elementary-educated persons actually declined (in constant dollars), while they climbed 13 per cent for college-trained persons.

Non-market returns

So far we have discussed the return to education which is realized by the individual in terms of his employment conditions. But some of the value of education to the individual accrues in other forms. For example, the fruits of literacy – an output of elementary education – include, in addition to consumption aspects, the implicit value of its non-market use. To illustrate: when a person prepares his own income tax return he performs a service made possible by his literacy. Were this service provided through the market, it would be priced and included in national income.[21]

Assume that roughly fifty million of the sixty million personal income-tax returns filed per year are prepared by the taxpayer himself. At a value of $5.00 per return, a low estimate of an

21. It could be argued that the service (like many others in national income and product) is not a final output, but a cost item (cost of tax collection), and thus should not be included in estimates of production; but since it is often difficult to distinguish clearly outputs from inputs in our national accounts, and since our national income and product accounts principally measure effort expended, it would be interesting to make some estimate of the market-value equivalent of the services performed by a person in preparing his own income-tax return.

Inclusion of the value of this non-market production as an educational benefit presupposes that this represents a net increase in the value of the individual's total non-market activities and that the opportunity cost of performing additional non-market production is essentially zero.

Richard Goode has suggested that, although the failure to consider non-market production leads to understatement of the return to education, 'nevertheless, there seems to be little danger that this omission will lead to an undervaluation of educational benefits in comparing time periods, countries, and population groups with different amounts of formal education'. He presents 'the hypothesis that the greater the amount of formal education the greater the proportion of goods and services acquired through the market. If this is true, estimates based on money earnings or national income statistics may exaggerate the contribution of education to real income differentials or growth'.

average charge by an accountant for preparing a not-too-complex return, we arrive at an annual market value of the tax-return services performed by taxpayers for themselves of $250 million. Relative to Schultz's estimate of total elementary-school costs of $7.8 billion in 1956,[22] this suggests a current-year return of 3.2 per cent of the current investment in literacy! And this is only one, obviously minor, form of return from literacy which the individual enjoys.

This attempt to place a value on a particular use of literacy is subject to at least the following criticism: were it not for the widespread literacy in this country we would probably not have the present type of income-tax system operating, and, therefore, we would adjust to illiteracy in a less costly way than having others (say, accountants) prepare tens of millions of returns. The adjustment might involve government tax assessments or a resort to another type of tax such as one on expenditures. This suggests that the literacy value estimate above is on the high side, in terms of the alternative tax collection cost in the absence of literacy.

I have attempted a very rough estimate of the alternative cost of collecting an alternative form of tax – a sales tax – which would not require such a literate population, in order to compare it with the collection cost of the income tax.[23] The assumption is that a principal reason for the relative tax-collection efficiency of the income tax is the work performed by the taxpayer in preparing his own return. For the year 1940, the all-states average cost of collecting state personal income taxes was $1.50 per $100 collected, while the comparable figure for the general sales taxes of states was $2.00 per $100 collected. In the same year, collection costs per $100 of federal personal income tax were estimated at $1,68,[24] while there was, of course, no federal sales tax.[25]

22. 'Economic growth', p. 64, Table 5.
23. This disregar ls the different distributive effects of the two forms of tax.
24. James W. Martain, 'Costs of tax administration: Statistics of public expenses', *Bulletin of the National Tax Association*, February 1944, pp. 132–47, as cited in Charles A. Benson, *The economics of public education*, Boston: Houghton-Mifflin Co., 1961, p. 145.
25. Estimation of collection costs is subject to the common difficulty of the allocation of joint costs; furthermore, we really know little about scale

In the absence of a superior alternative I have assumed that, as was true for the state tax-collection costs presented above, a federal sales tax would cost one-third more to collect than the federal personal income tax. Assuming the 1960 Internal Revenue Service estimate of collection costs, of approximately forty cents per $100, to apply to the personal income tax, then a one-third increase in the cost of collecting $50 billion (1959 individual income-tax receipts) would involve an additional $66 million – approximately 0.8 per cent of elementary-school costs.[26]

III

In this section we consider the benefits of education which are external to the student. If all the benefits of education accrued to the student, then, assuming utility-maximizing behavior and access to capital markets, there would be little reason for public concern about the adequacy of education expenditures – unless publicly supported education were an efficient way of altering the personal distribution of income in a desired way.

Income redistribution effects aside, it seems clear that access to the capital market is imperfect and also that a child, even at high-school or college age, is in a poor position to make sensible long-run decisions regarding the amount or type of education, though advice from teachers, counselors, and parents may improve the decision. But these imperfections hardly appear to justify the massive public expenditures in support of education – more than $19 billion in 1960, including capital outlays.[27] We are led to the position that, to understand why education is of public concern as well as to project demand for education and determine whether

---

economies in tax collection, or about the difference in degree of enforcement of state and federal taxes, so that it is dangerous to apply state cost figures to the federal level.

26. Actually we should note that a number of years of education is required to develop 'literate' people but also that, once developed, they presumably retain the knowledge. Were we to take into account the number of tax returns an average person may be expected to file during his lifetime, a higher rate of return would appear.

27. *Health, education, and welfare trends, 1961*, op. cit., pp. 52, 53.

expanded education is warranted on allocative-efficiency grounds, we should pay more attention to identifying and quantifying external benefits of education.[28] This section of the paper suggests a framework for analyzing these benefits and considers opportunities for measurement.

As economists, our interest in external benefits is typically related to the question of whether all benefits (as well as costs) of some action are taken into account by the decision-maker. The issue is whether the benefits are or are not captured by the decision-maker, since the assumption of profit maximization has the implication that benefits will be recognized by the decision-maker if, but only if, he is able to obtain them. Insofar as parents and children make joint decisions on purchases of education, with none of them being a very expert, experienced buyer, those benefits which are less apparent and indirect are likely to be overlooked. Parents thinking of their children may even neglect the less direct benefits to themselves, discussed below. Moreover, benefits to non-family members are probably not considered at all.

In principle, the recipients of external benefits from some activity (for example, education) should be willing to subsidize the activity and, indeed, should seek to subsidize it. The voting mechanism and taxation provide the means for subsidization. Analysis of voting behavior may shed some light on the question whether external benefits are recognized and have an effect on decisions. But regardless whether or not subsidies are actually paid by 'outsiders', we need to identify and measure the magnitudes of external benefits to determine the rate of return on resources devoted to education.

Persons receiving external benefits from a student's education may be divided into three broad groups, though the same people may be in more than one: (1) residence-related beneficiaries – those who benefit by virtue of some relationship between their place of residence and that of the subject; (2) employment-related beneficiaries – those who benefit by virtue of some employment relationship with the subject; (3) society in general.

28. It is true, however, that economies of scale (with respect to the number of students) would also be a sufficient explanation for the public interest in education.

Residence-related beneficiaries

Current family of the subject. While the purpose of schooling is obviously education, the manner in which it is provided may result in incidental, and even accidental, by-products; in the case of elementary education, such a by-product is child care. Schools make it possible for mothers who would otherwise be supervising their youngsters to do other things. For those mothers who choose to work, we have an estimate of the productivity of the child-care services – their earnings. This rests on the assumption that the mothers would not work if a sitter had to be hired but do work when the child is in school. If mothers would make other child-care arrangements in the absence of schools, then a better measure of value than earnings obtained would be the cost of hiring a baby sitter or making some alternative custodial arrangement.

In March 1956 there were 3.5 million working mothers in the United States with children six to eleven years of age.[29] Assuming that as few as one million of these mothers would not work except for the schools (the others being willing to let their children stay with hired persons or simply care for themselves), and assuming $2,000 as the earnings of each mother during the school year, the value of the child-care services of elementary school may be estimated as roughly $2 billion per year.[30] Estimating total resource costs (excluding capital outlays but including implicit interest and depreciation) of public and private elementary schools in 1956 at $7.8 billion,[31] we reach the startling conclusion that elementary-school support provided a return of

29. United States Bureau of the Census, *Marital and family status of workers: 1956* (Series P-50, No. 73, April 1957), p. 11, Table 3.

30. For those mothers who would be willing to hire baby sitters, obtainable for, perhaps, $1,000 per year, the value of the school child-care services is this alternative cost of $1,000, instead of $2,000. Of the 3.5 million working mothers with children six to eleven years old, approximately 1.5 million also had children twelve to seventeen. Some of the older children could conceivably care for the younger ones; but even considering the remaining 2 million, the assumption that one-half would not work except for the care provided by schools seems plausible and even conservative.

31. Schultz, 'Economic growth', p. 85.

25 per cent of cost in the by-product form of child-care services, alone.[32] This disregards the value of these services to mothers who do not choose to work; since the value is certainly greater than zero, the total value of the child-care is even more than 25 per cent of cost.

The increased production from working mothers tends to offset the foregone production from students in school. Various writers have emphasized students' foregone earnings as a cost of education, and have debated its magnitude, but have not considered the fact that some mothers' earnings are made possible by the fact that children forego earnings to remain in school.

Future family of the subject. When the student reaches adulthood and becomes a parent, the children will benefit from his or her education by virtue of the informal education which the children receive in the home. The presence and relevance of such education is recognized, but to my knowledge no attempts to estimate its value have been made. If scores on achievement tests could be related to educational attainments of parents, adjusting for variation in students' ability, we might obtain some information about the extent of education in the home. This might be translated into equivalent years in school, to which a value, perhaps average cost, could be attributed.

If we think of the investment–consumption distinction as involving whether or not benefits accrue in the 'present' (consumption) or in the 'future' (investment), then education has an investment component in the form of these intergeneration benefits.[33] If we generalize the conception of investment to include not

32. If working mothers employ housekeepers as substitutes and if they incur other additional costs in working (for example, transportation and additional clothes), these added costs should be deducted from the gross returns.

33. Schultz has also recognized this point: 'The education of women . . . reduces the subsequent effective costs of education because of the critical role that mothers play in motivating their children to obtain an education and to perform well while they are attending school. Thus, if we could get at the factors underlying the perpetuation of education, it is likely that we would discover that the education of many persons not in the labor force

only intertemporal benefits,[34] but also interpersonal benefits, then the child-care role of schools, discussed above, represents an investment in the productivity of mothers. Similarly, other interpersonal benefits examined below will constitute investment aspects of educational expenditures.

Neighbors. As we consider more extended groups, beginning with the individual receiving the education and then his family (present and future), we come to his neighbors. Education affects them at least in the following ways: by inculcating acceptable social values and behavior norms in the community children and by providing children with alternatives to unsupervised activities which may have antisocial consequences. The second is essentially of short-period significance – during the time the child is of school age. The first effect is clearly of long-period consequence, following the student as he grows, and as he moves. As the student achieves adulthood, and as he migrates, the social values developed in part through his education continue to affect his 'neighbors'.[35]

The hypothesis that education does affect neighbors might be tested by studying voting behavior on school issues among nonparents. We might expect that their voting would be influenced by the extent to which students emigrate after completion of school, so that any potential external benefits or costs to neighbors would be realized by persons in other communities. Perhaps some notion of the magnitude of external, neighborhood benefits – at least to the extent they are recognized – could be obtained in this manner.

---

contributes heavily to the effective perpetuation of the stock of education. To the extent that this is true, some part of the education not in the labor force contributes to this investment process' ('Economic growth', pp. 74–5).

34. Tax implications of the existence of intertemporal education returns have been discussed by R. Goode, 'Educational expenditures and income tax', in Mushkin (ed.), *Higher education.*

35. One writer points out: 'Education has effects on the caliber of voluntary community activities: choral groups, drama, clubs, local art shows, etc.' (Benson, op. cit., p. 349).

Taxpayers. Related to the effects of education on neighbors are the effects on those who pay (directly or indirectly) for the consequences of the lack of education. For example, insofar as lack of education leads to employment difficulties and crime, law enforcement costs will tend to be high. Thus may education provide social benefits by reducing the need for incurring these 'avoidance costs', to the advantage of taxpayers.

Education also benefits taxpayers in other communities. The migration of poorly educated persons having behavioral patterns and educational attainments differing from those prevailing in the new areas may necessitate additional effort and expense to permit the in-migrant children to adjust to the new school conditions.[36] Thus, people in areas of in-migration have a stake in the education of children in the areas of out-migration. People who are or may be in the same fiscal unit with an individual have a financial stake in his education.

Employment-related beneficiaries

The education of one worker may have favorable external effects on the productivity of others. Where production involves the co-operative effort of workers, flexibility and adaptability of one worker will redound to the advantage of others. Productivity of each member of the group influences the productivity of each other member. In such a case, each worker has a financial interest in the education of his fellow workers. Again, the relevance of this interdependence for the present context rests on the assumption that education develops the properties of flexibility and adaptability. Further analysis is required to determine the extent to which the assumption is valid, and, if it is, to estimate its significance.

Employers may also have a financial interest in the schooling and training of their employees. Much of education improves the quality of the labor force and thereby bestows some benefits to employers of the workers insofar as market imperfections or the

36. See, for example, C. F. Schmid, V. A. Miller, and B. Abu-Laban, 'Impact of recent negro migration on Seattle schools', *International Population Conference Papers*, Vienna, Union International pour l'Étude Scientifique de la Population, 1959, pp. 674–83.

'specific'[37] nature of the education result in failure of the employer to pay the marginal revenue product of a worker.

Society in general

Some of the benefits from education are enjoyed by individuals and groups that are reasonably identifiable, as we have seen. But some of the benefits are distributed broadly either spatially or temporarily, so that the nature of individual beneficiaries is obscure. These shall be considered under the heading, 'Society in general', which thus becomes somewhat of a residual category of benefits.

Literacy is not only of value to the individual possessing it and to employers but also is of value to others. Without widespread literacy the significance of books, newspapers, and similar media for the transmission of information would dwindle; and it seems fair to say that the communication of information is of vital importance to the maintenance of competition and, indeed, to the existence of a market economy, as well as to the maintenance of political democracy.

Along the same lines it should be noted that the substantial role played by checking deposits in our economy requires, among other things, generalized literacy and competence with arithmetic operations. It is not necessary to argue the issue of cause versus effect, but only to recognize the essentiality of literacy – a principal output of elementary education – to the present state of our economic development. Nor does saying this deny the possibility that other factors were also indispensable to growth.

Equality of opportunity seems to be a frequently expressed social goal. Education plays a prominent role in discussions of this goal, since the financial and other obstacles to education confronted by some people are important barriers to its

37. As the term is used by Gary S. Becker 'specific' training is that which raises the marginal productivity of the worker in one firm more than it raises his productivity in other firms. By contrast, 'general' training raises marginal productivity equally in many firms. Since, under competitive conditions, wage rates are determined by workers' marginal productivities in other firms, a worker with 'specific' training would be expected to receive a wage less than his actual marginal revenue productivity but more than his alternative productivity. [See Reading 9.

achievement.[38] If equality of opportunity is a social goal, then education pays social returns over and above the private returns to the recipients of the education.

Although the long-term effect of education on future earnings is surely the most powerful income distribution consequence of education,[39] there are also some short-term effects. These occur through the provision by schools of things traditionally considered to be private consumer goods and services – including subsidized lunch programs, musical instrument lessons, and driver-training courses.

Earlier we distinguished between the output of education in the form of the student's training and the output of the system or means by which the training was accomplished – the latter being illustrated by custodial or child-care services. The same distinction may be made with respect to higher education, the point being that the training of students is not the only output of schools; a joint product is the research activity of college and university faculties, from which society reaps benefits. It is undoubtedly true that were it not for the higher-education system the volume of basic research would be smaller. A question exists regarding the extent to which the value of the research is reflected in salaries and, thereby, in private returns. The relation of education to research and of research to social returns deserves more attention from economists.[40]

Training of persons in particular kinds of skills may result in important external benefits if there are bottlenecks to economic development. In the context of underdeveloped economies, one

38. Even if it were true that educating everyone would widen the personal distribution of earnings compared with what it would be with less education, it would not follow that additional education for some people would worsen their relative or absolute economic position.

39. The relation between education and income distribution has been studied by J. Mincer ('Investment in human capital and personal income distribution', *Journal of Political Economy*, August 1958, pp. 281–302), and L. Soltow ('The distribution of income related to changes in the distributions of education, age and occupation', *Review of Economics and Statistics*, November 1960, pp. 450–53).

40. For an interesting study of returns from research, see Z. Griliches, 'Research costs and social returns: Hybrid corn and related innovations', *Journal of Political Economy*, October 1958, pp. 419–31.

writer, while particularly noting the political significance of primary and higher education, and the prestige significance of the latter, argues: 'Secondary education is essential to the training of "medium" personnel (elementary teachers, monitors, officials, middle classes). The shortage of such people is today a real obstacle to economic development.'[41] But without perfect capital markets and appropriate subsidization programs, these socially valuable people may be unable to capture for themselves the full value of their contribution. Therefore, their earnings would understate the full benefits of their education.

IV

In the preceding pages I have asked: 'Who receive the benefits from education?' In addition, I have considered some of the limited possibilities for quantifying certain of the benefits. As plans are developed for future research I urge that more attention be directed to the spatial and temporal dimensions of these benefits.

While much work remains, we might summarize our findings. We have noted that some of the benefits of education are realized at the time the education is being received (that is, in the 'short' run); others, after the formal education has been completed (that is, in the 'long' run). Benefits to mothers, in terms of the child-care role of schools, and benefits to neighbors, in keeping children 'off the streets' are realized while the education is being obtained. Any benefits associated with subsequent employment of the student as well as benefits to the student's future children are realized later.

We have found, further, that benefits from education occur not only at various times but also in various places. The benefits of education do not necessarily accrue to people in the area or in the school district which financed the child's education. In particular, some of the benefits depend upon the individual's place of residence, which may change. Location of many residence-related

41. Michael Debeauvals, 'Economic problems of education in the underdeveloped countries', in International Association of Universities, op. cit., pp. 116–17.

benefits as well as employment-related benefits will be determined partly by population migration, though this is not generally true of benefits to family members and to society as a whole. While it is not necessarily true that total benefits will depend upon one's location, the point is that the particular beneficiaries will be a function of the location of the individual. Thus, the process of migration is a process of spatial shifting of some of the external effects of education.

Some interesting questions are raised simply by the recognition that external benefits of education exist, and that they are not all in broad, amorphous form; that is, that to some extent these benefits accrue to particular, rather well-defined, groups. Thus, to the extent that the education system at the elementary level is producing child-care services as an output, benefit–principle taxation would suggest that families of the children might pay for these benefits.[42] In general, a desire to use this taxation principle would imply attempts to identify various groups of education beneficiaries and to assess taxes in recognition of the distribution of benefits.[43]

It seems to me that there is a legitimate question concerning the justice of requiring broad, public support for education insofar as the benefits are narrow and private, except as an income-redistributive device. For example, to the extent that there is really no educational sacrifice involved in having children attend split-shift classes, so that the real motive for the abolition of split-shifts is to make life more comfortable for mothers who have all of their children in school at the same time, then a question of equity arises: should non-parents be expected to share the costs associated with the provision of these child-care services for parents? The answer may not be an unequivocal 'no', but the question deserves further consideration. Except for lack of information, or a disavowal of benefit–principle taxation, there is little rationale for failure of our education-tax system to recognize the existence of particular groups of beneficiaries.

There is another strong reason in addition to the alleged justice of benefit–principle taxation for identifying benefits and bene-

42. This point came out in a discussion with Julius Margolis.

43. This is not to argue that the benefit principle, in contrast to the ability-to-pay or some other principle, should necessarily prevail.

ficiaries. To the extent that the distribution of tax burdens for the support of education differs substantially from the distribution of education benefits, it is likely that education will be either under-supported or oversupported from an allocative-efficiency stand-point, given the existing preference structure and distribution of income and wealth.[44]

Both with respect to equity and to efficiency in education finance, the increasing phenomenon of migration needs to be recognized. Insofar as some of the benefits of education depend upon the location of the individual and insofar as this location is a variable over his lifetime, some of the benefits from education accrue to people who have played no part at all in the financing of this particular person's education. This would seem to be especially pertinent with respect to areas of substantial net in- or out-migration. Areas experiencing net in-migration might be expected, on benefit–principle grounds, to subsidize areas of net out-migration, particularly if highly productive people are involved. Subsidy in the opposite direction might be justified insofar as the in-migrants to an area are relatively unproductive compared to its out-migrants. Needless to say, there are good and powerful arguments in favor of keeping all the financing of education at a local level. However, a thorough analysis of the issue would seem to require recognition of the points raised here.

The analytic approach to benefit identification employed in this paper is one of many alternatives; it does appear to have the advantage of focusing on the time and the location of education benefits, and these are relevant to the study both of efficiency in the allocation of resources between education and other ends and of equity in the financing of education.

It is clear that even with much additional effort we shall be unable to measure all the relevant benefits of education. At the same time the following four points are worth noting, and they summarize the views expressed in this paper: (a) identification of benefits is the logical step prior to measurement and, therefore, recognizing the forms of benefits represents some progress; (b) determination of what it is we are trying to measure will make it easier to develop useful quantification methods; (c) some reasonable measures of some education benefits are possible;

44. However, an objective of education may be to change the distribution.

(d) even partial measurement may disclose benefits sufficiently sizable to indicate a profitable investment, so that consideration of the non-measured benefits would, *a fortiori*, support the expenditure decision.

In any event, and however difficult the measurement task is, it remains true that education expenditure decisions will be made, and they will be made on the basis of whatever information is available.

9 G. S. Becker

Investment in On-the-job Training

Excerpt from G. S. Becker, *Human Capital. A theoretical and empirical analysis, with special reference to education*, Columbia University Press. (1964), chapter 2, pp. 7–29.

The original aim of this study was to estimate the money rate of return to college and high-school education in the United States. In order to set these estimates in the proper context, a brief formulation of the theory of investment in human capital was undertaken. It soon became clear to me, however, that more than a restatement was called for; while important and pioneering work had been done on the economic return to various occupations and education classes,[1] there had been few, if any, attempts to treat the process of investing in people from a general viewpoint or to work out a broad set of empirical implications. I began then to prepare a general analysis of investment in human capital.

It eventually became apparent that this general analysis would do much more than fill a gap in formal economic theory: it offers a unified explanation of a wide range of empirical phenomena which have either been given *ad hoc* interpretations or have baffled investigators. Among these phenomena are the following: (1) Earnings typically increase with age at a decreasing rate. Both the rate of increase and the rate of retardation tend to be

1. In addition to the earlier works of Smith, Mill, and Marshall, see the brilliant work (which greatly influenced my own thinking about occupational choice) by M. Friedman and S. Kuznets, *Income from independent professional practice*, New York, N.B.E.R. (1945); see also H. Clark, *Life earnings in selected occupations in the U.S.*, New York (1937); J. R. Walsh, 'Capital concept applied to man', *Quarterly Journal of Economics*, February 1935; G. Stigler and D. Blank, *The demand and supply of scientific personnel*, New York, N.B.E.R. (1957). In recent years, of course, there has been considerable work, especially by T. W. Schultz; see, for example, his 'Investment in human capital', *American Economic Review*, March 1961, pp. 1–17. [See Reading 1.]

positively related to the level of skill. (2) Unemployment rates tend to be inversely related to the level of skill. (3) Firms in under-developed countries appear to be more 'paternalistic' toward employees than those in developed countries. (4) Younger persons change jobs more frequently and receive more schooling and on-the-job training than older persons do. (5) The distribution of earnings is positively skewed, especially among professional and other skilled workers. (6) Abler persons receive more education and other kinds of training than others. (7) The division of labor is limited by the extent of the market. (8) The typical investor in human capital is more impetuous and thus more likely to err than is the typical investor in tangible capital.

What a diverse and even confusing array! Yet all these, as well as many other important empirical implications, can be derived from very simple theoretical arguments. The purpose here is to set out these arguments in general form, with the emphasis placed on empirical implications, although little empirical material is presented. Systematic empirical work appears in Part Two.

In this chapter a lengthy discussion of on-the-job training is presented and then, much more briefly, discussions of investment in schooling, information, and health. On-the-job training is dealt with so elaborately not because it is more important than other kinds of investment in human capital – although its importance is often underrated – but because it clearly illustrates the effect of human capital on earnings, employment, and other economic variables. For example, the close connection between indirect and direct costs and the effect of human capital on earnings at different ages are vividly brought out. The extended discussion of on-the-job training paves the way for much briefer discussions of other kinds of investment in human beings.

I. On-the-Job Training

Theories of firm behavior, no matter how they differ in other respects, almost invariably ignore the effect of the productive process itself on worker productivity. This is not to say that no one recognizes that productivity is affected by the job itself; but the recognition has not been formalized, incorporated into economic analysis, and its implications worked out. I now intend to do just that, placing special emphasis on the broader economic implications.

Many workers increase their productivity by learning new skills and perfecting old ones while on the job. Presumably, future productivity can be improved only at a cost, for otherwise there would be an unlimited demand for training. Included in cost are the value placed on the time and effort of trainees, the 'teaching' provided by others, and the equipment and materials used. These are costs in the sense that they could have been used in producing current output if they had not been used in raising future output. The amount spent and the duration of the training period depend partly on the type of training since more is spent for a longer time on, say, an intern than a machine operator.

Consider explicitly now a firm that is hiring employees for a specified time period (in the limiting case this period approaches zero), and for the moment assume that both labor and product markets are perfectly competitive. If there were no on-the-job training, wage rates would be given to the firm and would be independent of its actions. A profit-maximizing firm would be in equilibrium when marginal products equaled wages, that is, when marginal receipts equaled marginal expenditures. In symbols

$$MP = W, \qquad (1)$$

where W equals wages or expenditures and MP equals the marginal product or receipts. Firms would not worry too much about the relation between labor conditions in the present and future, partly because workers would only be hired for one period and partly because wages and marginal products in future periods would be independent of a firm's current behavior. It can therefore legitimately be assumed that workers have unique marginal products (for given amounts of other inputs) and wages in each period, which are, respectively, the maximum productivity in all possible uses and the market wage rate. A more complete set of equilibrium conditions would be the set

$$MP_t = W_t, \qquad (2)$$

where t refers to the tth period. The equilibrium position for each period would depend only on the flows during that period.

These conditions are altered when account is taken of on-the-job training and the connection thereby created between present and future receipts and expenditures. Training might lower current receipts and raise current expenditures, yet firms could profitably provide this training if future receipts were sufficiently raised or future expenditures sufficiently lowered. Expenditures during each period need not equal wages, receipts need not equal the maximum possible marginal productivity, and expenditures and receipts during all periods would be interrelated. The set of equilibrium conditions summarized in equation (2) would be replaced by an equality between the *present values* of receipts and expenditures. If E_t and R_t represent expenditures and receipts during period t, and i the market discount rate, then the equilibrium condition can be written as

$$\sum_{t=0}^{n-1} \frac{R_t}{(1+i)^{t+1}} = \sum_{t=0}^{n-1} \frac{E_t}{(1+i)^{t+1}}, \qquad (3)$$

when n represents the number of periods, and R_t and E_t depend on all other receipts and expenditures. The equilibrium condition of equation (2) has been generalized, for if marginal product equals wages in each period, the present value of the marginal product stream would have to equal the present value of the wage stream. Obviously, however, the converse need not hold.

If training were given only during the initial period, expenditures during the initial period would equal wages plus the outlay on training, expenditures during other periods would equal wages alone, and receipts during all periods would equal marginal products. Equation (3) becomes

$$MP_0 + \sum_{t=1}^{n-1} \frac{MP_t}{(1+i)^t} = W_0 + k + \sum_{t=1}^{n-1} \frac{W_t}{(1+i)^t}, \qquad (4)$$

where k measures the outlay on training.

If a new term is defined,

$$G = \sum_{t=1}^{n-1} \frac{MP_t - W_t}{(1+i)^t}, \qquad (5)$$

equation (4) can be written as

$$MP_0 + G = W_0 + k. \qquad (6)$$

Since the term k only measures the actual outlay on training, it does not entirely measure training costs, for it excludes the time that a person spends on this training, time that could have been used to produce current output. The difference between what could have been produced, MP_0', and what is produced, MP_0, is the opportunity cost of the time spent in training. If C is defined as the sum of opportunity costs and outlays on training, (6) becomes

$$MP_0' + G = W_0 + C. \qquad (7)$$

The term G, the excess of future receipts over future outlays, is a measure of the return to the firm from providing training; and, therefore, the difference between G and C measures the difference between the return from and the cost of training. Equation (7) shows that the marginal product would equal wages in the initial period only when the return equals costs, or G equals C; it would be greater or less than wages as the return was smaller or greater than costs. Those familiar with capital theory might argue that this generalization of the simple equality between marginal product and wages is spurious because a full equilibrium would require equality between the return from an investment – in this case, made on the job – and costs. If this implied that G equals C, marginal product would equal wages in the initial period. There is much to be said for the relevance of a condition equating the return from an investment with costs, but such a condition does not imply that G equals C or that marginal product equals wages. The following discussion demonstrates that great care is required in the application of this condition to on-the-job investment.

Our treatment of on-the-job training produced some general results – summarized in equations (3) and (7) – of wide applicability, but more concrete results require more specific assumptions. In the following sections two types of on-the-job training are discussed in turn: general and specific.

General training

General training is useful in many firms besides those providing it; for example, a machinist trained in the army finds his skills of value in steel and aircraft firms, and a doctor trained (interned) at one hospital finds his skills useful at other hospitals. Most on-the-job training presumably increases the future marginal productivity of workers in the firms providing it; general training, however, also increases their marginal product in many other firms as well. Since in a competitive labor market the wage rates paid by any firm are determined by marginal productivities in other firms, future wage rates as well as marginal products would increase in firms providing general training. These firms could capture some of the return from training only if their marginal product rose by more than their wages. 'Perfectly general' training would be equally useful in many firms and marginal products would rise by the same extent in all of them. Consequently, wage rates would rise by exactly the same amount as the marginal product and the firms providing such training could not capture any of the return.

Why, then, would rational firms in competitive labor markets provide general training if it did not bring any return? The answer is that firms would provide general training only if they did not have to pay any of the costs. Persons receiving general training would be willing to pay these costs since training raises their future wages. Hence it is the trainees, not the firms, who would bear the cost of general training and profit from the return.[2]

These and other implications of general training can be more formally demonstrated in equation (7). Since wages and marginal products are raised by the same amount, MP_t must equal W_t for all $t = 1, \ldots, n - 1$, and therefore

$$G = \sum_{t=1}^{n-1} \frac{MP_t - W_t}{(1 + i)^t} = 0. \qquad (8)$$

Equation (7) is reduced to

$$MP_0' = W_0 + C, \qquad (9)$$

2. Some persons have asked why any general training is provided if firms do not collect any of the returns. The answer is simply that they have an incentive to do so wherever the demand price for training is at least as great as the supply price or cost of providing the training. Workers in turn would prefer to be trained on the job rather than in specialized firms (schools) if the training and work complemented each other.

or

$$W_0 = MP_0' - C. \qquad (10)$$

In terms of actual marginal product

$$MP_0 = W_0 + k, \qquad (9')$$

or

$$W_0 = MP_0 - k. \qquad (10')$$

The wage of trainees would not equal their opportunity marginal product but would be less by the total cost of training. In other words, employees would pay for general training by receiving wages below their current (opportunity) productivity. Equation (10) has many other implications, and the rest of this section is devoted to developing the more important ones.

Some might argue that a really 'net' definition of marginal product, obtained by subtracting training costs from 'gross' marginal product, must equal wages even for trainees. Such an interpretation of net productivity could formally save the equality between marginal product and wages here, but not always, as shown later. Moreover, regardless of which interpretation is used, training costs would have to be included in any study of the relation between wages and productivity.

(a) *Gross and net earnings*. Employees pay for general on-the-job training by receiving wages below what they could receive elsewhere. 'Earnings' during the training period would be the difference between an income or flow term (potential marginal product) and a capital or stock term (training costs), so that the capital and income accounts would be closely intermixed, with changes in either affecting wages. In other words, earnings of persons receiving on-the-job training would be net of investment costs and would correspond to the definition of *net* earnings used throughout this paper, which subtracts all investment costs from 'gross' earnings. Therefore, our departure with this definition of earnings from the accounting conventions used for transactions in material goods – which separate income from capital accounts to prevent a transaction in capital from *ipso facto*[3] affecting the

3. Of course, a shift between assets with different productivities would affect the income account on material goods even with current accounting practices.

income side – is not capricious but is grounded in a fundamental difference between the way investment in material and human capital are 'written off'. The underlying cause of this difference undoubtedly is the widespread reluctance to treat people as capital and the accompanying tendency to treat all wage receipts as earnings.

Intermixing the capital and income accounts could make the reported 'incomes' of trainees unusually low and perhaps negative, even though their long-run or lifetime incomes were well above average. Since a considerable fraction of young persons receive some training, and since trainees tend to have lower current and higher subsequent earnings than other youth, the correlation of current consumption with the current earnings of young males[4] would not only be much weaker than the correlation with long-run earnings, but the signs of these correlations might even differ.[5]

Doubt has been cast on the frequent assertion that no allowance is made in the income accounts for depreciation on human capital.[6] A depreciation-type item is deducted, at least from the earnings due to on-the-job training, for the cost would be deducted during the training period. Depreciation on tangible capital does not bulk so large in any one period because it is usually 'written off' or depreciated during a period of time designed to approximate its economic life. Hence human and tangible capital appear to differ more in the time pattern of de-

4. The term 'young males' rather than 'young families' is used because as J. Mincer has shown (in his 'Labor force participation of married women', *Aspects of labor economics*, Princeton for N.B.E.R., 1962), the labor force participation of wives is positively correlated with the difference between a husband's long-run and current income. Participation of wives, therefore, makes the correlation between a family's current and a husband's long-run income greater than that between a husband's current and long-run income.

5. A difference in signs is impossible in Friedman's analysis of consumer behavior because he assumes that, at least in the aggregate, transitory, and long-run (that is, permanent) incomes are uncorrelated (see his *A theory of the consumption function*, Princeton for N.B.E.R., 1957); I am suggesting that they may be *negatively* correlated for young persons.

6. See C. Christ, 'Patinkin on money, interest, and prices', *Journal of Political Economy*, August 1957, p. 352; and W. Hamburger, 'The relation of consumption to wealth and the wage rate', *Econometrica*, January 1955.

preciation than in its existence,[7] and the effect on wage income of a rapid 'write-off' of human capital is what should be emphasized and studied.

This point can be demonstrated differently and more rigorously. The ideal depreciation on a capital asset during any period would equal its change in value during the period. In particular, if value rose, a negative depreciation term would have to be subtracted or a positive appreciation term added to the income from the asset. Since training costs would be deducted from earnings during the training period, the economic 'value' of a trainee would at first increase rather than decrease with age, and only later begin to decrease. Therefore, a negative rather than a positive depreciation term would have to be subtracted initially.[8]

Training has an important effect on the relation between earnings and age. Suppose that untrained persons received the same earnings regardless of age, as shown by the horizontal line UU in Figure 1. Trained persons would receive lower earnings during the training period because training is paid for at that time, and higher earnings at later ages because the return is collected then. The combined effect of paying for and collecting the return from training in this way would be to make the age earnings curve of trained persons, shown by TT in Figure 1, steeper than that of untrained persons, the difference being greater the greater the cost of, and return from, the investment.

Not only does training make the curve steeper but, as indicated by Figure 1, also more concave; that is, the rate of increase in earnings is affected more at younger than at older ages. Suppose, to take an extreme case, that training raised the level of marginal productivity but had no effect on the slope, so that the

7. In a recent paper, R. Goode has argued (see his 'Educational expenditures and the income tax', in Selma J. Mushkin (ed.), *Economics of higher education*, Washington, 1962) that educated persons should be permitted to subtract from income a depreciation allowance on tuition payments. Such an allowance is apparently not required for on-the-job training costs or, as seen later, for the indirect costs of education; indeed, one might argue, on the contrary, that too much or too rapid depreciation is permitted on such investments.

8. See G. S. Becker, *Human Capital. A theoretical and empirical analysis, with special reference to education*, Columbia University Press, 1964, ch. 7, section 2, for some empirical estimates of 'depreciation' on human capital.

marginal productivity of trained persons was also independent of age. If earnings equaled marginal product, *TT* would merely be parallel to and higher than *UU*, showing neither slope nor concavity. Since, however, earnings of trained persons would be below marginal productivity during the training period and equal

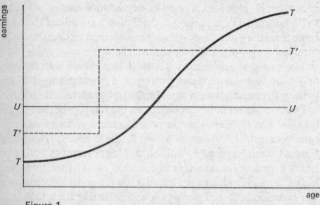

Figure 1

afterward, they would rise sharply at the end of the training period and then level off (as shown by the dashed line *T'T'* in Figure 1), imparting a concave appearance to the curve as a whole. In this extreme case an extreme concavity appears (as in *TT*); in less extreme cases the principle would be the same and the concavity more continuous.

Foregone earnings are an important, although neglected, cost of much investment in human capital and should be treated in the same way as direct outlays. Indeed, *all* costs appear as foregone earnings to workers receiving on-the-job training; that is, all costs appear as lower earnings than could be received elsewhere, although direct outlays, *C*, may really be an important part of costs. The arbitrariness of the division between indirect and direct costs and the resulting advantage of treating total costs as a whole [9] can be further demonstrated by contrasting school and

9. The equivalence between indirect and direct costs applies to consumption as well as to investment decisions. In my paper, *A theory of the allocation of time*, I.B.M. Research Paper RC 1149, 20 March 1964, an analysis

on-the-job training. Usually only the direct costs of school training are emphasized, even though opportunity costs are sometimes (as with college education) an important part of the total. A shift from school training to on-the-job training would, however, reverse the emphasis and make all costs appear as foregone earnings, even when direct outlays were important.

Income-maximizing firms in competitive labor markets would not pay the cost of general training and would pay trained persons the market wage. If, however, training costs were paid, many persons would seek training, few would quit during the training period, and labor costs would be relatively high. Firms that did not pay trained persons the market wage would have difficulty satisfying their skill requirements and would also tend to be less profitable than other firms. Firms that paid both for training and less than the market wage for trained persons would have the worst of both worlds, for they would attract too many trainees and too few trained persons.

(b) *Military personnel.* These principles have been clearly demonstrated during the last few years in discussions of problems in recruiting military personnel. The military offers training in a wide variety of skills and many are very useful in the civilian sector. Training is provided during part or all of the first enlistment period and used during the remainder of the first period and hopefully during subsequent periods. This hope, however, is thwarted by the fact that re-enlistment rates tend to be inversely related to the amount of civilian-type skills provided by the military.[10] Persons with these skills leave the military more

---

incorporating both direct and indirect consumption costs is applied to the choice between work and nonwork, price and income elasticities of demand for goods, the economic function of queues, and several other areas. [Now published in *The Economic Journal*, vol. 75 (1965), p. 299.]

10. See *Manpower management and compensation*, report of the Cordiner Committee, Washington (1957), vol. I, chart 3, and the accompanying discussion. The military not only wants to eliminate the inverse relation but apparently would like to create a positive relation because they have such a large investment in heavily trained personnel. For a recent and excellent study, see Gorman C. Smith, 'Differential pay for military technicians', unpublished Ph.D. dissertation, Columbia University, 1964.

readily because they can receive much higher wages in the civilian sector. Net military wages for those receiving training are higher relative to civilian wages during the first than during subsequent enlistment periods because training costs are largely paid by the military. Not surprisingly, therefore, first-term enlistments for skilled jobs are obtained much more easily than are re-enlistments.

The military is a conspicuous example of an organization that both pays at least part of training costs and does not pay market wages to skilled personnel. It has had, in consequence, relatively easy access to 'students' and heavy losses of 'graduates'. Indeed, its graduates make up the predominant part of the supply in several civilian occupations. For example, well over 90 per cent of United States commercial airline pilots received much of their training in the armed forces. The military, of course, is not a commercial organization judged by profits and losses and has had no difficulty surviving and even thriving.

What about the old argument that firms in competitive labor markets have no incentive to provide on-the-job training because trained workers would be bid away by other firms? Firms that train workers are supposed to impart external economies to other firms because the latter can use these workers free of any training charge. An analogy with research and development is often drawn since a firm developing a process that cannot be patented or kept secret would impart external economies to competitors. This argument and analogy would apply if firms were to pay training costs, for they would suffer a 'capital loss' whenever trained workers were bid away by other firms. Firms can, however, shift training costs to trainees and have an incentive to do so when faced with competition for their services.[11]

11. Sometimes the alleged external economies from on-the-job training have been considered part of the 'infant industry' argument for protection (see J. Black 'Arguments for tariffs', *Oxford Economic Papers*, June 1959, pp. 205–6). Our analysis suggests, however, that the trouble tariffs are supposed to overcome must be traced back to difficulties that workers have in financing investment in themselves – in other words, to ignorance or capital market limitations that apply to expenditures on education, health, as well as on-the-job training. Protection would serve the same purpose as the creation of monopsonies domestically, namely, to convert general into specific capital so that firms can be given an incentive to pay for training;

The difference between investment in training and in research and development can be put very simply. Without patents or secrecy, firms in competitive industries cannot establish property rights in innovations, and these innovations become fair game for all comers. Patent systems try to establish these rights so that incentives can be provided to invest in research. Property rights in skills, on the other hand, are automatically vested, for a skill cannot be used without permission of the person possessing it. The property right of the worker in his skills is the source of his incentive to invest in training by accepting a reduced wage during the training period and explains why an analogy with unowned innovations is misleading.

Specific training

Completely general training increases the marginal productivity of trainees by exactly the same amount in the firms providing the training as in other firms. Clearly some kinds of training increase productivity by different amounts in the firms providing the training and in other firms. Training that increases productivity more in firms providing it will be called specific training. Completely specific training can be defined as training that has no effect on the productivity of trainees that would be useful in other firms. Much on-the-job training is neither completely specific nor completely general but increases productivity more in the firms providing it and falls within the definition of specific training. The rest increases productivity by at least as much in other firms and falls within a definition of general training. A few illustrations of the scope of specific training are presented before a formal analysis is developed.

The military offers some forms of training that are extremely useful in the civilian sector, as already noted, and others that are only of minor use to civilians, i.e. astronauts, fighter pilots, and missile men. Such training falls within the scope of specific training because productivity is raised in the military but not (much) elsewhere.

---

see the remarks on specific training below and in section 4 of this chapter [not included in this excerpt]. Presumably a much more efficient solution would be to improve the capital market directly through insurance of loans, subsidies, information etc.

Resources are usually spent by firms in familiarizing new employees with their organization,[12] and the knowledge thus acquired is a form of specific training because productivity is raised more in the firms acquiring the knowledge than in other firms. Other kinds of hiring costs, such as employment agency fees, the expenses incurred by new employees in finding jobs, or the time employed in interviewing, testing, checking references, and in bookkeeping do not so obviously increase the knowledge of new employees, but they too are a form of specific investment in human capital, although not training. They are an investment because outlays over a short period create distributed effects on productivity; they are specific because productivity is raised primarily in the firms making the outlays; they are in human capital because they lose their value whenever employees leave. In the rest of this section reference is mostly to on-the-job specific training even though the analysis applies to all on-the-job specific investment.

Even after hiring costs are incurred, firms usually know only a limited amount about the ability and potential of new employees. They try to increase their knowledge in various ways – testing, rotation among departments, trial and error, etc. – for greater knowledge permits a more efficient utilization of manpower. Expenditures on acquiring knowledge of employee talents would be a specific investment if the knowledge could be kept from other firms, for then productivity would be raised more in the firms making the expenditures than elsewhere.

The effect of investment in employees on their productivity elsewhere depends on market conditions as well as on the nature of the investment. Very strong monopsonists might be completely insulated from competition by other firms, and practically all investments in their labor force would be specific. On the other hand, firms in extremely competitive labor markets would face a constant threat of raiding and would have fewer specific investments available.

These examples convey some of the surprisingly large variety of situations that come under the rubric of specific investment. This

12. To judge from a sample of firms recently analyzed, formal orientation courses are quite common, at least in large firms (see H. F. Clark and H. S. Sloan, *Classrooms in the factories*, New York, 1958, ch. 4).

set is now treated abstractly in order to develop a general formal analysis. Empirical situations are brought in again after several major implications of the formal analysis have been developed.

If all training were completely specific, the wage that an employee could get elsewhere would be independent of the amount of training he had received. One might plausibly argue, then, that the wage paid by firms would also be independent of training. If so, firms would have to pay training costs, for no rational employee would pay for training that did not benefit him. Firms would collect the return from such training in the form of larger profits resulting from higher productivity, and training would be provided whenever the return – discounted at an appropriate rate – was at least as large as the cost. Long-run competitive equilibrium requires that the present value of the return exactly equals costs.

These propositions can be stated more formally with the equations developed earlier. According to equations (5) and (7), the equilibrium of a firm providing training in competitive markets can be written as

$$MP_0' + G\left[\sum_{t=1}^{n-1} \frac{MP_t - W_t}{(1+i)^t}\right] = W_0 + C, \qquad (11)$$

where C is the cost of training given only in the initial period, MP_0' is the opportunity marginal product of trainees, W_0 is the wage paid to trainees, and W_t and MP_t are the wage and marginal product in period t. If the analysis of completely specific training given in the preceding paragraph is correct, W would always equal the wage that could be received elsewhere, $MP_t - W_t$ would be the full return in t from training given in 0, and G would be the present value of these returns. Since MP_0' measures the marginal product elsewhere and W_0 measures the wage elsewhere of trainees, MP_0' equals W_0. As a consequence G equals C, or, in full equilibrium, the return from training equals costs.

Before claiming that the usual equality between marginal product and wages holds when completely specific training is considered, the reader should bear in mind two points. The first is that the equality between wages and marginal product in the initial period involves opportunity, not actual marginal product. Wages would be greater than actual marginal product if some productivity was foregone as part of the training program. The second is that, even if wages equaled marginal product initially, they would be less in the future because the differences between future marginal products and wages constitute the return to training and are collected by the firm.

All of this follows from the assumption that firms pay all costs and collect all returns. But could not one equally well argue that workers pay all specific training costs by receiving appropriately lower wages initially and collect all returns by receiving wages equal to marginal product later? In terms of equation (11), W_t would equal MP_t, G would equal zero, and W_0 would equal $MP_0' - C$, just as with general training. Is it more plausible that firms rather than workers pay for and collect and return from training?

An answer can be found by reasoning along the following lines. If a firm had paid for the specific training of a worker who quit to take another job, its capital expenditure would be partly wasted, for no further return could be collected. Likewise, a worker fired after he had paid for specific training would be unable to collect any further return and would also suffer a capital loss. The willingness of workers or firms to pay for specific training should, therefore, closely depend on the likelihood of labor turnover.

(a) *Labor turnover rates*. To bring in turnover at this point may seem like a *deus ex machina* since it is almost always ignored in traditional theory. In the usual analysis of competitive firms, wages equal marginal product, and since wages and marginal product are assumed to be the same in many firms, no one suffers from turnover. It would not matter whether a firm's labor force always contained the same persons or a rapidly changing group. Any person leaving one firm could do equally well in other firms, and his employer could replace him without any change in profits. In other words, turnover is ignored in traditional theory because it plays no important role within the framework of the theory.

Turnover becomes important when costs are imposed on workers or firms, which are precisely the effects of specific training. Suppose a firm paid all the specific training costs of a worker who quit after completing it. According to our earlier analysis, he would have been receiving the market wage and a new employee could be hired at the same wage. If the new employee were not given training, his marginal product would be less than that of the one who quit since presumably training raised the latter's productivity. Training could raise the new employee's productivity but would require additional expenditures by the firm. In other words, a firm is hurt by the departure of a trained employee because an equally profitable new employee could not be obtained. In the same way an employee who pays for specific training would suffer a loss from being laid off because he could not find an equally good job elsewhere. To bring turnover into the analysis of specific training is not, therefore, a *deus ex machina* but is made necessary by the important link between them.

Firms paying for specific training might take account of turnover merely by obtaining a sufficiently large return from those remaining to counterbalance the loss from those leaving. (The return on 'successes' – those remaining – would, of course, overestimate the average return on all training expenditures.) Firms could do even better, however, by recognizing that the likelihood of a quit is not fixed but depends on wages. Instead of merely recouping on successes what is lost on failures, they might reduce the likelihood of failure itself by offering higher wages after training than could be received elsewhere. In effect, they would offer employees some of the return from training. Matters would be improved in some respects but worsened in others, but the higher wage would make the supply of trainees greater than the demand, and rationing would be required. The final step would be to shift some training costs as well as returns to employees, thereby bringing supply more in line with demand. When the final step is completed, firms no longer pay all training costs nor do they collect all the return but they share both with employees.[13]

13. A. Marshall (*Principles of economics*, 8th ed, New York, 1949, p. 626) was clearly aware of specific talents and their effect on wages and productivity: 'Thus the head clerk in a business has an acquaintance with men and things, the use of which he could in some cases sell at a high price to rival firms. But in other cases it is of a kind to be of no value save to the business in which he already is; and *then his departure would perhaps injure*

The shares of each depend on the relations between quit rates and wages, layoff rates and profits, and on other factors not discussed here, such as the cost of funds, attitudes toward risk, and desires for liquidity.[14]

If training were not completely specific, productivity would increase in other firms as well, and the wage that could be received elsewhere would also increase. Such training can be looked upon as the sum of two components, one completely general, the other completely specific; the former would be relatively larger, the greater the effect on wages in other firms relative to the firms providing the training. Since firms do not pay any of the completely general costs and only part of the completely specific costs, the fraction of costs paid by firms would be inversely related to the importance of the general component, or positively related to the specificity of the training.

Our conclusions can be stated formally in terms of the equations developed earlier. If G is the present value of the return from training collected by firms, the fundamental equation is

$$MP' + G = W + C. \qquad (12)$$

If G' measures the return collected by employees, the total return, G'', would be the sum of G and G'. In full equilibrium the total return would equal total costs, or $G'' = C$. Let a represent the fraction of the total return collected by firms. Since $G = aG''$ and $G'' = C$, equation (12) can be written as

$$MP' + aC = W + C, \qquad (13)$$

---

it by several times the value of his salary, while probably he could not get half that salary elsewhere.' (My italics.) However, he overstressed the element of indeterminacy in these wages ('their earnings are determined . . . by a bargain between them and their employers, the terms of which are theoretically arbitrary') because he ignored the effect of wages on turnover (ibid., fn. 2).

14. The rate used to discount costs and returns is the sum of a (positive) rate measuring the cost of funds, a (positive or negative) risk premium, and a liquidity premium that is presumably positive since capital invested in specific training is very illiquid; see the discussion in G. S. Becker, op. cit., ch. 3, section 2.

or

$$W = MP' - (1 - a)C.^{15} \qquad (14)$$

Employees pay the same fraction of costs, $1 - a$, as they collect in returns, which generalizes the results obtained earlier. For if training were completely general, $a = 0$, and equation (14) reduces to equation (10); if firms collected all the return from training, $a = 1$, and (14) reduces to $MP_0' = W_0$; and if $0 < a < 1$, none of the earlier equations is satisfactory.

A few major implications of this analysis of specific training are now developed.

Rational firms pay generally trained employees the same wage and specifically trained employees a higher wage than they could get elsewhere. A reader might easily believe the contrary – namely, that general training would command a higher wage relative to alternatives than specific training does, since, after all, competition for persons with the latter is apt to be weaker than for those with the former. This view, however, overlooks the fact that general training raises the wages that could be received elsewhere while (completely) specific training does not, so a comparison with alternative wages gives a misleading impression of the *absolute* effect on wages of different types of training. Moreover, firms are not too concerned about the turnover of employees with general training and have no incentive to offer them a premium above wages elsewhere because the cost of such training is borne entirely by employees. Firms are concerned about the turnover of employees with specific training, and a premium is offered to reduce their turnover because firms pay part of their training costs.

The part of specific training paid by employees has effects similar to those discussed earlier for general training: it is also paid by a reduction in wages during the training period, tends to make age–earnings profiles steeper and more concave, etc. The

15. If G'' did not equal C, these equations would be slightly more complicated. Suppose, for example, $G'' = G + G' = C + n$, $n \geq 0$, so that the present value of the total return would be greater than total costs. Then $G = aG'' = aC + an$, and

$$MP' + aC + an = W + C,$$

or

$$W = MP' - [(1 - a)C - an].$$

part paid by firms has none of these implications, since current or future wages would not be affected.

Specific, unlike general, training produces certain 'external' effects, for quits prevent firms from capturing the full return on costs paid by them, and layoffs do the same to employees. These, however, are external *diseconomies* imposed on the employees or employers of firms providing the training, not external economies accruing to other firms.

Employees with specific training have less incentive to quit, and firms have less incentive to fire them, than employees with no training or general training, which implies that quit and layoff rates are inversely related to the amount of specific training. Turnover should be least for employees with extremely specific training and most for those receiving such general training that productivity is raised less in the firms providing the training than elsewhere (as, say, in schools). These propositions are as applicable to the large number of irregular quits and layoffs that continually occur as to the more regular cyclical and secular movements in turnover; in this section, however, only the more regular movements are discussed.

Consider a firm that experiences an unexpected decline in demand for its output, the rest of the economy being unaffected. The marginal product of employees without specific training – such as untrained or generally trained employees – presumably equaled wages initially, and their employment would now be reduced to prevent their marginal productivity from falling below wages. The marginal product of specifically trained employees initially would have been greater than wages. A decline in demand would reduce these marginal products too, but as long as they were reduced by less than the initial difference with wages, firms would have no incentive to lay off such employees. For sunk costs are sunk, and there is no incentive to lay off employees whose marginal product is greater than wages, no matter how unwise it was, in retrospect, to invest in their training. Thus workers with specific training seem less likely to be laid off as a consequence of a decline in demand than untrained or even generally trained workers.[16]

16. A very similar argument is developed by Walter Oi in 'Labor as a quasi-fixed factor of production', unpublished Ph.D. dissertation, Univer-

If the decline in demand were sufficiently great so that even the marginal product of specifically trained workers was pushed below wages, would the firm just proceed to lay them off until the marginal product was brought into equality with wages? To show the danger here, assume that all the cost of and return from specific training was paid and collected by the firm. Any worker laid off would try to find a new job, since nothing would bind him to the old one.[17] The firm might be hurt if he did find a new job, for the firm's investment in his training might be lost forever. If specifically trained workers were not laid off, the firm would lose now because marginal product would be less than wages but would gain in the future if the decline in demand proved temporary. There is an incentive, therefore, not to lay off workers with specific training when their marginal product is only temporarily below wages, and the larger a firm's investment the greater the incentive not to lay them off.

A worker collecting some of the return from specific training would have less incentive to find a new job when temporarily laid off than others would: he does not want to lose his investment. His behavior while laid off in turn affects his future chances of being laid off, for if it were known that he would not readily take another job, the firm could lay him off without much fear of losing its investment.

These conclusions can be briefly summarized. If one firm alone experienced an unexpected decline in demand, relatively few workers with specific training would be laid off, if only because their marginal product was initially greater than their wage. If the decline were permanent, all workers would be laid off when their marginal product became less than their wage and all those laid off would have to find jobs elsewhere. If the decline were temporary, specifically trained workers might not be laid off even though their marginal product was less than their wage because the firm would suffer if they took other jobs. The likelihood of

sity of Chicago, 1961. Also, see his article with almost the same title in *Journal of Political Economy*, December 1962.

17. Actually one need only assume that the quit rate of laid-off workers tends to be significantly greater than that of employed workers, if only because the opportunity cost of searching for another job is less for laid-off workers.

their taking other jobs would be inversely related, and therefore the likelihood of their being laid off would be positively related, to the extent of their own investment in training.

The analysis can easily be extended to cover general declines in demand; suppose, for example, a general cyclical decline occurred. Assume that wages were sticky and remained at the initial level. If the decline in business activity were not sufficient to reduce the marginal product below the wage, workers with specific training would not be laid off even though others would be, just as before. If the decline reduced marginal product below wages, only one modification in the previous analysis is required. A firm would have a greater incentive to lay off specifically trained workers than when it alone experienced a decline because laid-off workers would be less likely to find other jobs when unemployment was widespread. In other respects, the implications of a general decline with wage rigidity are the same as those of a decline in one firm alone.

The discussion has concentrated on layoff rates, but the same kind of reasoning shows that a rise in wages elsewhere would cause fewer quits among specifically trained workers than among others. For specifically trained workers initially receive higher wages than are available elsewhere and the wage rise elsewhere would have to be greater than the initial difference before they would consider quitting. Thus both the quit and layoff rate of specifically trained workers would be relatively low and fluctuate relatively less during business cycles. These are important implications that can be tested with the data available.

(b) *Pension plans.* Although quits and layoffs are influenced by considerations other than investment costs, some of these, such as pension plans, are more strongly related to investments than may appear at first blush. A pension plan with incomplete vesting privileges[18] penalizes employees who quit before retirement and thus provides an incentive – often an extremely powerful one – not to quit. At the same time pension plans 'insure' firms against quits for they are given a lump sum – the non-vested portion of payments – whenever a worker quits. Insurance is needed for

18. According to the as yet unpublished National Bureau study of pensions, most plans have incomplete vesting.

specifically trained employees because their turnover would impose capital losses on firms. Firms can discourage such quits by sharing training costs and the return with employees, but they would have less need to discourage them and would be more willing to pay for training costs if insurance were provided. The effects on the incentive to invest in one's employees may have been a major stimulus to the development of pension plans with incomplete vesting.[19]

An effective long-term contract would insure firms against quits, just as pensions do and also insure employees against layoffs. Firms would be more willing to pay for all kinds of training – assuming future wages were set at an appropriate level – since a contract, in effect, converts all training into completely specific training. A casual reading of history suggests that long-term contracts have, indeed, been primarily a means of inducing firms to undertake large investments in employees. These contracts are seldom used today in the United States,[20] and while they have declined in importance over time, they were probably always the exception here largely because courts have considered them a form of involuntary servitude. Moreover, any enforcible contract could at best specify the hours required on a job, not the quality of performance. Since performance can vary widely, unhappy workers could usually 'sabotage' operations to induce employers to release them from contracts.

Some training may be useful not in most firms nor in a single firm, but in a set of firms defined by product, type of work, or geographical location. For example, carpentry training would raise productivity primarily in the construction industry, and French legal training would not be very useful in the United States. Such training would tend to be paid by trainees, since a single firm could not readily collect the return,[21] and in this

19. This economic function of incomplete vesting should caution one against conceding to the agitation for more liberal vesting privileges. Of course, in recent years pensions have also been an important tax-saving device, which certainly has been a crucial factor in their mushrooming growth.

20. The military and the entertainment industry are the major exceptions.

21. Sometimes firms cooperate in paying training costs, especially when training apprentices (see *A look at industrial training in Mercer County, N.J.*, Washington, 1959, p. 3).

respect would be the same as general training. In one respect, however, it is similar to specific training. Workers with training 'specific' to an industry, occupation, or country are less likely to leave that industry, occupation, or country than other workers, so their industrial, occupational, or country 'turnover' would be less than average. The same result is obtained for specific training, except that a firm rather than an industry, occupation, or country is used as the unit of observation in measuring turnover. An analysis of specific training, therefore, is helpful also in understanding the effects of certain types of 'general' training.

(c) *Monopsony.* Although a discrepancy between marginal product and wages is frequently taken as evidence of imperfections in the competitive system, it would occur even in a perfectly competitive system where there is investment in specific training. The investment approach provides a very different interpretation of some common phenomena, as can be seen from the following examples.

A positive difference between marginal product and wages is usually said to be evidence of monopsony power; just as the ratio of product price to marginal cost has been suggested as a measure of monopoly power, so has the ratio of marginal product to wages been suggested as a measure of monopsony power. But specific training would also make this ratio greater than one. Does the difference between the marginal product and the earnings of major-league baseball players, for example, measure monopsony power or the return on a team's investment? Since teams do spend a great deal on developing players, some and perhaps most of the difference must be considered a return on investment (even if there were no uncertainty about the abilities of different players).[22]

Earnings might differ greatly among firms, industries, and countries and yet there might be relatively little worker mobility.

22. S. Rottenberg ('The baseball players' labor market', *Journal of Political Economy*, June 1956, p. 254) argues that the strong restrictions on entry of teams into the major leagues is prima-facie evidence that monopsony power is important, but the entry or threat of new *leagues*, such as have occurred in professional basketball and football, is a real possibility. And, of course, new teams have entered in recent years.

The usual explanation would be that workers were either irrational or faced with formidable obstacles in moving. However, if specific[23] training were important, differences in earnings would be a misleading estimate of what 'migrants' could receive, and it might be perfectly rational not to move. For example, although French lawyers earn less than American lawyers, the average French lawyer could not earn the average American legal income simply by migrating to the United States, for he would have to invest in learning English and American law and procedures.[24]

In extreme types of monopsony, exemplified by an isolated company town, job alternatives for both trained and untrained workers are nil, and all training, no matter what its nature, would be specific to the firm. Monopsony combined with control of a product or an occupation (due, say, to antipirating agreements) converts training specific to that product or occupation into firm-specific training. These kinds of monopsony increase the importance of specific training and thus the incentive to invest in employees.[25] The effect on training of less extreme monopsony positions is more difficult assess. Consider the monopsonist who pays his workers the best wage available elsewhere. I see no reason why training should have a systematically different effect on the foregone earnings of his employees than of those in competitive firms, and, therefore, no reason why specific training should be more (or less) important to him. But monopsony power as a whole, including the more extreme manifestations, would appear to increase the importance of specific training and the incentive for firms to invest in human capital.

23. Specific, that is, to the firms, industries, or countries in question.
24. Of course, persons who have not yet invested in themselves would have an incentive to migrate, and this partly explains why young persons migrate more than older ones. For a further explanation, see the discussion in G. S. Becker, op. cit., ch. 3; also see the paper by L. Sjaastad, 'The costs and returns of human migration', *Investment in human beings*, pp. 80–93.
25. A relatively large difference between marginal product and wages in monopsonies might measure, therefore, the combined effect of economic power and a relatively large investment in employees.

10 R. S. Eckaus

Comment on Becker's Analysis of On-the-job Training

R. S. Eckaus, 'Investment in human capital: a comment', *Journal of Political Economy*, vol. 71 (1963), no. 5, pp. 501–5.

I. Introduction

The theoretical analysis of investment in human capital that recently appeared in this *Journal* performs a useful service by raising many relevant issues and in suggesting relationships.[1] Without wishing to ascribe to the author's results a greater degree of definitiveness than he himself claims, it seemed to this reader that certain of them were put forward with more certainty than is warranted. In general I do not want to question the logical validity of those results. Rather, it is their generality, whether they provide reasonably accurate descriptions of reality and good predictions, that I shall mainly discuss.

The analytic exemplar of the article is the discussion of on-the-job training, and it deserves to be the starting point of any criticism. From there this comment will pass briefly to some of the other issues raised.

II. Who Bears the Cost of On-the-Job Training when there are Perfect Markets?

On-the-job training is, for nearly all of Becker's analysis, quite distinct from the production processes of a firm in the sense that inputs into training are never, to any extent, inputs into production. The decision to train or not train is, therefore, one that can be isolated and based solely on the costs and returns associated with the training procedure. In this case, according to Becker, if

1. Gary S. Becker, 'Investment in human capital: A theoretical analysis', *Journal of Political Economy*, vol. 70 (1962) Supplement, pp. 9–49. Page numbers given in text in parentheses refer to this article.

one makes the customary assumptions associated with perfect markets, the individual worker will bear the burden of whatever training makes a *general* contribution to his productivity.

This conclusion is certainly correct under the assumptions. Becker's reasoning on this point occurs at several places in his article. The following quotation is intended to represent it:

Income maximizing firms in competitive labor markets would not pay the cost of general training and would pay trained persons the market wage. If, however, training costs were paid, many persons would seek training, few would quit during the training period, and labor costs would be relatively high. Firms that did not pay trained persons the market wage have difficulty satisfying their skill requirements and would also tend to be less profitable than other firms. Firms that both paid for training and less than the market wage for trained persons would have the worst of both worlds, for they would attract too many trainees and too few trained persons (p. 16).

A slight amplification of the argument may help demonstrate the dependence of the conclusions on the particular assumptions. The complete separability of training and production costs and the perfect mobility of labor make firms into nothing more than private schools for general training. Because of competition and free mobility workers would never accept less than their marginal product. As a result, firms could never possibly afford to 'invest' in any training that makes a general contribution to labor productivity because the full increment of any addition to their productivity would always be captured by workers. On the other hand, because training costs are separate and identifiable, firms can always collect the exact costs of the training offered.

According to Becker, since workers have permanent title to themselves, they face no special risks in perfect markets in investing in their own general training in order to increase their own productivity. The role of the firm in labor training under his assumptions is one of supplying information on costs and returns and of doing training. The production activities of firms are no more than sources of information. Workers would base their demand for general training on its properly discounted costs and returns. Firms would supply general training on the basis of the profitability of training activities only. The production levels and relative input proportions of the firm would, in turn, adjust to the decisions taken in the training 'market'.

Specific training is defined by Becker as training whose marginal productivity is higher in the firm giving the training than in other firms. The conditions of perfect markets are violated, at least on the employer side, since the training firms stands in a unique relation to its trainees. Otherwise, the assumptions of perfect markets are maintained.

'Special training' as defined by Becker would not improve the worker's productivity in other firms. As a result the firm giving such training would not face competition by other firms for the added skills of the workers who are made more capable by having had such training. Thus, no market mechanism would operate to give the worker the full benefits of special training.

The firm investing in special training would be aware, however, that if a worker left its employment it would lose its investment. How would the firm giving this type of training protect the capital created? Becker's answer to this is that the firm will always find it better to pay somewhat higher wages to eliminate labor mobility rather than to equate discounted returns and costs on investment in specific training taking into account the risks of losing workers (p. 20). Yet, if the firm wants to create some degree of labor immobility by paying higher wages, then it must regard such payments, as well as the costs of special labor training, as if they were similar to investments in physical capital with, perhaps, more than ordinary risks of losing their investment. Then the amount of the increment in wages that the firm would pay in order to confer immobility would be determined by a calculation of the returns to such a risky investment.

Suppose now that on-the-job training is an 'unavoidable' joint product with the firm's regular output, that is, that neither the marginal nor average costs of production and training are completely separable. Becker mentions this case without, I believe, developing its implications (p. 20). Under these conditions the previous conclusions require some revision.

When goods, education, and other outputs are produced jointly in 'fixed' proportions[2] then the marginal costs of each

2. 'Fixity' here may imply no more than some limit to the variability of the proportions of the joint output.

cannot be defined. Only the familiar equilibrium conditions for the firm must be met: that the marginal costs of both together must equal the sum of the prices of each. For each good, of course, the total quantity supplied must equal the total demanded. The costs of general training under these conditions need not be fully shifted to workers. It is, in fact, impossible to know exactly what these costs are. The firm produces; workers become better trained by example, by practice, and by maturing in a job situation. The amount that the firm will be able to extract from workers in compensation for the training is not determined by training costs. On the one hand, the firm cannot pay the worker less than his marginal productivity in goods production in any other line or the worker will make the move that his general training makes possible. On the other hand, the firm cannot avoid giving the training. The level of wages will, in turn, depend on the overall demand for labor and its supply, which will reflect the opportunities created by the training as well as opportunities in other sectors.[3]

Turning to special training as defined by Becker, if it were created in a process of joint production, the conclusions drawn above for the non-joint product case would still hold. There is no identifiable set of training costs, and there is no way for the firm to pass any part of the burden of total costs to the worker by paying less than the wages of untrained workers in alternative employment as long as there are perfect labor markets.

There are, no doubt, many instances of firms establishing facilities for training workers that are completely independent of their production facilities. However, this probably constitutes a small proportion of all on-the-job training. Apprenticeship programs, for example, are not entirely or even mainly in this category. The relatively informal, unorganized type of vocational training through casual instruction and as a joint product with actual work experience is, I believe, much more significant.

3. Of course, when general training is produced in variable proportions with output, no firm would undertake any marginal expense for training for which it was not reimbursed, just as in the non-joint production case.

III. On-the-Job Training in Less than Perfect Labor Markets

Let us now put aside the assumptions of perfect factor markets. Certainly it has often been argued that achievement of the results of perfect markets does not require that every participant conform to the assumptions. It does require, at least, a mechanism that rewards and punishes as if the assumptions were valid. The extent to which such a mechanism exists and operates will remain a matter of judgment. It may, however, assist in that judgment if some of the imperfections and their consequences are reviewed briefly to provide contrast with Becker's conclusions. Becker's conclusions that workers bear the cost of 'general' on-the-job training and firms the cost of 'specific' on-the-job training have the appeal of concreteness. Yet these conclusions, based on Becker's assumptions of perfect markets and the complete separation of production costs and training costs, must be abandoned as soon as the assumptions are dropped.

Becker does refer to market 'difficulties' (p. 31), but apparently he thinks that for practical purposes they do not vitiate his analysis. Yet if, for example, there is some degree of labor immobility, that is, not perfect, free, and frictionless response to wage differentials, his conclusion that firms will never bear the cost of the on-the-job general training which he defines no longer holds. Under 'perfect' conditions firms never would bear this cost because they could never collect any returns. But, if there is some degree of immobility, firms can collect part of the extra product training creates and therefore can consider such general training as if it were an investment in fixed capital. If, at prevailing wages, workers with the desired training do not present themselves in the numbers desired by the firm, based on its production plans, a firm may undertake to give and pay the costs of general training. In these circumstances they could rely on labor immobility to provide them with the necessary return on their investment. On the other hand labor immobility would reduce the need for firms to pay premiums above alternative wages in order to keep 'specially trained' workers.

The lack of knowledge of alternatives which characterizes job markets must be recognized and the role of union bargaining in setting wages and conditions of labor. These too would interfere with Becker's conclusions on the incidence of on-the-job training costs.

Becker argues that the difficulties of financing education are similar to those for financing 'comparable' investments in physical capital, reasoning, for example, that an eighteen-year-old would have just as much trouble financing physical capital as education (p. 42). Presumably the point of the story is that there is no more need to worry about imperfections in 'human' capital markets than in physical capital markets. But an argument based on such an example cannot be taken seriously unless Becker wants also to propose that eighteen-year-olds undertake as significant a part of investment in physical capital as in education.

Apart from money incomes there are social status features associated with particular occupations and their training. Workers may be willing to bear all or part of the costs of specific training or refuse to bear the costs of general training, or vice versa, depending on the status aspects.

It is true that Becker recognized that there are market imperfections and obstacles to the working of the price system that impair the arguments based on perfect markets. However, he seems to regard these as only minor qualifications to the main conclusions. External economies in on-the-job training that arise from the inability of firms to collect the full benefits of such training are, for example, brushed away by Becker in his original argument (p. 21) and never brought back by his qualifications. However, if training is an unavoidable joint product with goods production, or if firms, because of various imperfections, bear part of the cost of that training that is not 'joint', the price system will not necessarily fully reflect relative skill resource scarcities and costs of training.

IV. Conclusion

Economic analysis applied to labor and training can be an extremely powerful tool, as Becker shows in many interesting speculations about the sources of various labor and labor market phenomenon. He demonstrates, for example, the effects of differential amounts of education and training in creating a personal income distribution more skewed than the distribution of abilities.

Other conclusions, however, depend so strictly on the assumptions of perfect factor markets that the arguments, however ingenious, must be suspect. For example, differentials in occupational wage streams would, in perfect markets, reflect the differences in 'human investment'. In actuality relative differences may measure primarily the significant market imperfections among occupations.

Extension of the assumptions of perfect markets for goods to areas such as education raises the danger of creating an analysis that caricatures reality. The ghost of 'economic man' walks again when Becker argues that individual decisions on 'outside' investments, as in better diets, health, and congenial households, are made by comparison of their productivity with the productivity of investment in education.

214

11 M. Blaug

The Rate of Return on Investment in Education

Excerpts from M. Blaug, 'The rate of return on investment in education in Great Britain', *The Manchester School*, vol. 33 (1965), no. 3, pp. 205–51.

A mere acquaintance with the history of economic thought is sufficient to show that the science of economics is almost as subject to fashions as the art of dressmaking. At the present time, 'human capital formation', 'human resource development', or, simply, 'investment in human beings' is all the rage. As is so often the case with fads, the impetus has come from America. But studies of the returns from expenditures on education – to mention only the most important form of direct investment in the productivity of human beings – are not an American monopoly: the earliest work was done forty years ago in the Soviet Union and, in recent years, contributions have appeared in Mexico, Chile, Venezuela, and Israel. Rejection of this approach, however, does appear to be a national monopoly: Marshall's prescient comments notwithstanding, almost all the outspoken critics of what has come to be called the 'rate of return approach' to educational investment have been British; even the *Robbins Report*, while endorsing the investment-view of education in principle, expressed strong doubts on the side of measurement. The generally sceptical attitude in this country may account for the failure of the British Census of Population to secure the sort of information about earnings by age and education which is regularly collected by the decennial population census in the United States.

This paper is frankly intended as a defence of the investment approach to human resource development, with particular reference to formal education in a developed country such as Great Britain. It is not another survey of the literature.[1] Rather, it

1. For the few excellent examples of this genre, see W. G. Bowen, 'Assessing the economic contribution of education: An appraisal of alternative

attempts to meet the many objections that have been raised against rate-of-return calculations and to demonstrate that, so far as advanced industrialized economics are concerned, none of them is really convincing[2]. [. . .]

I. The Rate-of-Return Approach

Casual impression suggests that people who remain at school beyond the statutory leaving age attain, on average, higher lifetime earnings than people of similar ability and family background who enter the labour force as soon as they can. It is not immediately evident, however, that the extra future earnings outweigh the present costs incurred in staying at school. Therefore, the first task is to find a way of measuring the private yield of education, viewed as a type of investment by the individual in his own earning power. The standard method is to observe, for a particular year, and for different age cohorts, the net earnings differentials after tax that are associated with various amounts of education received, and then to calculate the internal rate of return which would equate the present value of these expected differentials, properly adjusted for income-determining factors other than education, to the private costs incurred in obtaining additional education. Social rates of return are derived from the private rates by allowing for the total public and private costs of

approaches', *Higher education. Report of the committee under the chairmanship of Lord Robbins* (*Robbins Report*). Cmd. 2154, London, 1963, IV, pp. 80–94, reprinted in *Economic aspects of higher education*, (ed.) S. E. Harris, Paris, 1964 [see Reading 5]. A. M. Rivlin, 'Research in the economics of higher education: Progress and problems', *Economics of higher education*, (ed.) S. J. Mushkin, Washington, 1962, pp. 360–73; F. Machlup, *The production and distribution of knowledge in the United States*, Princeton, 1963, pp. 110–20; T. W. Schultz, *The economic value of education*, New York, 1963, pp. 54–64; Lé Than Khôi, 'Le rendement de l'éducation', *Tiers-Monde*, janvier-mars, 1964, pp. 105–39; and M. J. Bowman, 'The new economics of education', *International Journal of the Educational Sciences*, vol. 1, no. 1 (1966), pp. 29–46.

2. I am indebted to G. S. Becker, M. J. Bowman, H. L. Elvin, P. R. G. Layard, A. T. Peacock, M. Peston, T. W. Schultz, M. Steuer, J. Wiseman, and M. Woodhall for suggestions and comments on an earlier version of this paper.

education, and by adding in earnings that are taxed away. In other words, lifetime earnings are estimated from cross-section data classified by age, and we solve for the discount rate at which the present costs of extra education would yield the prospective stream of extra earnings. The argument is usually confined to different *levels* of education, but the approach is equally suitable to different *types* of secondary schools, different *channels* of higher education, and even to on-the-job training as a substitute for formal education. Similarly, separate rates of return can be calculated for arts and science graduates, males and females, whites and non-whites, and natives and immigrants. Even in America, however, lack of data has so far held back research on the effects of different kinds as distinct from the effects of more or less education.

Before turning to the policy implications of the rate-of-return approach, which is our principal concern in this paper, we must pause for a moment to consider the significance of rate-of-return calculations for private behaviour. Some American writers have postulated the existence of a rational calculus of educational and occupational choice, that is, the ability to equalize the present values of alternative lifetime income streams, differing both in amount and time-shape. The student or his parent is conceived as choosing between no less than two lifetime income profiles, one with immediate but relatively low earnings which then increase only gradually over time, the other with no earnings for several years followed by steeply rising earnings after graduation; since future income means less than equivalent income now foregone, rational intertemporal choice involves the comparison and equalization, not of the *sums* of alternative lifetime income streams, but of their *present* values. As Adam Smith argued long ago, this implies relatively higher earnings in occupations that require additional schooling, or, turning it around, not obtaining additional schooling unless it leads to occupations with relatively higher earnings.[3]

3. 'When any expensive machine is erected, the extraordinary work to be performed by it before it is worn out, it must be expected, will replace the capital laid out upon it, with at least the ordinary profits. A man educated at the expense of much labour and time to any of those employments which require extraordinary dexterity and skill, may be compared to one of those

Are private educational decisions economically rational in this sense? How does one verify such an assumption? One way is simply to ask people. But although there is a vast body of social survey data that indicates that students are principally motivated by vocational considerations in deciding to stay at school beyond the compulsory leaving age,[4] the method of testing hypotheses by inquiring directly into personal motives is inherently unsatisfactory. It is not what students or their parents think they are doing but what they actually do that concerns us. It is preferable to check assumptions about motives by looking at the behaviour that is predicted by these assumptions.

The private rate of return on the costs of the three years required to complete secondary-school education in Great Britain in 1963 is about 13 per cent; the corresponding rate on three years of higher education is about 14 per cent.[5] These yields are about 50 per cent higher than those that can be earned by investing in equities and debentures. Even after allowing a considerable premium for the greater illiquidity and uncertainty of

---

expensive machines. The work which he learns to perform, it must be expected, over and above the usual wages of common labour, will replace to him the whole expense of his education, with at least the ordinary profits of an equally valuable capital.' Adam Smith, *The wealth of nations*, Bk I, pt I, ch. X.

4. E. Roper, *Factors affecting the admission of high school seniors to college*, Washington, D.C., 1949, p. 21; B. S. Hollinshead, *Who should go to college*, New York, 1952, pp. 138–85; C. C. Cole, Jr., *Encouraging scientific talent*, New Jersey, 1956, pp. 145–6, 163; M. Rosenberg, *Occupations and Values*, Glencoe, Ill., 1957, pp. 11–16; Ministry of Education, 15 *to* 18. *A report of the Central Advisory Council for Education, under the chairmanship of G. Crowther*. London, 1959, II, pp. 25–6; J. B. Lansing and C. Moriguchi, *How people pay for college*, Survey Research Center, Ann Arbor, 1960, pp. 119–46; W. D. Furneaux, *The chosen few*, London, 1961, pp. 58–62; J. N. Morgan, M. H. David, W. J. Cohen, and H. F. Brazer, *Income and welfare in the United States*, New York, 1962, pp. 356–7; *Robbins Report*, II(B), pp. 167–89; and R. Rice, 'The social and educational background and anticipated career prospects of a group of students in a college of advanced technology', *British Journal of Educational Psychology*, November 1964, pp. 264–5.

5. [See D. Henderson-Stewart, 'Appendix: estimate of the rate of return to education in Great Britain', *The Manchester School*, vol. 33 (1965), no. 3, pp. 252–62.]

investment in human capital, it appears that private rates of return on educational investment exceed the yield of risk capital in the business sector. Now, the *Robbins Report* demonstrated the existence in this country of an excess demand for places in higher education, defined as an excess of qualified school leavers who apply for admission over the number of qualified applicants admitted.[6] This finding is consistent with the assumption that students will not voluntarily choose additional education unless the extra years of school attendance promise a rate of return significantly in excess of the yield of alternative investment opportunities; in short, it is consistent with the hypothesis in question.[7] Unfortunately, given the artificial limitation on the supply of places in higher education in Great Britain, it is hardly surprising to find evidence of excess demand: until we know what determines the position of the social supply curve of places, we cannot infer from the existence of excess demand that the private demand curve for education is a function of the 'price' as defined by the yield of investment in schooling relative to the yield of all investment.[8]

6. For a definition of British 'higher education', see *Robbins Report*, I, pp. 12–13.

7. The reader may notice that we are switching back and forth between the language of the internal-rate-of-return or discounted-cash-flow approach (the rate which makes the algebraic sum of the discounted costs and benefits equal to zero) and that of the present-value rule (the value of the net returns when discounted to the present at a predetermined rate of interest), as if they were identical decision rules for ranking alternative investment proposals. But, in fact, the two criteria only lead to the same results if capital markets are perfectly competitive, if the contemplated proposals are completely divisible, if there are no interdependencies among the proposals, and if the benefits which are generated can be reinvested at their own internal rates of return up to the terminal date of the longer-lived alternative (for a review of the argument, see M. M. Dryden, 'Capital budgeting: Treatment of uncertainty and investment criteria', *Scottish Journal of Political Economy*, March 1963). It is obvious that the latter condition at any rate is violated with respect to earnings differentials associated with education, so that the strictly correct criterion, here as elsewhere, is the present-value rule, namely, that of accepting all income streams which have a positive present value at the market rate of interest. Nevertheless, this would give the same answers about educational choice in all the cases with which we will be concerned; the internal-rate-of-return criterion is employed in the text simply because it is more intuitively appealing.

8. Still, it is significant that the scarcity of university places in Great

Furthermore, a figure for a single year does not afford a very sensitive test of the hypothesis of a rational educational calculus. The American evidence, however, extends over two decades from 1939 to 1959 and, owing to the weight of private finance for higher education in the United States, there is virtually no rationing of places in American colleges. Looking at the private rates of return on investment in American high school and college education, as well as separate rates of return to additional years of high-school and college education for white males, women, and Negroes, it is interesting to find that all of these yields are in conformity with observed changes in school attendance rates and with differential rates of entry to college on the part of different sorts of students.[9]

There are, of course, many other explanations of the phenomena under investigation. A popular alternative hypothesis accounts for the post-war 'enrolment explosion' in most countries in terms of a radical shift in the taste for education, viewed as a consumer good. Unfortunately, this hypothesis will account for every observable change in the demand for education, whatever direction it takes. Another equally popular hypothesis is that a growing economy demands more skilled labour; students are perfectly aware of this trend and realize they require additional education. But this explanation turns into the rate-of-return hypothesis, provided one grants that students also realize that extra education is not free. Still another interpretation argues that the bulge in the birthrate and the changing social composition of secondary school students are entirely responsible for all the observed facts. The data, such as they are, are not yet capable of definitely rejecting any of the contending hypotheses. What we can

Britain first made itself felt in 1945–6 as a direct result of substantial grants for ex-service men and women under the Government's Further Education and Training Scheme (the British analogy to the American G.I. Bill). This extra demand had hardly been absorbed when the recommendations of the Minister of Education's Working Party on University Awards (1948) were put into effect, increasing the number and amounts of grants available to intending students to more than twice the pre-war levels, and thus sharply raising the private rate of return on investment in education.

9. See G. S. Becker, *Human capital. A theoretical and empirical analysis, with special reference to education*, Princeton, 1964, pp. 91–3, 95, 101, 103.

say at this stage is that it appears that students or their parents choose more education *as if* they were making a rational investment response to certain expected monetary and psychic returns. At any rate, no one has yet produced evidence that would falsify this assumption.[10]

The more interesting question is that of a possible conflict between the private demand for education as a function of prospective earnings and, hence, the demand from industry for educated people, and the public supply of school places as a function of the social rate of return on educational investment. The social as distinct from the private rate of return on three years of secondary schooling in this country is about 12·5 per cent; likewise, the social rate of return on six years of secondary and higher education is in the neighbourhood of 8 per cent. These yields are not very different from the rate of return which the State has come to expect from the nationalized industries. If the State decisions about education were rational in the same sense in which private decisions could be said to be rational, one might conclude that the recommendations of the *Robbins Report* were motivated by non-economic considerations. But that argument would beg the question: what is the maximand that determines the government's educational policy? When we calculate the social yield of education, we are not necessarily 'explaining' social decisions by testing some behavioural assumption, but rather attempting to clarify the nature of these decisions and, presumably, to affect them in some way. Thus, appraisals of the private and the social rate of return on investment in education call for quite different criteria of judgement. Neglect of this consideration has produced considerable confusion in the literature. Associated with this confusion is the argument that the private returns do not matter because the most important benefits of education are indirect and external to the educated individual. It is not always appreciated that even if this were true, it would still leave us with the task of explaining why people choose more or less education, or one kind of education rather than another: indirect economic benefits by definition do not determine individual choice. The indirect benefits of education, however, should enter into the calculation of

10. The problem is further explored in the author's paper: 'An economic interpretation of the private demand for education', *Economica*, May 1966.

the social rate of return which has another *raison d'être* than that of predicting behaviour. In what follows, we will rigidly distinguish between the private and the social level of discourse.

II. An Omnibus of Objections

A review of the literature on the subject shows that the various objections that have been advanced against rate-of-return calculations fall broadly into six classes: (1) education, earnings, endowed ability, individual motivation, and social class are all intercorrelated and no one has yet succeeded in satisfactorily isolating the pure effect of education on earnings; (2) it is assumed that people are motivated solely by consideration of the financial gains of additional school attendance, thus ignoring both the nonpecuniary attractions of certain occupations and the consumption benefits of education; (3) the calculations depend on the projection of future trends from cross-section evidence, thus neglecting historical improvements in the quality of education as well as the effect of the secular growth of education on prospective earnings differentials; (4) existing earnings differentials in favour of educated people reflect, not differences in their contribution to productive capacity, but rather long-established social conventions in an inherently imperfect labour market; hence, rate-of-return studies tell us nothing about the role of education in economic growth; (5) the direct benefits of education are quantitatively less important than the indirect spillover benefits and the latter are not adequately reflected in a social rate of return which simply relates income differentials before tax to the total resource costs of education; and (6) social rates of return have ambiguous policy implications because educational authorities have other goals than that of maximizing the net national product. We will now discuss each of these objections in turn.

III. Multiple Correlations among the Income-Determining Variables

The four leading critics of the rate-of-return approach – whom we will meet again and again in the following pages – all agree in denying the possibility of attributing a definite portion of the observed differentials in earnings to education alone.[11] There is a difficulty here and it must be conceded that most of the early contributions to the literature failed to standardize in any way for various income-determining factors other than education. But as early as 1954, one American study showed that the earnings of ex-students rose with additional years of college education even after adjusting for differences in I.Q. scores, class rank in high school, and father's occupation.[12] Since then we have been furnished with an exhaustive analysis of a national probability sample of heads of American households, isolating the pure effect of education on earnings with the aid of multivariate analysis that allows separately for all the various factors that influence the level of personal income: age, formal education, on-the-job training, sex, race, native intelligence, need-achievement drive,

11. According to J. Vaizey, 'There is a multiple correlation between parental wealth, parental income, access to educational opportunity, motivation in education, access to the best jobs and "success" in later life. Above all, there is sheer native wit and ability which will "out" despite all educational handicaps. It follows, then, that all the statistics may go to show is that incomes are unequal, and that education is unequally distributed; there may be no necessary causal relationship between education and income', *The economics of education*, London, 1962, p. 45; T. Balogh and P. P. Streeten agree: 'Expenditure on education is highly correlated to income and wealth of parents, to ability and motivation, to educational opportunities such as urban residence and proximity to educational centres, to access to well-paid jobs through family and other connections, any of which could either by itself or in conjunction with any of the others account for superior earnings', 'The coefficient of ignorance', *Bulletin of the Oxford University Institute of Economics and Statistics*, May 1963, p. 102. [See Reading 18.] The sole American critic carries the argument to its logical extreme: 'Amount of education is at least partly a matter of choice. As long as this is true, no matter how many factors have been considered, one can never be certain that there are not some unanalysed variables influencing the choice which in themselves are responsible for the income differential attributed to education', H. G. Shaffer, 'Investment in human capital: Comment', *American Economic Review*, December 1961, p. 1030 n. [See Reading 3.]

12. D. Wolfle, *America's resources of specialized talent*, New York, 1954; and D. Wolfle and J. G. Smith, 'The occupational value of education for superior high school graduates', *Journal of Higher Education*, April 1956, summarised by D. Wolfle in *Higher education in the United States. The economic problem*, (ed.) S. E. Harris, Cambridge, Mass., 1960, pp. 178–9.

parents' education, family size, father's occupation, religion, geographic region, city size, occupational choice, occupational mobility, mortality, unemployment, and hours of work.[13] Multivariate analysis assumes that variables do not interact with one another, so that their combined effect is simply the sum of their separate effects. Since the variables are themselves closely correlated, however, there is a tendency to remove too much and therefore to understate the pure effects of education, as the authors themselves are the first to point out.[14] Despite this built-in tendency towards over-adjustment, education emerges in this study as the single most powerful determinant of family income: to give a concrete example, factors other than age and education together 'explain' only 40 per cent of the gross unadjusted earnings differentials between high-school and college graduates in the age group 18–34, and only 12 per cent in the age group 35–74. As the authors conclude: 'objections to the use of simple average earnings of different age and education groups on the grounds of spurious correlation are correct but quantitatively not terribly important'.[15]

In his recent book on *Human capital*, Becker marshals all the available American evidence on the influence of ability, motivation, and home environment.[16] He observes that we now have five independent studies which standardize the earnings differentials between typical high-school and college graduates for various scattered measures of 'ability' and 'social class origins' – including a striking early study of the incomes of brothers with

13. Morgan, and others, op. cit., pp. 387–427.

14. For example, the most important factor determining the level of education achieved by the head of a household is not his I.Q. score or his ability measured in other ways, nor the income of his parents, but the educational attainment of his father (ibid., pp. 359–84, 391–2, 401–2). In drawing conclusions about the effects of education on earnings, this intergeneration effect is eliminated by assuming that a variable like father's education influences the earnings of the head of the household directly without affecting his terminal education age.

15. J. N. Morgan and M. H. David, 'Education and income', *Quarterly Journal of Economics*, August 1963, pp. 436–7. Owing to the tendency to over-adjust for ability and parental influences, they find only a modest rate of return of 4·6 per cent on school years completed for a 1960 cross-section of the United States.

16. Becker, op. cit., pp. 79–88.

different amounts of education[17] – all of which suggest that college education itself is the major determinant of the extra life-time income of college graduates. Allowing separately for I.Q., high-school-class rank, and father's occupation, Becker concludes that the ability-cum-social-class adjustment reduces the private rate of return on college education actually received by a typical college graduate from 13 per cent to 11·5 per cent, and the rate that may be expected by a typical high-school graduate from 13 per cent to just under 10 per cent, depending on whether we standardize the earnings of college graduates for the distribution of ability among college students or among high-school students. Similarly, Denison, using much the same material, has now concluded that 66 per cent of the gross earnings differentials between college and high-school graduates is due to education alone.[18] Translating Denison's figure into rate-of-return terminology, it appears that both authors agree more or less on the magnitude of the required adjustment, leaving education substantially unaffected as a generator of higher future earnings.

The British figures, given above, referred to earnings differentials *attributable* to education, that is, after multiplying the gross earnings differentials by the 'Denison coefficient' alpha, varying from 0·6 for secondary-school leavers to 0·66 for those with higher education, to take account of the fact that some of the observed differentials associated with extra education are attributable to individual differences in ability and family environment. In the absence of definitive British evidence, it is not clear whether it is legitimate to apply an American alpha-coefficient to British earnings: on the one hand, the stock of education embodied in the labour force is smaller in Britain than the United States, which argues for a premium on education in this country

17. D. E. Gorseline, *The effect of schooling upon income*, Bloomington, Ind. (1932).

18. E. F. Denison, 'Proportion of income differentials among education groups due to additional education: The evidence of the Wolfle–Smith survey', *The residual factor and economic growth*, (ed.) J. Vaizey, Paris, 1964, p. 97. In his book *The sources of economic growth in the United States*, New York, 1962, pp. 69–70, he assumed arbitrarily that the correct figure was 67·7 per cent, derived from an equally arbitrary figure of 60 per cent of the gross income differentials between elementary school graduates and all those with additional education.

and hence a higher value for alpha; on the other hand, the tripartite character of British secondary education suggests that the selective effects of social class determinants operate with much greater force here than in the United States, and this argues for a lower alpha-value. On balance, it is likely that an alpha-coefficient of 0·6 for secondary-school leavers is somewhat on the high side, given the finding that 'early leaving' is highly correlated with social class.[19] But, in the same sense, the true alpha-coefficient for university graduates is probably much in excess of 0·66. Once students have entered advanced sixth forms, the divisive influence of social-class membership, with all that it implies in differential home background, has largely ceased to operate: the evidence shows that it has very little effect in deciding whether a student in the upper sixth applies to a university, none at all in determining whether he is accepted or not, and very little in governing his performance in university courses.[20] Social-class origins is only one of the components of the alpha-coefficient; nevertheless, it is not to be doubted that students in higher education are more homogeneous with respect to measured ability than secondary-school students. In consequence, the social rate of return on investment in higher education in Great Britain, looked upon as a yield actually received rather than an anticipated yield, is nearer 9 than 6·5 per cent.[21]

Nothing we have said denies the fact that social-class origins, in this country as well as in the United States, largely determine who it is that obtains additional education; nevertheless, they do not explain why the better educated receive higher lifetime incomes. In other words, those who stay on at school voluntarily beyond the leaving age seem to require secondary and higher education to translate favourable home background and superior measured ability into higher earnings.[22] Summing up: it is perfectly true

19. The evidence for Great Britain is set forth in the *Robbins Report*, I, pp. 38–84.

20. See Furneaux, op. cit., p. 71; *Robbins Report*, pp. 52–3, and *Robbins Report*, II(A), pp. 135–6, 155–6.

21. See Henderson-Stewart, op. cit., chart III.

22. Needless to say, this is only true on average for given age cohorts. So long as abilities to learn, opportunities to learn, and quality of schools differ, some individuals with less education will earn more than their better educated contemporaries. Indeed, there is considerable variation in the

that better educated people have better educated parents, come from smaller homes, obtain financial help more easily, live in cities, are better motivated, achieve higher scores on intelligence and aptitude tests, attain better academic grade records, gain more from self-education, and generally live longer and are healthier. But unless we adopt Shaffer's methodological position that all correlations are worthless if they are not simple correlations, we must arrive at the conclusion that the critics are simply wrong when they state that 'there is no demonstrable connexion between education and later earnings which is also not as close as the connexion between birth and earnings'.[23] Apparently it takes a university graduate to believe that endowed ability is the major cause of the higher earnings of university graduates!

We have not quite finished, however, with the problems created by multiple correlations. Apart from all their other advantages, educated people also tend to receive more on-the-job training than less educated individuals.[24] Hence, earnings differentials attributable to education include the monetary returns to associated on-the-job training. Indeed, the same is true of other forms of human capital formation: for example, the income benefits of education differ for each different level of investment in medical care. Contrary to intuitive impression, however, this only biases one's estimates of the rate of return on education if the yield of these other forms of investment in human beings differs systematically from the yield of education. When the yields are the same, expenditures on labour training or health simply add as much to the costs as to the returns of human capital. In the absence of any knowledge of these other rates of return, therefore, there is no reason to think that we have necessarily over or underestimated, the rate of return on education.[25]

rates of return within age cohorts. (See H. P. Miller, 'Annual and lifetime income in relation to education', *American Economic Review*, December 1960, p. 963; Becker, op. cit., pp. 104–13.)

23. J. Vaizey, 'The role of education in economic development', *Planning education for social and economic development*, (ed.) H. S. Parnes, Paris, 1963, p. 40.

24. J. Mincer, 'On-the-job training: Costs, returns, and some implications', *Journal of Political Economy*, Supplement: October 1962, pp. 59–60.

25. Becker, op. cit., pp. 88–90. See also Mincer's brief discussion of the rates of return on formal education *versus* on-the-job training, op. cit., pp. 63–6.

IV. The Psychic Returns to Education

We will forego the pleasure of documenting the argument that rate-of-return calculations ignore the consumption-benefits of education and the nonpecuniary benefits of certain occupations that are only accessible to the highly educated: it has been mentioned not only by every critic but also by every advocate of the investment-approach to education. The standard method of dealing with the consumption aspects is either to subtract a notional consumption component from educational costs or to add some estimate of the consumption-benefits to the monetary returns.[26] In either case, of course, the effect is to increase the yield of investment in education.

However, the tacit premise that the psychic returns from consuming education are necessarily positive requires further examination. In the first place, the essential distinction that is being made is between present and future satisfactions, that is, between the enjoyment of education for its own sake and the anticipated enjoyment of a higher monetary and/or psychic income in the future. A large part of what is usually thought of as the consumption component of education is, in fact, forward looking, involving the consumption over time of the services of a durable consumer good; motivated as it is by utilities that accrue in the future, it is more akin to investment than to consumption. No doubt, this sort of consumption-benefit is positive and ought to be added to the rate of return on investment in education. But the same thing is not true of the current consumption of education, which, for all we know, may have negative utility for the average student.[27] And if this be granted, perhaps we ought to subtract something from the rate of return as conventionally calculated.

The more we think about it, the more we realize how arbitrary is any assertion about the consumption-benefits of education, whether they are reaped in the present or in the future. Since tastes are directly affected by schooling, we are faced with making

26. Schultz, op. cit., pp. 8, 54–6; Bowen, op. cit., p. 89.
27. The fact that the major single cause of drop-outs is poor educational performance suggests that there is enormous variation in the value that different students would assign to the present enjoyment of education.

intertemporal comparisons of utility with a yardstick that is itself constantly changing: the value for a sixth former of the future enjoyment of university education is surely different from his appraisal after university graduation? It is true that there is an extraordinary consensus on the positive psychic benefits of education, but it is a consensus of educated people whose taste for learning has been affected by the learning process itself. It is not so much that the belief that education makes for a richer life is a value judgement but that it is *ex post facto* and, hence, of a different kind from the *ex ante* value judgement that governs the choice to acquire more education. John Stuart Mill used to say that 'the uncultivated cannot be competent judges of cultivation', but he did not realize that the converse is just as true. Is it meaningful to ask someone with a Ph.D. to debate the proposition that ignorance is bliss?[28]

It could be argued that the decision to stay at school beyond the statutory age is typically made by parents, while the choice of subjects to study is left to the student. Hence, the decision to choose more or less education is, indeed, made by someone who places an unambiguously positive value on both the present and the future consumption-benefits of education. In this case, the question whether we have biased the rate of return downwards by ignoring the consumption benefits turns into a question of fact: do students and parents agree about the value of remaining at school beyond the leaving age?[29] It would seem that at this stage we simply do not know whether to add or to subtract the consumption-benefits from the investment-benefits of education. This is not to say that we can never find out. If people's choices

28. The discrepancy between expected and realized satisfactions is a familiar problem in welfare economics. It is usually slurred over by interpreting the standard assumption of constant tastes to mean perfect foresight on the part of each individual about his preferences for future as yet unexperienced satisfactions. Even if we accept this interpretation for general purposes, it seems inadmissible in treating the welfare aspects of education, for education alters rather than widens the range of choices.

29. Summarizing all the evidence of public opinion polls taken of cross sections of the American population as far back as possible, A. J. Jaffe and W. Adams conclude: 'A much smaller proportion of the children have attitudes and intentions favourable to college enrolment than do the parents': 'College education for U.S. youth: The attitudes of parents and children', *American Journal of Economics and Sociology*, July 1964, p. 273.

about education were found to be inconsistent with conventionally calculated private rates of return, it might mean that they were motivated by the consumption-benefits. For the time being, however, the consumption hypothesis may be ruled out by Occam's Razor.

As soon as we tackle questions of social policy, however, the consumption-benefits come back to plague us. If the electorate is persuaded that education is a good thing in its own right, the *social* rate of return computed from earnings differentials attributable to education must be viewed as a minimum figure, to which something must be added to reflect the value of education as a consumer good. This solution will not satisfy everyone, for there are educators who appear to believe that the economist's mania for quantifying everything will lead to a perversion of the human values of education. Be that as it may, the point of calculating the social rate of return is simply that it provides a summary of the measurable economic effects of education. If it is asserted that certain immeasurable effects are more important, it does at least permit separation of the positive and normative elements in such declarations of faith.

We come now to a different kind of psychic income from education: the nonpecuniary benefits of certain occupations which require more than average education. Nonpecuniary attractions as such create no special problems for our purposes: it is true that they give rise to compensating variations in earnings but this does not matter provided the nonpecuniary attraction is a feature of the job, equally attractive to all job applicants. Unfortunately, studies of the prestige-ranking of occupations suggest that more educated people attach a higher than average value to the nonpecuniary aspects of work. Thus, occupations with considerable nonpecuniary benefits are highly correlated with the distribution of education in the labour force, and to ignore this factor is to *under*state the private rate of return to education.[30]

It is not obvious that the magnitude of this bias is very large. Certainly, it is not significant enough to reverse the positive correlation between education and monetary earnings for given age groups. But once again, the problem takes on new colours when

30. Shaffer, op. cit., pp. 1031–2.

we consider the social rather than the private rate of return. From the viewpoint of social policy, nonpecuniary alternatives can be dismissed as a neutral factor. The reason for this, as Bowen explains, is that they affect only the supply and not the demand for labour, and, therefore, do not distort the relationship between earnings and a man's productive contribution to national output.[31] Employers can offer less for attractive jobs; hence, two jobs differing in their nonpecuniary attractions, but otherwise the same, will differ in relative earnings but this difference will simply reflect the relative scarcities of labour available for the two jobs. The only exception to this is the case where nonpecuniary attractions take the form of fringe benefits that impose extra costs on the employer – for example, paid holidays, expense accounts, subsidized housing, and so forth. Since it is likely that such fringe benefits occur more frequently in education-intensive industries, an upward adjustment is required in the social rate of return to education. Thus, nonpecuniary alternatives impart a downward bias to both the private and the social rates of return, but the two biases are not uniquely related because they spring from different causes.

V. Current Earnings and Lifetime Earnings

Rate-of-return analysis of education usually involves a time-series projection of earnings from cross-section data. [. . .]

The diffusion of more and more education in successive age cohorts tends, everything else being the same, to narrow earnings differentials at any age level. There is the danger, therefore, that future income differentials will, in fact, be smaller than those indicated by present cross-section statistics. This suggests that there may be an inherent upward bias in present methods of estimating the rate of return to investment in education, a fact which has played some role in sapping confidence about the entire approach.

The standard answer to this objection is to point to American evidence that the earnings differentials between high-school and college graduates have remained fairly constant since 1939, apparently because the demand for more educated workers has

31. Bowen, op. cit., pp. 83–4.

been rising at about the same rate as the supply of college graduates. Indeed, in the last decade, the differentials in the United States seem to have widened rather than narrowed.[32] Thus, it seems that cross-section data do not necessarily yield irrelevant results. But this conclusion is subject to one qualification. To the extent that the quality of education is improving all the time, so that each new cohort of school leavers is better educated than the last, estimates of lifetime earnings from current earnings do *under*state the expected rate of return on education. Balogh and Streeten seem to have this in mind when they say: 'Since the time-flow over a lifetime of the earnings of the educated is quite different from that of the uneducated, lifetime earnings now must be calculated as returns on education in the nineteen-twenties. To conclude from those returns anything about today's returns is like identifying a crystal radio set with Telstar.'[33] Unfortunately, we know very little about secular changes in the quality of educational output. We cannot even agree on the meaning of 'quality' in education, and so far there have been few serious efforts to measure it. Still, the best guess is that it has been improving at all levels.[34] But to compare it with improvements in the output of the radio industry over the last generation is to grossly exaggerate a well-taken point.

The possibility of error in the projection of lifetime earnings can be built directly into the calculated rates of return, in the form of an upper and lower limit for each stated error-factor.

32. H. P. Miller, 'Income in relation to education', *American Economic Review*, December 1960, pp. 967–9; and J. Morgan and C. Lininger, 'Education and income: Comment', *Quarterly Journal of Economics*, May 1964, pp. 346–8. The differentials in question refer to the *absolute* income on investment in education. Since the better educated receive higher earnings, a decline in relative earnings differentials is compatible with an increase in absolute earnings differentials. Surprisingly enough, however, relative earnings differentials associated with extra education seem also to have widened in the same decade. (See Becker, op. cit., pp. 52–5, 128–35, for a discussion of trends in the rates of return to education since 1900.)

33. Balogh and Streeten, op. cit., p. 102.

34. Some material indicators of the improvement are: the rise in the number of days attended per school-year; the growth in the number of qualified teachers; the rise in the real earnings of teachers; the rise in current expenditures per student; the rise in capital expenditures per student; and so forth.

Suppose we had over- or under-estimated next year's earnings differentials associated with extra education by one per cent, and the following year's differentials by another one per cent, compounding the error each year by a further one per cent; this mistake would mean that earnings differentials fifty years hence would in fact be more than 50 per cent greater, or about 35 per cent less, than what we had assumed. Nevertheless, this would only reduce the rate of return on investment in education by about one per cent, for the simple reason that the early years get a much heavier weight.[35] The rate of return is not sensitive to the entire age–earnings profiles of educated people; provided we correctly project the next five or ten years' earnings, significant shifts in earning patterns in three or four decades do not substantially affect the results.

When all is said and done, cross-section data have a distinct advantage over genuine life-cycle data in that they are free from the influence of the trade cycle and implicitly provide estimates in money of constant purchasing power. Furthermore, they reflect the way in which private choices are actually made; an average person forms his expectations of the financial benefits of additional years of schooling by comparing the present earnings of different occupations requiring various amounts of education, that is, by cross-section comparisons.

Cross-section earnings data have the further advantage of providing reliable estimates of the cost of student-time as a resource input in the educational system. The appropriate measure of this input is the earnings of people of similar age, ability, and prior education who are currently in employment, and this information can be read off directly from age–education–earnings data for a given year. Students' time is, of course, only one of the inputs, the others being the time of teachers and administrators, and the use of buildings, equipment, and materials. Although the latter are measured directly by 'what is put in', while the former is measured indirectly by 'what is done without', the distinction is one of statistical expediency, not of theoretical principle: after all, the actual money outlays on teachers, plant, and equipment are themselves only estimates of the goods and services foregone for other purposes. Admittedly, all these estimates, including that of

35. See Henderson-Stewart, op. cit.

earnings foregone, are only reliable indicators of opportunity costs for *marginal* changes. For example, for a major shift in resource allocation, such as raising the school-leaving age by a year, the use of cross-section earnings to estimate the value of students' time minimizes the consequent loss in output. Similarly, since there is evidence that the personal incidence of unemployment is correlated with the amount of education received, estimates of earnings foregone in a less than fully employed economy will tend to understate the loss in output from additional investment in education when this extra investment forms part of a general spending policy designed to secure full employment.[36]

All this may sound like a parade of well-worn truths but, alas, these truths have not won universal assent. According to Vaizey, 'the inclusion of income foregone in the costs of education opens the gate to a flood of approximations which would take the concept of national income away from its origin as an estimation of the measurable flows of the economy'. Furthermore, he adds, 'if income foregone is added to educational costs, it must also be added to other sectors of the economy (notably housewives, mothers, unpaid sitters-in, voluntary work of all sort)'; also 'it would be necessary to adjust the costs by some notional estimate of the benefits incurred while being educated, and these are usually considerable'.[37] Upon close inspection, it appears that this paragraph consists of a misunderstanding of national income accounting, followed by two non sequiturs.[38] To measure the net flow of goods and services in the economy is one thing; to measure the real cost of a particular activity is another. The fallacy of identifying the two is made apparent by substituting 'unemployment' for 'education' in Vaizey's leading sentence. The equivalent argument then reads: it would be wrong to include incomes foregone in a calculation of the cost of unemployment because measured national income does not include the goods

36. For a definitive discussion of these problems, see M. J. Bowman, 'The costing of human resource development', *The economics of education. Conference of the International Economic Association*, (eds.) G. E. A. Robinson and J. Vaizey, London, Macmillan, 1966. See also B. A. Weisbrod, 'Education and investment in human capital', *Journal of Political Economy*, Supplement: October 1962, pp. 122–3.

37. Vaizey, *Economics of education*, p. 43.

38. See Becker, op. cit., p. 74 n.

and services the unemployed would have produced if they had been working.

These have not always been Vaizey's views.[39] In recent writings, however, he has reiterated his objections to counting earnings foregone, and his views have received some endorsement.[40] All this is very surprising from an author who, in other contexts, seems perfectly amenable to 'a flood of approximations'. For example, after discussing and finally rejecting the rate-of-return approach in *The economics of education*, Vaizey turns suddenly to cost–benefit analysis of public works, explains the methods that were used to calculate the probable costs and anticipated benefits of the London–Birmingham Motorway, and concludes 'this is the most realistic procedure for calculating the returns to investment in education', without any indication of the fact that cost–benefit analysis is exactly the same thing as rate-of-return analysis![41]

We conclude that, whatever the temptation of making out the most appealing case for additional education expenditures by leaving out some of the costs, we must take account of the earnings foregone by students in calculating both the private and the social rate of return, and this, in fact, has been the standard practice.[42] The necessity of doing so in calculating the social yield

39. In *The costs of education*, London, 1958, p. 125, he admitted that 'the education accounts understate the true cost to the economy of the educational expenditure' by the amount of 'the wages that people would have earned'. And in an article on 'Education as investment in comparative perspective', *Comparative Education Review*, October 1961, p. 99, he actually estimated the incomes foregone by students in the United Kingdom but mistakenly added to this their maintenance costs. In this article he also remarked parenthetically that 'it is clearly important that investment in different levels of education should be compared with appropriate rates of return', (p. 101).

40. See Vaizey, *Planning education for social and economic development*, p. 40; R. F. Lyons, 'Formulating recommendations on educational needs', ibid., pp. 246–7; Balogh and Streeten, op. cit., pp. 101–2; S. E. Harris, 'General problems of education and manpower', *Economic aspects of higher education*, (ed.) S. E. Harris, Paris, 1964, pp. 13, 50–51, 56; J. Burkhead, *Public school finance. Economics and politics*, Syracuse, 1964, p. 5.

41. *Economics of education*, pp. 48–9.

42. See Schultz, op. cit., pp. 27–32. The memorandum submitted by H.M. Treasury to the Robbins Committee allows for the fact that students would consume more if they were working by deducting from earnings

is almost self-evident. But even with respect to the private yield, to ignore foregone earnings is to seriously misrepresent the nature of private decisions about education: it is foregone earnings that explain why so many able children from low-income families do not stay at school beyond the statutory age, despite the fact that the out-of-pocket costs of continuing school are minimal, particularly in this country. The American evidence suggests that foregone earnings constitute over half of the total resource costs of high school and college and about 75 per cent of the private costs borne by students. In Great Britain, foregone earnings represent 34 per cent of the total costs of higher education and nearly 100 per cent of the private costs, given the fact that student grants now cover nearly all approved fees and maintenance costs.[43] Standard grants for maintenance even cover about 40 per cent of earnings foregone but they still leave the average student paying indirectly for about 25 per cent of the total costs of higher education. In consequence, even free university education would not be completely free, and the private rate of return to university education is far from being infinitely high.

VI. A Non-Competitive Labour Market?

'The wage-system,' according to Vaizey, 'is in fact a system of administered prices. Therefore, these measurements of the rate of

---

foregone by students the difference between consumption as students and consumption if not students (*Robbins Report*, *Evidence*, I, pp. 1973–5). But this appears to be a mistake: the fact that an individual consumes less if he is a student does not reduce the loss of output involved in keeping him at school; what it does is raise the real income of the rest of the community at the expense of the student. Unless we argue that the welfare of students counts less heavily than the welfare of the employed population, there are no grounds for treating the asceticism of students as a reduction in the resource costs of education. Even from the point of view of the private calculus, reduced consumption is one of the sacrifices of alternatives which ought to be included in our estimates of what the student foregoes to stay at school.

43. *Robbins Report*, II(B), pp. 216–23; IV, pp. 148, 153.

return to education are measuring the consequences of a process of market imperfections so serious as to invalidate the results.'[44] Balogh and Streeten include the point about imperfect labour markets in a more comprehensive indictment of rate-of-return analysis: 'The American data, which are mostly used, do not provide evidence whether expenditure on education is a *cause* or *effect* of superior incomes; they do not show, even if we could assume it to be a condition of higher earnings, whether it is a *sufficient* or *necessary* condition of growth, and they do not separate *monopolistic* and *other forces* influencing differential earnings, which are correlated with, but not caused by, differential education.' To which they add, a page later: 'Much of the higher earnings is not a return on education but a monopoly rent on (1) the scarcity of parents who can afford to educate their children well and (2) the restrictions in members permitted into a profession in which existing members have a financial interest in maintaining scarcity.'[45]

The issue before us is, not whether there are imperfections in the labour market, but whether these are so significant as to invalidate rate-of-return calculations. It is not immediately evident where to draw the line, but, presumably, what is meant is a situation in which relative earnings do not correspond systematically to relative marginal productivities and, hence, do not uniquely reflect a worker's contribution to the national product. Do the critics really mean what they say? Vaizey, for example, having flatly declared that wages are administered prices, goes on to argue that a shortage of a particular skill leads to a rise in the earnings of that skill, or to queues of firms if market imperfections keep wages 'below what they would have been under free competition'.[46] Similarly, an excess supply leads to a decline in salaries: 'teaching has become a profession . . . whose relative salary position has deteriorated, reflecting a growing abundance of educated talent and a decline in the quality of teachers'.[47] Thus he, at any rate, concedes that the market mechanism governs the level of wages and salaries, even the salaries of teachers which,

44. Vaizey, *Economics of education*, p. 45.
45. Balogh and Streeten, op. cit., pp. 101, 102.
46. Vaizey, op. cit., pp. 105–6.
47. ibid., p. 110; also p. 112.

after all, are administered by the State.[48] And to say that the market forces impinge upon wages and salaries is equivalent to saying that earnings are being continuously brought into line with relative productivities.

Of course, it is not enough to assert that earnings by and large reflect the push and pull of market forces. Such a defence is so vague that no observation could refute it. The major testable implications of a competitive theory of wages and salaries are (1) that positive excess demand for a skill leads to a rise in its price and (2) that the price of a skill varies directly with the cost of acquiring it. If these implications were refuted by experience, we would indeed be justified in regarding earnings as administered prices. But, as a matter of fact, there is more than enough evidence to show that earnings do rise in a seller's market and, in addition, the very data in question show that higher earnings do accrue to people who have invested in acquiring special skills. In short, the shoe is really on the other foot: if relative earnings reflect, not relative productivities, but family connexions, traditional conventions, the snob-value of a university degree, nepotism, entry restrictions in trade unions and professional organizations, politically determined wage administration or any other market imperfection one might care to mention, how is it that more than 60 per cent of gross earnings differentials are directly attributable to education alone?

Rate-of-return analysis, despite what critics are always implying, does not assume that markets are competitive. On the contrary, it affords a test of the hypothesis that labour markets are competitive. The notion that a relatively high rate of return to education and training in some professions is due simply to

48. It must be kept in mind that 45 per cent of the 450,000 university graduates and about 60 per cent of the 750,000 people with full-time higher education in Great Britain in 1961 were public servants, that is, worked in education, health, civil service, local government, armed forces, nationalized industries, and government research establishments, with as many as 45 per cent of those with full-time higher education teaching in schools, colleges, and universities (see C. A. Moser and R. G. Layard, 'Planning the scale of higher education in Britain: Some statistical problems', *Journal of the Royal Statistical Society*, December 1964, Table 6). Thus, the yield of investment in higher education is decisively influenced by salary patterns in the public sector.

monopolistic restrictions on entry can be verified by a rate-of-return comparison between professions with similar educational qualifications but different entry restrictions. In fact, a pioneering study in this field did just that when it demonstrated that the life-time earnings of physicians in America exceeded that of othe. equally educated professionals, owing to the restrictive practices of the American Medical Association.[49] It is ironic that the critics who attack rate-of-return analysis because they believe labour markets are typically non-competitive close the door to one of the models that could test this belief.

We have been arguing as if rate-of-return analysis depended upon the absence of significant imperfections in the labour market. But, as a matter of fact, the only imperfections that really matter are those that are directly related to the education received by members of the labour force. For example, suppose it were true that trade unions raised wages in unionized industries relative to the unorganized sectors of the economy. Since the majority of union members have received little extra voluntary education, this sort of departure from a competitive labour market would not affect the rate of return to education. On the other hand, if business firms really do practise 'conspicuous consumption' of university graduates for reasons of prestige, paying them more than they are really worth, as is so often alleged, it is difficult to attach any meaning to a calculated rate of return on investment in higher education. But is it reasonable to believe that industry would waste £300 to £500 per worker on a quarter of a million people?

We come now to an objection which all the critics, and particularly Balogh and Streeten, have linked with the question of competitive labour markets: even if it is granted that more education leads to higher earnings, rate-of-return studies do not tell us whether education is 'a sufficient or necessary condition of growth'. The first point to emphasize is that rate-of-return analysis is not directly concerned with assessing the role of

49. M. Friedman and S. Kuznets, *Incomes from independent professional practice*, New York, 1946. For a similar treatment of scientists and engineers, see J. C. De Haven, *The relation of salary to the supply of scientists and engineers*, The Rand Corporation P-1372-RC. Santa Monica, 1958, unpublished.

education in economic growth. Instead, it is addressed to the more mundane question of efficient allocation of resources among competing uses. The reason that these two questions have become hopelessly confused in the literature is, no doubt, that Denison in *The sources of economic growth* used earnings differentials attributable to education as weights to construct an index of labour inputs.[50] What he did was to ascribe a definite part of the historical improvement in the quality of labour to additional education and then to treat these and other changes in quality as equivalent to changes in the quantity of labour. Of course, the level of education of the labour force has not increased uniformly for all age cohorts and so Denison introduced three-fifths of the observed income differentials between males of similar age, classified by years of education, as weights to combine the different cohorts into a composite index.[51] Denison's book presents a model of the American economy in terms of an aggregate production function obeying the condition of constant returns to scale; given this condition, the marginal product of every input will be a constant multiple of its average product and, therefore, the contribution of every input to total output will be identical to the input's relative share of national income. It is this corollary of a constant-returns-to-scale production function which imparts numerical precision to Denison's calculations of the various sources of economic growth, including education. It is perfectly possible to believe that earnings differentials are largely attributable to education, and even that education contributes to economic growth, without accepting the concept of an aggregate production function, much less that it is linear and homogeneous.[52] There is, indeed, no logical connexion between Denison's estimate of the fraction of growth attributable to education and the finding of a particular rate of return to investment in education. It would not be necessary to say this were it not that the sins of the former are forever being visited upon the latter.

50. [See Reading 5.]

51. For a more detailed explanation, see M. Abramovitz, 'Economic growth in the United States. A review article', *American Economic Review*, September 1962, pp. 769–71.

52. Denison later allows for increasing returns to scale as a separate source of growth but the basic model depends on the properties of a linear homogeneous production function.

Furthermore, rate-of-return calculations as such will never establish whether education is either a necessary or a sufficient condition for growth. It can at best create a presumption that education contributes to growth, for there is always the possibility, however unlikely, that it merely redistributes an income pool, which is growing for other reasons, from the uneducated to the educated. Analogously, if the growing use of computers in industry improved the quality of the existing capital stock, a positive rate of return on investment in computers would not imply that more computers would suffice to produce growth or that the economy would not grow at all without more computers. The really disputable issue is not so much whether education is one of the sources of growth, but whether it is a more significant source than physical capital or other types of social expenditures. And in this regard, what is important is not only the rates of return on investment in human and physical capital, but also the way in which these investments are typically financed. As Denison has remarked, even if the yield of education were less than the yield of business capital, it is possible that the diversion of resources from private industry to education would raise national income and contribute to economic growth as conventionally measured if, as seems likely, private investment tends to be financed out of savings whereas additional private and public funds for education tend to be financed out of consumption expenditures.[53] Of course, the effects of an increase in taxation on saving and spending depends on the character of the extra taxes and their incidence on particular income groups. Given the British system of educational finance, it would be difficult to associate any particular tax change with a change in educational expenditures so as to distinguish the tax-elasticity of saving and of consumption. Nevertheless, the general point is that it cannot be assumed even in a fully employed economy that an extra pound sterling for education would necessarily displace an equivalent amount of investment in physical capital.

Similarly, we cannot simply multiply the cost of education by the rate of return to education to obtain a measure of education's contribution to national income. The calculated yield of investment in education depends upon the age pattern of an average

53. Denison, *The sources of economic growth*, pp. 77–8.

differential lifetime earnings stream; it would have to be age-specific to be the type of coefficient which can derive the contribution of an investment to national income, once the cost of the investment is known. As Mary Jean Bowman observes, in her clarification of this analytical tangle: 'When the purpose is to measure education's contribution to national income growth, to discount returns is logically incorrect; what is relevant is the sequential current inputs of Eds ("embodied education") and their contribution as these emerge in a series of undiscounted presents.'[54]

Lastly, educational expenditures are counted in national income as consumption and, therefore, gross of depreciation and maintenance of the educational stock embodied in the labour force; this ignores the fact that the existing stock is being continuously used up as time passes. In other words, we include in *net* national income the *net* additions to the stock of physical capital, as a measure of the net returns from the use of physical capital, but the *gross* additions to the stock of human capital, with the result that the contribution of education to future productive capacity, whatever it is, is always smaller than the contribution of education to national income. To reinforce the point, no allowance is made in measured national income for student-time as an investment cost of education. It follows, for all the reasons given, that we cannot jump directly from calculations of rates of return on educational investment to conclusions about economic growth.[55]

VII. The Indirect Benefits of Education

Having rejected all existing methods of measuring the direct returns to education, Vaizey nevertheless affirms that 'expenditure

54. M. J. Bowman, 'Schultz, Denison, and the contribution of "Eds" to national income growth', *Journal of Political Economy*, October 1964, p. 453.

55. The converse also holds, contrary opinion notwithstanding: 'I am more agnostic on the matter of the contribution of education to economic growth than a number of recent converts to the cause. I am doubtful whether, in the long run, the concept of education as "investment" will prove much of a guide on what "ought" to be spent on education', J. Vaizey, 'Criteria for public expenditures on education', *Economics of education*, op. cit.

on education pays', by virtue of the fact that 'the indirect benefits of education are so great that its direct benefits are not necessarily the most important aspect'.[56] This point of view is widely shared, even by economists who, in analysing the returns to educational investment, have despaired of ever quantifying the indirect benefits of education. The critics, therefore, can hardly be blamed for seizing on this difficulty as the Achilles heel of the rate-of-return approach.

A careful specification of the variety of indirect benefits immediately reveals the cause of the despair that so many writers have voiced.[57] A less than exhaustive compilation of the indirect benefits of education that have been cited in the literature yields the following list: (1) the current spillover income gains to persons other than those who have received extra education; (2) the spillover income gains to subsequent generations from a better educated present generation; (3) the supply of a convenient mechanism for discovering and cultivating potential talents; (4) the means of assuring occupational flexibility of the labour force and, thus, to furnish the skilled manpower requirements of a growing economy; (5) the provision of an environment that stimulates research in science and technology; (6) the tendency to encourage lawful behaviour and to promote voluntary responsibility for welfare activities, both of which reduce the demand on social services; (7) the tendency to foster political stability by developing an informed electorate and competent political leadership; (8) the supply of a certain measure of 'social control' by the transmission of a common cultural heritage; and (9) the enhancement of the enjoyment of leisure by widening the intellectual horizons of both the educated and the uneducated. Merely to scan the list is to discover the difficulty: if all these are to be quantified, we are indeed defeated at the outset. But why demand

56. Vaizey, *Economics of education*, pp. 46, 150; see also Vaizey, *Planning education for social and economic development*, pp. 40, 51–2.

57. For a similar specification to the one that follows, see the suggestive paper by A. T. Peacock and J. Wiseman, 'Economic growth and the principles of educational finance in developed countries', *Financing of education for economic growth*, (ed.) O.E.C.D., Paris, 1966. (Reprinted in *Economics of education 2*.) See also M. J. Bowman, 'The social returns to education', *International Social Science Journal*, vol. 14 (1962), no. 4, pp. 647–60; B. A. Weisbrod, *External benefits of public education: An economic analysis*, Princeton, 1964, pp. 28–37.

more quantitative knowledge about the effects of education than economists are wont to demand from other economic phenomena? After all, we do not give way to despair because we cannot measure the total direct and indirect benefits of industrialization. We simply admit that economics is only 'part of the story', albeit an important part, and leave it at that. Surely similar humility is in order with respect to education.

To come to grips with the problem, we must distinguish the economic from the non-economic consequences and confine ourselves to the former. A minimum demand is that we quantify the effect of better-educated people on the earned income of the less educated. Ideally, we would like to quantify the economic benefits to each individual of every other individual having been educated. Unfortunately it is not immediately evident how many rounds of activity will be embraced in such an ideal calculation, with the result that interpersonal effects and intertemporal effects are straightway confused. Moreover, it is not easy to decide whether we mean that better educated people raise the total incomes of other people irrespective of their education, or the marginal incomes of other people as a function of their education. In short, even the simple concept of income spillovers is fraught with difficulties.[58]

Be that as it may, we will define the increments in the current earnings of $a, b, c, \ldots, n - 1$ from the additional education of n as the 'first-round spillovers'. It is universally believed that these are positive, though this is by no means obvious; we have not even begun to spell out the nature of these 'employment-related' external benefits, to use Weisbrod's language, but presumably they take the form of educated supervision raising the productivity of the less-educated members of a working team in industry.[59] If the first-round spillovers are positive, it seems to follow that we have underestimated the *social* rate of return. But this conclusion is not justified. If the discounted value of the

58. For example, Becker has shown that the old argument that the benefits of on-the-job training spillover to firms other than those providing it is subject to serious qualification, op. cit., pp. 17–18. [See Reading 9.]

59. Peacock and Wiseman in *Education for democrats*, London, 1964, pp. 19–20, are, to my knowledge, the first to question the order of magnitude usually assigned to the first-round spillovers from education.

direct income benefits minus tax exceeds the present cost of investing in additional education, private individuals are economically justified in making the investment, even if they have to borrow the funds. Similarly, the State is economically justified in investing in education if the annual expenditure on school places can be eventually recovered by increased tax receipts following upon the increase in earning power generated by additional education. This is the argument for calculating the social rate of return from before-tax earnings differentials as a percentage yield on the total private and public costs of education. The reported earnings differentials already embody the first-round spillovers; if we could somehow remove them, the absolute income differentials attributable to education would increase and, hence, the social rate of return would be higher. Therefore, we have actually *over*estimated the social yield if the social yield is narrowly interpreted as referring only to the *direct* economic benefits of education.

The use of the now well-established term 'social rate of return' is somewhat unfortunate since it includes only the direct and indirect private economic benefits, and not the cultural and political benefits of education – items (7), (8), and (9) in our list. But the point is that it does include all of the private financial gains from schooling, to whomever they accrue: there are no economic benefits from education to second parties which do not raise their earnings and thus generate increased tax receipts. Educated individuals cannot appropriate the first-round spillovers, but the State can and does *via* its taxing powers.[60] This is not to say that the distribution of tax burdens for the support of education is identical to the distribution of the private economic benefits of education, but simply that the incidence of the income tax broadly reflects the cash value of these benefits.

The 'second-round spillovers' – that is, items (2) to (6) in the list – are not so easy to deal with. It may be doubted that more education for the present generation acts to raise the earnings of

60. This argument ignores international and inter-regional spillover effects which can be very important for small countries or for federal systems of government. See Weisbrod, *External benefits of public education: An economic analysis* which deals with the spillover of benefits among American states.

the next generation, except in so far as the children of better-educated parents typically acquire more education themselves, or more education of a better quality; in either case, this tendency will be registered in time to come in the form of direct economic benefits. The intergeneration argument, if taken seriously, threatens to convert all the financial gains of education into indirect benefits.[61] Secondly, it is just as likely that certain kinds of education hinder the discovery of potential ability, impede the ability of the labour force to adjust to changing technology, foster the wrong sort of basic research, and increase the pressure on social services. Do the external diseconomies of the wrong sort of education outweigh the external economies of additional amounts of education? Surely, it would be presumptuous to give a definite answer to such a question in our present state of knowledge.

The second-round spillovers have so far defied measurement but they are, in principle, measurable. In his book, Becker argues that we can get an idea of their probable magnitude without measuring them directly. He begins by deriving the social rate of return from before-tax earnings differentials as a function of the total cost of education, including foregone earnings before tax. This figure, construed as a lower limit to the true social rate of return, amounts to about 12·5 per cent for the 1949 cohort of white male college graduates. As an upper limit, Becker takes the value of Denison's residual of 'advancement in knowledge' – that part of the increase in output that is not explained either by increases in the quantity of inputs or by improvements in their quality – and attributes all of it to education. This gives him an upper limit of 25 per cent. The difference between 12·5 and 25 per cent, he concludes, measures our ignorance of the external effects of education.[62]

Some of the second-round spillovers clearly involve the dissemination and not the creation of knowledge – for example,

61. There are great difficulties in applying the same argument to women whose earnings differentials attributable to education exceed those for men but whose working life is typically much shorter. Much of the economic benefit of educating women is, truly, an intergeneration benefit, reflected in the greater educability of their children.

62. Becker, op. cit., pp. 119–21.

items (4) or (6). Hence, these are already reflected in the lower limit of 12·5 per cent. For example, the costs of scientific research are in part included in the costs of higher education and the benefits are presumably reflected in time to come in earnings differentials. That is, Becker's procedure amounts to attributing another 12·5 per cent to items (3) and (5). That may well be correct, but it seems difficult to believe.[63] But these are quibbles. Becker's calculation of the upper limit implies more confidence in the numerical accuracy of Denison's model of economic growth than is warranted. The upper limit of 25 per cent may serve as a bench-mark for further argument, but it has little significance in its own right. For better or for worse, the direct economic benefits and the first-round spillovers of education remain at present the only ones capable of fairly accurate measurement; and this is the chief, if not the only, justification for concentrating on them.

It is possible, however, to gain some impression of the effect on the rate of return of various assumptions about the magnitude of the second-round spillovers. The frequently expressed opinion that the indirect benefits of education are more important than the direct benefits is tantamount to the assertion that we should multiply earnings differentials associated with education by an alpha-value greater than 1·2, instead of 0·6; in other words, that the social rate of return on six years of secondary and higher education is at least 13 rather than 8 per cent.[64] But this conclusion depends on the notion that second-round spillovers do not raise everyone's incomes, including those of the more educated, by equal absolute amounts. The critics of the rate-of-return approach appear to believe that this is precisely what happens.[65]

63. For a vigorous statement of the belief that 'the most important return from college education, viewed broadly, is additions to knowledge in contrast to transmission of existing knowledge', see H. Villard, 'Underinvestment in college education?: A comment', *American Economic Review*, May 1960, pp. 376–7. The question turns on the belief that additional spending on academic research would produce a more than proportionate increase in the value of marketable scientific results.

64. See Henderson-Stewart, op. cit., chart III.

65. This is frequently linked to an unstated objection to the use of earnings differentials, in any sense of the word, to measure the returns from education. For instance, Vaizey remarks that 'if all incomes were equal it

Yet it is difficult to envisage how this could come about. Take item (4) as a case in point: suppose general instead of specialized higher and further education would make it easier to retrain workers to take up new jobs; is it likely that this would not show up in absolute earnings differentials, say, by raising all earnings equi-proportionately? The idea that more education can raise earned income across the board without any differential impact on the more educated carries very little conviction.

For different reasons, we shall say nothing about the economic implications of literacy, political stability, and greater enjoyment of leisure – items (7), (8), and (9). It is obvious that a minimum degree of literacy is vital to the very existence of a market economy, and it is no less obvious that economic advance is impossible without a smoothly functioning political system. These are questions which can be and have been investigated by economists, and they may well be vital to the role of education in economic growth. They are not relevant, however, to allocative decisions which involve less than a total transformation of society: the rate of return to a literacy campaign of given size, yes, but not the rate of return to converting an illiterate society to a literate one. None of this denies the importance of the intangible benefits of education to the community at large. It is simply that these are not economic values at all in the ordinary sense and to assert that they are 'large' or 'small' is to dress up a personal value judgement. We all indulge in these judgements but it is clarifying to keep them separate from analysis of the measurable economic gains.

Recently, however, it has been argued that the trouble with rate-of-return analysis goes deeper than that of failing to quantify the intangible benefits of education: education is a 'public good' satisfying a 'social want' for which conventional value and capital

---

would appear to follow (from rate-of-return studies) that education as such has no direct return which is absurd; the return would be immeasurable by this method', *Economics of education*, p. 45. But, far from being absurd, the direct returns would indeed be zero in a society that no longer needed income differentials to encourage people to continue with their education or to induce employers to economize on scarce educated manpower. Even in such a society, however, education might still generate indirect benefits to the community by raising all incomes together.

theory breaks down completely; it is not simply that most production of education occurs outside the market but that, in the nature of the case, it could not be produced efficiently by a market process.[66] The peculiar characteristic of public goods is that their benefits are indiscriminate in the double sense that no consumer can be excluded from enjoying the benefits and that consumption by one person in no ways reduces the consumption opportunities of others. Hence, public goods cannot be priced by a market mechanism because consumers have no incentive to reveal their individual preferences for these goods; what is required is a political device like the ballot box to induce individuals to reveal their true preferences.[67] Clearly, therefore, if education is a 'public good' pure and simple, it is meaningless to calculate the rate of return, whether private or social.

The concept of a 'public good', however, is far more limited than appears at first. It is not enough to have joint consumption; the condition of equal consumption must apply to all, whether they pay or not. Furthermore, there must be no rationing problem in the supply of the good because a limitation on quantity is equivalent to a price, which creates the possibility of a solution by a price system. This leaves such things as lighthouses, national defence, noise and smoke abatement, clearance of areas that produce infectious diseases, as unambiguous examples of pure 'public goods', but not internal law and order, medical care, and education.[68] Education is not a pure 'public good' because its economic benefits are largely personal and divisible: below the statutory leaving age, it is possible to buy more education, and above the statutory age, the number of places in higher education are rationed out in accordance with examination results. It follows that there is nothing in the nature of education as an economic service that prevents meaningful comparison of its financial costs and benefits.

66. R. S. Eckaus, 'Economic criteria for education and training', *Review of Economics and Statistics*, May 1964, pp. 181–3.

67. The argument goes back to Italian writers on public finance in the 1890s but its modern formulation is due to P. A. Samuelson, 'The pure theory of public expenditures', ibid., November 1954, pp. 387–9, and R. A. Musgrave, *The theory of public finance*, New York, 1959, pp. 3–29.

68. See J. Margolis, 'The pure theory of public expenditures: Comment', *Review of Economics and Statistics*, November 1955, pp. 347–8.

It must be admitted, however, that it is not possible to confine all the benefits of education to those who have paid for it, nor is it possible to exclude the less educated from the spillover benefits of education.[69] Education, therefore, represents what might be called a 'quasi-public good' and to that extent great caution is called for in translating findings about the rate of return on educational investment into recommendations for public action. But the fact remains that education could be privately financed and even privately provided, and, in so far as the input and output of the educational system are bought and sold in the private market, the 'prices' of teachers and students do reflect the relative scarcities of the resources involved in schooling.

We conclude that it is very unlikely that the indirect benefits of education exceed the direct benefits, at least when benefits are interpreted in a strictly economic sense. Moreoever, the first-round spillovers are not ignored in rate-of-return analysis but enter into the calculation of the *social* rate of return. Lastly, knowledge of the social yield of education does not save the policy-maker the task of assessing the possible magnitude of the second-round spillovers or the duty of making value judgements about the non-economic benefits of education. Having broken the problem down into its separate components, however, the nature of the political decision will have been made explicit instead of implicit.

VIII. The Policy Implications of the Approach

If all the economic benefits of education accrued directly to ex-students, if there were no economies of scale in operating educational institutions, if capital markets were freely accessible to private individuals and if students were perfectly informed about job opportunities, there would be no need for public concern about the adequacy of educational expenditures. There is every reason to believe, however, that none of these conditions is fully met with. Furthermore, only part of the costs of education falls directly on students or their parents and, for this reason alone, the

69. If they could be excluded, it would be possible to charge them for the benefits, thus eliminating the spillover: see R. Turvey, 'On divergences between social cost and private cost', *Economica*, August 1963, pp. 309–13.

social rate of return on investment in education is different from the private rate. But of what practical use is knowledge of the social rate of return, given the fact that it neglects the second-round spillover of education?

Since the issue is one of allocating resources among alternative uses, the first difficulty is that of finding an appropriate comparison with the rate of return on education. For private decisions, the basis of the comparison is, presumably, the yield after tax on corporate equities and debentures. For social decisions, however, the relevant alternative rate is not so obvious. What we are after is the social opportunity cost of education: the value to society of the next best alternative use of the resources invested in education, or, to put it more stringently, the present value of the consumption stream that would be created by releasing the resources now invested in education. This implies the specification of a social time preference rate, expressing the government's valuation of the relative desirability of consumption at different points of time. Some economists have proposed that the rate of interest on long-term government bonds serves that function; others have pointed to the yield of private investment or to an average of market interest rates and business investment yields, but the issue remains unsettled.[70] The problem would be simplified if we knew the social yield of other types of government expenditures.[71] Pending such findings, however, it seems that the best candidate for expressing social opportunity costs is some compromise between the yield of investment in physical capital and the rate at which the State can borrow.

The before-tax return on all business capital in the United States in dollars of constant purchasing power averaged about

70. For a convenient review of the debate, see M. S. Feldstein, 'Opportunity cost calculations in cost–benefit analysis', *Public Finance*, vol. 19 (1964), no. 2, pp. 117–40, and P. D. Henderson, 'Notes on public investment criteria in the United Kingdom', *Bulletin of the Oxford University Institute of Economics and Statistics*, February 1965, pp. 55–89.

71. There is a considerable body of evidence, however, on the rate of return on investment in road transport and in the nationalized industries in this country, on defence and water resource development in the United States, and on electricity generating facilities in France. For the United Kingdom, see B. R. Williams, 'Economics in unwonted places', *Economic Journal*, March 1965, pp. 20–30.

12 per cent for the period 1947–57, compared to an after-tax rate of 8 per cent. The *social* rate of return to white male college graduates in the same period was at least 10 and at most 13 per cent; the corresponding rate to all college entrants, including drop-outs, women, and Negroes, varied between 8 and 11 per cent. On the basis of these calculations, Becker concludes that the yields of investment in business capital and in education fall within the same range and, hence, that the direct benefits of education alone cannot justify an increase in public expenditure on college enrolments at the expense of investment in business capital.[72] At the same time, college education is a profitable private investment for the average American student since he earns about 10 per cent after taxes on the private costs of four years in college. Likewise, it pays him to complete high school, which promises a rate of return of about 13 per cent. Indeed, even alternative rates as high as 10 per cent justify the average student in completing every level of education in the United States.[73]

Since the social returns to education equal the sum of the gains to all individuals, it might be thought that the social yield could not possibly be less than the private yield. But, on the contrary, while income taxes substantially reduce the level of the private yield, public subsidies to schools outweigh this effect and raise the private above the social yield. American college education forms an exception to this rule owing to the considerable earnings that are foregone by 18–22-year-old students. Nevertheless, even college education compares favourably with the after-tax yields

72. Becker, op. cit., p. 121. It must be noted, however, that the 8 per cent return on investing in business is after corporation income taxes but not after personal income taxes paid on the earnings from business investment. In that sense, it is not quite comparable to the after-tax earnings differentials on college education.

73. This is Lee Hansen's conclusion, after estimating the marginal and average social rates of return to education for every age from 6 to 21 and for every grade from elementary school to graduate school, as well as the private rates of return for every age from 14 to 21 and for every year of high school and college: 'Total and private rates of return to investment in schooling', *Journal of Political Economy*, April 1963. His figures do not allow for differences in native ability and family background, and, therefore, must be reduced by 1–3 per cent; this does not affect his principal conclusion. [See Reading 7.]

of alternative investment opportunities in the United States. This implies that both high-school and college enrolment would increase if better information were provided and all institutional restraints on private finance were removed. In other words, if the federal government wanted to get more resources into education for, say, non-economic reasons, it would need to do little else than to improve the flow of finance for students in the capital market. If, at the same time, it were concerned about equalizing opportunities to obtain higher education, it could raise private rates of return even higher by making more generous grants to students, possibly in relation to parental income.

This argument applies doubly to the situation in Great Britain. A comprehensive analysis of all fifty-three British Unit Trusts or mutual funds shows that returns on equity investment in the form of dividends and capital gains have averaged 12 per cent before tax in *real* terms for the period 1948–62, and about 8 per cent after tax.[74] The White Paper on the *Financial and economic objectives of the nationalized industries* (1961) lays down target rates of return on total net assets for the nationalized industries, the general import of which is that new projects in the public sector should earn at least 8 per cent. We may accept the latter figure as an indicator of the social opportunity costs of education. As mentioned earlier, the social rates of return in this country in 1963 are about 12·5 per cent to staying on at school until 18 years of age and about 8 per cent to staying on until the age of 21 to complete higher education.[75] The implications are that the social rate of return on British university education is not strikingly higher than the yield of alternative investment opportunities, but that there is substantial under-investment of resources in

74. A. J. Merrett and A. Sykes, *The finance and analysis of capital projects*, London, 1963, pp. 73–4.

75. Some readers may deny that the yield of British university education can be less than that of American college education, in view of the fact that only 4–5 per cent of the British working population are 'higher-educated', as against 9 per cent of the American working population. The explanation may lie in the much higher current cost per student in British higher education. In so far as this reflects superior quality of instruction, it should increase the returns no less than the costs. But much more re-search is needed before we can meaningfully compare rates of return to education in different countries.

secondary education and further education between the ages 15–18.[76]

As in the United States, the private rate of return to education in this country generally exceeds the social rate; and this tendency is even greater for higher education, which is not the case in America. About 90 per cent of the direct expenditures on teaching, research, administration, and buildings in British higher education are met from public funds; the figure is not very much lower in secondary education. For students in higher education, even indirect costs in the form of earnings foregone are largely subsidized by generous maintenance grants. The result is that British university students bear only 25 per cent of the total cost of university education, whereas secondary-school students bear about 65 per cent of the total cost of educating them. In consequence, the private rate of return on secondary education is only a little higher than the social rate, but the private rate of return on higher education considered separately is more than twice the social rate. These private rates create a *prima facie* case for charging more of the cost of higher education to the beneficiaries, at least if the benefit principle of taxation has any validity. But even if this principle be rejected, they justify renewed consideration of the case for government-guaranteed loans to students qualified for university entrance (possibly at subsidized rates of interest with repayment in the form of deductions through P.A.Y.E.).[77] Since this would conflict with the goal of 'equality of

76. It is worth noting that the rate of return of 12·5 per cent for staying on at school until the age of 18 is not just the yield of three years of extra education. Owing to the British system of selective secondary education, the 15-year-old school-leaver receives a different *kind* of education from the 18-year-old leaver. Hence, the 12·5 per cent is a return both to a different type and to a larger amount of education.

77. The *Robbins Report*, pp. 211–12, dismissed the arguments for loans to students, but see the evidence of some of the witnesses that appeared before the committee: *Evidence*, II, pp. 136–7, 146–52. See also W. Vickrey, 'A proposal for student loans' and R. Goode, 'Educational expenditures and the income tax', *Economics of higher education*, (ed.) S. J. Mushkin, pp. 268–305; and S. E. Harris, *Higher education, resources and finance*, New York, 1962, pp. 255–63, 291–304, which discusses the replies of some 200 American economists to a questionnaire on student loans. See also the instructive examples of loan schemes currently in operation in The Netherlands, Western Germany, and Sweden, *Robbins Report*, V, pp. 97, 116,

opportunity', loans to students in higher education ought to be coupled with an extension of maintenance grants to secondary-school students so as to encourage more of them to reach the levels from which university entrants are drawn.[78]

To come back to the more simple-minded implications of the social rate of return to higher education: is it really true that there is no case for additional public investment in higher education? Have we left anything out of our calculations? It has been suggested that we must add at each stage of the educational ladder the cash-value of the option to obtain still more education, suitably weighted by the probability of the option being exercised; in short, we must attribute to one level of schooling the expected value of the financial rewards obtainable from the next level to the extent that these rewards exceed the next best alternative investment opportunity.[79] In our case, this means adding the cash-value of the option to take up post-graduate education. But what happens when the financial rewards of the next level of education are less than the best alternative investment opportunity, as appears to be the case for secondary education in Great Britain? This implies a negative option-value,[80] with the result

---

146–7; and the recent American experience, Harris, op. cit., pp. 246–83. [For the author's subsequent thinking on student loans, see M. Blaug, 'Loans for students?', *New Society*, 6 October 1966, p. 539.]

78. So much for the accusation that rate-of-return studies of education necessarily have *laissez-faire* implications: in a recent article, Balogh inveighs against 'fallacious attempts to calculate the rate of return on capital investment in education for the individual. These have been evolved, I suspect, for political motives, in order to substantiate a plea for *laissez-faire* finance of education, to make it "pay for itself", to abolish free education and institute a system of giving loans to prospective students, to be paid back from the increase in their earnings as a result of their being educated' – 'The economics of educational planning: Sense and nonsense', *Comparative Education*, October 1964, p. 7. But as a matter of fact, the emphasis in rate-of-return analysis on the vocational aspects of education is conducive to a radical attitude towards educational reform.

79. Weisbrod, *External benefits of public education*, pp. 19–23, 138–43. [See Reading 8.]

80. The equation for the option value adds to the conventional rate of return for, say, secondary schooling, the difference between the yield of higher education and the yield of business capital, multiplied, firstly, by the proportion of secondary-school leavers who enter and complete university,

that one might make the mistake of rejecting the second level of educational system if one could not also go on to the third. The traditional method of dealing with interdependent investment projects is to lump them together and to calculate a rate of return on the aggregate; this is what we did in calculating the yield of six years of schooling required to complete higher education. If more was known about the financial rewards of postgraduate education in Britain, the same approach could be extended to staying at school until the age of 24 or 25.

It may be convenient at this stage to recall all the other factors that we have mentioned tending to produce biased estimates of the rates of return.

	Downward bias	*Upward bias*
Private rate of return	1. Lower rates of return to other types of human capital formation. 2. Future consumption-benefits(?) 3. Nonpecuniary preferences of educated people. 4. Improved quality of education. 5. The earnings differentials necessarily include the first-round spillovers.	1. Higher rates of return to other types of human capital formation. 2. Present consumption-benefit (?)
Social rate of return	1. As (1) above. 2. Consumption-benefits of education. 3. Nonpecuniary alternatives taking the form of fringe-benefits. 4. As (4) above. 5. As (5) above. 6. Earnings less than marginal productivities (?) 7. Second-round spillovers(?)	1. As (1) above. 2. Earnings exceed marginal productivities (?) 3. No allowance for depreciation of the educational stock embodied in the labour force.

It is evident that the bias is mostly one way even when we ignore the broader cultural and political benefits of education. In this way a case can be made, even on narrow economic grounds,

and, secondly, by the ratio of the costs of the two levels of education to permit addition of the corresponding rates of return.

for additional public expenditures in both secondary and higher education.

If this were all we could say with the aid of rate-of-return calculations, it would hardly justify the effort. Clearly, analysis of the economic effects of various *amounts* of education must be considered a first step in a more comprehensive approach which would include the effects of various *types* of education. In the United States, there is the problem of the very uneven quality of some 2,000 Institutions of Higher Learning.[81] In this country, there is the question of the many different channels of further and higher education, not to mention the variations that must exist in the social rate of return to different subjects.[82] In addition, there is out-of-school training whose costs may well be equal to one-half of total expenditures on formal education.[83] Nothing but lack of data inhibits calculation of the rate of return to each and every type of formal and informal education. So long as the analysis is confined to amount of formal education, the approach is not given a fair chance to show its worth.

A once-and-for-all calculation of the rates of return on investment in education can only throw indirect light on the causes of early leaving: it may be due to income disabilities, or to ignorance about the returns to additional education, or to imperfections in the capital market. But as soon as steps are taken to influence any of these causes of early leaving, rate-of-return calculations will disclose the effectiveness of the adopted policy. American studies now have the advantage of historical data for 1939, 1949, and 1959 which has, for example, made it possible to analyse the

81. For the first attempt to deal with this, see S. J. Hunt, 'Income determinants for college graduates and the return to educational investment', *Yale Economic Essays*, Fall, 1963, reprinted as Center Paper No. 34, Yale University Economic Growth Center, New Haven, 1964.

82. For example, the social costs of science students in universities is twice that of art students (*Robbins Report*, IV, p. 110) whereas their lifetime earnings differentials differ much less.

83. This is Mincer's finding for the U.S.A., op. cit., p. 63. However, his estimates do not come directly from the accounting data of firms and do not catch the costs of training which are borne by firms rather than by workers in the form of lower wages. A much lower figure was once calculated for Great Britain by P. J. D. Wiles: 'The nation's intellectual investment', *Bulletin of the Oxford University Institute of Statistics*, November 1956, p. 284.

impact of the G.I. Bill for veterans.[84] Similarly, rate-of-return analysis as such cannot tell us whether education should be privately or publicly provided and financed, but it alone is capable of summarizing the economic impact of changes in the mix of private and public finance. In the same way, it permits rapid calculation of the economic effect of such policy measures as raising the school-leaving age, eliminating some channel of further or higher education, altering the level of student grants, and the like. Moreover, when the same approach has been further extended to the other social services, it is bound to clarify the really important issue of the efficient allocation of resources between additions to the stock of physical capital and the stock of human capital.

Policy makers are frequently attracted to manpower forecasting as an alternative technique of educational planning, on the grounds that it avoids all the subtleties of rate-of-return analysis and, in addition, does not commit one to the assumption that earned income is an accurate measure of a worker's contribution to the net national product. But the simplicity of the manpower approach is largely a function of its narrow view of the economic ends of education. Like rate-of-return analysis, it neglects the consumption-benefits and most of the second-round spillovers of education; in addition, it almost always ignores the costs of producing different types of educated manpower, implying that educational inputs are free goods. Of course, manpower planning is not concerned with optimizing behaviour and its central objection to rate-of-return analysis is that it can at best indicate the desirable direction of change in educational policy, not its required magnitude. Unfortunately, it is precisely in spelling out the magnitude of a required change that manpower forecasting so often falls to the ground, owing largely to its failure to take account of the possibilities of substitution between different skills as a function of relative wage rates. If the allocation of resources to education were governed entirely by market forces, rate-of-return studies would have full scope but centralized manpower planning would have little meaning. Despite the importance of public provision and finance of education, however, manpower forecasting is only a useful exercise if students and their parents

84. See H. P. Miller, 'Income and education: Does education pay off?', *Economics of higher education*, (ed.) S. J. Mushkin, pp. 129–47.

are in fact poor choosers, and if elasticities of demand for particular skills, and therefore elasticities of substitution between skills, are typically less than unity. By its failure to pay any attention to money costs and earnings, manpower planning stands condemned as a brand of technological determinism.

But these are not deficiencies inherent in the manpower approach and the fact remains that it tries to grapple with one of the significant second-round effects of education which is only inadequately reflected in rate-of-return calculations. The two methods are complementary and, unless we assume that the production of highly qualified manpower is the only economic purpose of an educational system, even the most accurate manpower forecasting would not dispense with the need for rate-of-return analysis.[85]

Is a relatively low return on teachers' training a signal to stop educating more teachers? Is a modest social rate of return on higher education a reason for discouraging students from going to university? These questions have answers, but not until they are considered in the round. As one American critic of the rate-of-return approach put it: 'it might prove detrimental to the best interest of society (measured in terms other than aggregate economic returns on investment) to have government policy determined (or even substantially influenced) by an investor's point of view'.[86] It might, but we will never know until we see what sort of policy follows from 'an investor's point of view'. Surely, it makes more sense to advocate something on non-economic grounds after, and not before, the implications of an economic point of view are clearly understood?

85. The strongest argument for manpower planning is simply that there is the strong possibility, given the long gestation period of certain critical occupations demanding specialized education, of cobweb cycles with periods of gluts and low salaries succeeding periods of shortages and high salaries, and so on *ad infinitum*. If we had historical data on the rates of return to individual fields of study, we could test this cobweb hypothesis by checking whether the various yields fluctuated over time.

86. Shaffer, op. cit., p. 1033.

Part Four
The Manpower-Forecasting Approach

Educational planning is as old as state education itself: over a hundred years ago some of the American states went in for decennial reviews of educational needs and Royal Commissions in Britain drew up reports on the state of elementary, secondary, and university education. What is new in educational planning in our own day is the degree to which more and more countries are subordinating the expansion of the educational system to the prospective demand of industry and government for highly qualified manpower, a prospective demand which is forecast with ever more sophisticated techniques. Sparked off by various international organizations, the interest in manpower planning and forecasting has now spread around the world and received official endorsement almost everywhere in both developed and underdeveloped countries.

The readings in this section begin with a general statement of the case for 'manpower analysis in educational planning' by Herbert S. Parnes, Professor of Economics and Director of the Center for Human Resource Research at the Ohio State University. The most controversial aspect of the manpower-forecasting approach is the translation of projected manpower demands into desired supplies of educational output. In his second paper, Parnes outlines the difficulty and suggests some methods of attacking the problem.

Claus A. Moser and Richard G. Layard provide a post-mortem of various manpower forecasts that have been made in Great Britain since the war and, at the same time, paint a typical picture of manpower planning problems in advanced economies. They link their discussion to the recommendations of the *Robbins Report on Higher Education*, having served respectively as Statistical Adviser and Senior Research Officer to the Robbins Committee on Higher Education. C. A. Moser is Professor of Social Statistics and Director of the Unit for Economic and Statistical Studies on Higher Education at the London School of Economics; R. G. Layard is now Deputy Director of that Unit. Kenneth J. Arrow, Professor of

Economics at Stanford University, and William M. Capron, Senior Staff member in the Economic Studies Division at the Brookings Institution, analyse the scientist–engineer 'shortage' in the United States, which they contend, is being remedied by ordinary market forces and hence requires no planning solution.

The best example to date of the manpower-forecasting approach to educational planning is the Mediterranean Regional Project of the Organization of European Co-operation and Development (O.E.C.D.), inspired by the work of H. S. Parnes. The first phase of this project has now been completed and evaluated by R. G. Hollister, Assistant Professor of Economics at the University of Wisconsin. The essay in question is his own summary of the report that he prepared for the O.E.C.D.

12 H. S. Parnes

Manpower Analysis in Educational Planning

H. S. Parnes, 'Manpower analysis in educational planning', *Planning education for economic and social development*, ed. H. S. Parnes, Paris, O.E.C.D., 1964, pp. 73–80.

I should like to do three things in this paper: first, to explore the role and the limitations of manpower forecasting in educational planning; second, to present an overview of a 'manpower requirements approach' to estimating a society's needs for education; and, third, to discuss some of the methodological aspects of manpower analysis. Thus, the first topic raises the question of the relevance of manpower considerations to educational planning; the second presupposes a favourable answer to the first and suggests the broad outlines of a manpower approach; and the third treats some of the technical problems that are involved.

The Role of Manpower Forecasting

The rationale for according manpower forecasts a prominent role in assessing educational needs is perfectly straightforward. It runs something like this: a nation with plans or aspirations for economic development cannot afford to slight the preparation of its human agents of production. The creation of a new steel works, for example, is meaningless unless provision is also made for the scientists, engineers, managers, technicians, skilled workers, clerical staff, etc., necessary to operate it. Since one of the functions of the educational system in a society is to provide its work force with the abilities required for productive activity, it follows that that system must be reasonably well geared to the production requirements of the economy. Moreover, it is the *future* pattern of manpower requirements that must guide to-day's educational decisions. The reason is that the 'lead time' in producing qualified manpower is exceptionally long. When one considers the time involved in constructing new school facilities, in training new teachers, and in filling up the educational pipeline in order to expand significantly the number of university graduates, it becomes clear that the educational planner must have in mind the prospective patterns of manpower requirements at least a decade or two in advance. Thus the need for long-term forecasts of manpower needs.

The objections that are sometimes raised to the foregoing statement of the case for manpower forecasting are of two general kinds: one ideological and the other quite practical. Some persons have such a profound feeling that the 'true' purpose of education is to contribute to an individual's personal development that they regard as almost immoral an approach to educational planning that is essentially economic in its orientation and which seems to use society's needs for a 'human capital' as a basic criterion. On the other hand, there are those who profess no philosophical objections to the manpower approach, but who feel that the impossibility of making valid long-term forecasts of manpower needs makes this approach dangerous, the more so because individual careers can be wrecked if youngsters pay too much attention to faulty official forecasts. It is necessary to examine the validity of each of these positions.

On the philosophical question, first let me admit to my own bias, which is that decisions with respect to how much and what kinds of education a society should have, should not – indeed must not – be made in terms of economic considerations alone. The institution of education serves a number of individual and social purposes in any society, and all of these must be kept in mind when policy decisions are made. It is not enough, either, to differentiate the role of education in contributing to the development of the individual and its role in satisfying the *economic* needs of society. Actually, there is an economic and a non-economic dimension to education both in its individual and its social role. Even if one were to take the extreme view that the only purpose of education is to enable individuals to achieve self-fulfilment, one could not logically exclude vocational considerations, for the prospects of finding remunerative employment are hardly irrelevant to the fullest enjoyment of life. Nor is it true that from the vantage point of society the only considerations are economic. The role of education in moulding the human resources of an economy to fit the requirements of its productive resources is quite obvious. But no less important is the contribution of education in providing the citizenry with an understanding of the technological, economic, social, and political forces that influence their lives. Such understanding is a necessary condition for a viable political democracy, and may also make a contribution to economic development that is quite independent of specific vocational preparation.

In other words, to argue that manpower considerations are relevant to educational planning is by no means to hold that the only, or even the principal, function of education is to promote economic development. The emphasis that has been placed in the Mediterranean Regional Project on the so-called 'cultural approach' to educational planning testifies to the recognition of the other objectives of educational policy.[1] But having said this, it is clear that by no realistic standards can the question of what the educated are to do when they complete their formal schooling be neglected, and this is simply another way of emphasizing the need for manpower forecasts.

Granting the importance of manpower forecasts for the purpose of ascertaining needs for education, the more difficult question is whether such forecasts can be made with sufficient confidence that we are justified in basing educational plans upon them. The sceptics call attention to the large margins of error that are likely at virtually every stage of the forecasting process: the estimate of gross national product fifteen years in advance; the distribution thereof among the various sectors and branches of the economy; the estimation of future manpower structure within each of the branches; and the equation of occupations with required educational qualification. Isn't it a dangerous delusion, they are inclined to ask, to pretend that we can answer questions like these with confidence?

A complete answer to objections of this kind cannot be given at this point, for it would involve a detailed examination of the various steps in the forecasting process, and these are the subjects of the five lectures that follow. The technical difficulties involved in each of these stages, and the degree to which they

1. See Herbert S. Parnes, *Forecasting educational needs for economic and social development*, Paris, O.E.C.D., 1962.

make suspect the final result, are matters which each of you must ultimately decide. There are, however, several considerations that I think are important in assessing the contribution that manpower forecasts can make to educational planning, and I should like to comment on these now.

In the first place, I should like to suggest that, so long as one grants that manpower considerations are one of the elements that *ought* to influence educational decisions, then all such decisions, if they purport to be rational, involve manpower forecasts, whether or not they are explicitly made. That is to say, a decision to expand enrolments in the pure and applied sciences at the university level implies the belief that employment opportunities for the graduates of such faculties are going to be expanding more rapidly than for the graduates of, say, colleges of law; or at least that the additional scientists and engineers are going to be somehow more useful to the economy than the alternative expansion that could have been planned in the output of lawyers. Otherwise, the decision does not make much sense. Thus, the question is not whether forecasts are to be made, but the extent to which they are going to be as systematic as possible and are going to be based on all of the evidence that can be marshalled. If the allocation of resources to education were governed entirely by market forces, the necessity for centralized decisions on such matters would, of course, disappear. Under these circumstances, the question whether new facilities and personnel for engineering schools should be developed would be the resultant of numerous individual decisions making themselves felt on the market, with each youngster (or his family) presumably making an individual 'forecast' to guide his action. But since no country apparently contemplates this as a serious possibility, governments are unable to escape the responsibility of forecasting.

The second point to be made concerning the manpower forecasts that underlie educational planning is that they do not, or at least should not, purport to be pure unconditional forecasts. That is, they are not so much predictions of what *will happen* in the manpower field as indications of what *must happen* if certain targets for economic growth are to be realized. This brings us to a consideration of what is meant by 'manpower requirements' in this context. In particular, it is necessary to differentiate between the term manpower requirements as used here and the 'demand for labour' as that concept is traditionally used by economists. To the economist, demand for a particular category of labour e.g. metallurgist, machinist, secretary – is actually a schedule of relationships between quantities of labour and a series of possible wage rates. That is to say, employing establishments are conceived to be willing to hire varying quantities of workers depending on the wage that must be paid them – more at a lower wage than at a higher one. Supply, incidentally, is used in the same way to refer to the numbers of workers who would make themselves available at a corresponding series of wage rates – more at a higher than at a lower wage. The number of workers in a particular occupation at a given moment of time, as well as the wage they receive, is conceived by the economic theorist to be a function of these supply and demand schedules. If the number of workers that employers wish to hire at existing wage rates is greater than the number available at those rates, the consequence in a competitive labour market is a rise in the wage, which reduces the number demanded and increases the number supplied until equilibrium is achieved. From this point of view, the number of workers employed at a particular moment of time is a measure both of the supply and the demand.

From the foregoing it should be quite clear that estimating future manpower requirements in the context of educational planning is not at all the same thing as forecasting future demand in the market sense. Rather, the idea of manpower requirements as used here relates to the functional (occupational) composition of employment that will be necessary if certain social and/or economic targets are to be achieved.[2] The concept, in other words, is more a technological than an economic one.

With respect to some categories of manpower this concept is both easy to illustrate and to defend. In the case of medical personnel, for example, it is perfectly meaningful to ask how many doctors will be required if given standards of medical care are to be achieved. In education, the number of teachers required to

2. Compare the definition of a 'manpower shortage' suggested, and discarded, by David M. Blank and George J. Stigler, *The demand and supply of scientific personnel*, New York, National Bureau of Economic Research, 1957, p. 23.

teach a given number of students is also a meaningful question. Other examples relating to protective service occupations, government service personnel, etc., readily suggest themselves. Even in these cases, however, 'requirements' cannot be quantified except in terms of certain assumptions about the organizational structure and about the technology that will be employed in the particular industry. For example, the number of teachers required will be affected by the extent to which educational television is used, the degree to which subprofessional clerical assistants are provided, etc. In the case of physicians, required numbers will be a function not only of the standard of medical care that is aimed for, but also of the particular division of duties between physicians on the one hand and supporting medical personnel (nurses, medical technicians, etc.) on the other.

In the case of those activities accounting for the large majority of jobs in an economy, targets for future production establish the criteria for assessing the volume and pattern of manpower requirements. There is, of course, no unique relation between output in an industry and either the total labour force or its occupational composition. The substitutability of factors of production means that a given quantity of textiles can be produced either by utilizing a large number of workers operating hand looms in their homes or a smaller number of workers on power-driven looms in a factory. In the latter case, not only is the output per worker higher than in the former, but the functional composition of the work force is also quite different. Loom-fixer, engineer, timekeeper, and personnel director are examples of new occupations that would probably not exist in the simpler organization of the productive process.

Thus, within limits, a given level of labour productivity in a branch of activity (output per man-hour), dictates the required technology and the manpower structure (at least in terms of broad categories). This seems to be the only meaningful sense in which one can speak about the shifts in manpower structure necessary to produce given rates of economic growth. Increases in output per worker (which are the principal source of improvement in *per capita* income) occur primarily as the result of changes in production techniques, and it is the latter that dictate the functional composition of the work force. It must be admitted that the foregoing can be regarded only as an hypothesis, but the similarities in broad occupational composition trends among countries as productivity rises lend it considerable credence.

The final point that needs to be kept in mind in considering the possibility of making manpower forecasts is that such forecasts do not need to be extremely detailed in order to be useful for purposes of educational planning. It is doubtful that even the most confident of manpower forecasters would advocate an attempt to blueprint fifteen or twenty years in advance the number of persons required to be trained in every specific occupation. Even if the pattern of requirements could be predicted with that degree of precision, we simply do not know enough about the mobility of workers from occupation to occupation to permit the requisite supply forecasts. Fortunately, however, this degree of precision is not really necessary. At the lower end of the occupational hierarchy – in the semi-skilled, unskilled, and many of the service occupations – there is almost complete transferability among jobs, at least so far as educational qualification is concerned. These do not need to be differentiated at all. At higher levels, it is true that carpenters and electricians are not interchangeable, and even less are chemists and economists. But merely differentiating among occupations requiring different amounts of education, and between those requiring general and those requiring scientific–technical preparations, would be of great value in guiding the allotment of educational expenditures among the several levels and branches of the educational system.

I do not mean to deny the importance of estimating future supplies and requirements in specific occupations when such estimates can be made with confidence. Clearly the greater detail in the forecasts, the more detailed can the educational planning be. Moreover, in the case of some occupations, notably teachers, a detailed estimate is indispensable. What I am saying, however, is that if reliable detailed estimates cannot be made, all is not lost. There is much to be gained by long-term forecasts in terms of rather broad occupational groups.

To summarize all of the foregoing, I would conclude that manpower forecasts of the kind that I have described are both necessary and possible for sound educational planning. They are only one guide, to be sure, but they are essential if the proper structuring of educational expenditure is to be achieved. One ought not to delude oneself into thinking that one can foretell with precision the distribution of manpower in an economy fifteen years in the future. But any action with respect to education implies that at least some guesses have been made as to the effect of economic development on the distribution of employment opportunities. Since this is so, it is clearly desirable that these guesses be made as systematically as possible, and in the light of all the relevant data. And the process of making these systematic guesses is what I would mean by manpower forecasting in this context.

The Manpower Requirements Approach. An Overview

Now, granting the importance of manpower forecasts, how are they to be made, and exactly how are they to be used as a basis for educational planning? This is a long and complex subject, the several facets of which will be dealt with in the lectures that follow. I should like here simply to sketch a bare outline of what might be called a 'manpower requirements approach' to educational planning, and leave to the speakers that follow the important task of describing the relevant techniques.

There is, of course, no single, universally accepted method of making manpower forecasts for purposes of ascertaining needs for education. Probably most exercises of this kind have involved predicting the requirements for high-level personnel, e.g. engineers, and numerous techniques have been used or advocated. These include asking employers to estimate their prospective requirements; extrapolating past trends in the growth of the profession; and correlating the number of employees in the occupation with total employment, population, *per capita* or total national income, or some other such variable, using the regression equations thus derived to estimate the total stock of engineers needed as of the forecast date. This quantity is then compared with a forecast of the supply of engineers as of that date, calculated on the basis of the current stock, withdrawals, and inflows from existing educational institutions. Prospective shortages or surpluses are thus identified.

When hasty estimates for a specific occupation must be made, such methods cannot be ruled out. However, they suffer from several limitations. For one thing, they provide no basis for evaluating the realism of the specific forecast in the light of the total structure of employment. That is, if forecasts for all occupations were to be made independently of one another by these methods, their total could very well depart significantly from the anticipated size of the total labour force. Moreover, such a piece-meal approach does not provide a basis for *total* educational planning. For the latter purpose, it is necessary to examine the future occupational structure of the entire labour force, and to relate this to categories of educational qualification corresponding to the various levels and branches of the educational system. Making the forecasts of requirements and of supplies in terms of educational qualifications has yet another advantage: it avoids the difficult problem posed by mobility among occupations. Estimates of future supplies of manpower by *occupational category* require assumptions about the movement of workers from one occupational category to another. If, on the other hand, the estimates are in terms of *educational qualification*, these are unaffected by movement among jobs for which (presumably), the same educational preparation is appropriate.

If one accepts the foregoing point of view, the elements that are involved in forecasting manpower requirements and supplies as a basis for ascertaining the required expansion in the various levels and branches of the educational system, can be outlined as follows:

(a) prepare an inventory of manpower for the current year, differentiating between the employed and the unemployed, and cross-classifying the labour force by occupation and industry, by occupation and education, and by educational attainment and age. These data are important in that they provide the bases for the forecasts of both future requirements and future supplies of manpower by educational qualification;

(b) estimate the size of the labour force for the forecast year. This constitutes the total supply of manpower, i.e. sets the upper limits for the summation of specific manpower requirements. Estimates of 'needs' in the various occupational categories cannot in total exceed the estimate of the total labour force; nor can

271

they be substantially below this figure without implying large-scale unemployment;

(c) estimate total employment in each sector and branch of the economy for the forecast year. It should be noted that this step is essential only because occupational structure differs from one industry branch to the next. If occupational structure were identical and could be expected to remain identical in all branches of activity, there would be no need for industrial differentiation. One could move directly from the forecast of the labour force to forecasts of occupational requirements. It is also true that, even with inter-industry differences in occupational composition, there would be no need for industry breakdowns if (1) the increase in total employment during the forecast period were spread proportionately among all industry branches and (2) there were no change in occupational structure (or equal percentage changes) in each industry branch. To put all this in positive terms, the reason for the necessity of industry breakdowns is to permit account to be taken of either or both of the following factors in assessing the future occupational composition of the labour force:

— different rates of growth of industry branches whose occupational structures vary, and
— differences among industries in future trends in occupational composition;

(d) within each sector and branch of the economy, allocate total employment for the forecast year among the various categories of the occupational classification system. Aggregating the requirements for each occupational category in all sectors and branches gives the total stock of manpower required for the forecast year classified by occupational category;

(e) convert the data on requirements by occupational category into data on requirements by educational qualification, using as categories the several levels and branches of the educational system. This is necessary even if the occupational classification system has been prepared with a view to relating occupation to educational qualification, for very few occupational categories can be expected to be homogeneous with respect to required educational qualification;

(f) estimate the anticipated supply of personnel with each major type of educational qualification for the forecast year on the basis of:

— present stocks;
— anticipated outflows from the existing educational system,
— losses due to death, retirement, and withdrawal from the labour force;

(g) compute the change in annual outflow from the various levels and branches of the educational system necessary to create balance in the forecast year between the forecast of requirements (e) and the forecast of supplies based on existing educational outputs (f);

(h) calculate the enrolments in each level and branch of the educational system necessary to achieve the required annual outflows.

The foregoing provides the basic data for planning educational investment on the basis of manpower objectives. The required expansion in enrolments in the various components of the educational system may be used to estimate the requirements for additional teachers and educational facilities, which in turn provide the basis for estimating costs. Needless to say, it is considerably easier to mention each of these steps in the process than to resolve the methodological problems involved in carrying them out.

13 H. S. Parnes

Relation of Occupation to Educational Qualification

H. S. Parnes, 'Relation of occupation to educational qualification', *Planning education for economic and social development*, ed. H. S. Parnes, Paris, O.E.C.D., 1964, pp. 147–57.

I should like, in this discussion, to focus on the problem of translating long-term forecasts of occupational structure into requirements for personnel with varying amounts and types of education. The question, in other words, is this: if one knows the required occupational structure of the labour force for some future date, is it possible to indicate the required distribution of that labour force by level and type of education and training?

Nature of the Problem

To begin with it is essential to examine briefly the conceptual difference between a classification by occupation and a classification by educational qualification. The former focuses upon the function performed in the productive process, i.e. the particular configuration of tasks or operations that the worker is expected to perform. The latter, on the other hand, looks to the amount and kind of instruction and training that the individual has been successful in acquiring. While these two classifying principles are related, they are clearly not the same thing. The link between them is provided by the assumption that certain types of general and vocational education develop patterns of skill and knowledge that are essential for the performance of corresponding occupational functions.

This type of statement of the presumed relation between educational qualification and occupation has the advantage of permitting us to see clearly to what extent it is possible, conceptually, to specify the educational inputs that are required to produce a worker for a particular occupation. If every occupation were perfectly homogeneous with respect to the required patterns of skill and knowledge, and if a given pattern of skill and knowledge could be acquired only through a particular educational background, it would be possible to estimate, on the basis of a forecast of occupational structure, the minimum number of years of education and training of various types necessary to meet the future manpower requirements of the economy.

These two conditions prevail only with respect to a limited number of occupations, most of which involve some kind of legal certification. The medical professions and the teaching professions are examples in almost all countries. But once one moves outside the relatively few occupations for which there are legal educational requirements, it becomes very difficult indeed to establish rigid links between education and occupation. One reason for this is that no occupational category is perfectly homogeneous with respect to required patterns of skill and knowledge. If one deals in terms of broad categories of occupations, such as 'skilled manual workers', 'sales personnel', or 'clerical workers', this is perfectly evident. But even such specific occupations as 'statistician', 'chemist', 'carpenter', or 'waiter' are really abstractions from a large number of individual jobs whose functional content may be quite diverse. It is instructive to examine the distribution of personnel by educational attainment in a few selected occupations in the United States (see Table 1).

It will be noted from Table 1 that while there is a pronounced modal group in most of the seven occupations, there is nevertheless considerable dispersion. In the case of the two professional occupations (authors and mechanical engineers), about half of the men had completed university (16 years of school). But as many as a fourth of the authors and a third of the engineers had not gone beyond secondary school (12 years). Among photographers and bank tellers, completion of secondary school was by far the most typical educational attainment, but almost a tenth of each group had completed university, while a third of the photographers and more than a sixth of the tellers had not finished secondary school. Among carpenters, a majority had not gone beyond primary school (8 years) but a fifth had had some secondary education and an equal proportion had completed secondary school. Salaried managers and salesmen in manufacturing industries showed the most pronounced dispersion in educational background. About a fourth of the managers were university graduates and another fifth had had some university training. But almost three out of ten had not completed secondary education. The distribution of salesmen was rather similar, except that a somewhat smaller number had completed university.

Table 1

Percentage Distribution of Males in Selected Occupations by Number of Years of School Completed, U.S., 1950

Occupation	Number reporting education	8 or fewer	9–11	12	13–15	16 or more
Authors	9,780	3.7	5.8	15.0	28.2	47.2
Mechanical engineers	107,340	9.1	7.2	16.2	17.0	50.5
Salaried managers in manufacturing	374,940	14.7	14.1	29.3	18.9	23.0
Photographers	43,260	14.3	18.0	40.8	18.4	8.5
Salesmen in manufacturing	293,190	14.5	15.5	33.6	20.3	16.0
Bank tellers	34,380	6.4	11.7	51.1	22.2	8.6
Carpenters		56.9	21.2	17.4	3.6	.9

Source: Computed from data in U.S. Bureau of the Census, 'U.S. Census of Population: 1950, Vol. IV', *Special Reports*, pt I, ch. B, Occupational Characteristics, Table 10, Washington, U.S. Government Printing Office, 1956.

The foregoing data are not conclusive, because they relate to the actual educational *attainments* of incumbents of the occupations rather than to the educational *requirements* of the job. Nevertheless, they strongly support the common-sense proposition that even within relatively specific occupations there is a wide range of jobs that differ considerably in their demands upon the worker and, consequently, in the amount of education and/or training he must have.

It might, of course, be argued that this problem would disappear, or at least be significantly reduced, if more homogeneous occupational categories were used, i.e. if several levels of each occupational title were differentiated. While this is doubtless true to some extent, the question is purely academic, for there is no real possibility of obtaining manpower data for the entire economy in terms of such refined categories.

Not only are the occupational categories in terms of which forecasters must work too heterogeneous to permit unique relations between them and educational qualification to be established, but it is also true that even quite specific patterns of skill and knowledge may be acquired in different ways. Formal and informal on-the-job training, apprenticeship programmes, self instruction, and simply experience in related occupations may substitute in varying degrees for formal education in preparing workers for specific jobs. Finally, individual differences in native ability are also relevant in this context, for the existence of such differences may mean that varying amounts, if not kinds, of education may be necessary in order to achieve the same level of proficiency in a given occupation.

The foregoing considerations have definite implications for the occupational classification system used in forecasting manpower requirements and, whatever classification system is used, for the process of converting occupational into educational requirements. Concerning the occupational classification, the implication is that it is impossible to develop a classification in terms of required educational attainment. It is tempting, of course, to consider the possibility of a grouping of occupations on the basis of the amount and types of education they require. If this could be done, the problem of converting a distribution of the labour force by occupation into a distribution by educational qualifications would disappear; or, rather, the conversion would be built into the occupational structure. Once manpower forecasts by occupation had been made, the required educational qualifications would be automatically obtained. But for the reasons that have been explored above, this is not possible.

There may be some merit in grouping occupations so as to be as homogeneous as possible with respect to educational qualification, but in any case most of the categories will be associated with a *range* of educational qualification rather than with a specific level and kind. The degree of dispersion around the average will, to be sure, vary depending upon how detailed the occupational classification system is and, for any given degree of detail, will differ among occupations. Some occupations for which entrance requirements are legally established in terms of prescribed education will have little or no dispersion; others, in which hiring requirements are formally established and in which there are strong institutional pressures for uniformity in these requirements (e.g. college professors in the United States) will also tend to have little dispersion. On the other hand, for occupations which generally have no formal hiring requirements (proprietors of firms is the extreme example) or for which such requirements as may exist are generally not established primarily with respect to educational attainment (skilled workers in the United States) the variation can be expected to be greater.

Granted that there will be a range of qualifications associated with each occupational category, one might ask why the *average* requirement for each category cannot serve the purpose of educational planning. The answer is relatively simple. While data on average requirements might be useful for calculating the total number of man-years of schooling that need to be provided, they tell us nothing about the distribution of that number among the various levels of education, and this is precisely what we need to know in order to plan enrolments in the various components of the educational systems. Such data do not even permit us to estimate the total required investment in education, since the cost per student varied considerably among the several levels.

An example will perhaps make this clear. Of the close to five million persons classified as 'managers, proprietors, and officials' in the United States Census of Population of 1950, the median number of school years completed was a fraction over 12. If one used *average* schooling as a criterion, one would plan to give all future managers a secondary school education. But this would ignore the more than half-million persons in this occupational category who had university degrees and the additional three-fourths of a million with some university training.

The problem, then, of converting occupational forecasts into estimates of the numbers of persons with various educational qualifications turns out to be one of estimating the *proportions* of each occupational category who should be expected to have each level and type of education. How may this be done?

Use of Data on Educational Attainment

One obvious approach is to obtain data on the *current* distribution of each occupational category by educational attainment and to apply these proportions to estimates of future requirements. If three-fourths of the current number of engineers are university graduates and one-fourth graduates of higher secondary technical schools, then the number of engineers required in the target year would be expected to be composed of 75 per cent with university degrees and 25 per cent with higher secondary certificates.

The difficulty with this approach, of course, is that it assumes that the current labour force is 'properly' or 'optimally' educated for the existing occupational structure. Thus, while it would permit the planning of education to keep pace with changes in occupational structure, it would operate to perpetuate existing imbalances between occupational structure and educational attainment. This imbalance, it should be noted, may operate in either direction. In the agricultural sector that is so prominent in most underdeveloped and developing economies, it would be a disastrous error to assume that the existing educational qualifications of the labour force are adequate. There is reason to believe that agricultural productivity could be significantly increased if the numerous small farmers had at least some judiciously designed technical education. On the other hand, there may be 'over education' from a purely functional point of view in some occupations as the result of the traditional over-emphasis on 'liberal arts' curricula in the higher education systems of many of the less developed countries.

Despite the limitations of this approach it is imperative that data on the current educational qualifications of occupational categories in the economy be collected and analysed, for even if such data are unreliable indicators of what 'should be', they are none the less indispensable for discovering the current deficiencies in occupational preparation.

Another approach to relating occupation to educational qualification is on the basis of data for other countries – presumably more advanced than the planning country. An example is provided by a study made in 1957 by the Commonwealth of Puerto Rico on needs for manpower and education in 1975. The research group made the assumption that by the target date most Puerto Rican industries would have levels of productivity approximating those of the corresponding United States industries as of 1950. It was further assumed that if comparable occupational groups are to have equal levels of productivity, they must also have equivalent educational characteristics. Hence, educational qualifications of the several major occupation groups in the United States in 1950 were used as standard for their Puerto Rican counterparts as of 1975.[1]

If one is interested in ascertaining educational needs from a purely manpower point of view, there are obvious dangers in the use of comparative data of this kind for an economically more advanced country. The principal problem is that it is impossible to be certain that data on the actual *educational attainment* of the several occupational categories accurately reflect *educational requirements*. Another way of saying this is that data on educational attainment do not reveal what proportion of the education incorporated in the work force represents 'investment' and what proportion represents 'consumption'. There are many goods that may be considered either capital goods or consumer goods depending on their use in particular instances. Every teacher of introductory economics has thought of numerous illustrations – e.g. the bottle of ink, which is 'capital' if it happens to be on the desk of the book-keeper in an enterprise, but a consumer's good if it is in the home of the same individual. This may cause some initial confusion to beginning students of economics, but the concept is none the less clear, and if it were interesting to do so one could quantify the amount of ink utilized in the productive process as distinguished from the amounts used in consumption. But in the case of education, although economists have by analogy used the same concepts, it is not at all clear how one decides what proportion of an individual's education is 'necessary' for the performance of his job.

Despite this limitation, comparative international data on the educational characteristics of occupational categories provide use-

1. *Puerto Rico's manpower needs and supply*, Commonwealth of Puerto Rico Planning Board, Bureau of Economics and Statistics in co-operation with the United States Department of Labor, Bureau of Employment Security (1957), pp. 32–6.

ful clues for assessing educational needs in the light of occupational structure. Unfortunately, the available data are rather limited. I have been unable to find data for any advanced country that show the distribution of occupational categories by level *and type* of education and training. There are data, however, for Canada, England and Wales, France, India, Italy, Japan, and the United States for various years during the past decade showing number of years of school completed, type of school certificate, or school leaving age. Differences in educational and occupational categories among these countries make it extremely difficult to make comparisons in terms of standardized occupational and educational attainment categories. Nevertheless, an attempt has been made to do this by James Blum, and the results are shown in *The Mediterranean regional project: Forecasting educational needs for economic and social development.*[2]

Some of Mr Blum's data for Canada, England, France, and the United States are presented in Table 2, which shows the proportions of personnel in each major occupation group who have completed thirteen or more years of school. Data such as these, even though rough, have some usefulness. For one thing, they permit realistic assumptions to be made about the relationships among occupational groups in terms of educational qualification, for it will be noted that the relative ranking of the major occupation groups is fairly uniform from country to country. Secondly, they would at least discourage naïve assumptions about the relation between occupation and education, for example, that all occupations in the professional or managerial categories require university training. Finally, they may be used to establish guide lines for actual quantification. A developing country, for example, might feel safe in using the proportions indicated for one of these countries as upper limits for its own requirements. Using Canada as a model, this would mean that not more than two-thirds of workers in the professional category, or more than a fifth of those in the manager category, should be expected to require over 12 years of schooling from the viewpoint of man-power considerations alone.

Both of the approaches that have been mentioned thus far rely

2. H. S. Parnes, *Forecasting educational needs for economic and social development*, O.E.C.D., Paris, October 1962.

on the actual educational attainments of workers in various occupations as measures of required educational qualification. What are the possibilities of arriving at the 'ideal' distribution of educational qualifications for given occupational categories?

Table 2

Proportion of Workers with Thirteen or More Years of Education by Major Occupation Group, Selected Countries

Occupation group	Canada (1951)	England and Wales (1951)	France (1954)	United States (1950)
Professional workers	65	64	51	78
Semi-professional workers	38	23	41	45
Administrative, executive, and managerial workers	19	23	20	32
Clerical workers	14	12	5	20
Sales workers	12	6	3	20
Service, sport, and recreation workers	5	6	1	6
Farmers, farm managers, and workers	2	5	*	4
Other workers	3	1	1	5

* Less than 0.5%.

Source: Herbert S. Parnes. *Forecasting educational needs for economic and social development*, O.E.C.D., Paris, October 1962.

Is it possible, in other words, to define the educational background required for various occupations in the light of the characteristics of the *jobs* themselves rather than on the basis of the characteristics of the *workers* who currently fill them?

Use of Data Based on Job Analysis

One interesting attempt to specify the amount of education and training required by specific jobs is a study made by the United States Bureau of Employment Security, in which trained job analysts coded a sample of 4,000 jobs drawn from the United

States Dictionary of Occupational Titles according to the 'General educational development' and 'Specific vocational preparation' required by each.[3] General educational development was scaled into seven levels, each of which was described and illustrated with respect to three variables: reasoning development, mathematical development, and language development. Specific vocational preparation was divided into nine levels, each expressed in terms of the amount of time necessary to 'learn the techniques, acquire information, and develop the facility needed for average performance in a specific job-worker situation'.

The limitations of these results for estimating educational requirements on the basis of data on occupational structure are numerous, even for the country for which the basic data were developed. For one thing, the estimates of general educational development and specific vocational preparation represented only the judgements of the job analysts. Secondly, and probably even more important, is the difficulty of relating the various levels of general educational development and specific vocational development to the several levels of the educational system. For instance, according to the B.E.S. study the general educational development required of a secretary is level four, which implies one or more of the following capabilities:

Reasoning development: Apply common sense understanding to carry out instructions furnished in written, oral or diagrammatic form. Deal with problems involving several concrete variables.

Mathematical development: Make arithmetic calculations involving fractions, decimals, and percentages.

Language development: Comprehension and expression as of the level of popular magazines.

Now the question is how much education does this imply?

Another difficulty stems from the fact that the specific vocational preparation time as coded by the Bureau of Employment Security may reflect not only formal vocational education, but also apprenticeship, in plant training programmes, on-the-job

3. *Estimates of worker trait requirements for 4,000 jobs*, United States Department of Labor, Bureau of Employment Security.

training, and even experience gained in related jobs. Finally, the general educational development and the specific vocational preparation are coded separately, and it is not clear if, or how, they should be combined. Thus, to take the example of the secretary once again, the requirement is for between six months and one year of specific vocational preparation. Is this in addition to the number of years of school assumed to be required for the general educational development, or is it a part thereof?

Despite these difficulties (which he recognizes), Professor Richard Eckaus has used the B.E.S. data in conjunction with census data showing occupational composition by industry, to analyse – in global terms rather than by occupational group – the general educational requirements and the specific vocational training requirements for the United States labour force and for specific industry groups for 1950.[4] His analysis, incidently, indicates that in 1950, 7.4 per cent of the jobs in the American economy required four or more years of university education and that an identical proportion of the employed labour force had this amount of education. Eckaus does not attempt to ascertain, however, to what extent the supply and the requirements for college graduates are matched in the various occupational categories.

Professor Eckaus' analysis of educational requirements is in terms of industry groups. The same procedure, however, could be used to establish the required educational distribution of occupational categories. Despite the limitations, the approach is deserving of additional experimentation. However, the basic data required for the analysis would take considerable time to develop. There are less ambitious and less time-consuming approaches to the problem of ascertaining an optimum educational level for particular occupational categories. Perhaps the simplest type of investigation would be to make an interview survey of a sample of establishments employing substantial

4. R. S. Eckaus, 'On the comparison of human capital and physical capital'; also *Economic criteria for education and training*, unpublished manuscript. The former paper appears in *The economics of higher education*, Selma Mushkin (ed.), Department of Health, Education, and Welfare, Washington Government Printing Office, 1962. [The latter paper has now been published in the *Review of Economics and Statistics*, vol. 46 (1964), no. 2, pp. 181–90.]

numbers of workers in the occupations in question. The interview schedule might include questions on:

(a) the educational qualifications of present employees in the occupations under investigation;

(b) formal hiring requirements that the establishment imposes, or would like to impose, for the occupations in question;

(c) employer judgements about the general level of adequacy of existing staff in terms of job preparation;

(d) employer opinions about the optimal and minimal levels and types of preparation required for efficient job performance (occupations in which the range between the optimum and the minimum requirements are substantial) provide a basis for compromise when the *desired* level of educational expenditure must be scaled down to the *possible*; and

(e) employer opinions about the likely changes in job content in the foreseeable future and the implications thereof for desired educational qualification.

The conclusions that emerge from such a survey will depend on how ambitious the investigation has been. At the very least, one can hope for impressionistic notions as to the range of educational qualification that should be associated with a particular group of occupations. In a more elaborate survey, it might be possible to quantify the proportions of personnel in the occupational category who should be expected to have each level and type of education.

A somewhat more refined study, relying less on impressions of employers, would involve a careful analysis of the relation between (a) precise job content; (b) extent and nature of education, training and experience, and (c) performance on the job. Within each occupation, carefully defined in terms of actual functional content, a sample of employees would be drawn. Detailed information on the education and training (including all specialized courses as well as general educational attainment) and the work experience of each employee would be obtained by interview. In addition, one or more measures of the worker's job performance would be obtained, which might take the form of ratings by the employee's supervisors. Correlations between the measures of job performance and the extent and nature of formal and informal preparation for the job might then permit conclusions relative to the 'ideal' type of preparation for the occupation. [. . .]

Conclusion

What I have said up to this point should make it clear that the translation of occupational requirements into needs for personnel with various levels and types of education is not a simple matter. But while it is necessary to call attention to the problems and to caution against simple mechanical procedures, one must not conclude that the task is an impossible one. There are, after all, a good many occupations at the top of the occupational hierarchy – particularly in the scientific and technical categories – for which educational requirements are reasonably unambiguous, and these groups are among the most crucial for educational planning. With respect to the others, which to be sure account for the large majority of the labour force, the link between education and occupation is not nearly so direct. Nevertheless, the several techniques that have been suggested, perhaps used in combination, can provide a basis for making realistic estimates of the required structure of the labour force by educational qualification.

14 C. A. Moser and P. R. G. Layard

Estimating the Need for Qualified Manpower in Britain

Excerpts from C. A. Moser and P. R. G. Layard, 'Planning the scale of higher education in Britain: some statistical problems', *Journal of the Royal Statistical Society*, Series A, vol. 127 (1964), part 4, pp. 493–513.

[. . .]

I. Type of Forecast Needed

In considering what type of forecast of manpower requirements might be useful, various classifications are relevant:

(i) Special (for one particular occupation) or general (covering many or all occupations).

(ii) Short-term (up to one year), medium-term (up to five years) or long-term (five years or more).

(iii) Demand (the numbers who will be offered employment at particular salaries) or needs (the numbers required for the attainment of some economic or other targets).

(iv) Conditional or unconditional. (A conditional forecast of demand is tied to specific assumptions about other variables, e.g. national income. If these other variables take a different course the forecast cannot be said to have been falsified, though it can be dismissed as irrelevant. An unconditional forecast, though it may be worked out on the basis of many assumptions, is put forward as a best guess at what will happen. Forecasts of needs are normally conditional to particular targets.)

The question is which type of forecast in each case might be most useful for the planning of higher education.

(a) Coverage and detail

As a background, we show in Table 1 estimates of the present stock of higher-educated manpower. In 1961, there were nearly 1,100,000 people in the labour force who had received a higher education; 450,000 had been to university, 240,000 to training colleges or colleges of further education, and the rest had studied in further education (mostly part-time) or by private study (including correspondence courses).[1] In terms of subjects, those educated in university comprised 160,000 who had studied science and technology, 220,000 who had studied arts and 70,000 doctors and dentists. Those who had studied in further education or by private study comprised 100,000 scientists and technologists with degree-level qualifications, 100,000 others who had studied technology but only to the level of H.N.C. or equivalent, and 200,000 with qualifications (mostly awarded by professional associations) in subjects such as commerce, law, architecture, and surveying.

For planning the future scale of higher education, estimates of manpower requirements would ideally include all the fields covered in Table 1. Though there are obvious difficulties in estimating the needs (outside teaching) for people educated in arts and commerce, one has to recognize that the needs for people in the different categories are related to each other, and in some cases to needs outside the range of higher education (e.g. the need for scientists and technologists is related to that for technicians and craftsmen). In fact, it is of key importance in manpower forecasting to allow for the extent to which people with different educational qualifications can be substituted for each other in given jobs, and this seems to indicate the need for a comprehensive general forecast.

As to degree of detail, the right-hand column of Table 1 (amplified so as to separate scientists from technologists) would constitute a minimum requirement. It would also be desirable to

1. In 1961, about 3·4 per cent of the working population had received a full-time higher education (see *Higher education. Report of the committee under the chairmanship of Lord Robbins 1961–63.* London, H.M.S.O., 1963. Cmnd 2154, Four Part V). By 1981, the proportion is expected to reach about 6·2 per cent. A large part of this increase will result from the expansion of higher education that has already occurred and a part from the further expansion recommended by the Robbins Committee. By 2025, 15 per cent of the working population will have had a full-time higher education, even if there is no expansion in the proportion of the age group entering higher education beyond that recommended by the Robbins Committee for 1980

have some indication of the numbers needed with different periods of working experience, for there might otherwise be a danger of producing a supply that was sufficient in aggregate but

Table 1

Numbers in the Working Population Who Have Completed Higher Education, Great Britain, April 1961

Thousands

	Educated full-time in			Educated in part-time further education	Educated by private study	Total
	Universities	Teacher training	Further education			
	(1)	(2)	(3)	(4)	(5)	(6)
Teachers						
Qualified scientists and technologists	40			10		50
Others (arts, etc.)	70	240				310
Others						
Qualified scientists and technologists	120		20	70		210
Others educated in technology			10	90		100
Doctors and dentists	70					70
Others (arts, commerce, etc.)	150		30	70	100	350
Total	450	240	60	240	100	1,090

Notes: (1) Colleges of Advanced Technology are included with Further education.
(2) Qualified scientists and technologists are those with degree-level qualifications as defined by the Committee on Scientific Manpower (General Register Office, 1962, Appendix A).

deficient in senior or junior people. If the balance between full-time and part-time higher education were to be influenced by calculations of manpower needs, this would involve the further problem of distinguishing between requirements for manpower with these different kinds of education. This may not be easy, but manpower forecasting can hardly avoid the issue of how much education requires to be formal and how much can be given on the job, with or without formal part-time instruction. It is also an open question whether forecasts can be meaningful without assumptions about curricula, but this aspect of educational planning is not discussed in this paper.

(b) Time span

Even if accuracy will diminish with distance, manpower forecasts must cover a series of years reaching some time ahead. People have working lives of up to half a century and the stocks of persons with particular qualifications are determined by outputs over the previous forty years or more. Thus short-run variations in the output of qualified people have comparatively small effects upon trends in stocks, and to adjust the flows of people from year to year on the basis of short-term forecasts involves the dangers of either failing to foresee requirements that will, if tackled over a short period, prove impossible to meet, or of ignoring the imminence of a surplus. Forecasts should therefore aim to cover as long ahead as possible, but the detail to be expected will diminish as the time period lengthens. This may not be a major drawback, since long-term decisions have to be taken largely in terms of faculties, and in the short run it may often be comparatively easy to switch the allocation of facilities between subjects within a faculty.

There is also a minimum time interval within which there is little point in making forecasts. This is the period for which the stock of qualified manpower is already broadly determined. Two factors affect the length of this period. One is the interval between the ages when students decide what final qualifications to attempt and when (if successful) they achieve these qualifications. In this country, the total output of higher education is partly determined by decisions about whether to enter the sixth form taken at the age of 16 (i.e. at least five years before the age of completing higher education). Subsequent decisions about actual entry to higher education at the age of 18 also play their part. Similarly, the balance in numbers between arts, physical sciences and biological sciences is partly determined by decisions taken at the age of 14, and very largely by the age of 16. The division within physical sciences between pure science and technology, and within biological sciences between pure science and medicine, is determined by the age of 18, while the division between branches of technology is often not made until the end of the first year of higher education, if then.

The other factor is the time it takes to modify plans for the provision of educational facilities. The planning and erection of buildings in higher education may take about four years, and, to the extent that new buildings are required, the output of higher education is pre-determined by at least five years, and longer if the buildings are required for students not already in their final year. There are also difficulties connected with staffing and administration, which may introduce a time lag between the conception of a plan and its execution. In general the time lag is greatest in relation to the total provision of higher education; for changing the balance between subjects it may be much less. It follows again that detailed forecasts should be for comparatively short periods ahead and less detailed ones for as far ahead as possible (say, up to twenty years).

(c) Forecasts of need and forecasts of demand

Manpower forecasts can deal either with needs or with probable demand. Both have their uses, but they must be distinguished. Needs specify what ought to happen; demand relates to what actually occurs, though it may, of course, be wrongly predicted.

The concept of need is elusive, for all needs are relative, and what one might look for is some yardstick by which to compare the country's needs for higher-educated manpower of different kinds with, for example, the need for housing, roads or machinery. An approach to this problem is through the idea of education as an investment, which contributes to the future output of goods and services, involves a definite cost and has consequently a (private and social) yield which can be compared with that on other forms of investment.[2] Thus one might choose to define the

2. The literature on the economics of education is large, and particularly useful discussions will be found in Mushkin (1962), Vaizey (1962), and Bowen (in *Robbins Report*, Four, Part III). [See Reading 5.]

number of qualified people needed in the labour force as the highest number that would give an adequate yield on the cost of educating them. However, such a definition would be extremely difficult to apply. Apart from the difficulty of deciding what yield is to be considered as adequate, there is the problem of assessing the future (or the past) yield on different types of education – the more so since a given output can be produced by many alternative combinations of types of manpower and capital. Yet, conceptually at any rate, there must, for a particular output, be an optimum combination of factors of production depending, from the national point of view, on the costs of education and of the other factors and on their potential contributions to output. This would specify for each type of manpower a single figure of the number needed.

By contrast the concept of demand might be understood as relating to a schedule showing the numbers who would be offered employment at each of a series of different relative salaries. Forecasts of demand are not often, it is true, expressed in this form; they usually relate, explicitly or implicitly, to the number who would be employed at current relative salaries.

There is no clear relation between future needs and future demand at current relative salaries. In the first place, salary differentials may not accurately reflect the total (private and social) benefits of education. For example, the salary which employers are prepared to pay may not allow for the external economies resulting from education; while it may allow for the ability of graduates, which is in part independent of their education. Nor can one expect a constant relationship over time between salary differentials and total benefits. Moreover, even if current differentials exactly reflected the benefits of education, the yield might still be excessive or inadequate. In other words, current differentials might be a function of current over-supply or under-supply. In terms of national needs, it might therefore be right to plan for a supply which differed from anticipated demand at current relative salaries.

Forecasts of demand may be chiefly relevant to the planning of higher education in so far as they answer the question: 'If you produce such and such a number of qualified people, how will they be employed?' If demand were expected to grow at the same rate as the stock of graduates, one would expect graduates to be employed at the same relative salaries as now (and, perhaps, in roughly similar kinds of occupations). But if the two grow at different rates, one would expect changes in the pattern of graduate employment and remuneration. It is sometimes supposed that if the stock grew faster than the demand this would mean graduate unemployment. Normally, however, this would only follow if graduates preferred to be unemployed to working in less well-paid occupations. It should always be relatively easy for the better-educated members of the community to find employment of some kind, provided they are willing to accept the salaries and type of work offered.[3]

II. Examples of Forecasts of Manpower Requirements

To illustrate the kinds of questions which manpower planners have been asked to solve, and the difficulties of doing so, we shall give examples of some forecasting methods, taking first two special forecasts (for teachers and scientific personnel) and then one type of general forecast. Perhaps inevitably the methods used (particularly for the special forecasts) take into account only some of the considerations outlined above.

(a) Forecasts for school teachers made by the Ministry of Education

Apart from uncertainties about future birth rates, it is comparatively easy to forecast the number of school teachers needed to achieve certain targets for class sizes in the schools, and the Robbins Committee used such estimates as a basis for recommendations for the expansion of the teacher training sector. The forecasts were conditional forecasts of need, and covered the years up to 1980. For simplicity, only those made for

3. As is pointed out by Trow (1964), 'In America, there is a marked inverse relation between education and unemployment, ranging from over 8 per cent among Americans who have not completed high school to 1·4 per cent among college graduates.' The relevance of this evidence in the present context would be diminished if there had been no decline in graduate salary differentials. On this latter point there is conflicting evidence (Vaizey, 1962, p. 105).

maintained primary and secondary schools in England and Wales will be discussed here.[4]

After estimating the number of children who will be in the schools in given years, the next step was to make assumptions about the appropriate size of classes. At present there are statutory maximum permitted class sizes in England and Wales of 40 in primary schools and 30 in secondary schools. But these maxima may be, and are, exceeded if, 'owing to the shortage of teachers, it is not possible to comply with the regulation'. However, existing estimates of the need for teachers all assume that these policy objectives constitute a minimum basis of needs. It is also usual to estimate, as a possible additional objective, the number of teachers who would be needed to eliminate primary classes over 30.

The next step is to calculate the overall pupil–teacher ratios which would be needed to eliminate all classes above the maximum. Finally, these ratios are applied to the forecasts of school population to derive estimates of teachers needed (the figures are shown in *Robbins Report*, One, Part IV, Table 25).

The estimates thus depend not only on the accurate projection of the birth rate and the trend to stay on at school, but also on assumptions about the required standard of provision. There is little evidence on the value of teaching provided in different sizes of class, and the present maxima are essentially matters of judgement. They can be accepted as giving a measure of needs only in the sense that they relate to definite targets fixed by the government.[5] They also provide, as it were, a guarantee that so long as the supply of teachers does not exceed the forecast need, those who are trained as teachers will normally be able to find a teaching job. But they do not directly prescribe any particular

4. See the *Robbins Report* (One, pp. 136–42). The forecasts were made by the Ministry of Education and involved bringing up to date forecasts made by the National Advisory Council for the Training and Supply of Teachers (1962).

5. In the case of teachers and public servants generally, there is no measurement of the value of their services other than the cost of employing them. Ideally, the output of teachers might be valued as part of a valuation of the output of the educational system, but at present there are not the means of doing this. Against this would be set the cost of training and employing the teachers.

course of action. For, in the first place, present policy is only formulated in terms of a minimum requirement: there is no suggestion that once oversize classes are eliminated all needs have been met. In the second place, there are at present many oversize classes, and no specific date has been fixed for their abolition. There is, however, a presumption that they should be abolished as soon as possible.

It was in the light of this presumption that the Robbins Committee approached their task. It was clear that unless drastic efforts were made to increase supply, the abolition of oversize classes would not occur before 1980. The Committee concluded that provision in training colleges should be expanded as rapidly as objective circumstances permitted, and the Ministry of Eduction were requested to provide estimates of the maximum possible rate of growth (see *Robbins Report*, One, pp. 140 and 141). The supply implications of this growth are shown in detail in *Robbins Report* (One, Part IV, Table 28).

It would have been desirable to have made separate estimates for graduate teachers of mathematics, physics, and chemistry. Unfortunately the requisite data were not at the time available, but it is to be hoped that calculations for special subjects will be undertaken by those responsible.

Other examples of studies in the field of public services in Britain concern teachers in higher education, teachers in further education, doctors, and dentists,[6] all of these depending essentially on the projection of some basic population variable and then some assumption about standards of service.

(b) Forecasts of the committee on scientific manpower

In estimating manpower requirements in industry, the problems tend to be more difficult if only because the personnel involved contribute less immediately to the required end which is in this case the output of goods and in the former the provision of personal service. As an example concerned with the industrial

6. See the *Robbins Report* (Three, Part IV); National Advisory Council on the Training and Supply of Teachers (1961); Committee to Consider the Future Numbers of Medical Practitioners and the Appropriate Intake of Medical Students (1957); Committee on Recruitment to the Dental Profession (1956). See also Gales and Wright (forthcoming) for a survey of manpower forecasts for different branches of the social services.

sector, we shall take the series of forecasts for scientists and technologists made by the Committee on Scientific Manpower.

The Committee has been associated with five forecasts since 1956.[7] Two (in 1956 and 1961) were of a long-term character, while three (in 1956, 1959, and 1962) were directed to needs over the subsequent three years. From the present point of view, the main interest lies in the long-term forecasts.

(i) *The first long-term forecast* (1956). The first long-term forecast projected needs for 1966 and, more tentatively, for 1970. The method was first to make an assumption about the course of industrial output and from that to derive the manpower requirements. No attempt was made to *forecast* the future course of output, but it was thought 'appropriate to work on the basis of an average increase of industrial production at the rate of 4 per cent per annum'. As the Committee said, 'the result gives an estimate . . . of the number of scientists and engineers, which we believe would be necessary to permit an increase in total industrial output amounting to 4 per cent per annum'. It is thus not a forecast of probable demand, but a conditional estimate of numbers needed to obtain a selected objective.

The numbers needed were derived on the assumption that scientists and engineers in industry should grow in a fixed ratio to the volume of output: in other words, that the proportion of scientists and engineers in the labour force would need to rise at the same rate as productivity. In the event, the index of industrial production rose between 1956 and 1959 not by 4 per cent per annum but by an average of 2·1 per cent. At the same time, the number of scientists and engineers grew by an average of 8·5 per cent per annum. The Committee concluded that it was unsatisfactory to forecast requirements in relation to output and, in their next long-term forecast, a different method was adopted.

It may be worth commenting on the discarded method. First, it would be unlikely that any relationship between output and qualified manpower would hold in the short run, irrespective of fluctuations in the rate of growth of output. But this does not mean that there may not be a long-term relationship. Secondly,

7. See Office of the Lord President of the Council (1956) and Advisory Council on Scientific Policy (1959, 1961, and 1963).

even if there appears to be no constant ratio between output and qualified manpower, there may well be a relationship of some other form. For example, in both Sweden and the Netherlands, forecasts of the requirements for engineers have been made in relation to output. In both cases the forecasts were based, unlike those of the Committee on Scientific Manpower, on a published series of past data. These data suggested a linear relationship between output and the number of engineers, but with the number of engineers rising faster than output.[8]

There remain two difficult problems associated with the use of this type of information. First, one cannot be certain that the number of engineers employed has been a cause of the output achieved. The second problem comes from extrapolating past trends into the future. Since there are many ways of producing a given output, one cannot assume that past trends in the relationship between output and the employment of engineers will necessarily be maintained.

(ii) *The second long-term forecast (1961)*. The Manpower Committee's second long-term forecast (made in 1961 and relating chiefly to 1970) was not linked to an assumption about the future course of industrial output or the economy generally.

The industrial component of the forecast was based essentially on a series of judgements. The first step was to estimate the total employment within each industry. Employment in manufacturing industry was estimated by assuming that the proportion of the total labour force employed in manufacturing would remain constant; the Committee then estimated the distribution of employment between industries 'on the basis of the evidence obtained in our review'. The next step was to estimate the density of qualified manpower required within the total labour force of each industry. These estimates were based on discussions with

8. For Sweden, see Moberg (1959), pp. 51–7; for the Netherlands, see de Wolff (1962), p. 96. The Swedish forecast was made by the Federation of Industry for the 1955 Royal Commission on Higher Education; the subsequent forecasting work undertaken by the Royal Labour Market Board has been based on a variety of methods. The Dutch forecast was made by the Central Planning Bureau but represents only one of the methods used. The data on Sweden related to employment and output in private industry, the data on the Netherlands related to total employment and national income.

industry. Many considerations were taken into account and in certain leading industries it was assumed that by 1970 'the density of employment of scientific manpower . . . will rise to the level which already characterizes the best firms in that group'.

From the resulting estimates, taking all sectors of the economy together and allowing for the expansion of higher education then envisaged, the Committee concluded that 'by 1965 supply and demand of manpower should not be much out of balance and that a surplus may exist after that date'. They emphasized, however, that though there might be an overall surplus, this could conceal shortages in particular subjects.

The forecast raises a number of problems, the first concerning the nature of what is being forecast. It is in fact described as a forecast of demand, though there was no explicit assumption about relative salaries and certain elements of the forecast (e.g those relating to teachers) involved estimates of need. We shall return to this question later.

A second difficulty concerns the methods used in forecasting the densities of qualified manpower in industry. These are not explained in detail, but the Report states that 'the most important assumption made, on the basis of inquiries, is that the speed of absorption of qualified manpower in technologically advanced industries tends to slacken off when a density is reached at which the technologies concerned are fully "manned up". Thereafter the rate of absorption would tend to be governed by the size of the industry and by replacement until such time as far-reaching but unknown technological changes (which are apt to be long-term processes) present an entirely new industrial situation. The Committee had grounds for assuming that technological "breakthroughs" as such within a large industry would not normally involve those industries in taking on significant additional resources of manpower.'

This line of thought is given as the basis for the assumption already quoted that in some industries 'the density of employment of scientific manpower . . . will rise to the level which already characterizes the best firms in that group'. Taken together these two passages seem to imply that, in general, the more advanced firms will not increase their densities of qualified manpower, while the less advanced firms will level to these same densities (or go out of business). There are, in fact, reasons for doubting whether either of these events will occur; and in most of the fields where forecasts have been based on assumptions of levelling, such a process has in the event accounted for only a small part of change.[9]

The assumption quoted can, however, be taken, in a different sense, to mean that by 1970 the *average* density of qualified manpower in all firms will be the same as that which now prevails in the best firms. This method of forecasting has considerable possibilities. The difficulty is to know when the best will become the average. Here research could throw light on probabilities, for if data were available over a series of past years one could determine the typical time taken for this to happen.

There is, however, a further problem concerned with the methods used for projecting densities of qualified manpower. The 1961 Report did not discuss in detail what factors affect the demand for scientists and technologists, though the passage quoted above was largely concerned with the impact of techniques of production. The position is complicated. About 40 per cent of scientists and technologists in manufacturing industry are employed in work directly connected with current production; about 40 per cent are on research and development and, though a good proportion of these are concerned with modification of existing techniques, some are employed to discover new ones; a further 20 per cent are engaged in management. Between 1959 and 1962 the numbers employed grew fastest in management and slowest in research and development. This suggests that different factors affect the demand for scientists and technologists in different branches of activity, and in future separate forecasts may well be needed for each activity.

This raises the general problem, which applies both to the industrial and other sectors, of forecasting the demand for scientists in occupations where their qualifications are not directly required for the job. Table 2 analyses the occupations of

9. It is interesting to note from the latest Report (Advisory Council on Scientific Policy, 1963, p. 46) that in establishments with 500 or more employees, which have much higher densities of qualified manpower than other establishments, these densities rose as fast between 1959 and 1962 as in other establishments.

scientists and technologists as shown by the 1961 Census. It shows that of 260,000 occupied scientists and technologists, 210,000 were judged by the Committee on Scientific Manpower to be employed in occupations 'likely to be closely related to their scientific education'. In addition, there were 17,000 who were working as technicians, 10,000 who were managers in service trades or administrators (e.g. in the Civil Service), 8,000 who were in non-scientific professions such as the churches or journalism and 15,000 who were otherwise employed, e.g. as commercial travellers.

Of the 15,000 in the latter group and the 17,000 technicians some were presumably people who for personal reasons of one kind or another proved unsuited to positions of greater responsibility; some 'wastage' of this kind is inevitable, and needs to be allowed for in any forecast. Others in these groups may well be using their qualifications to good advantage. But more needs to be known before adequate forecasts can be made of the numbers who should be allowed for in these groups of employment.

No less difficult is any attempt to forecast the requirements for scientists in, for example, the administrative civil service or the non-scientific professions. There is, in many of these fields, no demand for scientists as such, and the number who will be employed at particular salaries may depend on the relationship between demand in other sectors and the available supply. How many it is desirable should be employed is another matter and one that involves a strong element of judgement.

Even in the first group, described by the Manpower Committee as involved in occupations 'likely to be closely related to their scientific education', these problems are present. For example, 26,000 of the managers in mining, manufacturing, and construction are scientists or technologists. There are many others who are arts graduates and others who have no higher education. How is one to assess the number of managers who will be required to have had a scientific education? Even in the case of school teachers there is some difficulty in deciding how many science graduates are required.

The 1961 Report was not very explicit in discussing these problems. It purported to estimate immediate 'demands for employment', and on this basis estimated that a surplus of scientists might be anticipated. This possibility, it said, should be welcomed. 'It should make possible a rational, as opposed to an emergency, use of the scientific disciplines. It should mean that at long last

Table 2

Occupations of Qualified Scientists and Technologists in the Working Population, Great Britain 1961

Thousands

	Scientists	Techno-logists	Total
A. Occupations likely to be closely related to their scientific education:			
Teachers	42	8	50
Postgraduate students	8	2	10
Managers in mining, manufacturing, and construction	6	20	26
Others (e.g. research, technical supervision of production)	43	81	124
Sub-total	— 99	— 111	— 210
B. Technicians	4	13	17
C. Other managers and administrators	3	7	10
D. Other professions (e.g. clergy, journalists)	6	2	8
E. Others (e.g. commercial travellers, workers)	6	9	15
All	118	142	260

Source: Advisory Council on Scientific Policy (1963), Table 3, and General Register Office (1962), Table 3.

Notes: (1) All personnel managers (numbering 450) have been included in Group C.

(2) It was inadvertently stated in Advisory Council on Scientific Policy (1963) (para. 20) that sales managers were included in Group C; they were in fact included in the figures for Group A.

(3) See Note 2 to Table 1.

we shall have a supply of qualified manpower with a scientific training for management, administration, and the professions generally, in addition to those who up to the present have been drawn inevitably into vocational employment.' In fact, however, the forecasts already provided for a large number of managers and administrators with scientific training.[10] And in these activities there is no clear line between what employers will consider as necessary and what as desirable, and no escape from the fact that scientific qualifications can to a greater or lesser extent be substituted for others.

In conclusion, it should be noted that the Committee's most recent (1963) report, giving the results of the short-term forecast up to 1965, has modified the conclusions of the 1961 Report, for three main reasons. In the first place, the most recent Survey (see below) suggested that the increase of qualified manpower (and especially of technologists) required within the areas surveyed will exceed the total forecast increase in supply. Secondly, the 1961 Census revealed the existence of far more qualified people not covered by the regular surveys of manpower than was formerly supposed. Some, but not all, of these extra personnel are included in Groups C to E in Table 2. If allowance is to be made for a growth in the number of qualified people not covered by the survey, the shortage will be that much greater. Thirdly, there was the government's adoption of the National Economic Development Council's target of a 4 per cent per annum rate of growth. The 1961 Report was not based on an explicit assumption about growth rates, but the Manpower Committee, in its later report, argued that the government's decision about the National Economic Development Council's target was likely in the long term 'to increase the demand for scientific manpower'. They concluded that 'the rough balance between total supply and demand, which in our 1961 Report we thought might be achieved by 1965, is likely to be delayed'.

(*iii*) *The medium-term forecasts* (*1956, 1959, and 1962*). The Committee on Scientific Manpower have made three medium-term forecasts. These should be mentioned, though as was suggested earlier such forecasts are of less use in planning the overall scale of higher education than in indicating what adjustments are de-

10. It should be noted that the information available about current stock at the time the 1961 Report was published did not cover many of the scientists and technologists in Groups C to E in Table 2. But it covered most of the scientists and technologists engaged as managers in mining, manufacturing, and construction.

sirable in the balance between subjects. For example, the latest forecast has undoubtedly been of service in drawing attention to impending shortages of mathematicians and of electrical engineers.

The method used in the three-year forecasts has been to ask employers how many people having scientific and engineering qualifications they 'would aim to employ in three years' time, assuming . . . that the required number of recruits will be available'. No assumption has been stipulated about relative salaries, nor about the course of economic growth.

The main difficulty about such unconditional questions is that different employers are likely to make inconsistent assumptions. They may differ in their assessments of the growth of the economy as a whole or of individual industries (for example, the motor industry may make different assumptions from the sheet-steel industry which supplies it). Even if consistent assumptions were made about the growth of different industries, firms would still be likely to make inconsistent assumptions about their individual shares of the market.

One solution might be to specify to employers the assumptions on which to make their estimates of manpower requirements. But in the short run this may not give a more realistic forecast of requirements than is obtained from an unconditional question. For it is only sensible to ask employers to use assumptions in making forecasts if their actual behaviour is likely to be consistent with the assumptions put forward. For the long run the position is different. The long-term behaviour of employers will be influenced by the general course of events and only a central body could begin to consider whether the assumptions of separate employers about the pattern of growth were plausible in aggregate. This is the method used in a study by the U.S. Department of Labor (1961): employers in the chemical and electrical engineering industries were asked, as a check against forecasts obtained by econometric methods, to estimate their requirements for scientists and engineers ten years ahead and the assumptions which they used were discussed in detail with the Department. A long-term study of this kind may have considerable value. If a forecast of needs were required, this would of course have to be based on explicit targets, even in the short run.

*(c) General forecasts in the O.E.C.D. Mediterranean regional
   project*

From the point of view of educational planning, special forecasts are of limited use, particularly if they are based on different
assumptions about the growth of productivity. For productivity
affects the requirements for people with higher education
throughout industry and commerce and sets the context for
expenditure on the public services (e.g. the services of teachers).

The difficulties of forecasting the future growth of national income are well known. Moreover, in so far as the supply of qualified manpower itself affects national income, there is a logical
problem in deducing the demand for qualified manpower from a
forecast of the level of national income; both cannot be deduced
from each other.

These problems do not apply to a conditional forecast of manpower needs related to a target for national income. We shall
take as our third example the methods of making such forecasts
evolved by the Organization for Economic Co-operation and
Development and six member countries in the so-called Mediterranean Regional Project of educational planning.[11] The forecasts
relate to the manpower needed at all levels of occupation to
achieve certain specified objectives up to 1975. The following are
put forward as examples of the minimum number of categories
for which a forecast should give estimates: university graduates
(science curricula/other curricula); higher secondary school
graduates (scientific and technical/commercial and general);
lower secondary school graduates; less than eight years of schooling. The actual categories vary from country to country and,
where possible, the forecast is made in more detail. The main aim
is to make it possible to plan the relative rates of expansion at
different levels of education and, broadly, as between arts and
science.

The first step is to set a target for national income and then to

11. This is a joint project of the O.E.C.D. and six member countries to
draw up educational plans for those countries. Certain common elements
are used in all plans and in addition the O.E.C.D. consultants suggest various
alternative details of methodology within this framework (Parnes, 1962,
and Parnes (ed.), 1963). Broadly similar methods were used in SVIMEZ
(1960).

make estimates of its composition in terms of output for the various sectors of the economy, and for different industries. These can be made directly, or they can be derived from estimates of the pattern of final demand (i.e. of consumers' expenditure, government expenditure, investment, and exports), these being converted into estimates of output by methods of input–output analysis of the kind being developed by Professor Stone in his growth model at Cambridge (Stone, 1962).[12] At the same time other objectives of national policy (besides a general target of growth) may need to be taken into account.

The next step is to estimate future total employment within each sector and industry. There are different ways of approaching this, of which the most obvious but not necessarily the most reliable is through estimates of future productivity.

Future employment within each sector and industry is then divided into occupational categories, occupation meaning the combination of duties, tasks, and functions performed by a worker, irrespective of his education. The forecast of occupational distribution in each sector and industry can be made in several ways. One approach is simply to project past trends, either as a function of time or as a function of output or as a function of both. Another approach is to adopt as targets the occupational structures prevailing in other countries with higher levels of output per head; or to set targets (in a similar way to the estimates of the Committee on Scientific Manpower) by reference to the occupational pattern in the most advanced firms in each industry. The outcome is a forecast of the numbers needed in each occupation.

The final stage is to translate this into a forecast of the numbers required to have had each level and type of education. One method is through an analysis of the skill requirements of each occupation. Another is based on projecting the present pattern of, or trends in, the *actual* qualifications of workers in different occupations.

12. The first report of the National Economic Development Council, *Growth of the United Kingdom economy to 1966* (1963a), Tables 1 and 6, provides an example of a direct estimate of future output and employment in seventeen selected industries. The estimates were based on the views of the industries themselves, but were checked against 'a tentative projection . . . of the industrial structure of the economy in 1966 in the 4 per cent case, based on provisional estimates of final demand' (para. 114).

Again an alternative is to adopt the pattern of qualifications in each occupation in a more advanced country or in the most advanced firms or industries in the country of study.

Since Britain is now committed to a specific target of economic growth, systems of manpower assessment of the general type proposed by the Organization for Economic Co-operation and Development deserve serious consideration. But they involve many problems, which must now be briefly summarized.

III. Problems of Forecasting Manpower Requirements

(a) Lack of data

On the practical side, there is in Britain a serious lack of relevant data, which influenced the Robbins Committee in not attempting a general assessment of manpower needs. In the first place, there were no comprehensive data on occupational distribution for any year after 1951. Secondly, the 1951 Census gave no information on types of educational qualifications, though it gave data on terminal ages of full-time education. The 1961 Census included an additional question on higher scientific and technological qualifications, but not on qualifications in other fields or at lower levels. It is to be hoped that in the 1966 Census this question will be extended to cover all qualifications. Moreover, for an adequate evaluation of manpower requirements it is important to examine the interrelations not only between education and occupation but also between these and age and salaries, and this would require an elaborate survey. It is to be hoped that a large-scale survey with this objective will be undertaken.

(b) Problems of methodology

We have referred in passing to many methodological difficulties of manpower forecasting, and it is worth summarizing what seem to be some of the crucial problems. To begin with, there are the difficulties of forecasting technical change and popular taste, both of which have profound effects on the pattern of growth of the economy. More specifically within the manpower field, there are the problems of projecting the occupational structure and the pattern of educational qualifications in each occupation.

In estimating occupational distribution, the major difficulty lies in assessing the effect of technical change. What, for example, will be the impact of automation? An examination of past occupational trends may throw some light on this, but one cannot assert with confidence that these trends will be maintained. For example, the proportion of the labour force in clerical occupations has been growing throughout this century but technical changes could well reverse this trend (Leicester, 1963). Nearly all fields of activity are influenced by technical change. But there are some whose role is largely to generate such change (e.g. pure research) and in these it is perhaps even more difficult to assess the optimal levels of employment.

Beyond this there is the question of the educational requirements of particular occupations. This is a special case of the problem of the substitution between factors of production – between capital and labour, and between people with different educational and other characteristics – to which we have already referred.

In some occupations (for example, doctors or teachers) there is a minimum educational qualification which is required by law or by convention. These are generally occupations where all the practitioners require for some of their work a minimum specific level of knowledge. Even here, of course, there is room for argument about what type of course is really needed and how long it should take. But in some occupations the area of uncertainty is much wider. In relation to managers, for example, a problem arises partly because the degree of responsibility held by those classified as managers varies widely, and partly because, even for managers with similar responsibilities, there is no clear-cut type or level of education which it was agreed they would require.

A first step in attempting to elucidate these questions would be to examine the pattern of qualifications actually held (now and in the past) by members of each occupation. But the difficulty is that, in the labour force as a whole, the pattern of qualifications is a reflection of past educational trends. It may be that many occupations employ too few qualified people because of a dearth in supply, or too many because of an excess. There has, for example, been a rapid increase since the war in the number of graduates (and especially of arts graduates) in industry and in the executive grade in the Civil Service, but this is not to say that graduate qualifications are necessarily the most suitable for the work. Some people would say that in this, and other cases, educational qualifications are being used as a way of selecting people for their ability rather than for their education.

To decide what pattern of qualifications is the most desirable, one must know the effects of substituting one type of qualification for another, other things being equal. In attempting this, there are major difficulties not only of measuring the effects, but also of isolating the contributions of education from those of natural ability and working experience.

There is also the further complication that substitution can occur not only within occupations, but also between occupations. As an example of the former, one might want to consider the use as managers of graduates as against non-graduates. Equally one might want to know the effects of a combination of, say, one technologist and three technicians as against two of each; or of one technologist compared with one arts graduate and a technician. Thus one needs to discover the educational requirements (or combinations of requirements) not for particular occupations but rather for particular sets of tasks. As things are, many occupations involve a wide range of tasks: the work of dentists ranges from highly skilled surgery to routine extractions, and school teachers often spend time supervising meals as well as teaching. One cannot assume that the allocation of tasks between occupations is immutable.

For most tasks there may be a minimum level of skill required to perform them at all, but this does not mean that a task should be performed by the least skilled person capable of doing it. People with more than this minimum may vary in the speed and effectiveness with which they can perform the task and those more highly skilled may do it more effectively than those less highly skilled. In the case of people with higher education there is the further point that they not only perform tasks that are put before them but they often discover new tasks to be undertaken.

It is thus obviously an enormous problem to try to specify what educational qualifications are 'needed' in the labour force. The problem of forecasting 'demand', as opposed to need, is easier only in the sense that the present position can be observed. But the problems of forecasting future developments are just as great. There is thus little force in the argument (occasionally advanced in discussions of the Robbins Report) that even if one did not aim to show how many graduates the country needed, one should at least show how the graduates who will result from expansion will be employed. [. . . .]

IV. Problems of Translating Manpower Requirements into Flows through the Educational System

Finally, we consider some problems which arise in translating manpower needs into requisite patterns of output from the educational system.

If it is decided that manpower criteria should largely determine educational provision, it is desirable that figures of manpower needs should be estimated (or interpolated) for a series of single years. The annual output of the educational system has then to provide for changes in stock and for losses over the year.

For any particular type of manpower there will, however, be cases where the trends in output required will be so unstable that the educational system could not aim to follow them in detail. If a manpower need has been growing at a constant rate and is expected to go on doing so, then output will also require to rise at a more or less constant rate. This poses no technical problems. But if the trend of manpower needs is variable, then sudden changes will be required in output. An accelerated rate of growth in manpower needs will require a more than proportionate rate of increase in output; a levelling off will require a more than proportionately reduced rate of growth or even a decline in output. This arises from the fact that the stock of manpower is determined by output over the last forty years or so, and the annual change in the stock is largely dependent on the difference between current output and output forty years ago.

In practice the requirements for particular types of manpower are unlikely to grow at constant rates of increase. At one time the need for one particular type of manpower may be increasing rapidly, and in a succeeding period it may tend to level off, while another need emerges sharply. One could think of various examples as between different specialities of science and engineering.

This creates serious problems for educational planning. For it will generally be difficult to achieve sudden increases in the flow of people with certain qualifications, and perhaps even more difficult to achieve sharp reductions, partly because the teachers are already there and are enthusiastic to maintain their subject, and partly because of difficulties in altering the use of buildings or equipment.

These are important reasons why educational plans could never be derived mechanically from forecasts of manpower needs. In addition, as we have indicated, such forecasts are at present unreliable and, even when better methods and data are available, they will remain subject to uncertainties. There are three implications for educational planning which we should like to mention. First, if students are educated in a way that fits them for more than one branch of activity, they will be more likely to find suitable and productive employment during their lives. Secondly, a substantial part of the educational system will need to be concerned with retraining. Thirdly, it will be easier to meet new manpower needs in a system that is rapidly expanding than in one where output is stable. [. . .]

V. The Relation between the Demand for Places and the Need for Qualified Manpower

We have considered two methods of gauging the number of places required in higher education: the first, to meet the demand for places, the second, to meet the needs for qualified manpower. In this final part, we consider briefly the relationship between these two approaches, which raises problems both for the researcher and for the policy-maker. Our main concern is with the former.

In theory at least, one can imagine certain conditions under which the demand for places would adjust itself automatically to the 'needs' of the economy. This would seem to require that the following conditions were satisfied (or that divergence from them were proportionate and counterbalancing):

(i) The lifetime salary differential for graduates would need to reflect exactly the marginal productivity of higher education;

(ii) the cost of higher education would need to be borne exclusively by the student;

(iii) potential students in deciding whether to stay on at school and enter higher education would need to act on an assessment of life-time salary prospects in relation to costs;

(iv) this assessment would need to be correct.

In practice, none of these conditions is likely to apply,[13] but financial prospects obviously have an important effect on the decisions of potential students about whether to try for higher education, and the future growth of the market for new graduates will affect the future demand for places. If the market demand for graduates were to expand less fast than their stock, one might expect a narrowing of the graduate salary differential and, eventually, a reduced rate of growth in the demand for places. Conversely, if market demand grew faster than stock, one might expect an increased differential and an upturn in the demand for places. Thus the rate of growth in the demand for places may, to some extent, adjust itself to the rate of growth in the demand for graduates. Similarly, students' faculty preferences may, to some extent, follow the pattern of market demand.

For these reasons, a forecast of the provision needed to meet anticipated demand for places should properly take into account a forecast of the economy's demand for graduates.[14] Equally, a forecast of the places required to satisfy manpower needs will be of little practical use, unless there is also a forecast of the demand for places which shows that a sufficient demand can be encouraged to fill the places indicated.

This raises the critical question of our ignorance of the extent to which the demand for places is influenced by policy. Some writers have suggested that the influence of policy is so strong that it makes little sense to try framing policy to meet the demand (Parnes, 1962, p. 64). This is perhaps a rather extreme view, and it is worth noting that in the last ten years, there has in this

13. There are some who argue that circumstances should be altered so that they more nearly apply (for example, Peacock and Wiseman, 1964).

14. As already mentioned, future demand at current relative salaries does not necessarily correspond with the number of graduates needed.

country been a remarkably stable trend in the proportion of the age group achieving given school-leaving qualifications, though this has been a period of sharp, and apparently relevant, policy changes. And it is interesting that, in the view of the French *Commission de l'équipement scolaire, universitaire et sportif*, 'there can be no question of halting or speeding up the general growth of secondary and higher education that is bound to result' from general factors of the kind discussed in section 2.3 (b) above (Poignant, 1963, p. 216).

The Robbins Committee took an intermediate position. As regards policy factors outside higher education – such as the school-leaving age or the provision of maintenance grants for sixth-formers – they could not make specific recommendations, and formed their estimates in the light of what seemed the most likely developments. But on matters of policy within the field of higher education, they were explicit. Thus, in making their estimates of the demand for places they made it clear that these depended on the assumption that policy on student maintenance would remain unchanged. They justified this assumption on the grounds that the nation should not risk discouraging able young people from entering higher education – an argument in tune with their judgement that the kind of expansion recommended was necessary to attain the growth targets set by the National Economic Development Council.[15]

By implication, however, the Committee assumed that it was easier to modify the pattern of demand between sectors and faculties than to influence its overall level. It goes without saying that any 'modification' of the demand for places would, in our society, be acceptable only if individual freedom of choice were maintained, and a good deal probably depends on the information (regarding places and prospects) available to those making the choice. There is probably a fair range of flexibility here in what boys and girls wish to do, and this explains why the Robbins Committee, while accepting expected demand as determining the overall number of places, took some account of manpower con-

15. In its second publication, *Conditions favourable to faster growth*, (1963b), the N.E.D.C. itself expressed the view that 'economic growth is dependent upon a high and advancing level of education' (para. 1), but emphasized the lack of established evidence on this point.

siderations in allocating places between sectors and faculties. A very similar procedure was adopted as part of the 4th French Plan (Poignant, ibid.).

But, even at this level, considerable practical difficulties may arise, as recent experience in this country shows. Since the Second World War, there has, in this country, been a fairly deliberate national policy on the provision of university places. In the immediate post-war period, this was based largely on manpower considerations. In 1946, the Barlow Committee[16] recommended an immediate doubling of the output of scientists and technologists, together with a substantial expansion in arts. This expansion was soon achieved, largely owing to the pressure of demand for places from ex-servicemen. During the first ten years after the war, the number of places increased a good deal faster in scientific subjects than in arts subjects and there is evidence that the demand for places followed the same pattern (U.G.C., 1948, p. 29, and the *Robbins Report*, Table 45). This swing of demand towards science may well have been encouraged by the doubts, regularly expressed by the University Grants Committee, about the employment prospects for arts graduates (U.G.C., 1948, p. 40, and U.G.C., 1953, para. 29).

Since 1955, the policies of the University Grants Committee appear to have given increasing weight to considerations of the probable demand for places. They have suggested that two-thirds of the additional provision should be for science and technology. This policy was arrived at essentially by examining the 'A'-level trends, but was confirmed by reference to the forecasts of the Committee on Scientific Manpower and of committees concerned with medical subjects (U.G.C., 1964, paras. 198 and 470). But no specific steps were taken to encourage the continuation of the 'A'-level trend towards science, and since 1959 it appears that the trend has altered in the direction of arts (the *Robbins Report*, Table 45). The result has been that the balance of demand does not correspond with the balance of provision and there is a greater pressure on places in arts than in scientific subjects (Universities Central Council on Admissions, 1964).

It seems to follow that if attempts are to be made to encourage

16. Committee appointed by the Lord President of the Council (1946).

certain types of demand and discourage others, there is need for a much better information service for schools (such as exists in, for example, Sweden), and for some conscious planning of the balance between specialities not only in higher education but also in the schools. The school plans for the immediate future would, because of the time lag involved, need to be related to the higher education plans for the more distant future.

There remains the policy question of what weights one would give, in framing policy on higher education, to considerations of manpower needs and of the demand for places if both could be adequately measured. There are many grounds for trying to consider both approaches (together, of course, with considerations of cost and staffing). Higher education has important consequences for national economic development; it is also expensive. For both reasons a nation could argue that future provision should up to a point be adjusted to manpower needs. Even looked at in less explicitly economic terms, there is a case for trying to ensure that those who have received higher education will find jobs offering a reasonable outlet for their qualifications. As for the demand for places, one can advance many arguments why this should influence the policy-maker – some based on grounds of education seen as consumption, others on the harmful effects of excessive competition on the educational system, others again based on grounds of fairness to children irrespective of sex or the size of the age group in which they are born.

How these arguments balance against each other is a matter of judgement for the policy-makers. There would normally be a strong case for providing at least as many places as are needed on manpower grounds, assuming that these can be assessed and that they are related to national targets that have already been decided on. This may, on occasion, make it desirable to try to stimulate the demand for places. Conversely, if the demand for places (based on current policies) is expected to be higher than is needed on manpower ground, the policy-makers must judge how strong a case there is for meeting it on social and educational grounds.

In conclusion, we must stress that decisions as to how much weight to put on the demand for places and how much on mapower needs cannot be made on purely technical grounds. The instruments of measurement are likely to remain too blunt to provide precise information for the eventual political decision. But if the country is moving into a period of more systematic economic planning, it may well be that manpower considerations will come to play a more important part in educational planning than hitherto. For these considerations to be at all securely based will require far better information at national level than is yet available as well as more intensive research.

References

ADVISORY COUNCIL ON SCIENTIFIC POLICY, COMMITTEE ON SCIENTIFIC MANPOWER (1959) *Scientific and engineering manpower in Great Britain 1959.* H.M.S.O.

ADVISORY COUNCIL ON SCIENTIFIC POLICY, COMMITTEE ON SCIENTIFIC MANPOWER (1961) *The long-term demand for scientific manpower.* H.M.S.O.

ADVISORY COUNCIL ON SCIENTIFIC POLICY, COMMITTEE ON SCIENTIFIC MANPOWER (1963) *Scientific and technological manpower in Great Britain 1962.* H.M.S.O.

CENTRAL ADVISORY COUNCIL FOR EDUCATION (ENGLAND) (1963) *Half our future.* H.M.S.O.

COMMITTEE APPOINTED BY THE LORD PRESIDENT OF THE COUNCIL (1946) *Scientific manpower.* H.M.S.O.

DOUGLAS, J. W. B. (1964) *The home and the school.* MacGibbon & Kee.

GENERAL REGISTER OFFICE, GENERAL REGISTRY OFFICE, SCOTLAND (1962) *Census 1961, Great Britain, Scientific and technological qualifications.* H.M.S.O.

LEICESTER, C. (1963) 'The composition of manpower requirements', in *Economic growth and manpower.* British Association for Commercial and Industrial Education.

MINISTRY OF HEALTH, DEPARTMENT OF HEALTH FOR SCOTLAND (1956) *Report of the Committee on Recruitment to the Dental Profession,* H.M.S.O.

MINISTRY OF HEALTH, DEPARTMENT OF HEALTH FOR SCOTLAND (1957) *Report of the Committee to Consider the Future Numbers of Medical Practitioners and the Appropriate Intake of Medical Students.* H.M.S.O.

MOBERG, S. (1959) 'Methods and techniques for forecasting specialized manpower requirements', in *Forecasting manpower needs for the age of science.* Organization for European Economic Co-operation.

MUSHKIN, S. J. (ed.) (1962) *The economics of higher education.* U.S. Department of Health, Education, and Welfare.

THE NATIONAL ADVISORY COUNCIL ON THE TRAINING AND SUPPLY OF TEACHERS (1961) *Teachers for further education.* H.M.S.O.

THE NATIONAL ADVISORY COUNCIL ON THE TRAINING AND SUPPLY OF TEACHERS (1962) Seventh Report, *The demand and supply of teachers 1960–80.* H.M.S.O.

NATIONAL ECONOMIC DEVELOPMENT COUNCIL (1963a) *Growth of the United Kingdom economy to 1966.* H.M.S.O.

NATIONAL ECONOMIC DEVELOPMENT COUNCIL (1963b) *Conditions favourable to faster growth.* H.M.S.O.

NATIONAL INCOMES COMMISSION (1964) Report No. 3. *Remuneration of academic staff in universities and colleges of advanced technology.* H.M.S.O.

OFFICE OF THE LORD PRESIDENT OF THE COUNCIL, MINISTRY OF LABOUR AND NATIONAL SERVICE (1956) *Scientific and engineering manpower in Great Britain.* H.M.S.O.

PARNES, H. S. (1962) *Forecasting educational needs for economic and social development.* Paris: Organization for Economic Co-operation and Development.

PARNES, H. S. (ed.) (1963) *Planning education for economic and social development.* Paris: Organization for Economic Co-operation and Development.

PEACOCK, A. T. and WISEMAN, J. (1964) *Education for democrats.* London: Institute of Economic Affairs.

POIGNANT, R. (1963) 'Establishing educational targets in France' in PARNES, H. S. (ed.) *Planning education for economic and social development.* Paris: Organization for Economic Co-operation and Developme␣t.

STONE, R. (1962) *A computable model of economic growth.* Chapman and Hall.

SVIMEZ (ASSOCIAZIONE PER LO SVILUPPO DELL'INDUSTRIA NEL MEZZOGIORNO) *Trained manpower requirements in the next fifteen years.* Rome, 1961.

TROW, M. (1964) 'A question of size and shape', *Universities Quarterly,* **18,** 2.

U.S. DEPARTMENT OF LABOR, BUREAU OF LABOR STATISTICS (1961) *The long-range demand for scientific and technical personnel.* Washington: National Science Foundation.

UNIVERSITIES CENTRAL COUNCIL ON ADMISSIONS (1964) *First Report 1961–63.* London: U.C.C.A.

UNIVERSITY GRANTS COMMITTEE (1948) *University development from 1935 to 1947.* H.M.S.O.

UNIVERSITY GRANTS COMMITTEE (1953), *University development, Report on the years 1947 to 1952.* H.M.S.O.

UNIVERSITY GRANTS COMMITTEE (1964), *University development, 1957–1962.* H.M.S.O.

VAIZEY, J. (1962), *The economics of education.* Faber and Faber.

WILLIAMS, B. R. (1963), 'University expansion in the short-term', in *Home universities conference*. The Association of Commonwealth Universities.

DE WOLFF, P. (1962), 'Employment forecasting techniques in the Netherlands', in *Employment forecasting*. Paris: Organization for Economic Co-operation and Development.

15 K. J. Arrow and W. M. Capron

Shortages and Salaries: The Engineer–Scientist Case in the
United States

K. J. Arrow and W. M. Capron, 'Dynamic shortages and price rises: the
engineer–scientist case', *Quarterly Journal of Economics*, vol. 73 (1959),
no. 2, pp. 292–308.

The frequent and loud complaints of a shortage of engineers and
scientists heard over the past eight years or so might be taken as
indicating a failure of the price mechanism and indeed have frequently been joined with (rather vaguely stated) proposals for
interference with market determination of numbers and allocation. It is our contention that these views stem from a misunderstanding of economic theory as well as from an exaggeration of
the empirical evidence. On the contrary, a proper view of the
workings of the market mechanism, recognizing, in particular,
the dynamics of market adjustment to changed conditions, would
show that the phenomenon of observed shortage in some degree
is exactly what would be predicted by classical theory in the face
of rapidly rising demands.

In this paper we present a model which explains the dynamics
of the market adjustment process and apply the conclusions
drawn from this analysis to the scientist–engineer 'shortage'.

Equality of supply and demand is a central tenet of ordinary
economic theory, but only as the end result of a process, not as a
state holding at every instant of time. On the contrary, inequalities
between supply and demand are usually regarded as an integral
part of the process by which the price on a market reaches its
equilibrium position. Price is assumed to rise when demand
exceeds supply and to fall in the contrary case.[1] A shortage, in the
sense of an excess of demand over supply, is then the normal concomitant of a price rise.

1. See, for example, Marshall's well-known analysis of the equilibrating
process on the corn market, *Principles of economics*, 8th ed., pp. 332–4.
P. A. Samuelson has shown the fundamental importance of the law of supply
and demand in stability analysis; see *Foundations of economic analysis*, pp.
263, 269–70.

318

If we assume stability of the market mechanism, the shortage observed during the equilibrating process is transitory and tends to disappear as the price approaches equilibrium. If, however, the demand curve is steadily shifting upward at the same time, the shortage will persist, and the price will continue to rise. We argue that the interaction of rising demand with price movements which do not instantaneously equate supply and demand provides a plausible interpretation of the recent history of the engineer–scientist market in the United States from about 1950 to date. We also suggest a more detailed account of the price-adjustment mechanism than the bare statement that price varies according to the inequality between supply and demand.

I. Shortages and Price Rises

In what follows, we use the terms supply and demand to mean the aggregation of *the choices made by all firms and individuals in equilibrium at a given price* on a given market. Thus for a firm, the quantity demanded or supplied at a given price is that which maximizes profits. The equilibrium of each firm does not, of course, imply the equilibrium of the market, since the aggregate of the decisions of all firms need not lead to equality of supply and demand. At any given moment, the decision made by a firm or individual need not be optimal from its point of view at the given price, since economic agents require time to make decisions and to learn. It is assumed that each agent gradually corrects its errors, but in the process the firm or individual will not, by definition, be on its demand or supply curve. We hold that the process by which an economic agent moves towards its own internal equilibrium is an integral part of the process by which the market as a whole comes into equilibrium.

In Marshall's formulation, two equilibria were distinguished, short-run and long-run. A movement along a long-run demand or supply curve manifests itself as a shift in the short-run curve. Market price at any moment may diverge from *both* equilibrium prices. In comparative static analysis all that is shown is that under certain assumptions about the nature of supply and demand functions, price will tend to move toward both short-run and long-run equilibrium price, given a shift in one or both of these functions. Over short periods of time, in which we are interested, the shift of the short-run demand or supply functions can be taken as exogenous trends, and will be so treated in this paper. Our analysis is, in Marshallian terms, short-run; but it differs from the neoclassical analysis in that we are presenting a model which explains not only the direction of price adjustment (i.e., toward equilibrium) but the rate of adjustment in the face of continued shifts in the short-run functions.

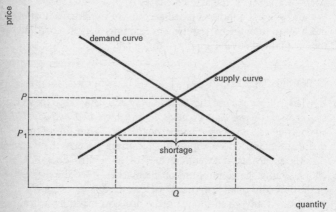

Figure 1

For purposes of comparison we draw the usual price-quantity diagram (see Figure 1). If P_1 is the initial price, we expect the existence of a shortage to raise the price gradually to the equilibrium value P. During the process the shortage decreases to zero. The shortage can persist only if the price is held at some value such as P_1 by an outside force, such as price control. In that case we have a shortage due to a fundamental imperfection of the market.

Now suppose that we have a market which is initially in equilibrium. For concreteness, we may think of it as the market for engineers and scientists. Suppose further that the price of a commodity that uses engineers in its production has increased. Assume further that each firm producing this commodity was in equilibrium before the increase in the commodity price, that is, that it had as many engineers as it wished to hire at a given salary level. Under the new conditions, the number of engineers that it would pay the firm to hire at the previous salary has gone up, and therefore the market demand has risen. The change from the old situation to the new is illustrated in Figure 2. Here D_1 represents

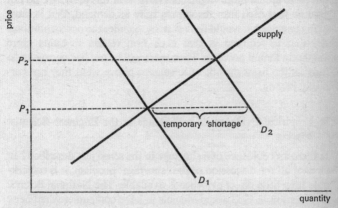

Figure 2

the original demand curve for engineers. Curve D_2 represents the new demand arising from some change in external conditions, in this instance the rise in the price of the commodity in whose production the engineers are engaged. Recall that for present purposes we define demand as the amount which the firm would choose to buy after careful calculation. At any given moment of time the firm may not be fully aware of what its demand (in our sense) is and seek to hire more or fewer engineers. But we do assume that the firm will gradually become aware of any such errors and correct them.

In Figure 2, P_1 represents the equilibrium price when the demand curve is D_1. Let us assume that in fact P_1 was the price prevailing just before the shift in the demand curve. After the demand curve has shifted to D_2, the price that would bring supply and demand into equilibrium is P_2. But movement to this price or salary level typically will take time.

Consider the situation of a firm just after the shift of the demand curve to D_2. A comparison of Figures 1 and 2 shows a strong analogy, not to say identity. At the moment of the shift, the market is experiencing a shortage, which is in many respects comparable to what it would face under price control. Each firm seeks to hire additional engineers at the price it currently pays, but there are no more engineers available at this price. We do not assume that each firm recognizes fully its demand, that is, how many engineers it would be best to have under the new conditions. All that is required is that each firm realize it wants more engineers than it now has. Then there will be unfilled vacancies so long as the firms do not raise salaries above what they are currently paying.

II. Empirical Evidence of a Shortage in the Engineer–Scientist Market

Is there any evidence of a shortage in the sense just described? In view of all the discussion of the 'shortage' problem, it is remarkable how little direct evidence is available. The National Science Foundation in 1953 asked officials in large companies whether or not they were experiencing a shortage of engineers and scientists for research and development purposes,[2] but no clear operational definition of the term 'shortage' was supplied to these officials. It is plausible to suppose that a respondent would interpret the term to mean the existence of unfilled vacancies with salaries equal to those of engineers and scientists now employed by the firm and performing equivalent services. At least half of the firms reported that they were unable to hire enough research scientists and engineers to meet their needs, although, except for the aircraft industry, there was no industry in which all firms reported such a shortage.

The picture given by the National Science Foundation study is similar to that given by G. W. Beste in a study of the chemical industry.[3] Referring to the Ethyl Corporation, Beste states, 'We

2. See National Science Foundation, *Scientific Manpower Bulletin No. 6*, 1 August 1955.

3. G. W. Beste, 'A case study of the shortage of scientists and engineers in the chemical industry', presented at the second meeting of the National Committee for the Development of Scientists and Engineers, 21 June 1956.

employ 370 chemical engineers today but need an additional 39. This 39 represents the accumulated deficiency of the last five years.'[4] The meaning of the term 'deficiency' is not explained, but it is perhaps fair to assume that it means the inability to fill vacancies at salaries then being paid to employees. If Beste and the respondents to the National Science Foundation's survey have understood the term 'shortage' in this way, there is then fragmentary evidence of a shortage as manifested by unfilled vacancies, but this shortage is not large. Such a situation is to be expected when the demand curve has shifted and the price does not immediately rise to the level that would equate supply and demand.

III. The Process of Adjustment in the Market

We will trace briefly the sequence of events that will be observed in the market as a result of the shift in the demand curve from D_1 to D_2. At the moment, any individual firm may not have fully calculated how many more engineers it could profitably hire, but we may suppose that it will be aware of wanting more engineers than it now employs. It will begin by seeking to hire more engineers at the going salary but will find that there are none to be had. Its advertised vacancies find no takers; its offers are refused. The firm becomes aware that in order to hire additional engineers it must pay higher salaries, and it will now have to calculate whether or not the additional product derivable from additional engineers will be sufficient to cover the higher level of salaries. In the situation envisaged, the firm will indeed eventually decide to hire some additional engineers at a higher salary, but the decision will take time. First, there must be recognition of the need for higher salaries, then approval must be obtained from various echelons of management, and finally orders must be issued to hire.

Thus the time lag in the firm's reaction is spent partly in learning about the supply conditions in the market and partly in

4. Actually, this deficiency turns out to be largely the product of the two years, 1955 and 1956. It is typical of the lack of historical perspective in the engineer–scientist shortage discussion that such short-run phenomena are made the basis for discussion of long-run policies.

determining the profitability of additional hiring under the new supply conditions. This, however, is only one step in the process of adjustment. First of all, the firm may not yet have fully adjusted to the new demand curve; it has hired some more engineers than before but possibly not as many as would achieve maximum profitability. But second, even if the firm has hired as many as would be profitable at the new salary level, the market as a whole would still not be in equilibrium, because the firm is now paying a lower salary to its old employees than to the new ones, and there is really more than one price being paid for the identical services rendered by different individuals. The multiplicity of prices is characteristic of disequilibrium situations, but in any well-developed market it cannot persist indefinitely. What happens is that other firms, also experiencing shortages, bid for the services of the engineers belonging to the firm we have been considering. While old employees will probably have some reluctance to move, this reluctance is certainly not absolute and can be overcome by a sufficiently high salary offer. That engineers do change jobs in sufficient numbers to suggest a responsiveness to market forces has been shown by Blank and Stigler.[5] However, we would again expect a lag in information.[6] An employed engineer may not be in touch with current salary offers, and it may take some time before he is aware that the salary he is receiving is below what he might receive elsewhere. We would, however, certainly expect that he will become informed eventually, and that the discrepancy between his actual and his possible salary will tend to be reduced over time. While some individuals will not be tempted to move even in the presence of considerable possible salary increases, many would be willing to

5. David M. Blank and George J. Stigler, *The demand and supply of scientific personnel*, New York, National Bureau of Economic Research, 1957, pp. 29–30.

6. We might note that in some markets such as the organized exchanges for securities or commodities information is available very quickly, indeed almost instantaneously, but this is clearly accomplished only because it has been found worthwhile for those who buy and sell on these markets to pay the costs of the operation of such exchanges. No such exchange exists for scientists and engineers, and one can understand why: the product is not homogeneous, and each unit of supply is controlled by a different owner (i.e. the individual scientist or engineer himself).

do so; either they will in fact move or the hiring firm, to keep them, will raise their salaries to the competitive level. Thus the initial tendency within the firm for new employees to enjoy higher salaries than old ones will gradually be overcome as the salaries of the latter are raised in response to competition.

There is another mechanism which will work to eliminate salary differences within a firm but at the expense of slowing down the firm's willingness to raise salary offers for new personnel. Salary differences within the firm are certain to be a source of morale problems to the extent that they are known, and clearly complete secrecy is out of the question. There will be pressure on the firm to increase the salaries of all its employees (in the same category) to the new higher levels. The lag in adjustment of the salaries of already-employed engineer–scientists is thereby reduced, but on the other hand the firm is more reluctant to increase its salary offers to new employees because it realizes it must incur the increased cost not only for the new employees but also for the old ones. In effect the additional cost of the salary rise is recognized by the firm to be much greater if it has to extend the increase to all employees.

The total lag in the response of salaries to a shortage (in the sense of an excess of demand over supply) is then compounded out of the time it takes the firm to recognize the existence of a shortage at the current salary level, the time it takes to decide upon the need for higher salaries and the number of vacancies at such salaries, and either the time it takes employees to recognize the salary alternatives available and to act upon this information or the time it takes the firm to equalize salaries without outside offers.

IV. A Model of Dynamic Shortages and Price Rises

While there is, strictly speaking, no one market price during the process of adjusting supply to increased demand, a multiplicity of prices being characteristic, we may focus attention on the average price being paid for engineering services. The preceding discussion makes clear that the average price will tend to rise so long as there is an excess of demand over supply, but it will not rise instantaneously to the level that will bring supply and mand into equality (P_2 in Figure 2). Further, the forces that induce price rises will clearly operate more strongly the greater the excess of demand over supply. Hence we find it reasonable to accept the usual view that the rate of increase of price per unit of time is greater the greater the excess of demand over supply. As a corollary, price will cease rising when the price is such that demand equals supply. Recall that demand and supply at any given price are defined as the quantities demanded and supplied after complete rational calculation.

Call the ratio of the rate of price rise to the excess of demand over supply the *reaction speed*. Then the amount of shortage will tend to disappear faster the greater the reaction speed and also the greater the elasticity of supply (or demand).[7]

Let p be the (average) price, k the reaction speed, D demand, S supply, and t time. The movement of the market over time is determined, in the above model, by the following relations (using linear approximations for the demand and supply functions):

$$\frac{dp}{dt} = k(D - S), \tag{1}$$

$$D = -ap + c, \tag{2}$$

$$S = bp + d. \tag{3}$$

Equation (1) expresses the assumption in the text about the relation between price rises and the difference between supply and demand; equations (2) and (3) are simple assumptions about the nature of the demand and supply functions, as represented graphically in Figures 1 and 2.

Let X represent the shortage, i.e. $X = D - S$. From (2) and (3),

$$X = -(a + b)p + (c - d). \tag{4}$$

Differentiate (4) with respect to time; then

$$\frac{dX}{dt} = -(a + b)\left(\frac{dp}{dt}\right).$$

7. See K. J. Arrow, 'Price-quantity adjustments in multiple markets with rising demands', The RAND Corporation, P-1364-RC, 7 May 1958, to be published in *Proceedings of the First Stanford Symposium on mathematical methods in the social sciences* (Stanford University Press).

If we then substitute from (1) and replace $D - S$ by X, we have,

$$\frac{dX}{dt} = -k(a + b)X. \tag{5}$$

Thus for any given shortage X, the speed of convergence is greater the greater $k(a + b)$. In particular, other things being equal, the smaller the value of b (which is closely related to the elasticity of supply), the slower will be the convergence of the shortage X to zero.

We have thus far been sketching a way of looking at the response of the market to a single shift of the demand curve; we have suggested that the price will tend to move to the new equilibrium but with a lag. This analysis has been preliminary to our main purpose, which is to consider a situation of *continuing* change in demand (or supply). We will suggest that this has been the case for engineer–scientists in the period beginning about 1950. If, for example, the demand curve is rising steadily, then as the market price approaches the equilibrium price the latter steadily moves away from the former. There will be a chronic shortage in the sense that as long as the rise in demand occurs buyers at any given moment will desire more of the commodity at the average price being paid than is being offered, and the amount of the shortage will not approach zero. The price will increase steadily and indefinitely but always remain below the price that would clear the market. This condition will continue as long as demand is increasing.

The steady upward shift in demand may be represented by adding a trend term to the demand as given by (2),

$$D = -ap + c + et, \tag{6}$$

where t represents time and e the rate of increase of demand with time for any given price. Let X be the amount of shortage, i.e. $D - S$. From (3) and (6),

$$X = -(a + b)p + (c - d) + et. \tag{7}$$

Differentiate all the terms of (7) with respect to time.

$$\frac{dX}{dt} = -(a + b)\left(\frac{dp}{dt}\right) + e. \tag{8}$$

327

The Manpower-Forecasting Approach

In view of the definition of X, (1) can be written,

$$\frac{dp}{dt} = kX. \tag{9}$$

Substitute from (9) for dp/dt into (8).

$$\frac{dX}{dt} = -(a+b)kX + e. \tag{10}$$

Assume that at the beginning, there is no shortage, so that $S = D$, or $X = 0$. Then from (10) we see that $dX/dt > 0$, so that the shortage X starts increasing and must continue to increase (since if dX/dt ever reached zero, it would remain at zero thereafter). It is also easy to see that,

$$\lim_{t \to \infty} X(t) \frac{e}{(a+b)k}, \tag{11}$$

so that the shortages tend to a limit which is greater the greater the rate of increase of demand and the slower the speed of adjustment would have been with an unshifting demand schedule.

Let p' be the rate of increase of prices, i.e., dp/dt. Differentiate (9) with respect to time, and then substitute from (8).

$$\frac{dp'}{dt} = k\frac{dX}{dt} = -k(a+b)p' + ke. \tag{12}$$

By the same reasoning as with (10), p' must be increasing over time and approaching a limit. Since it is zero to begin with, it follows that p' must be positive for all t, so that, by the definition of p', the price p must be increasing steadily.

Let p^* be the price at any time which would clear the market, that is, which would make $X = 0$. In view of (7), p^* satisfies the equation,

$$0 = -(a+b)p^* + (c-d) + et. \tag{13}$$

Multiply through in (13) by k.

$$0 = -k(a+b)p^* + k(c-d) + ket. \tag{14}$$

Let q be the excess of the market-clearing price over the actual price, i.e., $q = p^* - p$. Substitute from (7) into (9).

$$p' = -k(a+b)p + k(c-d) + ket \tag{15}$$

Subtract (14) from (15) and use the definition of q.

$$p' = k(a+b)q \tag{16}$$

Since p' is positive and increases from zero to a limit, the same must be true of q. Thus the actual price will always remain below the market-clearing price and indeed the gap will actually widen with time, but the two time paths will approach parallelism.

The discussion to this point has dealt with a single market. In the real world there are a number of related markets. Firms in different industries, in different localities, etc., may in any given case compete for the services of engineer–scientists of certain specified skills. Therefore the firms in any one industry will find that the supply available to them depends not only on their own salary offers but on the salary levels in all industries buying similar skills. In short, the demand for engineer–scientists comes from a whole series of inter-related markets. This situation cannot be represented graphically, but the general conclusions just drawn remain valid.

In the market for engineer–scientists or for any other commodity we expect that a steady upward shift in the demand curve over a period of time will produce a shortage, that is, a situation in which there are unfilled vacancies in positions where salaries are the same as those being currently paid in others of the same type and quality. Such a shortage we will term a *dynamic shortage*. The magnitude of the dynamic shortage depends upon the rate of increase in demand, the reaction speed in the market, and the elasticity of supply and demand. The reaction speed in any particular market depends partly on institutional arrangements, such as the prevalence of long-term contracts, and partly on the rapidity with which information about salaries, vacancies, and availability of personnel becomes generally available throughout the market. In the case of an organized exchange, such as those for securities or certain agricultural products, we should expect the information to be passed on so rapidly that the reaction speed is virtually infinite and dynamic shortages virtually nonexistent.[8] In the following section we will advance evidence for the hypothesis that the engineer–scientist market for the last seven or eight years has shown a dynamic shortage in the sense just defined.

8. Thus, in Marshall's example of the corn market (op. cit.) the adjustment process took a day. In the market for scientist and engineers the 'day' will be much longer – say, several weeks or even months.

V. Dynamic Shortage in the Engineer–Scientist Market

The preceding analysis has been very abstract. Though we have referred to the market for engineer–scientists for the sake of concreteness, actually everything said would be equally applicable to any other market. We want to argue here that because of the character of the engineer–scientist market and the demands made on it over the last few years, the magnitude of the dynamic shortage may well have been sufficient to account for a great proportion of the complaints. It should be made clear that we are not arguing that the market is subject to unusual imperfections. Rather the very way in which the market performs its function leads to the shortage in this particular period.

A dynamic shortage is a possible explanation of the observed tensions in the engineer–scientist market because (1) there has been a rapid and steady rise in demand, (2) the elasticity of supply is low, especially for short periods, and (3) the reaction speed on the engineer–scientist market may, for several reasons, be expected to be slow. The hypothesis stated in the previous section would imply that under such conditions a dynamic shortage could be expected. And we believe that such a shortage would largely explain such reactions as intensified recruiting and attempts at long-range policy changes observable in the industries affected.

(1) The market on which the tensions seem to be focused is not the engineer–scientist market in general but the market for engineers and scientists for research and development purposes. It is a matter of common knowledge that there has been a very rapid increase in demand in this market. During the year 1951 the total number of research engineers and scientists in industry rose from 74,028 to 91,585, an increase of 17,557 or 23·7 per cent.[9] Such an increase is clearly capable of putting a strain on the smooth functioning of almost any market.

The increase in demand is, in turn, to be explained chiefly by

9. See U.S. Department of Labor, Bureau of Labor Statistics, *Scientific research and development in American industry: A study of manpower and costs*, Bulletin No. 1148, 1953, Tables C-5 (p. 62) and C-11 (p. 68). This source gives the January 1952 employment and the percentage increase; the other figures were calculated from these two.

the action of the government in contracting for research and development work by private industry. The increase in the number of research engineers and scientists employed on government contracts during the year 1951 was 15,547,[10] so that virtually the whole increase in employment of research engineers and scientists was due to government demand. The importance of the increase in government demand as the chief explanation of shortages has also been stressed by some observers, such as C. B. Jolliffe, of the Radio Corporation of America.[11] Jolliffe also states that the type of research and development done on military contract is more complicated than the usual industrial work. This would imply that there is some differentiation between the markets for engineer–scientists in military and in other research and development, so that the full force of the increased demand would fall on the former.

(2) The elasticity of the supply of engineer–scientists with respect to price changes may be expected to be small but not zero over short periods of time, owing to the length of time it takes to train new personnel. Over longer periods, higher salaries will certainly elicit a greater supply, though again because of the importance of non-economic factors in choosing a career and because of the uncertainty of rewards in the distant future, the responsiveness of supply will be less than for commodities such as manufactured goods. Hence while it would be totally incorrect to deny the influence of price on supply, the responsiveness is sufficiently low to add to the possibility of a dynamic shortage.

(3) There are three reasons why it might be expected that the speed of reaction in the engineer–scientist market would be slower than that in the markets for other commodities, such as

10. ibid., Table C-13 (p. 70), shows that the number employed on government contracts in January 1952 was 45,425 and that this figure was an increase of 52 per cent over that of January 1951. The figure in the text is calculated from these two.

11. C. B. Jolliffe, 'Electronics: A case study of the shortage of scientists and engineers', delivered to the President's Committee for the Development of Scientists and Engineers, 21 June 1956. In discussing his own company, Jolliffe says, 'We could use one thousand more right now without any question. Where could we use them? Mainly on military contracts because it is here – rather than in consumer and industrial electronics – that the pinch is tightest' (p. 6).

manufactured goods, or even than in other labor markets. They are the prevalence of long-term contracts, the influence of the heterogeneity of the market in slowing the diffusion of information, and the dominance of a relatively small number of firms in research and development.

Typically, for the engineer–scientist already employed by the government, a university, or a private industrial firm, there will be no instantaneous adjustment in the price he receives even in the face of demand changes, since contracts are not subject to daily renegotiation. Even in the absence of specific contractual elements of this sort, reaction is slowed down because of the greater job security which comes with long service with a particular employer. Professorial tenure is an extreme and institutionalized form of this phenomenon.

We have remarked earlier that the market for engineer–scientists is not a single one. The heterogeneity of the market may interfere with the diffusion of information because an individual engineer–scientist may not know to which market he belongs. He may be aware that an associate is getting a higher salary, which may suggest that he ought to look around for another position. But he may very well wonder whether the associate's higher salary is perhaps due to superior ability or to the fact that somewhat different skills are being rewarded more highly at the moment. Because of his doubts he may be delayed in ascertaining his alternative opportunities. Thus the length of time before he actually does achieve a higher salary, either from another firm or from his own, will be longer, and the reaction speed will be correspondingly less.

Finally, one special characteristic of the market for engineers and scientists in research and development is that the typical buyer is large; in particular a single buyer, the government, directly and indirectly accounts for about half of the total demand.[12] Up to a certain point a large firm with large competitors has an incentive to keep salaries down rather than bid engineer-

12. Bureau of Labor Statistics Bulletin No. 1148, op. cit., presents some relevant figures for 1951. In that year, seven companies spent 26 per cent of the total expenditures on research and development in industry (p. 21), and the government financed 46.8 per cent of all such expenditures (Table 4) in addition to research performed directly by the government.

scientists away from competitors. Any one firm in an industry dominated by a few large ones will fear that increasing salaries in order to attract more scientists and engineers may set off competitive bidding that will end up with no substantial change in the distribution of scientists and engineers among firms but a considerably higher salary bill. This is especially likely to be the attitude of firms if the total supply of the engineer–scientists for which they are competing is not likely to change much in response to higher prices.

The desire to avoid competitive bidding sometimes takes the form of 'no-raiding' agreements, drawn up among otherwise competing firms in the same industry. Such a situation is alleged to exist to some extent in the electrical equipment and electronics industries, dominated by General Electric, Westinghouse, and the Radio Corporation of America, and in aircraft, where a handful of firms account for the bulk of the research and development and of output.

But in no case do the large firms dominate the research and development market to such an extent that 'no-raiding' agreements or other devices to limit competition in hiring can be effective indefinitely. If nothing else happens, the competition of smaller firms forces the large firms to match their offers. There is no evidence that attempts by large firms to avoid competitive bidding can in the long run prevent the market price from reaching its equilibrium level. But they certainly can slow down the speed with which prices will rise in response to an excess of demand over supply and so, in accordance with the analysis of the preceding section, increase and prolong the dynamic shortage.

VI. Alternate Definitions of a Shortage

It is not our purpose here to present an exhaustive review of alternative concepts of shortage. However, it is appropriate to call attention to the discussion of the alleged shortage of scientists and engineers presented in the recently published, important study of the engineer–scientist market by Blank and Stigler.[13]

After considering several definitions of the term 'shortage', the authors settle on the following: 'A shortage exists when the

13. Blank and Stigler, op. cit., p. 9; ch. II, p. 2.

number of workers available (the supply) increases less rapidly than the number demanded *at the salaries paid in the recent past*. Then salaries will rise, and activities which were once performed by (say) engineers must now be performed by a class of workers less well trained and less expensive.'[14] Blank and Stigler rely primarily on a comparison of the earnings of engineers with the earnings of other professional groups and wage earners in order to test the hypothesis of a shortage of engineers. By definition a shortage exists if the relative earnings of engineers have risen.

The authors look at such data as are available going back to 1929, in more detail at the period since 1939, and in still greater detail at the post-World War II period. They say:

We may summarize these pieces of information on engineering earnings as follows. Since 1929, engineering salaries have declined substantially relative to earnings of all wage earners and relative to incomes of independent professional practitioners. Especially since 1939 engineering salaries have declined relative to the wage or salary income of the entire group of professional, technical and kindred workers, as well as to the working population as a whole. After the outbreak of the Korean War there was a minor increase in the relative salaries of engineers (and of other college trained workers), but this was hardly more than a minor cross-current in a tide. Relative to both the working population as a whole and the professions as a separate class, then, the record of earnings would suggest that up to at least 1955 there had been no shortage – in fact an increasingly ample supply – of engineers.[15]

The Blank–Stigler conclusion that there has been no significant shortage must be viewed not only in the light of their definition but also in the context of their major concern with long-run trends, not short-run phenomena. It might be pointed out, however, that it is only in the post-Korean era that there have been any complaints of shortages in this market. Therefore even if one is primarily concerned with the broad sweep of events, it seems proper to suggest that the period of real interest as far as possible shortage goes is that of the last few years, and with this interest in mind one may legitimately view 'the minor cross-current' as being significant. The reason that Blank and Stigler adduce for dismissing the evidence of a shortage (by their own definition as

14. ibid., p. 24. Italics by Blank and Stigler.
15. ibid., pp. 28–9.

tested by their own data) in the years since 1950 is that the relative change in salaries of engineers has been so slight that the shortage could not have been serious. But concluding that the market is a free, competitively working market, they do not consider the suggestion put forward here, namely, that even though there may be no obvious imperfections in the market, there may be a considerable lag in the adjustment of salaries in response to changes in demand.

It is worth noting just what the Blank–Stigler data do show. By their definition a shortage exists whenever the price of a given commodity rises. From 1950 to 1956 they show a rise in average starting salaries for college graduates with an engineering degree of 51.5 per cent.[16] Since increases in starting salaries for college graduates in other fields have been roughly comparable (though none are quite so high for this same period), this merely indicates, by their definition, that there has been a shortage of college graduates in general, i.e., a rise in their relative wages. (The same table shows that, for the period 1950–55, starting engineers' salaries increased by 38.0 per cent compared with an increase for manufacturing wage earnings of 31.8 per cent.)

Blank and Stigler acknowledge that there has been considerable talk about a shortage of engineers and scientists, but having concluded that there has not in fact been a 'shortage' of the price-rise type of any significance, they make no attempt to explain all the talk except to point to the use of the word 'shortage' as embodying some social criterion. It may be their hypothesis that the recent complaints of 'shortage' have been based solely on this use of the term.

As we have recognized elsewhere,[17] there are other possible explanations for at least some of the public concern over the 'shortage' of scientists and engineers in recent years. It should be emphasized that many of those who have discussed this problem have been using the term 'shortage' in a very different sense from that we have employed here. In particular, careful reading of such statements indicates that the speakers have in effect been saying: There are not as many engineers and scientists as this nation should have in order to do all the things that need doing such as

16. ibid., Table 14, p. 28.
17. Alchian, Arrow, Capron, op. cit.

maintaining our rapid rate of technological progress, raising our standard of living, keeping us militarily strong, etc. In other words, they are saying that (in the economic sense) demand for technically skilled manpower *ought* to be greater than it is – it is really a shortage of *demand* for scientists and engineers which concerns them. A somewhat different implicit definition of shortage which has been applied asserts that since we are not producing scientists and engineers at as fast a rate as the Soviet Union we have a 'shortage'. Still another explanation of the complaints may be found if one recalls the servant shortage of World War II days. In that situation, there is no evidence that the market did not respond to changed supply and demand conditions; alternative opportunities for employment developed for those who had previously been servants; the higher wages in these alternate lines of employment lured many to these occupations so that, *at the price they had been paying for household help*, many families found they could no longer find such people. Rather than admit that they could not pay the higher wages necessary to keep help, many individuals found it more felicitous to speak of a 'shortage'. There is reason to think that at least some of the complaints of shortage in the scientist–engineer market have the same cause. Indeed, in any market when there is a relatively sudden and dramatic change in either demand or supply which results in large price increases, we may find complaints of a 'shortage' while people get used to the fact that the price has risen significantly.

VII. Conclusion

It is our view that the model of dynamic shortage developed in this paper is useful in helping to understand the behaviour of the market for scientists and engineers in the past several years. The very rapid increase in demand in the market during this period has led to 'shortage' conditions resulting basically from a failure of the price of such services to adjust upward as rapidly and by as large an amount as warranted by the increasing demand, given the supply schedule of such services. This lag in adjustment, so far as we can see, can be attributed to a significant extent, not to any successful overt attempt to control prices artificially, but to certain inherent characteristics of supply and demand conditions and of the operation of the market. While the relative rigidity of supply in the short run is unpleasant (from the buyers' standpoint), and the price rise required to restore the market to equilibrium may seem to be very great, it is only by permitting the market to react to the rising demand that, in our view, it can allocate engineer–scientists in the short run and call forth the desired increase in supply in the longer run.

16 R. G. Hollister

An Evaluation of a Manpower-Forecasting Exercise

R. G. Hollister, 'A technical evaluation of the O.E.C.D.'s Mediterranean Regional Project and conclusions', *The World Year Book of Education 1967. Educational Planning*, J. A. Lauwerys, G. Z. Bereday and M. Blaug (eds.), Evans Bros., 1967, pp. 161–70.

The O.E.C.D.'s Mediterranean Regional Project is the most significant effort to date of educational planning based on the manpower-requirements approach. Anyone familiar with the literature in this field prior to the MRP could not help being struck by the abundance of arguments and assertions in the face of an almost total lack of empirical evidence. Both advocates and opponents of manpower planning emphasized various theoretical strengths or weaknesses of the method, unhindered by any reference to quantitative knowledge.

In creating the MRP, the O.E.C.D. took the first step from theory to reality; the MRP showed that it was possible to base educational planning on manpower forecasting. Seeking to capitalize on this gain, the O.E.C.D. undertook to supplement the individual country reports of the MRP with a technical evaluation of the project.

The Technical Evaluation was both a challenge and an opportunity.[1] The challenge was to evaluate the project itself and the opportunity was furnished by the data generated by the MRP that could be used to review the current state of manpower planning methods.[2] An evaluation of the full range of technical elements in the MRP would have required resources nearly equal to those devoted to the MRP itself. Therefore, the Technical Evaluation was necessarily narrow in focus. In order to

1. R. G. Hollister, *Planning education for manpower needs: A technical evaluation of the first stage of the Mediterranean Regional Project*, O.E.C.D., 1966.

2. In the terminology of operations research, this provided an opportunity to *calibrate* the manpower-requirements–educational-planning model, i.e. to determine real, as opposed to theoretical, values for various model parameters.

serve a double purpose, that of the project itself and of manpower methods in general, the evaluation was concentrated on the central problem of estimating manpower requirements and deriving educational targets from those manpower estimates.[3] The procedure followed was to isolate some of the criticisms that had been made of the manpower-forecasting approach to educational planning and then to assess the strength of these criticisms in the light of the MRP data. Thus, the topics on which the Technical Evaluation focused can be outlined in terms of a set of questions raised by the critics.

There are two major questions: (1) is the impact of manpower requirements on the educational system quantitatively significant enough to justify the considerable effort involved in making detailed estimates of requirements? (2) if the answer to (1) is yes, are present methods so inaccurate that, for all practical purposes, requirements cannot be estimated? Further questions spring from (2) concerning the possible sources of weakness in present forecasting methods:

1. Are occupational–input coefficients (the number of workers in a certain occupation per unit of output) at a given point in time fixed, or are they variable, and what difference would it make if they are in fact variable? This is the so-called 'substitution problem'.

2. To what extent do uncertainties about changes in productivity (changes in output per man due to changes in technology) affect estimates of manpower requirements?

3. To what degree must the economic structure and the labour force be disaggregated (e.g. into economic sectors, industries, firms, broad skill groups, or detailed occupation categories) if reliable estimates are to be made?

4. How serious is our ignorance of the exact relationship between a given occupation and the educational background 'required' for it and what difference does this ignorance make to the usefulness of educational targets derived from estimates of manpower requirements?

3. Some other technical and policy aspects of the MRP are evaluated in: *An experiment in planning by six countries*, O.E.C.D., 1965 and *Financial implications of the MRP targets*, O.E.C.D., mimeographed, 1965.

I. Methods of Evaluation

The character of the technical evaluation was shaped as much by the selection of particular methods of analysis as by the choice of topics. The methods were chosen both because they were commensurate with the limitations of the data and, more importantly, because they reflected a particular attitude towards planning. This attitude, as will be seen below, emphasizes a careful consideration of the nature of the uncertainties underlying the particular plan.

In order to indicate the nature of the methods used, it is helpful to put down in symbolic terms the procedure that was used in most of the MRP plans to arrive at estimates of the number of workers required in a particular occupation by 1975. The figure was arrived at by multiplying together four estimates for the target years as follows:

$$\begin{aligned}\text{Workers in occupation i in sector j} = &\frac{\text{employment in occupation i in sector j}}{\text{Total employment in sector j}} \times \frac{\text{employment in sector j}}{\text{GDP originating in sector j}} \\ &\times \frac{\text{GDP originating in sector j}}{\text{total GDP}} \times \text{total GDP}[4]\end{aligned}$$

Then by adding all sectors for each occupation, the total number in the occupation required for the economy in the year 1975 is obtained.

The simplest of the two methods used was *sensitivity analysis*. Sensitivity analysis is carried out simply by taking a key variable, parameter, or assumption, changing it slightly, and then reworking the estimates to see what effect that change has on the final result, i.e. to see how sensitive the results are to changes in the selected element. For example: sensitivity analysis could be carried out on the estimates of occupational requirements, calculated as shown above, by changing the estimated value of total GDP in the target year, first by, say, +10, then by −10 per

4. GDP stands for Gross Domestic Product, a measure of the total economic output of a country.

cent and then working out the new estimates for the number of workers required. A comparison of these new, hypothetical estimates with the original ones would indicate the sensitivity of the occupational estimates to the assumed level of GDP.

The other method used, *sources-of-change analysis*, is similar but slightly more involved. Analysis of sources of change is carried out by attributing a certain portion of the change in a total figure to changes in the component elements which make it up. For example: most of the MRP plans provide an estimate of the change in the number of workers in a given occupation (and economic sector) from 1960 to 1975 and portions of this change can be attributed to changes over the period in each of the four elements that, multiplied together as shown above, determine the final estimate of the total.

It is fairly clear how these methods may be used to seek answers to the questions which have been outlined above. In the technical evaluation, data from the MRP Reports both for projections from 1960 to 1975 and for the historical period 1951–61 were subjected to sensitivity analysis in order to throw light on the substitution problem and the difficulty of translating occupation into education. The analysis of sources of change was used to trace out the roles played by assumptions about productivity and disaggregation in the determination of the occupational structure.

The importance of these methods extends beyond their direct usefulness in answering the questions posed. In the technical evaluation it was argued that these methods could be usefully incorporated into the planning procedure itself. The methods are useful because they facilitate the careful consideration of the nature of the uncertainties that lie behind particular estimates and because they highlight the importance of specifying alternatives and the choices amongst them.

Sensitivity analysis can be used in at least three different ways. First, testing preliminary estimates by sensitivity analysis would help planners focus their attention for further study upon those parameters, variables, and assumptions to which final estimates appear particularly sensitive. This would allow improvement of estimates by a series of successive approximations. The second and third uses are closely related to the function which estimates, such as those presented in the MRP are to serve. If these estimates enter into documents which are to aid decision-makers – for instance, Ministers of Education and Labour – they should allow for the exercise of the decision-makers' judgement, i.e. they should present alternatives for choice. The second use of sensitivity analysis, then, would be for the presentation of such alternatives: at points where uncertainty remains about key parameters, the parameters could be varied over the range of uncertainty and the decision-maker would be allowed to make judgements about the most reasonable values within this range, or he would be able to adjust policy decisions in view of the degrees of uncertainty about estimates.

The third use of sensitivity analysis would also generate sets of alternatives for decision-makers. In this use the analysis would be viewed as a crude substitute for the type of cost–benefit analysis which is commonly suggested as a basis for decision-making in the public sector. Recognition of the difficulties of quantifying the 'benefits' or 'output' of education was perhaps the major factor leading to the creation and acceptance of the manpower-requirements approach. Granted such difficulties, there is some room in this approach for a type of pseudo-cost–benefit analysis through sensitivity analysis. For instance, in all the MRP plans assumptions were made about the ratio of pupils to teachers and pupils per classroom. These ratios were generally taken to be a rough index of quality. It would be quite simple to vary these ratios and calculate the effect of the variations on total costs. Decision-makers would have their own opinions about the degree to which lowering the pupil-teacher ratio would improve the quality of the education and they would be able to balance these assessed benefits against the explicitly defined increase in costs.

The analysis of source of change could be used by planners in the process of developing their plans to clarify which factors and assumptions played a major role in determining their final estimates of such things as change in occupational structure. This would allow them to go back and examine more carefully the most important elements in their estimating process or to hedge their final estimates in view of the degree of uncertainty which dominates their results through various assumed or estimated factors.

II. Conducting the Evaluation

Having indicated the topics on which the technical evaluation focused and the methods of analysis used, I will sketch very briefly the way in which the analysis was carried out, and then turn in more detail to a listing of some of the conclusions which emerged from the study. A description of a lengthy analysis in a limited space must necessarily be compressed. Readers who find that compression has been achieved at the cost of ease of comprehension can only be asked, with apologies, to consult the more extended discussion in the text of the study itself.

In order to determine the dimensions of the impact of manpower requirements on the total change in educational output over a given period (the first major question raised above), it was found useful to think of the total required change in educational output over the period as composed of three elements: (1) that increase in educational output which is necessary to keep pace with the growth of the labour force in such a way that the 'average' educational level of the labour force remains the same at the end of the period as it was at the beginning; (2) the change in educational output that is required to allow for the necessary adjustment in occupational distribution of the labour force; and (3) the change in educational output that is necessary because of changes in the amount and kind of education associated with each occupation.

Now it is easy to see, conceptually at least, that for any given period any one of these three elements might be static and therefore require no change in educational output, e.g. the labour force might not grow at all over the period and thus the first element would be zero. Thus we can judge the impact of the elements by comparing the actual required change over the period with what the required change in educational output would have been if one or more of the elements remained static, i.e. equalled zero. This is clearly a form of sensitivity analysis.

Manpower requirements can be easily identified with elements (2) and (3), since it is the change in occupational distribution and the kind and amount of education associated with each occupation that reflects the changing economic and technological context. Thus, a measure of the impact of manpower requirements is obtained by comparing the change in educational output required when all three elements changed, with what the requirements would have been if (2) and (3) had remained static (equal to zero). The results of comparison made in this way are reported below.

The substitution problem necessitated more complex analysis and yielded more equivocal results. First, occupational coefficients (number of workers in a given occupation and given sector per unit of output in that sector) were calculated for several occupations and sectors for four different countries in the same year. Then these coefficients were compared in order to get some indication of how variable coefficients in each sector were. This test showed coefficients to be quite variable. There are good reasons to be cautious about interpreting the results of this test as establishing unequivocally the existence of important substitution possibilities (these reasons are carefully spelled out in the text of the study). However, they were taken as suggesting the existence of such flexibility and the analysis was extended in an attempt to provide a rough illustration of how much difference such variability could make in projected requirements.

Sensitivity analysis was used, again, to carry out this illustrative example. A percentage range of coefficient variability was established from the inter-country comparisons sector by sector in the base year, 1960, and then this percentage range was applied to the projected occupational coefficients of one of the countries in order to see how sensitive the final educational requirements were to variation of the coefficients within this range.

The question of the importance of changes in productivity and the problem of disaggregation were approached in a single piece of analysis. This was done by applying analysis of sources of change to the change in the occupational distribution of the labour force over a given period. As noted above, the estimates of numbers in an occupation in 1975 were obtained by multiplying together four component estimates. The change in the numbers in an occupation between the base year, 1960, and 1975 can therefore be looked upon as the result of changes in each of the components between 1960 and 1975. The total change can therefore be attributed to changes in component parts. Recalling the equation written out above, it can be seen that productivity change can be related to changes in the second component, $\dfrac{\text{employment in sector j}}{\text{GDP originating in sector j}}$, since this is simply the inverse of labour productivity in the sector. Disaggregation can be associated with the third component, $\dfrac{\text{GDP originating in sector j}}{\text{total GDP}}$, since this term represents the disaggregation of the total output measure into sectoral output measures.

An analysis of source of change will indicate the relative importance of each of the components; it will provide some insight into the relative importance of the problems connected with productivity change and disaggregation in terms of their associated components.

Finally, in order to determine the seriousness of our ignorance about the relationship between a given occupation and the education associated with it, the analysis used to answer the impact question was extended. The procedure was simply to combine sensitivity analysis and analysis of sources of change to determine the importance of changes in element (3) (the change in educational output that is necessary because of changes in the amount and kind of education associated with each occupation) relative to that of element (2). Since there is not much knowledge about how one should expect these elements to change, projected changes had to be based on somewhat arbitrary assumptions. The analysis showed how large a role these assumptions played in determining the final results, and thereby indicated the seriousness of any errors in the assumptions.

III. Conclusions

With apologies for this cryptic summary of the analytical procedures, I must now turn to a description of some of the conclusions which were drawn from the results.

1. The analysis showed that manpower requirements have a significant impact on educational output. In both projected MRP data for 1960–75 and in the historical data for 1951–61, over 50 per cent of the change in required educational output was determined by manpower requirements, above and beyond the

increase in educational output required to keep pace with the growth of the labour force. Thus, the direction of the manpower-requirements approach to educational planning, as spearheaded by the MRP, seems reasonable. As further results of the study showed, however, much work remains to be done to improve the reliability and sophistication of manpower forecasting.

2. On the basis of the analysis of the MRP data, the problem of taking into account substitution possibilities (flexibility in occupational coefficients) seems important. An illustrative example in the study indicated that as much as a 20 per cent change in requirements of higher education in one of the MRP plans could result from allowances for substitution possibilities. This conclusion need not be regarded with complete dismay. It suggests that care must be taken in forming and interpreting manpower-requirements estimates, but it also suggests that there is a wider range of choice than had been supposed among patterns of educational outputs which would be compatible with a given set of economic targets. It is by this avenue, perhaps, that consideration of relative costs of various educational programmes could enter into the manpower-forecasting procedures.

3. The problem of productivity estimates looms large, and while it is a problem which is of concern for a wide range of economic analysis, developments in research in this field should be carefully examined in the light of their relevance to manpower requirements. It is also worth considering whether the process of estimating manpower requirements should be integrated more fully into the total economic planning process. If there is, as one would suppose, a relation between the skill mix of labour and its productivity and if, in addition, there is a range of substitution alternatives, then the planning of economic outputs should take into account the effects of alternative skill mixes on productivity and output, and the relative costs of such alternatives in terms of educational expenditure.

4. The question of the desirable degree of aggregation remains open. The analysis of the MRP plans suggested that disaggregation of GDP to economic sectors did not contribute significantly to the estimates of occupational distribution. This does not mean that in every case disaggregation will not be useful; in fact, it can be argued that the results suggest that the pay-off from disaggre-

gation has not yet been realized. However, it should be remembered that there is no guarantee that the effort to disaggregate data will yield better estimates than could be obtained from aggregate information.

5. The most serious problem which emerges from the analysis in the Technical Evaluation results from lack of knowledge about the education associated with each occupation. The analysis showed that the final results of estimates of required educational outputs for some of the MRP plans were highly sensitive to the assumptions about occupation-education relationships and the role they play in determining the change in the stock of education embodied in the labour force. The manpower-requirements approach rests on insecure foundations until the results of such research are available.

In all of the analyses, the advantages of sensitivity analysis and the analysis of sources of change as tools in manpower and educational planning became evident. These methods allow planners to evaluate their estimates in the light of the uncertainties of various elements of the estimating procedure. Carrying out such analyses in the process of developing plans will help planners to review the development of their estimates. Usually in planning, estimates are developed sequentially; there is, therefore, a need at various stages to reconsider the structure of the plan as a result of the simultaneous variation of the sequentially developed elements. In sum, the methods allow planners to understand more fully the nature of the plans they develop and they allow them to develop plans which represent more honestly the underlying uncertainties of their analyses.

It also follows from the results of the technical evaluation that there is a great need for two types of follow-up plans of the MRP type. First, it is desirable that at the same time as attempts are made to implement plans, further data should be systematically collected and a means provided to 'correct' continually the plan projections in the light of the newly-accumulated evidence. Second, it is important that follow-up studies be made which analyse in detail the actual developments of the economy and educational system and compare them with the developments estimated in the plan. Only this type of basic research can make the methods of estimating manpower requirements more sophisticated and effective. This is certainly the way to gain even greater benefits from the MRP experience.

Because of the efforts made by those involved in the MRP, it will be much easier for future planners to accomplish similar plan developments. The MRP experience has made the pitfalls clearer, but it has also made the potential gains from a man-power-requirements approach concrete and visible. Hopefully, others will follow this path away from empty theorizing, towards hard empirical action, and hopefully, the technical evaluation has indicated that this approach to educational planning can be frank, more flexible and increasingly sophisticated.

Part Five
Educational Planning in Developing Countries

However remarkable has been the recent growth of interest in educational planning in developed countries, the whole-hearted endorsement of educational planning in all underdeveloped countries in the last decade is without precedent in the history of state education. With very few exceptions, every ministry of education in poor countries around the world is today engaged in implementing short-term educational plans and drawing up long-term ones. There is broad agreement that educational planning should be carried out as an inherent part of general economic planning but no consensus has yet emerged on what precise meaning to attach to the relationship between educational and economic planning. The readings in this section are designed to convey the flavour of the controversy with special reference to low-income countries.

Charles Arnold Anderson, Professor of Sociology and Director of the Comparative Education Center at the University of Chicago, and Mary Jean Bowman, Associate Professor of Economics at the same university, start us off with a penetrating discussion of the scope and relevance of educational planning, stressing the conflict between the goals of social equality and maximum economic benefits. They also provide another review of the controversy between manpower forecasters and cost–benefit analysts. Thomas Balogh, Economic Adviser to the British Government and Reader in Economics at the University of Oxford, and Paul P. Streeten, Professor of Economics and Acting Director of the Institute of Development Studies at the University of Sussex, go over the same ground, but arrive at conclusions diametrically opposite to those of Anderson and Bowman. It appears, as Anderson and Bowman remark in their paper, that 'both manpower planning and rate-of-return approaches have severe limitations. The contrasts between them have roots deep in the ways men look at political–economic systems and in the controls over those systems that are attempted in practice'.

Philip J. Foster, Associate Professor in the Department of

Education and Assistant Director of the Comparative Education Center at the University of Chicago, analyses the question of vocationally oriented education in Africa in a cost–benefit framework and argues, paradoxically enough, that academic-type schooling for Africans is in fact 'vocational' in character, in the sense that it paves the way to the best-paid and the most prestigious jobs in the economy. His essay throws considerable doubt on the proposition that schools are effective instruments for promoting social change in developing countries.

17 C. A. Anderson and M. J. Bowman

Theoretical Considerations in Educational Planning

C. A. Anderson and M. J. Bowman, 'Theoretical considerations in educational planning', *The World Year Book of Education 1967. Educational Planning*, J. A. Lauwereys, G. Z. Bereday, and M. Blaug (eds.), Evans Bros., 1967, pp. 11–37.

There is widespread agreement today in academic and governmental circles that public decisions regarding education should be made 'planfully' rather than *ad hoc*. This consensus extends beyond saying that government should be the principal financial support and even beyond saying that administration of education should be centralized in one or a few agencies equivalent to a ministry. It is widely agreed that public decisions regarding education should take into account policies and developments in other sectors of the society and vice versa.

But there is no equally firm agreement on precisely what 'planning' is or should be. Clarity is not aided by recognition among scholars that no government has ever 'really' planned comprehensively, except possibly in wartime. Certainly at present there is nothing like 'the theory of planning' and even less is there 'a theory of educational planning'.

There are, however, theoretical or analytical correlates – systematized analytical propositions – of one versus another approach to economic and educational planning. This paper will outline and comment on some of the main variants of these schemes':

Defining planning and educational planning

The Oxford Dictionary, in one of its meanings, says to plan is 'to devise or design (something to be done, or some action, etc., to be carried out); to arrange beforehand.'

Dror's statement is more definite even though formulated 'for the purposes of administratives sciences':[1]

1. Y. Dror, 'The planning process', *International Review of Administrative Sciences*, vol. 29, no. 1, vol. 46–58 (1963), pp. 50–52.

the process of preparing
a set of decisions
for action in the future,
directed at achieving goals,
by optimal means.

There are several key elements common to these or other serviceable formulations. (1) They specify orientation to the future. (2) There is an orientation to action (rather than to such other aims as acquiring knowledge or communicating information). (3) The definitions imply the preparing or designing of something and therefore are in some degree concerned with deliberative endeavours. Prediction as such is not planning, and neither is forecasting or 'foreshadowing'.

The orientation to action implies that planners presume that their plans will be passed upon and, if approved, implemented. However, implementation is not part of planning itself. Thus Dror drew a sharp distinction on this score:

Planning is substantially – and, in most cases, also formally and legally – a process of preparing a set of decisions to be approved and executed by some other organs. Even if the same unit combines planning functions with authority to approve and execute, these are distinct, though interdependent, processes which must be kept analytically separate.

The analytical distinction between planning and approving or implementing is both important and in some ways troublesome. Planning that is effectively oriented to action cannot ignore the means by which plans may be implemented or executed, whether these are merely implicit in the situation and the planning documents or are explicitly specified as part of a plan. A continuing planning process with operational relevance will entail continuous feed-backs of experience, including experience in the implementation (or non-implementation) of prior plans or phrases of plans. Morever, practising planners may often seek to involve policy-makers in the planning process as a first step in a strategy to ensure implementation; one could even construct a social–political theory of this sort of planning. But to define planning in such a way as to include as an essential component actual acts of implementation may lead to endless disputes that confuse what is 'really' planning with who does it, or with whether plans are accepted by the policy-making authorities. Similar are the many arguments that confound the idea of what planning is with questions concerning particular varieties of planning and planning situations, such as: How detailed must specifications be to be 'plans'? By what methods must they be made? What are the powers and the instruments of implementation? Since this cluster of issues receives so much attention in the literature, however, some clarifying comments are in order. Most of the discussions revolve around supposed economic planning, but that area is entangled in politico-ideological controversies. Thus, should planning be identified with a command economy in which the actions of each individual or operating unit are specified by a central authority? In actuality, no such economy has ever existed.

Is a system planned if a few priority projects or sectors are centrally controlled while other sectors take whatever is left? Does it make a difference whether co-ordination of activities in the remaining sectors is relegated to a market system (Meiji, Japan), or erratically manipulated by a series of *ad hoc* and often mutually inconsistent inducements and 'directives' as in Soviet Russia? What about French 'projective' or 'indicative' planning that combines widespread participation by non-official persons, persuasion, and substantial governmental investment in key sectors? In Yugoslavia, decentralized decision-making approximates syndicalism, and Dutch planning pays little attention to details while relying heavily on individual and private decisions.

Indeed, is systematic preparing of plans for future action 'planning' when the basic strategies are limited to manipulating a few monetary and fiscal instruments? Or, should we view as planning only the designing of decisions for action that are specified in 'real' rather than in monetary units? It is possible to plan to give people opportunities to plan for themselves and to induce them to do so in ways that enhance collective goals – which was the essence of Benthamism.

Each of the foregoing distinctions is important and must be examined when comparing the theoretical foundation of one approach to planning with another. But it is misleading and logically unsound to distinguish what is from what is not planning in terms of the instruments of control, utilization of real rather than monetary specifications, emphasis upon tactical details rather than broad strategies, or the extent to which plans are executed.

The dictionary definition used the word to 'design' and Dror distinguished between planning and decision making:

> While planning is a kind of decision-making, its specific characteristic in this respect is its dealing with a set of decisions, i.e. a matrix of inter-dependent and sequential series of systematically related decisions.

The adjective 'sequential' could be troublesome if we were to take it as excluding all endeavours that did not specify action sequences as part of the decision sets, and it may be better to be more permissive so far as sequence specifications are concerned. Dealing with sequences or not in the designing of a plan is then viewed as an important characteristic that distinguishes some planning methods and theoretical frameworks from others. However, the interdependence among a number of related decisions that thus make up a 'set' becomes an integral part of the definition of planning of any kind.

Even when planning is limited in scope to a few priority projects or sectors only (or even to a single project), decisions must be made in sets that have some minimal internal consistency. This distinction between decision-making and planning ('designing') is implicit in most writing on the subject, even when it is not made explicit. In this sense, even if in no other, planning is a 'rational' process. Note, however, that the word process must be emphasized. The mutual consistency is one of intent and appropriate rational procedures on the part of the planners; realization of that intent is not an essential ingredient of the definition. At the same time, the specification of intended consistency provides a key link between a definition of planning and a theory of planning.

This element in the definition points to an interesting conclusion in paradoxical form. Dutch economic planning is total economic planning even though it deals with a few parameters only; Soviet planning, which goes into much more detail, is not total economic planning. In Soviet practice priority projects are genuinely planned, with care given in ensuring that decisions are mutually consistent, but the *ad hoc* backing and filling with respect to the rest of the economy is not planning by even the broadest definitions. The bounds of a plan, then, are identified by the limits within which mutual consistency is sought, by the scope of the set of decisions. This is quite another matter from the questions of materials or financial planning or of the degree of detail considered by the planners. There is a pragmatic connection, however; it is impossible to devise a consistent plan for a whole economy when all quantities are expressed in physical terms.

Finally, there is one element in Dror's definition that we exclude from the definition of planning. This is his specification of decisions directed to achieving goals by 'optimal means'. This optimization clause, even when interpreted merely as an intent (i.e. apart from concrete realization of optimality) would exclude from 'planning' virtually all of the activities that have actually been so labelled. Planning entails exploration and examination of alternatives, and selection among them; but none of these alternatives will be truly 'optimal'. To strive for optimization would be a negation of operationally effective planning as an action-oriented process in a dynamic world. The search is for the best alternative that can be identified or discovered with a reasonable output of time and effort in search and comparison, but this will never be the best in any absolute, truly optimal sense. In practice planners' decisions come closer to the notion of 'satisficing' than of optimizing behaviour.

Summing up, we are defining planning essentially as Dror did, but without the limiting proviso of optimization. *Planning is the process of preparing a set of decisions for action in the future.* Though it is action oriented, the planning operation is distinct from approval and implementation, neither of which is essential to the definition. Planning is not distinguished from nonplanning by the persons doing it. Neither is it identified by how it is done except that mutually conflicting specifications are eliminated. This definition fits 'educational planning' as well as 'economic planning' and it fits any other sectoral or substantive orientation to the planning endeavour.

The scope and goals of educational planning

We may begin, then, by defining educational planning as 'the process of preparing a set of decisions for future action pertaining to education'. But this is only an initial step toward delineating the theoretical foundations of educational planning.

It is essential in the first instance to distinguish two very different situations. We can – and this is usual – treat educational planning as an adjunct or subhead of general economic planning. Or we can deal with educational planning in its own right, with economic elements taken only as an aspect of it. In the first case educational planning derives from, or more correctly constitutes merely an extension of, manpower planning. This approach reflects an orientation to planning of production and employment, and the goal becomes manpower production. The theoretical foundations of educational planning are then shared with those that underlie manpower planning – provided the latter pays attention to flows and sequences of adjustment and is not restricted to drawing blueprints for target dates. Since educational planning in practice is so often considered mainly in this context, the relations of education and manpower policy will be treated with some care.

When the aims and operations of education are considered in their own right as a focus of planning, the aim can be as manifold and complex as the functions education is expected to perform. Manpower considerations become merely one aspect of educational planning with no necessary priority over other goals. The focus comes to be more on people, less on production of 'human resources'.

A recent Latin American seminar promulgated an ambitious statement of educational planning that could be matched elsewhere:[2]

The overall planning of education is a continuous, systematic process, involving the application and co-ordination of social research methods, and of principles and techniques of education, administration, economics and finance, with the participation and support of the general public in education for the people, with definite aims and in

2. U.N., Santiago Conference, 1962, *Overall planning of education* (mimeo), pp. 15–16.

well-defined stages, and to providing everyone with an opportunity of developing his potentialities and making the most effective contribution to the social, cultural and economic development of the country.

As a description of any concrete act of educational planning, that statement has no validity. It is obviously of no use as a definition. Perhaps it was intended only as an idealized statement of what educational planning ought to be; with minor revisions it could serve as a plank in a political platform in many countries. In scope, it encompasses the entire range from planning flows of students, providing buildings and equipment, and training teachers to a detailed working out of curriculum and teaching methods. Cultural and economic, equity and efficiency goals, are all included. Systematic procedure is emphasized: 'a continuous, systematic process,' and the 'co-ordination of research methods . . . with definite aims'.

We may interpret the phrase 'application and co-ordination of social research methods, and of principles and techniques of education, administration, economics, and finance' to imply application of theories from each of these spheres. But one does wonder just how men with all these assortments of knowledge (and the 'general public' thrown in) are to be integrated into a planning team. Or is the statement intended in fact to include the school principal's planning with respect to assignment of duties of his staff, and the teacher's planning of lesson sequences and home work assignments? Evidently one of the major defects of the statement is that taken literally it would include the total operations of an educational system.

On the other hand, the statement is equally interesting for what it leaves out. There is no mention of the need to analyze the functions of education, and there is no reference to education other than in schools – an omission that is common enough. The statement is representative also in ignoring the aim of developing strategies to encourage innovations in education, including decentralized innovation as well as experiments sponsored by central agencies. And there is no mention of planning to take account of uncertainties.

Even within the conventional limitations, the quoted statement provides no suggestion of anything like a theory or logic of planning, precisely because it attempts to say everything so indiscriminately. There is no indication that the authors perceived that choices have to be made rather than just 'co-ordinated'. In other words, we are told to look systematically in many directions at once, but beyond an implied requirement of consistency there is no hint of any underlying rationale of educational planning in all this.

Educational Planning and Social Democratization

Why does the question of inequality arise?

A recent Unesco report on educational planning points out the need for both educational and other capital investments and then goes on to say that this situation 'requires that their educational systems shall provide that equality of opportunities which democracy proclaims'.[3] But this is not a well-founded conclusion; to agree that widespread schooling is needed for democratic government or that economic productivity presupposes heavy investment in training carries no implications whatever about educational equality. Why, then, does this assumption gain such widespread support?

(1) Equality of educational opportunity has been widely proclaimed as a 'universal human right'. At least in form, this faith is set forth in societies with the most diverse political systems.

(2) Many countries happen to have become independent just when relative equality in educational opportunity is approaching realization in the nations looked to as models, and these aims are adopted by governments of new nations.

(3) By an association with the idea of the hoped-for modernized production, many conclude that equality of opportunity must play the same part everywhere that it does today in the advanced countries. One would hardly deny that a population will be better prepared for modern life if half rather than a tenth receive eight years of schooling. But these resources have alternative uses. There is a wide gap between conclusions about motivation and training and decisions about how to dispose of inadequate resources. Modernization requires that education be given a central

3. UNESCO, 'Elements of educational planning', *Educational Studies and Documents*, no. 45, 1962, p. 5.

place, to be sure, but educational policy has to be related to the stage of economic development. Just as absence of industrial conflict is no criterion of labour commitment,[4] so equality of educational opportunity is an equivocal guide to prudent investment policies. Each of the key terms in most discussions on this topic proves to be ambiguous unless it is considered in a context of sequential social change. But there is also an inherent conflict between the ideal of equity and certain other basic values that also play a key part in national development.

Equity versus efficiency

Equity. If a given group, such as rural children, make up 60 per cent of the total population of children and occupy 60 per cent of the places in primary school, we would say there was an equitable distribution. But this is a very crude test, and it is easy to show that each of the four following variants of this rule has different implications for policy.

(a) An equal amount of education for everyone. No country has ever adopted such a goal. Moreover, when an educational system approaches this condition beyond the level of compulsory education, qualitative variations begin to be strongly emphasized.

(b) Schooling sufficient to bring every child to a given standard. If this norm is formulated weakly, virtually all children can be brought up to a minimum standard; thus the essence of compulsory attendance laws is that no one is to be allowed to lack the basic minimum. (If performance standards, not merely years of attendance, are specified, this will require repeating of grades and remedial teaching.) Persistence in school beyond the minimum prescribed level will then be brought under other norms setting standards that only a fraction of the children will be expected to attain.

(c) Education sufficient to permit each person to reach his potential. Only a wealthy society would try to meet this stipulation in anything like its full implications, for every individual has very great potentials in some direction. Hence the potentials in whose development the society is willing to invest become limited by convention, usually to the more 'academic' sorts. Educational

4. W. E. Moore and A. E. Feldman, *Labor commitment and social change in developing areas*, 1960, p. 17.

plans in all countries rest on assumptions, often unexamined, as to which potentials shall be invested in.

(d) Continued opportunities for schooling so long as gains in learning per input of teaching match some agreed norm. The norm is usually defined in terms of ambiguous passes on an examination or the judgment that carrying a large number of children into higher grades will be too costly in relation to their predicted learning. 'It just isn't worth while to keep them in school any longer.' When this criterion is examined closely it raises questions about the presumed outcomes of school, questions of learning *versus* teaching, and choice among various sorts of training.

Efficiency. Whereas equity is a goal or end in each of its variants, efficiency is a rationality concept: to get the most out of the least, whatever the nature of the rewards or ends may be. In its broadest meaning it is thus coterminous with the whole of rational decision theory, but here we are using it in much more limited ways. The first two efficiency criteria listed start from the assumption that learning as such is taken as the goal, and any given total of resources invested in education will then be most 'efficiently' used when the total aggregate of learning is maximized. The first variant is simply another way of expressing the fourth of the criteria listed under equity.

(a) Selection of individuals for further schooling should be based upon how much additional learning can be predicted for one *versus* another person. Those for whom the greatest increment in learning is predicted will be the first chosen, and so on to the point at which the assigned resources are all taken up. Extending this to include decisions as to how many resources should go into education, we may set a learning-rate cut-off point. It is universally accepted that the number of children capable of profiting from any given kind of training will diminish as the level of schooling rises. Some can learn more than others, and the higher skills do not need to be as plentiful as the lower ones – at least so long as we define education in bookish terms. But it now becomes evident that the equity status of the fourth criterion listed under that head is tenuous. Unless, and perhaps even if, we define education academically this is in fact an efficiency criterion sometimes dressed up in equity clothing. High-level people are needed, few have the potentials, so we concentrate resources on the talented. But to speak of equity in terms of 'talent' is equivocal, with no more intrinsic merit than race or social class or religious orthodoxy. Moreover, the idea of maximizing learning in a generalized formulation tends to become narrowed to refer to learning that will ultimately maximize a man's economic productivity.

(b) Priority should be given to groups or localities where given educational efforts will evoke the largest response in attendance and in demand for further schooling. This is a pragmatic criterion that relies upon demonstrated aspirations and upon the willingness of a population to sacrifice (at least leisure). It takes advantage of the fact that subpopulations displaying the greatest interest in schooling are likely also to have developed relatively favourable environments for learning among their children, and to have acquired and continued to create extra-school learning opportunities that support the school's efforts.

As a crude decision rule this one favours those subpopulations that are already most developed and violates at least some notions about equity – unless we insert a premise about group 'merit'. The criterion becomes much more complex if we specify it further to distinguish the source or agencies responsible for providing the educational resources. So far as central government is concerned, it may then ask: at which points would an introduction or expansion of centrally financed educational endeavour evoke the greatest response in expanded demands for education over and above what would develop in the absence of such an effort? The answer may then be quite different. In no case is this criterion likely to direct substantial investments to the most laggard communities until near-universal schooling is in sight, but this way of specifying the question implies a strategy that will partially resolve the conflicts between equity and efficiency considerations. The generalized form of the criterion tends to be realized by local interests and resources: gradients of interest and ability to support schooling go together, interest corresponding broadly to the gradients of economic development within the country, to the numbers of jobs requiring schooling, and to the willingness of populations to supplement public with private funds. At the same time, local responses to and requests for experimental efforts by the central government in less favoured areas can direct planners to the spots in which further central assistance would bring the greatest results. And where costs of elementary schools are borne in the main by local districts, the central budget will permit more allocation of funds to special schemes to provide facilities for zealous individuals from laggard areas – such as centralized boarding schools for middle-school or secondary-school pupils.

(c) The third efficiency criterion is explicitly economic, whereas the others were not necessarily so: invest in education where the expected ratio of gains in economic output to costs is highest and extend these investments so long as the economic benefit–cost ratios exceed ratios in alternative uses of resources. In a free market system a crude short-run approximation to this rule tends to hold among individuals. However, as a social planning criterion it requires estimation of public as well as private costs and returns. Also, in its conventional formulations even a socially assessed economic benefit–cost criterion ignores the processes of change and the effects of current investments in education upon future decision alternatives.

Only the second criterion even begins to bring the dynamics of educational and economic developments into focus. On the other hand, demands for schooling can and do sometimes outpace the aggregate development of job opportunities, a fact that does not enter into either of the first two criteria except as they may be modified to take it explicitly into account. It is only this third criterion that in fact specifies the margins at which decisions are made to invest in education or in something else: even the first criterion was oriented to the allocation of given total resources within education, taking the limits of educational effort as quite arbitrarily established. Unfortunately, the marginal social benefit–cost test is difficult to apply in practice, it requires major overhauling before it can be dynamized, and it is only in part compatible with equity norms.

Some dilemmas of democratization

The new nations, where we find the greatest enthusiasm for educational planning, must build a resilient policy along with a productive economy. Officials are tempted into politically-based assumptions concerning the pay-off from schooling, impelled also by demands to 'correct' geographic imparities in educational opportunities. But if rapid economic return is given priority, the second efficiency-criterion presumably would be more appropriate. Equity norms would come in to temper decisions based on the efficiency test and also to ensure that a ground is laid for longer-run developments in the presently unpromising areas, and that economic polarization does not become frozen.

Finally, any chosen policy raises troublesome questions about compulsion *versus* freedom of choice in education. Balancing equity against economic efficiency is easier if a planner can work within given manpower specifications and shut his eyes to the fact that he is rationing qualified individuals out of the kind of schooling they prefer. Such compulsion can be harmonized with equity only by blatant casuistry. Moreover, restriction on free choice of career can have serious effects upon efficiency through its effects upon motivation. It is only in the more advanced societies that equity can be regarded as essential to or even consistent with economic efficiency, but societies at every level need to be aware of the risks of controlling individuals' choices of careers by means other than salary structures.

Educational planning for production of manpower

The essential single-mindedness of a manpower-directed approach to educational planning facilitates analysis of its theoretical bases. However, orientation to manpower production does not necessarily imply that educational planning is a part of extension of highly detailed sectoral manpower planning. Models in which only general levels of manpower are specified are also relevant. There are important differences in how human resource development in agencies other than schools is taken into account, if at all. Furthermore, 'rate of return' analysis with its decision criteria might be regarded as a branch of manpower-oriented educational planning, though the methods and presuppositions are very different.

The logic of detailed manpower planning

The essential ingredients of detailed manpower plans in all of their variants are: (1) specification of the composition of manpower 'needs' or 'requirements' at some future date (or, less often, sequence of dates); (2) specification of manpower availabilities, which includes estimation of losses (by retirement and death) on the one hand, flows of new manpower out of educational institutions on the other; (3) a reconciliation of (1) and (2). Within this context, educational planning becomes the scheduling of flows of human raw material through the educational agencies and out into the economy as various specified kinds of manpower. In a first approximation, at least, the 'educational system' is taken usually to be the school system, and the rest of the human-resource development programme is likely to be planned, if at all, under other sector headings.

A characteristic of detailed manpower planning that must be faced before scrutinizing its theoretical assumptions is the single-valued nature of all its measures, whether of requirements for particular types of manpower or of its availability. There are no prices and no demand or supply schedules in the economic sense. Rather, in Parnes' words, 'the idea of manpower requirements . . . relates to the functional (occupational) composition of employment that will be necessary if certain social and/or economic targets are to be achieved. The concept, in other words, is more a technological than an economic one.'[5] The use of 'technological', which has become common among educational and manpower economists, means simply single-valued quantitative forecasts. It does not in fact escape economic content, however; instead it carries the economic implication of *ex ante* zero demand elasticity; even if we substitute 'highly inelastic' for 'zero', this is a very strong assumption that goes well beyond zero elasticity *ex post* or after arrival at any given point in time. All changes over time in the numbers of men employed at any given skill or occupation are thereby implicitly interpreted as shifts of demand, and changes in pay rates are irrelevant. Parnes puts it as follows:[6]

. . . so long as one grants that manpower considerations are one of the elements that *ought* to influence educational decisions, then all such decisions, if they purport to be rational, involve manpower forecasts,

5. H. S. Parnes, 'Manpower analysis in educational planning' in H. S. Parnes (ed.), *Planning education for economic and social development*, O.E.C.D., 1963, p. 76. [See Reading 12.]

6. H. S. Parnes, op. cit., p. 75.

whether or not they are explicitly made. . . . Otherwise, the decision does not make much sense. Thus, the question is not whether forecasts are to be made, but the extent to which they are going to be as systematic as possible and are going to be based on all the evidence that can be marshalled. If the allocation of resources to education were governed entirely by market forces, the necessity for centralized decisions on such matters would, of course, disappear. Under these circumstances the question whether new facilities and personnel for engineering schools should be developed would be the resultant of numerous individual decisions making themselves felt on the market, with each youngster (or his family) presumably making an individual 'forecast' to guide his action. But since no country apparently contemplates this as a serious possibility, governments are unable to escape the responsibility of forecasting.

The second point to be made concerning the manpower forecasts that underlie educational planning is that they do not, or at least should not, purport to be pure unconditional forecasts. That is, they are not so much predictions of what will happen in the manpower fields as indications of what must happen if certain targets for economic growth are to be realized.

Summing up, the detailed manpower-planning approach to educational planning starts off with the proposition that manpower production is the most important function of an educational system, that it is more prudent to estimate future manpower requirements systematically than to guess at them, and that forecasts of manpower needs (however defective) can be accurate enough to be useful guides. It assumes that skill demands are highly inelastic, and infers from this both the necessity for *detailed* manpower planning and a justification for its technological, non-economic techniques. Presumably this is the basis upon which Parnes justifies technological methodology even as he speaks of forecasts made 'as systematic as possible' and 'based on *all* of the evidence that can be marshalled' (italics ours).[7]

Proponents of detailed manpower planning usually argue that a long lead time is needed, and that manpower forecasting for educational planning purposes must therefore have medium to long time horizons. Further, they assume that students (or their parents) are unwise choosers and forecasters and that central

7. From the above quotation.

authorities must determine (directly or indirectly) the numbers of places in various schools and curricula without regard to prospective students' demands. Deviation from this position is seen as a concession to other, 'social' educational goals.

Pushing back all these characteristics, we can begin to construct the implicit theoretical framework at the core of the detailed manpower approach to educational planning.

(1) The first assumption has already been explicitly identified – the assumption of *ex ante* near-zero elasticities of demand for skills (*ex ante* near-zero skill substitutabilities).

(2) The period of specialized training in the more critical skills is taken to be long (irrespective of the length of prior general education). It is no accident that proponents of manpower planning refer so often to physicians in illustration of this point. No one assumes that the training period for medicine is typical, though no one would disagree that medical education requires a relatively long lead time. Medicine is also less problematic on the requirements-forecasting side than many other high-level specialities – at least if one does not raise questions about the 'need' for many fully-fledged physicians at all. In the usual case the future requirements for physicians are in large part derived from demographic predictions, their payment is often socialized, and the demand for doctors is comparatively unaffected by changing production technologies.

(3) It is explicitly asserted that a long lead time is required to provide the facilities in plant and personnel needed to train the new cohorts of manpower. This proposition, if true, adds to the time lapse involved in (2), provided that (4) is also applicable.

(4) Production coefficients in the formation of each type of manpower are taken to be highly fixed. In part this is just a particular facet of the assumption of inelastic demands for human skills: inelastic skill substitutabilities among teachers in various curricula and also between teaching and other activities. However, rigid educational production functions would imply also inflexibility in pupil–teacher ratios, in per student allowance of classroom and laboratory space, and so on. Plans often stipulate adjustments on this score, however, especially with regard to teacher–pupil ratios and teacher qualifications at the lower levels of school in underdeveloped countries. Few plans

give serious attention to the possibilities of substitution between skill acquisition in schools and by other means.

(5) It is assumed that the pace of change in manpower requirements is both rapid and irregular and/or that there are critical educational decisions entailing large investments that are both indivisible and specialized in their educational uses. Assuming manpower-production goals as predominant, either of these situations will call for unevenly spaced large decisions with relatively long-planning horizons. Unless one, or both, of these conditions prevails, the relevance of points (3) and (4) to the argument for detailed manpower forecasting well into the future is decidedly weakened. An even pace of change would allow for feedback adjustments at the margins at which decisions must be made. Hence, there would be little need for looking beyond the period of specialized training itself. Furthermore, if skill demands change relatively smoothly, the presumption against heeding student choices (as a major guide for expanding educational programmes) is greatly weakened. Emphasis upon educational decisions that entail large and indivisible investment is encouraged by two additional circumstances: the tendency to set manpower targets at intervals of several years ahead: and the association of manpower planning with *centralized* educational planning.

(6) Few manpower planners actually claim a high degree of accuracy in their forecasts. In the last analysis, they rest their case for detailed forecasting upon the claim that systematic attempts to forecast are better than no attempts at all. In the background, however, is the belief that with better data and increased knowledge we will be able to identify systematic deterministic relationships between economic development and manpower requirements, even though the sets of requirements at any given economic level will differ with the industry mix. The major part of the manpower-planning efforts in practice has been directed toward finding those coefficients.

Forecasting efforts to date have not been marked by startling success, and the practitioners are becoming more self-critical. Recent discussions in France have raised doubts about the validity of plans and Swedish investigators have identified gross errors of prediction in that country. A recent self-assessment from the Soviet Union reports that there is comparatively little difficulty in projecting manpower requirements in the service industries or in estimating replacement requirements in 'productive industries'. There has been almost no success in projecting changes in skill requirements in the same production industries.[8] These failures are variously attributed to inept implementation (in realizing 'targets') or to inability to identify the pertinent technical coefficients of demand shifts. A few doubters have questioned the underlying assumptions of technological determinism.

The foregoing assumptions give us a structural model characterized by technologically determined rigidities and inflexibilities in both the formation and the use of human skills, yet at the same time one marked by dynamic and uneven technological change. It is over-simplified in that practitioners will rarely adhere rigorously to the tenets of a logical construct – which is a very fortunate thing. Nevertheless, this model is both the starting point of detailed manpower planning and a close approximation to the way the planner proceeds right up to the end.

The model has several further implications that should be examined. It puts quite out of consideration any significant market adjustments to re-allocate available manpower among uses, and it automatically diverts practitioners from considering long-term strategies to facilitate more efficient future short-term adjustments in manpower utilization. It slurs over awkward problems of future obsolescence of the skills of today's output of new manpower and evades the question of whether the proposed programmes of training increase that obsolescence. It pays no attention to any systematic efforts to compare costs of human resource formation of one kind or another with the returns to such investments, or to a comparison of costs and returns to human-resource *versus* other investments. Practising planners of course cannot ignore costs as constraints upon education expenditures, but that is not an assessment of returns in relation to costs.

8. V. E. Komarov (compiler), 'Training of qualified manpower', (Selections prepared for forthcoming UNESCO *Readings on education and economic development*). [Now published as M. J. Bowman, M. Debeauvais, V. E. Komarov and J. Vaizey (ed.), *Readings in the economics of education*, Paris, U.N.E.S.C.O., 1968, pp. 732–41.]

The basic assumptions of the model tend also to constrain manpower-oriented educational planning within relatively conventional limits; in particular, there is a tendency to place responsibility for almost the whole of manpower development upon the schools, even when the skills involved are highly specialized. This bias is not inherent in the logic of manpower planning, but it is a likely by-product of the techniques used. Only in a few countries like Japan, where the traditional loci of formal education have been quite different, are educational agencies other than schools likely to receive careful attention. The other exceptions occur where manpower planners are informal and essentially non-methodological in their approach; Harbison is an example.

Manpower planning in its most elaborated and technical variants has been confined to industrially advanced countries, and it is primarily in this context that the logical model we have outlined has evolved. The less-developed countries, it is said, have the greatest need of manpower planning. But it is acknowledged that manpower planning is especially difficult in such economies because of the (hopefully) rapid and unpredictable rate of change in manpower requirements. Obviously one cannot extrapolate forecasts in those countries. Accordingly, there is greater use of comparisons with advanced countries in deriving estimates of demand shifts, and there is more reliance upon informal and unsystematic judgments. (Notice, however, that French manpower planning, with all of its elaborate refinements, also uses informal judgments.)

But let us set aside these problems of forecasting and accept for the moment the assumptions of high degrees of technological determinism. Several undebatable factors differentiate the less from the more developed economies. For one thing, the fifth assumption listed above is highly realistic when applied to a small and underdeveloped nation: the pace of change in manpower requirements must indeed be both rapid and irregular if economic growth is to be significant, *and* (not merely or) decisions with respect to the higher levels of education do entail investments that are large relative to total resources (and to existing facilities) and in a major degree indivisible. However, the first approximation of a closed economy in which most manpower requirements will be met by 'home production' is quite inapplicable at precisely those levels of skill to which manpower planning is directed. In addition, the chances are very large that high proportions of the home-produced manpower at the higher levels will emigrate. These conditions substantially alter the context of educational planning even when its dominant orientation is to manpower production, and the most critical decisions are of a very different character.

Tinbergen, fixed coefficients, and the 'transition' problem

Detailed manpower forecasting, like the detailed economic plans of which it is a part, has been geared to specified target dates, ignoring the paths by which such targets are approached over time. This is partly an accident of history, but it has also been a pragmatic necessity. The tasks of detailed planning are so great as to preclude elaboration of sequences as well – quite aside from the fact that in practice 'plans' have frequently come out of the shop after the period for their implementation has already begun. Development of ever bigger and faster computers and techniques for their use may change this. There is much talk in France at present of remaking four-year target-date plans each year, in an overlapping series that permits feed-back corrections along the way, which is a step in the direction of planning sequences. However, it is not the same thing. It does not examine the implications of its own technical coefficients for the path toward target-date plans. Is there in fact an incompatability inherent in the planner's model that was concealed by jumping from the present to a future equilibrium date without considering the path from now to then?

Although Tinbergen and Correa specified manpower requirements by general levels of education only, this is the question to which they directed attention.[9] Their approach is distinctively of the manpower planning type in several respects. Manpower requirements for the non-education sector are derived technologically from assumptions with respect to national income growth rates (as in French detailed manpower planning); factor combinations within the educational system are fixed, and so are educational input–output ratios (teachers, equipment, etc., per

9. H. Correa and J. Tinbergen, 'Quantitative adaptation of education to accelerated growth', *Kyklos*, vol. 15 (1962), no. 4, pp. 776–86.

pupil year at each educational level). They demonstrated that under such assumptions (which are less restrictive than with more detailed manpower planning) there can be and frequently (typically?) will be problems of 'transition' disequilibria. In other words, there are hidden incompatibilities in any manpower planning methods that disregard the paths by which the economic and educational systems move from the present to a planned future target-date equilibrium.

To the plodding realist who has approached educational planning from the education end to analyse the demography of an educational system, the sequential outcomes of injections at one point or another and the problems of internal bottlenecks (especially in teacher supplies) – following these through in a concrete case without benefit of any particular mathematical or economic model – the tremendous impact of the Tinbergen–Correa contributions upon planning lore and practice must seem puzzling. The realistic plodder knew well enough that there were problems of bottlenecks, that you could not go in straight lines from here to there, and that many compromises had to be made. He may even have followed through the implications of extrapolating from an initial crash programme to expand education in an undeveloped country, and thereby discovered how explosive the statistics could look – and so could the events. At the most such a man is likely to appreciate the Tinbergen–Correa contribution as a rather tidy but limited sort of check-sheet for the inexperienced, and he will certainly want to add to it. The economist who is used to thinking about accelerators, and who will quickly see the conventional accelerator aspect of uneven educational expansion, may not react very differently, especially if he is used to thinking as much in neo-classical as in Keynesian terms. But this is to under-estimate the implications of Tinbergen's work because it ignores the nature of the process by which most of us, and intellectuals in particular, make a bit of progress in our thinking. To comprehend the impact of Tinbergen's work it is necessary to look at it through the eyes of the technicians and theoreticians of manpower and economic planning. Seen in that perspective it forces concern for a new dimension at the logical heart of their work. It is not merely a new and unrealistic sort of planner's gadget that has to be altered almost out of recognition before it will fit – though that is happening too.[10]

The rate-of-return approach

This approach is central to investment-decision theory. Yet it seems to have been anathema to most planners. The weaknesses of the technological determinism that undergirds most manpower planning are by-passed or listed as caveats and then forgotten. Rate-of-return analysis, on the other hand, is typically ignored; planners who do not ignore it are content merely to attack its obvious weak points and then discard it. Nevertheless there is a small group of determined economic theorists and researchers who continue to uphold this approach and who are making efforts to demonstrate its empirical relevance.

Viewing education as investment in human-resource development (which is also the manpower planner's view), they ask: how are we to compare the relative advantage of such investment with other uses of resources? How should investment in one increment to educational endeavour be assessed in relation to another educational programme? The answer must take account of the time path, not merely the timeless sums, of benefits accruing from the one or the other investment. It is the same in essence as the answer to any other comparison among investment alternatives: whichever yields the higher rate-of-return will be chosen. Many of the attacks on this approach miss the mark and fail to recognize that the same objections may be charged equally against the more pervasive methods of manpower planning. Five common criticisms of rate-of-return analysis assert that it:

(1) Ignores the non-economic benefits of education. Answer: so does manpower planning.

(2) Catches only direct but not indirect economic returns. This is equally true of manpower planners; moreover the latter do not build any cost estimates into their models and make no attempt to measure even direct economic returns.

10. See, e.g. G. Williams. 'Planning models of educational requirements for economic development as applied to Greece', in J. Tinbergen *et al.*, *Planning models of educational requirements for economic development*, O.E.C.D. (mimeo), 9 Septemper 1963. [Now published in *Econometric models in education*, Paris, O.E.C.D., 1965, pp. 77–93.]

(3) Assumes pure competition. False; in fact rate-of-return analysis helps spot the monopolistic restrictions and points to where they need correction. By repeating assessments at intervals, it could become an increasingly useful tool for this purpose. (Neither rate-of-return analysis nor manpower-requirement estimates are once-for-all affairs; as a planning device each becomes more useful and interesting as it is repeated.)

(4) Is impractical because the necessary data are not available. This argument is circular. The data needed for first approximations are no more difficult to obtain than those normally used in manpower planning; these data are lacking because few people have been interested in their use for planning purposes.

(5) Ignores income effects of ability, motivation, and family status that are correlated with schooling. This charge is more awkward to meet especially where comparisons are being made between returns to investment in the formation of physical and of human capital, though the problem is not statistically insurmountable.

Up to this point nothing has been brought forth that strikes at the theoretical foundations upon which rate-of-return comparisons rest as guides for planning. If the foregoing criticisms were all, the rate-of-return approach would win. It provides a rational model, capable of empirical application, for comparing the economic productivity of one *versus* another investment in educational programmes, and for comparing the productivity of investments in education with those in physical capital. Manpower planning has no such tidy rationale, and is not in fact an optimizing model at all. However, the above criticisms are not all. To them we must add the following:

(6) Rate-of-return analysis does not incorporate systematic assessment of linkages between educational and economic developments over time. Rate-of-return estimates use cross-section age–income data to measure the life–income streams associated with one or another level or kind of schooling, but the time patterns used in this way are not historic or development-time. Manpower planning, by contrast, takes as its central problem the estimation of growth rates and their implications with respect to manpower 'requirements' at a future date.

(7) It is objected further that central decisions with respect to educational policy necessarily involve lump changes, in scale units too large to justify use of the marginal cost and return measures on which the logic of rate-of-return analysis is founded. This argument is sometimes over-pressed, and we have raised some questions about it earlier in quite another connection – as part of the discussion of conditions that would call for a long lead time in educational planning. However, estimates of rates of return at a particular time can at best no more than suggest a direction of change, not a magnitude; to assume that they alone are sufficient to indicate how big a big and discontinuous alteration of the educational system should be is a serious error.

(8) It is objected also that market prices, with or without an 'incomes policy', are faulty indexes of the productivity of such people as doctors and nurses, and that administered prices (wages, salaries) in a command economy are not measures of productivity for anyone. A rate-of-return devotee would respond that if and where this is the case one would use shadow prices for both cost and return estimates. But this leaves unanswered the question whether, in such circumstances, it is more practicable to start from quantity or from shadow-price evaluations.

Evidently both manpower planning and rate-of-return approaches have severe limitations. The contrasts between them have roots deep in the ways men look at political–economic systems and in the controls over those systems that are attempted in practice. Matching the insights from such different approaches is not easy. On the other hand, we may find keys to unlock some of the doors if we look more carefully at a question that is politically neutral in itself; the implications of substitution and demand elasticities and inelasticities.

The importance of substitution elasticities

Underlying objections (6) and (7) and even, in part, objection (8) to rate-of-return analysis as a planner's guide, is the assumption of inelasticities all along the line, the technological determinism of manpower planning models. Planning applications of rate-of-return analysis in any formal or routine manner would entail one of the following two choices. One could make correspondingly extreme assumptions of the opposite kind: *ex ante* highly elastic demands for skills and hence high skill substitution elasticities. Or, one could think in terms of the production of human beings, each of whom embodied a large diversity of skills: high flexibility in allocation of *individuals* among jobs, whatever the elasticities of substitution among particular skills.[11] Despite confounding by political ideologies, or perhaps partly because of that, the contrast between the manpower and the rate-of-return protagonists in their assumptions concerning substitution elasticities is at the heart of the dispute.

The National Manpower Council included among its indicators of shortage the desire to hire more men than can be found *at existing prices* and the desire to get better-quality people than are available *at current rates of pay*.[12] In this over-simplified form, these propositions resemble the common technicians' view in that pricing is not introduced as an equilibrator. Conversely, an 'excess' is expressed by unemployment of a skill (not necessarily of the skilled person) at a going rate of pay.

If both supply and demand for skills were in fact highly inelastic, crude counts of men seeking jobs and of job vacancies would give us measures of excess or shortage that would be modified very little by introducing pricing to equilibrate the market. In the short run neither the pricing process nor any other mechanisms available to central planners would be equal to the task. Under such conditions, the way in which shortage and excess are conceived and the way alternatives are compared in the planning process would make very little difference; shortages would in any case reveal themselves in the unemployment of the factor(s), human or physical, with which they are complementary in the production process. Approximations to this sort of extreme situation are sometimes cited to illustrate the limitations of a pricing mechanism to guide decisions and the tendencies (given inelasticities) for over-adjustments to appear, now in one direction and now in the other. Rate-of-return analysis is then alleged to be too delicate an instrument, suitable only for optimizing at

11. Rigid complementarity between education at school and on-the-job learning is not precluded by the rate-of-return approach.

12. National Manpower Council, *A policy for scientific and professional manpower*, Columbia University 1963, pp. 143–6.

fine decision margins but liable to distortion in the big decisions. Such an allegation rests upon a mistaken analogy between hog-cycle phenomena (the cobweb theorem) and the quite different matter of use of rate-of-return analysis as a planner's tool. Nevertheless, to the degree that short-term fixed-factor pro-portions are approximated in a dynamic setting, we are in trouble. The burden upon planners and market-adjustment mechanisms alike will become intolerably severe, whatever the models or methods of planning unless we train individuals capable of doing a variety of things or of learning quickly to do them.

For the unquestioned high priority, definitely intra-marginal decisions in a world of high inelasticities and rapid change, rate-of-return analysis is clearly irrelevant. So is overall manpower planning, with its attempted neat fits and consistency tests. This point is often missed in discussions of Soviet practice. Establish-ment of priority claims on manpower resources to meet the needs (or wants) of favoured projects, as in the Stalinist period in Russia, is not overall manpower planning at all. It is workable only because or to the extent that there is technical flexibility with respect to utilization of resources, human and non-human, in the left-out, non-priority spheres of life.

Toward designs for decision

Decision implies choice,[13] and preparation of a set of decisions implies both tests of internal consistency within the set and (at least informal) consideration of alternative decision sets. As soon as we go beyond the manpower orientation, some of the alterna-tives will involve choices that shift priorities among the goals of educational planning. These might include, for example, varia-tions of emphasis upon equity *versus* economic efficiency and alternative compromises to resolve some of the conflicts between them.

Whatever the goal priorities, assessments of benefits foregone, in the broadest sense, are at the core of decision making.

13. For a discussion of the dimensions of choice and 'opportunity costs', see M. J. Bowman, 'Costing of human resource development', *The economics of education: Proceedings of a conference of the International Economic Association*, (eds.) E. A. G. Robinson and J. E. Vaizey, London, Macmillan, 1966.

For whom the choices are made, at whose cost: In economic analysis it is important to consider choices from the viewpoint of a student (or his family) and from that of a business firm that trains its employees. These are essential considerations for the educational planner as well; incentive structures and private behaviour are parameters, elements that he may seek to alter but that also constrain what he can do. Even in a command economy the central planner must take account of private decisions and motivations. However, in this paper we are not dealing with planning by families or firms as such. The 'for whom, at whose cost' dimension centres on the equity-efficiency problem; the educational system both distributes opportunities and sifts out talent in the public interest.

The scale units in which decisions are made and alternatives compared: Comparisons may be made among alternatives that involve only small, marginal shifts in numbers attending college, for example; on the other hand decisions might involve large proportionate increases in the student body.

When planners' decisions entail smooth and gradual changes only, there can be continuous reassessments and feed-back to guide subsequent decisions at the new margins; in such situations we can use measurements that are not suitable when the changes are large, discrete, and non-reversible (because large). In the latter case assessments of alternatives have to be in larger-scale units. It is then essential to distinguish cases in which it would be possible to sum small-unit measures to arrive at totals from cases in which measurements must be in lumped units. This problem arises *ex ante* only; *ex post* aggregations at any level incorporate the working out of interdependencies that would have invalidated simple summation of micro *ex ante* estimates. But planning is an *ex ante* activity. This problem of scale units is a basic point of dispute between most manpower planners and the economists who think in terms of 'rate of return'. Large-unit scale of public action is one of the considerations that underlie the manpower planners' pragmatic use of technologically deterministic models.

The transferability potential: There are important differences between services that are (a) in fact marketed, (b) potentially marketable, and (c) not potentially marketable or even transferable. For the first we have approximate measurements, at least, ready to hand. For the second we can construct cardinal measures, in principle and in practice, to a far greater degree than is usually assumed. The measurement problem is most recalcitrant for the third case: non-transferable benefits achieved or foregone. The case for maximizing individual freedom of choice is greatly strengthened when these non-measurable elements in returns to education are considered. They cannot be systematically planned in any other way, but to ignore them is to create a bias against them in the planning itself.

The time dimensions of benefits achieved and foregone: This involves not merely one as against another date, but comparisons along different time paths. It is a matter not only of the problems of time sequences and internal consistency of plans noted earlier in this paper, but of time preferences also – choices between sacrifices now in order to have more later *versus* speedier returns at the expense of later and greater ones. These perspectives lead also into consideration of the ways in which present choices condition the range of available future alternatives, which brings us to the fifth and sixth dimensions.

The pace of change: This should not be confused with the problem of lump decisions. This dimension has components that are autonomous and others that are endogenous to the projections made by planners, in several respects. Coefficients used by manpower planners incorporate conditional projections of the pace of change in economic structure and productivity, but this is the superficial side of the picture. The realized pace of change will determine also the pace of skill obsolescence in ways that manpower planning commonly neglects. Lying behind the pace of change are social and political pressure for educational expansion and the momentum that these may build up. Numerous decision problems in educational planning are bound up with adaptations to the pace of change, its speed and unevenness.

The knowledge and uncertainty dimensions of choice: These should be distinguished from problems of measurability related to scale units and the absence of transferabilities. This dimension is associated with the future-oriented nature of planning, the distance of the planning horizon, and the pace of change. Yet it is analytically distinct and carries its own implications for the rationale of planning methods.

The institutional constraints upon decisions: This is a matter of identifying the room for manoeuvre in the development of educational plans. Early in this paper we took note of (and set aside as fallacious) the arguments that we have planning only if the planners possess control instruments of the sorts found in 'command economies'. That argument overlooks the fact that the command system also constrains planning; it prohibits the use of instruments of indirect control or direction through manipulation of opportunities and incentives in a market economy.

Paradoxically, perhaps, many economists tend to regard 'economic' constraints as 'objective' whereas all other constraints are 'subjective'. This is a gross illogicality that stems from a particular disciplinary perspective. Institutional constraints are not separable into economic, political, and so forth, rather they inevitably inject biases against experimentation outside specified limits, though the direction and degree of these biases differ from one society and situation to another. It is the prevalence of certain institutional constraints that explains why educational planners have given so little explicit attention to designs that would encourage innovative behaviour – including innovation in developing an educational system. Institutional constraints are of course bound up with preconceptions concerning every aspect of education and its relation to society. These preconceptions range, for example, from reified theories of economic progress and development to reified psychological theories of the nature of human learning, and even to perceptions of what gives a nation 'status' in the world today.

Concerning shortage and excess

All the elements in educational decisions can be in principle expressed in quantitative terms, whether or not they are easily measurable in practice; more of this versus more of that, more quality versus more people 'put through' classrooms. A conceptual clarification of what is meant by 'shortage' and 'excess' is logically prior to any reasoned attempt at manpower-oriented educational planning.[14] Curiously, this question rarely gets explicit attention, partly because most planners are 'technicians' who ignore the operation of markets as adjustment mechanisms. However, the market economists' identifications of shortage or excess on the basis of a rise or fall in price, or even of a rise or fall relative to incomes in other occupations, are also arbitrary and unsatisfactory. Even within a narrowly economic framework and a market system, such approaches ignore costs (benefits foregone). Rate-of-return analysis has the advantage that it incorporates considerations of cost, whatever its limitations in other respects.

But what about social ends and social benefits that are not incorporated in market measures? The National Manpower Council, among others, attempted to define excess and shortage for a wide variety of situations; it gave up in defeat, summing up with the sound but unhelpful assertion that ultimately 'shortage' and 'excess' are social judgments.[15] We would argue that shortages and excesses are manifestations of past faulty allocations of scarce resources among alternative investments; the allocations are faulty relative to some preferred and feasible (but not necessarily optimal) set of alternatives. Viewed in this way, the estimation of prospective shortage and excess of human skills falls into place as a basis for decisions among human investment alternatives.

Education as a value in itself is included in the analysis, but as an end product, like other end products, to which more or less resources are allocated. The differences do not lie in time perspectives, for consumer returns to education (or political or social returns) may have quite as extended a time horizon as returns associated with increased productivity of 'human resources'. If we take indirect economic effects of the diffusion of schooling into account, even the distinction between investment in formation of a producer's good (human producer capital) and other aspects of returns to education becomes blurred. The critical

14. M. J. Bowman, 'Educational shortage and excess', *Canadian Journal of Economics and Political Science*, vol. 29 (1963), no. 4, pp. 446–61.

15. op. cit.

difference here lies in difficulties of measurement. There is every practical reason to begin with the more measurable variables and then extend the analysis to incorporate the less measurable and the unmeasurable.[16]

For and against consistency

Early in this paper we stressed consistency within decision-sets as an element in defining what planning is. Consistency tests are an explicit part of manpower planning and of the Tinbergen models. The rate-of-return technique is not planning in this sense; it is only one criterion that would be utilized by astute planners. This difference is more than accidental.

Emphasis upon rate-of-return criteria has been more prevalent among American economists, who would give the market mechanism a larger part of the job of co-ordination. Starting from this more 'open' orientation, a few selected instruments of public policy can be utilized to induce and to guide market processes in the desired direction. At the same time there can be provision also for limited public enterprises and of subsidies for social infra-structure. Consistency in planning could be there in such an open system, but it would work itself out in less visible forms. Certainly consistency is a requisite, if we mean by planning a realistic appraisal of alternatives and of impossibilities and the development of strategies and tactics that are mutually supportive. To be consistent will be to co-ordinate the components of decision-sets to provide order rather than chaos and to reconcile competing ends.

But what about the emphasis upon consistency as we find it

16. Michael Kaser approximates such a procedure in his attempts to analyse social investments. However, he argues for putting all non-market values on the 'benefit' rather than the 'cost' side of the ledger. The arbitrary and narrow definition of costs in such a treatment confuses thinking about the nature of choices and what is foregone and impedes effective treatment of the timing of the cardinally measurable returns to one as against another investment. Nevertheless, he has made a beginning in efforts to include a broad range of ordinal as well as cardinal variables within a systematized planning process. For a recent example of his approach, see his *The analysis of costs and benefits of social programs*, prepared for the November 1963 meeting of the European Expert Group on Problems and Methods of Social Planning, Economic Commission for Europe (mimeo.). See also M. J. Bowman, 'Costing of human resource development', op. cit.

represented in formal models of manpower planning? There is a case against, as well as a case for, consistency. When it becomes a planner's fetish, it strengthens biases toward technocratic values. The problem is not that errors of forecasting are so great as to make scrupulous concern with detailed consistency irrelevant. Nor is the objection only that this sort of an image of what planning 'should be' has led in the past to patch-work attempts to conceal planning failures. More important is what consistency leaves out. And this brings us back to unmeasured values. Are they pushed outside the realm of choice because they are 'invisible'? How does one then devise a consistent plan that will both stimulate and neatly harness creativity and innovative energy? (Or is the planner by nature suspicious of innovation?) Where do the observed rising productivity coefficients come from, for that matter?

Planning for a dynamic future requires planning for flexibility, both in the human resources we create and in the scope for future revision of plans. It must be evident also that however skilled the planner-technicians, most important of all is men wise enough not only to plan for others but also to plan so as to encourage others to plan for themselves, whether in a socialist state or a welfare state. In the end, that might prove to be the important guide to educational planning even when economic development is the sole goal. It is assuredly essential if the non-measurables are to be given adequate scope.

18 T. Balogh and P. P. Streeten

The Planning of Education in Poor Countries

T. Balogh and P. P. Streeten, 'The coefficient of ignorance', *Bulletin of the Oxford University Institute of Statistics*, vol. 25 (1963), no. 2, pp. 97–107.

Carefully directed social expenditure can have a much higher total yield (including all secondary effects) than types of expenditure which may result in some imposing visible structure, but whose effects on output in other sectors of the economy are zero of negative. Expenditures on the health, education, and feeding of workers, on the provision of information, the creation of skills, etc., can raise output considerably, if properly directed and linked with improved equipment and appropriate institutional reforms. But these expenditures have for long been recalcitrant to theoretical treatment because

(a) they are permissive, creating opportunities for output growth without being its sufficient condition;

(b) their direct output is often not easily measurable;

(c) their effects are widely diffused;

(d) their effects are spread over a long time;

(e) there exists no determinate functional relationship between inputs and outputs, partly because success is contingent on complementary measures;

(f) independent value, as well as instrumental value, is attached to both the initial expenditure and the resultant flow of satisfactions;

(g) considerations of 'deserved social rewards' enter into the determination of costs (e.g. teachers' salaries);

(h) they cut across the traditional distinction between investment and consumption (on which many growth theories are built), according to which a sacrifice in current consumption can make future consumption greater than it would otherwise have been;

(i) they are frequently correlated with other causes of higher productivity from which they are not easily separated.

Although many of these considerations apply, perhaps to a lesser extent, also to expenditure on physical capital, they are more glaring when social expenditure is considered and therefore social expenditures have been, until recently, unpopular with model builders. But the bias which emphasizes allegedly measurable, separable, and determinate, and neglects other types of relationship is unwarranted. Actions about whose results it is possible to make only the vaguest guesses may be much more important than actions whose trivial effects are precisely foreseeable. The challenge of estimating the returns on certain types of social expenditure has been accepted, but in the process of analysing them the same mistakes have been made which have vitiated the use of more traditional concepts and relations, both in analysis and in their application to development planning.

In the last few years models have been constructed which attempt to isolate the contribution to growth made by expenditure on research, education, health, provision of information, etc. The starting-point has usually been the addition of one term to the Cobb–Douglas production function. $Y = aK^\alpha L^\beta H^\gamma$ where Y is national income, K capital, L labour, and H a ragbag term for 'human factor' including 'improved knowledge', improved health and skills, better organization and management, economies of scale, external economies, changes in the composition of output, etc., a, α, β, and γ are constants, and $\alpha + \beta = 1$. Thus whatever is not caught in variations of K and L is attributed to H. 'Improvement in knowledge' is a name for what has rightly been called 'coefficient of our ignorance'.[1]

Whatever the value of these models for advanced Western countries, and however welcome the attempt to get away from preoccupation with physical investment, their application to the problems of underdeveloped countries has bred confusion.[2]

1. Mr E. F. Denison, in his book *The sources of economic growth*, Committee for Economic Development, 1962, simultaneously assumes a linear homogeneous production function and perfect competition in order to use average return per unit of factor as a measure of its marginal value product, and attributes a substantial proportion of 'residual' growth to economies of scale.

2. For a brief discussion of and reference to these attempts, see John Vaizey, *The economics of education*, London, 1962, ch. 3. For criticism of the application of these models to underdeveloped countries, see T. Balogh,

The reasoning behind these new models can be briefly summarized: the increased use of one factor of production, while others are kept constant and 'knowledge' and 'skills' are given, will yield diminishing marginal returns. If the growth of national product over several decades is such that the expansion of land, labour, and capital does not account for the whole increase, the remainder must be due to 'investment in human beings'.

Another approach has attempted to estimate the returns in the form of higher earnings to the educated in relation to expenditure on their education in the U.S.A. Both these approaches and others have seemed to show that the returns to this type of 'investment' are substantially above the returns to physical investment. The conclusion is then drawn that expenditure on education and on other ways of improving knowledge and skills should be carried out by planners in other countries, and particularly in underdeveloped countries.[3]

'Balance in educational planning: Some fallacies in current thought', *The Times Educational Supplement*, 8 June 1962, and 'Misconceived educational programmes in Africa', *Universities Quarterly*, 1962.

3. Thus Mr Adiseshia, Unesco's Acting Director-General at a United Nations Association in Cambridge said: 'So my thesis is that accelerated economic growth is, to a large degree, a function of adequate and commensurate development of human resources . . . the expenditure in formal education, in training, in mass media, and in research and development leads to increased returns both to the individual and to the community. . . . The return from education over a twelve-year period to the individual, expressed in terms of the relation between the amount invested by him and/or his parents and his higher earnings in the future, can be averaged at 16 per cent gross or, if allowance is made for income forgone while at school or college, the net average would be 11 per cent. Similarly, a two-year training course increases future earnings by around 6 per cent gross or 3 per cent net.' *War on want*, Pergamon Press (1962).

Paul G. Hoffman, the head of the United Nations Special Fund, was reported in the *New York Times* of 21 October 1962, to have said: 'Possibly the greatest change in my own thinking is my widening recognition of the financial return from secondary education. Leadership must come from people with at least twelve years of schooling.' John Vaizey, in a letter to *The Times*, 14 March 1963, quoting the study of Edward F. Denison. 'Of an average percentage rate of growth in GNP from 1929 to 1957 of 2.93, education contributed 0.67 – far more than any other factor. In 1957 the typical United States male adult worker over twenty-five years of age had two and a half times more education than his counterpart in 1910. The

The pitfalls and fallacies in this admittedly over-simplified chain of reasoning are too numerous to be discussed here in detail. In the models of an aggregate production function a relationship, based on static economic models, is *assumed* between capital, labour, and output; the historically *observed* relationship in *advanced* countries is seen to diverge widely from the *assumed* relationship, and the difference is *postulated* to be due solely to 'improvements in knowledge'. This conclusion is then bodily *transferred* to a totally different technical, historical, cultural, religious, institutional, and political setting. Even if improved knowledge were a necessary condition for production growth, it might yield output only if incorporated in machines, exploited in specific ways, or combined with other policies, but not if occurring in isolation. Nor is education a homogeneous input. The teaching of Sanscrit has different results from the teaching of land cultivation. The teaching of book-keeping may increase the efficiency of manual labour, while the teaching of certain religions may reduce it. Isolation of 'education' from other measures ignores the importance of co-ordinating policies, and aggregation of all types of 'education' obscures the type of education required for development. The concept therefore suffers both from illegitimate isolation and from misplaced aggregation.[4]

Similar objections must be raised to the models attempting to calculate the returns to education by discounting the excess earnings of the educated over those of the uneducated. The American data, which are mostly used, do not provide evidence as to whether expenditure on education is *cause* or *effect* of superior incomes; they do not show, even if we could assume it to be a condition of higher earnings, whether it is a *sufficient* or a *necessary* condition of growth,[5] and they do not separate *monopolistic* from *other forces* influencing differential earnings which are correlated with, but not caused by, differential education.

---

implications for Britain are obvious. . . .' The recent emphasis on expenditure on education has occasionally been accompanied by an equally unwarranted depreciation of the importance of physical capital.

4. [See Paul Streeten 'The use and abuse of models in development planning' in K. Martin and J. Knapp, *The teaching of development economics*, Frank Cass, Ltd, 1967. (Authors' additional note.)]

5. Industrialization in Britain preceded general compulsory education.

The calculations based on these data ignore both the indirect (financial and non-financial) returns accruing to others than the educated individual, and the direct non-financial returns to the individual. On the other hand, they pay a good deal of attention to 'income forgone during study' which constitutes a large proportion of the costs of 'investment'. But neither the income foregone by other groups in society (housewives, voluntary workers, people such as some university teachers – accepting a lower income than they could get in other occupations), nor the non-financial benefits enjoyed during education are estimated. Since the time-flow over a lifetime of the earnings of the educated is quite different from that of the uneducated, lifetime earnings now must be calculated as returns on education in the nineteen-twenties. To conclude from those returns anything about today's returns is like identifying a crystal radio set with Telstar.

Assuming that the ratio of returns to costs reflected something significant, it would be rash to attribute it to education. Expenditure on education is highly correlated to income and wealth of parents, to ability and motivation, to educational opportunities such as urban residence and proximity to educational centres, to access to well-paid jobs through family and other connections, any one of which could, either by itself or in conjunction with any of the others, account for the superior earnings.

But monopolistic elements enter not only in the differential advantages enjoyed by the children of wealthy parents, but also in reaping the rewards of an education. How much of the differential earnings of lawyers and doctors is due to 'investment in men' and how much to restrictive practices concealed as requirements of qualifications? Much of the higher earnings is not a return on education but a monopoly rent on (1) the scarcity of parents who can afford to educate their children well and (2) the restrictions on members permitted into a profession in which existing members have a financial interest in maintaining scarcity.

If anybody attempted to use these models for calculating the returns to education in many underdeveloped countries, he would discover even higher rates of return. All this would show, however, is that pay scales in the civil service, in universities, and in the professions are still governed by the traditional standards of a feudal or colonial aristocracy and by natural or artificial restrictions. It would provide no clue as to how public money ought to be distributed between 'investment' in 'physical capital' and in 'people'.

This approach, though logically weak, not only appeals to the snobbery and flatters the self-esteem of the educated, appearing to provide an economic justification of existing income differentials, but also buttresses vested interests. The specific measures that would be required to make expenditure on technical and agricultural education effective are painful, they violate vested interests and run into numerous inhibitions of the planners and obstacles put up by the planned. What a relief then to be served by econometricians with an elegant model, and how convenient to elevate a statistical residual to the engine of development, thus converting ignorance into 'knowledge'. Instead of having to specify *which type of education combined with what other measures* (such as investment in improved methods of cultivation, provision of the right equipment), creating skills and ability and willingness to work efficiently, and *complemented by what other* policies reforming attitudes and institutions (land reform, reform of the credit system, the civil service, price guarantees, transport), one item is singled out, either as the necessary and sufficient condition, or as a principal strategic variable of development. But the wrong kind of education, or the right kind unaccompanied by the required complementary actions, can check or reverse the process of development. An unemployed or unemployable intelligentsia can be a source of revolutionary rather than economic activity, and young people brought up to despise manual work can reinforce the resistances to development.[6] Growth rates derived from the experience of the United States cannot be used to calculate the returns on education in the entirely different setting of underdeveloped countries. The same

6. 'Wilfrid Malenbaum, for instance, found that unemployment in India varies directly with the degree of higher education. See 'Urban unemployment in India', *Pacific Affairs*, vol. 30 (1957), no. 2, p. 146. Quoted in Gustav Ranis, 'Economic development: A suggested approach', *Kyklos*, vol. 12 (1959), fasc. 3, p. 445. In Mexico experiments have shown that investment in rural schools may not result in increased production or changed attitudes. For a discussion of the hostility to development generated by education and intellectuals, see Joseph A. Schumpeter, *Capitalism, socialism and democracy*, pp. 152 ff.

'input' could result in refusal to work on farms, an increase in urban unemployment, subversion, and collapse. The wrong type of education can also produce a ruling élite which gives the wrong kind of advice, as well as setting up ideals that stand in the way of development. It can encourage ignorance of and contempt for the professional and technical qualifications which are a condition of economic development.[7]

Aggregation of all 'investment in human capital' and its separation from 'investment in physical capital' not only obscures the complementary nature of most subgroups of the two, but also serves as an intellectual and moral escape mechanism from unpleasant social and political difficulties.

New types of models are beginning to appear in which the returns yielded by expenditure on research and development, on training in management and administration, perhaps even on psychological treatment to transform tradition-bound into 'achievement-motivated' personalities are calculated. But as long as crucial distinctions are blurred by aggregation, crucial connections severed by isolation, and historical and geographical differences neglected, the results will be useless or misleading.

One group of critics has attacked the sordidly mercenary approach to activities of high intrinsic value, saying that it is a perversion of values to calculate rates of return on what is, or should be, the ultimate end of all production. But these criticisms miss the point. The chief conclusion of most of the recent researches is that not enough is spent on education. The high independent value of education itself and of the consequent flow of independently (i.e. not instrumentally) valued satisfactions may be used as an argument against not spending enough, but it cannot be used as an argument against spending at least as much as would yield a return equal to that on physical capital. It could, of course, be said that once mercenary calculations are admitted,

7. The importance of the *type* and *composition* in contrast to the *total* of social expenditure is particularly glaring in the field of health: expenditure on death control which simply reduces mortality rates has a negative effect on *per capita* growth rates in many underdeveloped countries, whereas expenditure on birth control and improved health which raises vigour and reduces apathy has a positive effect. The same is true of expenditure on education. Education which breeds religious aversion and snobbery yields a selection mechanism and policies which have income-depressing effects.

the relative values of different kinds of education will be assessed by the wrong standards, and that the sense of the *value* of education will be lost, the more accurately its *price* is known. Already some authors argue that the returns on education in certain countries are lower than those on physical capital.

But the fact that we attach both independent and instrumental value to certain activities and that we attempt to estimate, if and when this is possible, the instrumental value, need not detract from the independent value. If the two reinforce each other, there can be no cause for complaint, and if they don't, it is surely rational to know the costs of policies promoting independent values.

The objection to the models is therefore not that they degrade education and equate human beings to machines. Better knowledge of the productive potential of human beings would raise, not lower, human dignity, human choice, and human freedom. The objection is that the models approach the problem in the wrong way.

The fault isolation of one tributary to the stream of production and the aggregation of different channels, some of which flow in opposite directions, some of which are stagnant, and some of which do not contain any liquid, does not imply a disparagement of the need for detailed quantitative planning, including the planning of education, which has particularly long gestation periods. Whether a particular theoretical model is worth constructing depends upon whether we can give sufficient precision to the definition of the parameters and the variables and whether we can estimate the numerical relations between them. The rigour which is claimed for mathematical models is an illusion if the terms which they contain have no clear reference to the relevant items.

In the process of criticizing misplaced aggregation, such as that which lumps all education into a single category, we are led to the formulation of less general concepts: education is subdivided according to where it takes place, in what subjects, at what level and to whom. The purpose of such decomposition, disaggregation, and subdivision is not to restrict analysis to less general concepts. We are, indeed, first tying to get rid of ragbag terms which do not correspond to anything observable and to replace them by 'boxes' that can be 'filled'. But as the boxes are being filled and as we gain fuller empirical knowledge, we may look forward to the formulation of new aggregates and to the reconstitution of the decomposed material in a different form. The new 'packages' or 'boxes' will differ from the old. Some of the new distinctions will cut across the old ones.[8] Thus when we examine the forces determining labour utilization in underdeveloped countries ('unemployment' and 'under-employment' are as misleading as 'education'), we shall discover that certain forms of education improve the quality of work and its efficiency, as well as, by improving hygiene and sanitation, the duration of work. Capital equipment may extend the duration (co-operation enforcing discipline) and efficiency. Instead of separating 'equipment' from 'labour' and aggregating each, we may arrive at a new abstraction in which skill and knowledge are infused through the introduction of machines.[9]

The formulation of long-term plans of economic development for underdeveloped countries which must incorporate the planning of education, must meet, in addition to these conceptual, certain other requirements.

(i) A long-term plan must embrace a study of how and how far traditional educational patterns have contributed to the failure of social and economic progress in the past. The study must discover whether the attitudes which are hostile to economic progress have been the result of a specific structure of education, and what modifications of that structure are needed to accelerate development. In both the formerly British and the formerly French territories a disdain of technical education has grown up which has been strengthened by the low status of technical

8. [See Paul Streeten, 'The use and abuse of models', op. cit. (Authors' additional note.)]

9. An interesting attempt to construct a model in which all productivity change is embodied in new investment was made by Professor Robert M. Solow, who, in the words of Arthur Smithies, 'is like a Pied Piper who can play different tunes'. This particular tune is the exact opposite to those which separate 'disembodied' knowledge and other improvements from capital accumulation. 'Technical progress, capital formation and economic growth', *Papers and proceedings*, *American Economic Review*, May 1962, pp. 76–86, Professor Kenneth Arrow and Messrs N. Kaldor and J. A. Mirrlees also have proposed a model of this type in *Review of Economic Studies*, June 1962.

schools and the restricted openings for their pupils. So long as the Civil Service and the appointments controlled or influenced by it are the preserve of the non-technically educated, the best ability will be diverted into non-technical education. This will both justify and strengthen the initial disdain and render progress more difficult. On the basis of this study of obstacles a new educational structure can be planned which will raise the status of those who meet the requirements of accelerated growth. Thus both diversion of the best talent and an increase in the supply of the required skills will be achieved.

(ii) The second requirement is a concrete idea of the size and composition of long-term development, based upon knowledge of the concrete endowments of the economy and a clear formulation of specific objectives and ideals. From these the future pattern of manpower distribution can be derived and thus an indication of the measures and the timing needed for educational development. The long gestation period of much education and training requires that starts are made now in order to reap results after fifteen, twenty, and twenty-five years. Neither general formulae of ill-defined and irrelevant aggregates and their unverifiable relationships, nor even the occupational composition experienced at comparable stages of development in advanced industrial countries are of much use.[10] Past experience of non-Soviet countries relates to spontaneous growth (or its failure). It cannot be assumed that deliberate efforts to accelerate growth

10. The most promising approach is that adopted by Mr Pitambar Pant of the Indian Planning Commission: 'To conclude, planning for education involves careful analysis of a number of issues . . . [the] planning [of education] should be approached from the point of view of long-term objectives of the society. In other words, the objectives and programmes of education should be related to the requirements of the future plans. Secondly, it is not very meaningful to talk in terms of aggregates, when the equation of supply and demand has to be worked for each separate category of personnel. For only to a limited extent are these variously qualified graduates interchangeable. A comprehensive plan should identify clearly the various categories of trained manpower required, and it is the main function of the educational process to give to properly selected boys and girls the best education and suitable environment to fit them for creative endeavour in future.' *Indian Journal of Public Administration*, vol. 7, no. 3, p. 330. [Such manpower planning cannot take the place of, but should be supplemented by, appropriate forms of cost–benefit analysis. (Authors' additional note.)]

by a series of policies would show the same requirements. The problem is to overcome *specific* difficulties, which differ from country to country and from time to time, while historical experience from now advanced countries points to broadly *similar* categories. From the long-term plan the quantities and types of educated personnel in detailed categories can be derived. Since changes in technology, demand, international policies, etc., will continually change these requirements, the long-term plan should be a 'rolling' plan, reviewed continually and at least annually, and adapted to new information. It should provide the framework for the five-year (or seven-year) plans and for the annual budgets, so that policies which will not bear fruit until after more than five or seven years are not neglected. To avoid superimposing new rigidities upon often already rigid economies, all three plans, the annual budget, the 'plan' and the perspective plan should be reviewed continually, and carried forward, so that they apply always to the next year, five years, fifteen years.

(iii) A number of measures will have to be taken which lie outside the scope of conventional economic considerations. Thus if training takes place abroad, the return of the trained men may have to be insured; if they have acquired the required skills, it will be necessary that they use them in isolated rural areas and reluctance to live there has to be overcome; the type of training provided must fit the available technology and not be appropriate to a more advanced form, etc.

(iv) Because of the narrow margins of tolerance and the closeness of many underdeveloped countries to misery and starvation, it is crucially important that minimum needs are estimated and that the required combination of measures is planned and executed. Failure to execute complementary measures can spell disaster. The isolation of 'educational' expenditure distracts attention from the urgent need, not only to select the right type of education, but also to combine it with the provisions of better seeds, drainage, and fertilizers, with land reform and price stabilization, with improvements in transport and birth control, with the improvements of rural amenities, with a reform of recruitment to the Civil Service and business management. The waste involved in not planning for the required complementarities and pushing education too far, can be detrimental to development.

(v) The detailed planning of education and training will have to make explicit political judgements about the distribution of the benefits between classes and over time. One of the costs of raising output later above what it would otherwise have been is the use of resources now to support the educational system required at a later stage. Since the social rate of time discount will tend to be high in countries where many are on the verge of starvation, extreme care is required in the expenditure on education. Financially conservative advice will be politically difficult and unpopular and may in many areas give rise to accusations of racial discrimination. Efforts are therefore needed to remove prejudices against quick-yielding and applied types of education. Education has to be used to get the right kind of education accepted. The larger the area for which collective planning can be initiated, the greater will be the scope for, and the less will be the danger of, indivisible highly specialized institutions which are expensive, not directly related to current progress, but imposing and prestige-yielding. The division of labour, in this field too, is limited by the extent of the market, and the larger and richer the area the more scope is there for specialized units conducting 'basic' research. Although it is true that the practical use of 'pure' research is unpredictable and that conscious direction of education and research to 'applied' fields does not always yield higher returns earlier than some initially 'pure' research, it cannot be denied that it takes time between a discovery, its application by engineers and its exploitation by entrepreneurs and their followers. Only a large and rich economy with a low rate of time discount can afford to devote much energy to basic or pure scholarship. It must not be forgotten, moreover, that the adaptation of *known* techniques by poor developing countries could raise substantially their real income.

The choice of the distribution over time is related to the choice between types of education with a high ratio of instrumental to independent value and those with a low ratio. The pursuit of knowledge for its own sake, wherever it may lead, is highly valued in many cultures, but it is not costless. This decision will in turn depend upon the political judgements made about the rate of growth of real income compared with that of leisure and the form in which leisure is to be enjoyed. These political value judgements will not be given once for all, but will themselves change as the plan is executed. But without a specification of concrete valuations and concrete manpower requirements, the calculation of 'returns to education' suppresses these value judgements in a pseudo-scientific formulation, buries the factual judgements in misplaced aggregation and severs crucial connexions by illegitimate isolation.

19 P. J. Foster

The Vocational School Fallacy in Development Planning

P. J. Foster, 'The vocational school fallacy in development planning', *Education and Economic Development*, C. A. Anderson and M. S. Bowman (eds.) Aldine Publishing Co., 1966, pp. 142–63.

In current controversies regarding the relationship between the provision of formal education and the economic growth of underdeveloped areas, few issues have been debated with more vehemence than the question of the desirability of providing technical, vocational, and agricultural instruction within the schools. So far as Africa is concerned, the controversy has been sharpened by the recent publication of a series of observations by the British economist, Thomas Balogh, on the conclusions of the 1961 Conference of African Ministers of Education at Addis Ababa.[1]

Briefly put, Balogh's views may be stated in the following manner: Since between 80 and 95 per cent of Africans are dependent upon agriculture, the essential need in African education is the development of large-scale technical and agricultural programs within the schools at all levels: 'The school must provide the nucleus of modern agriculture within the villages' and play a central role in the general raising of standards of living within the subsistence sector. Present educational facilities constitute an obstacle to rural progress because people are not trained for agriculture, and academic systems of formal education are the chief determinant of attitudes hostile to the practice of rural agriculture. Schools are regarded as primarily responsible for the flight from the rural areas to the towns. Balogh's views, stated in perhaps more measured terms, are paralleled in a recent United

1. UNESCO, United National Economic Commission for Africa, *Conference of African States on the development of education in Africa*, UNESCO/ED/181, Addis Ababa, 1961. Balogh's observations are to be found in 'Catastrophe in Africa', *Times Educational Supplement*, 5 January 1962, p. 8; and 9 February 1962, p. 241. Also in 'What schools for Africa?', *New Statesman and Nation*, 23 March 1962, p. 412.

Nations publication in which it is observed that one of the chief educational priorities in economically developing areas is 'the creation of a fully integrated system of agricultural education within the general framework of technical and vocational education'.[2]

Although only two examples of this trend of thought are given here, it is possible to indicate numerous current publications dealing with education and economic development that accord high priority to schemes for agricultural, vocational, and technical education as against the provision of substantially more 'academic' types of instruction. In the following pages I hope to show that these views are generally fallacious and ignore a series of crucial variables that must be taken into account if any realistic proposals for stimulating economic growth are to emerge. In developing the discussion I shall use examples from Ghana, which is not altogether unique among African territories in spite of the relatively high level of *per capita* income that it enjoys.

It should be said at the outset that there is no disagreement with two of Balogh's contentions. First, it seems clear that agricultural development and a rapid rise in rural incomes must definitely be accorded priority in all development schemes. Apart from the probability that such growth must precede even limited industrial development, there is the immediate question of raising the bare subsistence basis upon which many African cultivators are obliged to exist. Second, it is likely that such programs must depend in part upon the provision of technical and agricultural education as a necessary but by no means sufficient condition of growth.

However, in spite of vague general agreement on the desirability of such programs, there is a virtual absence of explicit dicta regarding their nature. For example, what would an educational scheme adjusted to developmental needs look like? What role would the schools themselves play in such a program? At what stage in formal education should specifically vocational subjects be begun, and how would technical and agricultural schools be

2. United Nations Committee on Information from Non-Self-Governing Territories, *Special study on educational conditions in non-self-governing territories*, New York, 1960, p. 8.

integrated with the general system? Then there is the problem of the content of studies; frequently vocational curricula are ill-designed to serve the needs of developing economies. Agreeing on the need for agricultural development does not lead us directly to any particular specifications for educational content or organization. Even assuming that well-validated prescriptions existed, it is equally apparent that these would vary considerably with the degree of effective centralized control exerted by governments. This latter factor seems to be rarely considered by educational planners, yet it is probably the single most crucial variable in determining the effectiveness of an agricultural or a technical program.

Having entered these caveats, our major disagreement with Balogh lies in the 'strategy' that he proposes and the degree to which he places reliance upon *formal* educational institutions in instituting change. Secondly, Balogh tends to view vocational and general education as substitutes for each other rather than to see them as essentially complementary and hardly substitutable.

There is, perhaps, a general tendency to accord to the schools a 'central' position in strategies designed to facilitate economic development. To some extent this reflects an appreciation of the relative lack of alternative institutions that can be utilized, but it stems partially from the notion that schools are particularly manipulable institutions. It is widely believed that schools can readily be modified to meet new economic needs and, more particularly, to accord with the intentions of social and economic planners. I shall argue, on the contrary, that schools are remarkably clumsy instruments for inducing prompt large-scale changes in underdeveloped areas. To be sure, formal education has had immense impact in Africa, but its consequences have rarely been those anticipated, and the schools have not often functioned in the manner intended by educational planners.

I. The Colonial Experience in Ghana

If there is anything surprising in Balogh's views it lies not in their originality but in the degree to which they reproduce with virtually no modification a series of arguments that were first stated in equally cogent fashion by the Education Committee of the Privy Council in 1847.[3] So far as Ghana, in particular, is concerned, the viewpoint was forcefully advanced in the Appendix to the Report of the Commission on the West Coast of Africa in 1842 and by a succession of colonial governors and educators thereafter.[4] Indeed, stress on the provision of vocational and agricultural education was included *without exception* in every major document related to educational development in the Gold Coast up till the grant of independence in 1957.

In spite of this, by 1959 the structure of the Ghanaian educational system was essentially that prevailing in most of British Africa: an expanding base of primary- and middle-school education of a predominantly academic variety capped by a group of highly selective grammar schools and a university college modeled closely upon British prototypes.[5] In that year only about 1 per cent of all persons enrolled in formal educational institutions were receiving instruction in vocational, technical, or agricultural subjects. The paradox in Ghanaian education has been the emphasis placed on vocational and agricultural training in all documentary sources and the relative absence of it within the actual system of education.[6]

3. The text of this early document is to be found in H. S. Scott, 'The development of the education of the African in relation to Western contact', *The Yearbook of Education*, Evans Bros., 1938, pp. 693–739.

4. There is considerable literature on this point but a few major examples may be cited. See the report of the Commissioner in the Appendix to the 'Report of the Committee on the West Coast of Africa', *Parliamentary Papers*, vol. 11, 1852. Also Gold Coast, *Report of the Committee of Educationalists*, Accra, Government Printer, 1920; Jesse Jones, *Education in Africa: A Study of West, South and Equatorial Africa by the African Education Commission*, New York, Phelps Stokes Fund, 1922; Gold Coast, *Report of the Education Committee*, 1937–41, Accra, Government Printer, 1942. This list cannot present numerous additional statements of this nature and there should be no need to refer the reader to the famous policy statements of the Advisory Committee on Education in the Colonies. However, in Appendix I to this paper we have included a selection of statements from these earlier documents [not reprinted here].

5. Ghana, Statistical Reports Series I, No. 6, *Education Statistics 1959*, Accra: Office of the Government Statistician, 1959.

6. The Ghanaian Ministry of Education, like most African Ministries, does not include in its reports technical and vocational training being undertaken in special schools connected with Railways and Harbors, the Public Works Department, etc.

A priori, it might be suspected that no serious attempt was ever made to implement schemes for agricultural and vocational training in the schools or that such proposals remained stillborn as the result of disinterest in them by the colonial rulers. In the case of Ghana this argument can be totally dismissed. There is ample documentary evidence throughout the latter half of the nineteenth century and the early twentieth that strenuous efforts were being made by both government and missions to establish agricultural schools, devise special agricultural curricula, and provide technical and vocational education. The development of academic secondary schools upon the British model was regarded with disfavor, as being inappropriate for the economic needs of the Gold Coast. Agricultural education was regarded as the key to economic development in that area. Particularly in the case of the activities of the Basel Mission, a system of schools based on agricultural and technical education was attempted which was probably unrivaled in any other territory in Africa.[7] Yet all of these earlier experiments were unsuccessful, and the educational history of the Gold Coast is strewn with the wreckage of schemes corresponding to Balogh's proposals.

In practice, the demand by Africa for western education was and is predominantly oriented toward the provision of more academic-type schools. This preference springs, I contend, from a remarkably realistic appraisal of occupational opportunities generated within the exchange sector of the economy as a result of European overrule. So far as the clientele of the schools was concerned, the primary function of formal education was to enable individuals to move from subsistence activities to occupations within the European-dominated sector. An examination of opportunities within that sector throughout the colonial period reveals that *relatively* there was a greater demand for clerical and commercial employees than for technically trained individuals. Opportunities certainly existed in technical fields and in agriculture, but they were inferior to the other alternatives. Access to most of the highly paid occupations was, therefore, achieved

7. For a succinct account of the activities of the Basel Mission, see W. J. Rottman, 'The educational work of the Basel Mission', Appendix A.I to *Special reports on educational subjects*, vol. 13, part 2, H.M.S.O., 1905, pp. 307–18.

through academic type institutions. Those who criticize the 'irrational' nature of African demand for 'academic' as opposed to 'vocational' education fail to recognize that the strength of academic education has lain precisely in the fact that it is pre-eminently a *vocational* education providing access to those occupations with the most prestige and, most important, the highest pay within the Ghanaian economy. The financial rewards and the employment opportunities for technically trained individuals were never commensurate with opportunities in the clerical field. Since the graduates of the academic school were manifestly more advantageously placed,[8] the pressure for 'academic' education reflected fairly accurately the demands for alternative types of skill within the exchange sector of the economy. One of the major ironies of the situation is that while proponents of technical education were criticizing the neglect of technical provision in the schools, the products of such technical institutions as existed were often experiencing difficulties in obtaining employment. Frequently those persons entered occupations unrelated to the training they had undergone.[9]

This form of 'wastage' among trained manpower is endemic in underdeveloped countries.

1. Initially, trained individuals may be produced for whom there is no actual demand so far as the market is concerned. There may be a considerable 'surplus' of these trained men where 'new nations', in their desire to emulate more economically developed areas, invest considerable sums in the training of technicians before they can be utilized in the existing economy.

2. Second, a real demand may exist for trained personnel, but at the same time scarce personnel are not utilized and skilled workers are involved in tasks not directly relevant to their professional accomplishments. This would appear to occur more commonly in government service and we shall draw attention to it specifically in later pages.

3. Third, skilled personnel may not enter the type of job for which they have been trained because opportunities seem so much

---

8. See also I. M. Wallerstein, *The emergence of two West African nations: Ghana and the Ivory Coast*, Columbia University Press, 1959, p. 241.

9. See Gold Coast, *Report of the Education Department*, 1935, para. 332; also Gold Coast, *Legislative Council Debates*, 1933, pp. 5, 94; and 1935, p. 5.

greater in alternative occupations. Thus, for example, many graduates of the Basel Mission schools who received agricultural and industrial training entered clerical employment. Here the most saleable component of their education experience was literacy, not trade training, and the former was thus utilized in the job market.[10] Wastage of skills must always be considered in assessing programs of vocational training.

To be sure, such wastage has also been characteristic of developed countries, but in the case of many of the 'new nations such a phenomenon is particularly undesirable in view of the limited resources available.

We do not intend here to underestimate non-economic factors that contributed to African demand for academic schools though these, in fact, reinforced the pattern we have described above. The European colonial élite itself acted as a reference group for African aspirations; emulation of that élite led to a pressure for 'parity' between metropolitan and colonial institutions. Since the colonial élite provided only a partial image of western society and was composed overwhelmingly of administrators and government servants educated primarily in academic institutions, African demand for education was understandably oriented to the acquisition of that kind of education that was perceived to be the key to European-type occupational roles. In this the Africans were acting astutely. One of the striking features of most post-colonial economies is the domination by government agencies of well-paid and high-status employment opportunities. Since such institutions, through recruiting primarily upon the basis of 'universalistic' criteria, stress the possession of an academic formal education, a higher premium is placed upon such schooling than occurred in early stages of development in most western societies.

In this context, one of the most striking differences between many of the new nations and the western world at earlier periods of its development is their lack of mobility opportunities lying outside the formal educational structure. Systems of apprenticeship, opportunities to open small enterprises, etc., all provided institutionalized modes of social and economic ascent in western society. The relative absence of those sorts of alternatives to

10. Rottman, op. cit., p. 300.

formal education in many new nations sometimes produces the paradoxical result, as in Ghana, that educational requirements for obtaining employment are now as high, if not higher, than in the former metropole itself, notwithstanding a very low level of diffusion of formal education in the population as a whole.

Thus when colonial peoples were involved in unequal competition with resident Europeans for a limited number of high-status jobs, it was considered imperative to obtain qualifications virtually identical to those prevalent in the metropole. This was a perfectly rational estimate of the relative advantages of alternative types of education; in the competition for scarce job opportunities nonmetropolitan curricula were by definition inferior.

It is important to note, however, that the termination of colonial overrule has made virtually no difference to the overall structure of occupational opportunities within the exchange sector. To be sure, Ghanaians are less involved in direct competition with Europeans for high-ranking posts within the administration. However, in the nongovernmental sector there has been little change in the premium placed on academic training; indeed, there has been an intensification of certain features apparent in the colonial period. At present, out of a total employed labor force of 2.56 million not more than 13.7 per cent (or 350,000) are employed full-time in the 'modern' sector of the economy. It has been calculated that the rate of growth in wage employment opportunities amounts to just over 4 per cent per annum; though this estimate is probably too low, a rather generous estimate of employment growth would be 20 to 25 thousand per annum.[11] On the other hand, the annual output of the middle schools alone has now risen to over 30 thousand per annum.

Parallel with this, however, has been the fact that government employment has absorbed an increasing proportion of the labor force: 42 per cent in 1951 and 51 per cent in 1957. The progressive enlargement of existing government agencies and the creation of new public corporations has, if anything, tended to

11. These estimates have been computed from the 1960 *Population Census of Ghana*, Advance Reports of vols. 3 and 4; Ghana, *Quarterly Digest of Statistics*, Accra, Office of the Government Statistician, 1959; and Ghana, *Economic Surveys*, 1955–8, Accra, Government Printer, 1959.

favor employment for clerical and administrative workers. Since, relatively speaking, the balance of job opportunities has shifted even more in favor of clerical employment, there is a mounting demand for the academic secondary school education that provides access to such positions.[12]

What is implied here is that although considerable attention has always been paid to the so-called problem of 'white-collar' unemployment in West Africa, there has been little realization that opportunities for technical employment have been even more limited and certainly more poorly paid. In virtually every African territory there appears to be a current stress upon the need for the provision of technical education upon a massive scale to meet the 'needs' of the economy. Sometimes such demands are based upon the conclusions of manpower surveys, the source of whose projections may not be too clear. Yet a sober inspection of the actual structure of job opportunities within an economy such as that of Ghana gives no reason to suppose that the products of technical schools can be absorbed soon on a large scale.[13] In actuality, we are not faced by the problem of white-collar unemployment at all but by a far more serious form of generalized unemployment.

II. The 'White-collar' Myth and Vocational Aspirations

There is no doubt that unemployment among school-leavers has reached alarming proportions in West Africa. Investigations by Callaway in Nigeria and by the present writer in Ghana confirm its extent and incidence and give no reason to suppose that it is likely to diminish in the near future.[14] However, the crucial question is not the amount of such unemployment but the delineation of significant factors determining its incidence. It has been frequently asserted that the problem has its source in the

12. This trend in demand for academic secondary education is, of course, indicated most sharply by the growth of private and proprietary secondary schools in Ghana which by 1961 numbered no less than fifty-two schools.

13. No data exist on the occupational destinations of the products of technical institutes, but in 1961 there was some concern that the products of Junior Technical Institutes, in particular, were experiencing difficulty in finding adequate employment.

14. Arch C. Callaway, 'School leavers in Nigeria: 1', *West Africa*, no. 2286 (25 March 1961), p. 325.

reluctance of literate individuals and school graduates to enter manual occupations and in their unrealistic search for white-collar employment, which they believe to be commensurate with their status as 'educated men'.[15] In this interpretation unemployment is conceived to be 'frictional' in nature, and the schools are perceived to be the villains of the piece; it is inferred that the type of education to which students are exposed (specifically, the the curriculum of the schools) largely determines their vocational aspirations and operates as an independent variable in setting the level of vocational choice. This has been a favorite theme for well nigh a century. Balogh, for example, specifically attributes the present employment crisis in Nigeria to the provision of a parti-cular form of academic elementary education that has generated unrealistic employment expectations for clerical work, caused a flight from the rural areas, and fostered a disdain for manual occupations.[16] If this diagnosis of the problem were correct, the solution would be simple: change the curricula to provide in-struction based upon agriculture and technical subjects, and the aspirations of young people will, in consequence, be directed to-wards agricultural activities; the flight from the land will be checked and the volume of 'frictional' unemployment will correspondingly diminish.

This reasoning is largely fallacious.[17] It has already been pointed out by others that the idea that children's vocational aspirations can be altered by massive changes in curriculum is no more than a piece of folklore with little empirical justification.[18]

15. This view is to be found throughout the literature. For a recent ex-ample see Ghana, *Economic Survey 1958*, p. 24.

16. Balogh, op. cit., *Times Educational Supplement*, 9 February 1962, p. 241.

17. We do not wish to imply here that the problem of the 'unemployed intellectual' who refuses to accept a type of employment 'below his status' is a myth in all areas. There is little doubt that this phenomenon was clear enough in India. However, this is a very different thing from saying that such attitudes were a result of the kind of formal western schooling under-gone by students. They probably stemmed from a much older tradition of Brahmanic intellectualism. However, in the case of West Africa, this would not appear to be the case, and there is a very high correlation between perceived prestige and perceived income variables.

18. Callaway, 'School leavers in Nigeria: 3', *West Africa*, vol. 2288 (8 April 1962), p. 371.

In Nigeria and Ghana the graduates of the primary and middle schools do work with their hands and they often seek employment as general laborers. Conversely, it is possible to show that

Table 1

Occupational Choices of Form IV Children in Ghana Middle Schools (N = 210)

Occupational category *	(1) Free choices		(2) Job expectations		Difference between (1) and (2)	
	Percentage	Number	Percentage	Number	Percentage	Number
I Higher professional	11.0	23	5.2	11	−5.8	−12
II Lower professional	10.0	21	1.9	4	−8.1	−17
III Teacher	0.9	2	3.8	8	+2.9	+6
IV Clerical and allied	8.1	17	10.0	21	+1.9	+4
V Artisans and skilled workers	51.0	107	22.4	47	−27.6	−60
VI Commercial	1.9	4	9.5	20	+7.6	+16
VII Semiskilled and unskilled	3.3	7	35.2	74	+31.9	+67
VIII Uniformed services	2.4	5	4.8	10	+2.4	+5
IX Fishermen and farmers	10.5	22	6.7	14	−3.8	−8
X Miscellaneous and unclassified	0.9	2	0.0	0	−0.9	−2
No Answer	0.0	0	0.5	1	+0.5	+1
Total	100.0	210	100.0	210		

* The occupational categories were:

Higher professional: Doctor, lawyer, minister of religion, etc.

Lower professional: Nurse, dispenser, draughtsman, journalist, agricultural officer, surveyor, etc.

Teacher: All teaching roles within the primary, middle, secondary or technical institutions.

Clerical and allied: Clerk (unspecified), cashier, bookkeeper, typist, bank clerk, librarian, letter writer, etc.

Artisans and skilled workers: Electrician, motor mechanic, plumber, carpenter, mason, printer, painter, shoemaker, locomotive engineer, tailor, etc.

Commercial: Petty trades and small-scale shopkeepers.

Semiskilled or unskilled workers: Laborer (various), messenger, bus conductor, watchman, steward, quarryman, miner, cook, etc.

Uniformed services: Police, army, Builders Brigade.

Fishermen and farmers, Miscellaneous and unclassifiable: Musician, boxer, artist, jockey, etc.

even where students have been educated in agricultural or technical schools, a high proportion of them have never entered those occupations for which they were trained but have gravitated to alternative employments offering greater opportunities. These observations would tend to throw some doubt on programs whose efficacy depends on the notion that the schools exercise a decisive influence upon vocational aspirations of students. However, more definite empirical evidence is available to suggest that in Ghana, at least, the disdain for manual labor believed to be so typical of the products of formal education is not at all in accord with fact.

In December 1959 the author drew a sample of 210 boys from the fourth forms of nine academic-type middle schools in Accra. These students were in their final month of studies preparatory to seeking employment or, in a few cases, continuing their education in other schools. They were asked, first, what kind of employment they would most like to obtain if they were *completely free* to choose. This enabled children to fantasy as much as they wished regarding their careers. Then they were asked what type of employment they actually *expected* to be able to obtain.

The findings in no sense indicate a predisposition to favor professional and white-collar employment (Table 1). Even where children were free to respond as they wished, no fewer than 62 per cent favored artisan employment or farming (even in an urban center such as Accra). Only 30 per cent favored employment in varying levels of white-collar activity (categories I–III). The most instructive section of the table, however, concerns job expectations. The pupils displayed a remarkable level of realism. Although 51 per cent expressed the hope of ultimately becoming skilled artisans, only 22 per cent *expected* to be able to do so, and 35 per cent were fully reconciled to entering semiskilled or unskilled occupations. These observations (which confirm an earlier study by Barnard) would seem to indicate that there is little foundation to theories attributing to the curriculum a major influence on vocational aspirations.[19]

It seems clear that mass unemployment among school-leavers in many new African nations is due to dysfunctions existing between the gross rate of school output and the slow expansion of occupational opportunities of all types within the exchange sector. It may be easy enough to increase the output of the

19. G. L. Barnard, 'Gold Coast children out of school', *Oversea Education*, vol. 23 (1957), no. 4, pp. 163–72.

schools but it is far more difficult to expand employment opportunities. The operative fact here is not that graduates will not accept certain types of employment but rather that the schools (irrespective of what they teach) have been shrewdly used as the gateway into the 'emergent' sector of the economy. The schools themselves can do little about this. So long as parents and students perceive the function of education in this manner, agricultural education and vocational instruction *in the schools* is not likely to have a determinative influence on the occupational aspirations and destinations of students. Aspirations are determined largely by the individual's perception of opportunities within the exchange sector of the economy, destinations by the *actual* structure of opportunities in that sector. The nature of educational instruction has little to do with the process, and the schools are unfairly criticized for creating a condition for which they have not been responsible – except insofar as they turn out too many graduates.

The reasons why graduates do not return to subsistence or quasi-subsistence agriculture has, of course, little to do with a disdain for farming that is created by an academic education. In 1961, a questionnaire was administered by the present writer to more than 700 Ghanaian male students in twenty highly selective academic secondary schools. The students were asked to rate twenty-five diverse occupations in terms of two criteria, occupational prestige and perceived income (Table 2). In practice, farming was rated sixteenth in prestige rankings (above middle- and primary-school teaching and office work, for example) and tenth in perceived income. Even among these advanced students farming is still rated moderately high. However, only one per cent of the students wished to become farmers in spite of the fact that it was rated higher in terms of both prestige and income than was primary- or middle-school teaching, which no less than 34 per cent of the students expected to enter.

It would seem that the factors inhibiting the 'return to the land' lie primarily in the institutional milieu of farming. Initially, of course, in certain areas of Ghana (such as Ewe territory) acute population pressure and land fragmentation pose the problem of getting people away from the villages and into alternative employment, or at least into areas where land is available. In other localities suitable cash crops that might provide the basis for reasonable cash incomes to supplement subsistence activities have not yet been discovered. However, even in areas where

Table 2

Secondary Student Perceptions of the Occupational Hierarchy (N = 775)

Occupation	(1) Prestige rankings			(2) Income rankings		
	Mean score	S.D.	Rank	Mean score	S.D.	Rank
Medical doctor	1.12	0.31	1	1.24	0.47	1
University teacher	1.16	0.38	2	1.28	0.51	2
Lawyer	1.45	0.64	3	1.40	0.55	3
Chief	1.89	0.78	4	2.47	0.80	8.5
Author	1.97	0.80	5	2.25	0.86	6
Secondary school teacher	2.05	0.51	6	2.23	0.58	5
Clergyman	2.96	0.84	7	3.10	0.95	15
Merchant or business-man	2.50	0.73	8	1.92	0.79	4
Nurse	2.60	0.64	9	3.01	0.57	13
Political party worker	2.70	0.93	10	2.38	0.90	7
Government clerk	2.71	0.59	11	2.78	0.58	11
Soldier	2.78	0.81	12	3.00	0.64	12
Actor	2.81	0.90	13	2.47	0.94	8.5
Chief's counsellor	2.82	0.74	14	3.21	0.79	17
Policeman	2.94	0.73	15	3.21	0.55	17
Farmer	2.95	0.96	16	2.75	1.06	10
Office worker	2.96	0.60	17	3.03	0.56	14
Middle school teacher	3.00	0.50	18	3.21	0.51	17
Primary school teacher	3.25	0.67	19	3.53	0.65	21
Motorcar fitter	3.59	0.73	20	3.35	0.77	19
Petty trader	3.62	0.75	21	3.36	0.82	20
Shop assistant	3.80	0.66	22	3.84	0.64	23
Carpenter	3.84	0.73	23	3.73	0.75	22
Farm laborer	4.47	0.70	24	4.51	0.63	24
Streetcleaner	4.74	0.56	25	4.73	0.53	25

cash-crop farming can be moderately profitable, it takes place within a neotraditional framework. The farmer is not only obliged to reside in areas whose amenities are demonstrably inferior to those of the urban areas, but he is necessarily involved in the obligations and constraints of traditional rural structure. The demands of kin and the constrictions of traditional land tenure with its usual concomitant of endless litigation combine to make 'progressive' farming a hazardous endeavor. In effect, if we are to really appreciate the factors that militate against individuals entering agriculture, we must examine the neotraditional institutional complex in which agricultural activities take place. It is probably in this complex and in the structure of accompanying incentives that the primary variables lie – not in the deficiencies of agricultural instruction in the schools nor in the 'academically' oriented values of students. Young people do not object to farming *per se* or to the desirability of entering 'modern' farming.[20] They are perfectly aware, however, that this is precisely what the institutional framework does not offer. Vocational instruction in agriculture by itself cannot induce youth to take up farming until an institutional complex exists which makes the utilization of new techniques profitable and meaningful. This reluctance would still prevail even if it were evident that such instruction was the principal mode of raising agricultural production. A high priority for research is indeed the delineation of those disincentives which spring from the neotraditional complex of institutions surrounding agriculture.

We have argued so far that the vocational aspirations of children and the occupations which they enter are almost exclusively determined by factors which lie outside the schools. Indeed, in terms of the actual opportunities open to them, the students' perceptions are remarkably realistic. It follows, therefore, that no amount of formal technical, vocational or agricultural instruction alone is going to check the movement from the rural areas, reduce the volume of unemployment, or indeed necessarily have any effect on the rate of economic development. Those factors which really give the impetus to early economic growth are far more subtle than the proponents of vocational education suppose. We would suggest that the crucial variables lie, instead, in the structure of incentives within the economic system and in the degree to which the institutional milieu is supportive of entrepreneurial activity. Without such a milieu no

20. See also Callaway, loc. cit.

amount of vocational instruction can be effective since the skills acquired will not be utilized. To put the issue more colloquially, in the initial stages technical and vocational instruction is the cart rather than the horse in economic growth, and its development depends upon real and perceived opportunities in the economy. The provision of vocational education must be directly related to those points at which some development is already apparent and where demand for skills is beginning to manifest itself.

III. Difficulties of Manpower Planning

In this respect, there may be some dangers attached to large-scale high-level manpower estimates which have recently been derived in some African areas. The bases upon which these projections are made are sometimes not clear and some of the assumptions about the rate of growth in the exchange sector of the economy seem to be questionable. In one instance such estimates have formed the basis for a large-scale system of general and vocational schools to meet these hypothetical manpower needs.[21] There is a tendency to talk of the 'needs' for development as if they were quite independent of the actual structure of job opportunities in the economy. This is daring planning, but it need hardly be said that if the rate of growth of the economy is not sufficient to absorb the products of a vastly expanded educational system, then the unemployment situation will become even worse. The production of large numbers of specifically trained individuals does not, at the same time, create employment opportunities for them.

Furthermore, the calculation of varying shortfalls for different types of specific skill is a hazardous endeavor, particularly in areas where there is an absence of any really satisfactory or meaningful data to make such projections realistic. Cumulative errors in the projection of a whole range of manpower needs can ultimately add up to an alarming misallocation of scarce resources, particularly when these are invested in the establishment of highly expensive vocational institutions. In certain sectors dysfunctional shortfalls will exist, while in other sectors surpluses

21. Nigeria, Federal Ministry of Education, *Investment in education* (the Ashby Report), Lagos, 1960.

will be produced; even accurate estimates may go awry when occupational wastage occurs.[22]

Perhaps the most disturbing feature of the manpower approach lies in the accent upon large-scale planning independent of the market. Large-scale planning involves large-scale miscalculations, which can be disastrous in economies with such limited resources. Major miscalculations, which are inevitable, then force either wasteful adjustments to conceal the magnitude of the errors or major reversals of policy, or both. At best, large-scale planning in the output of specific skills may induce subsequent extensive imposition of controls upon the trained men by something approximating to forced labor allocation. Certainly this writer can lay no claim to being an expert on manpower, but these dangers are not easily dismissed.

It might be more fruitful to encourage small-scale vocational training schemes closely associated with actual ongoing developments and quite divorced from the formal educational system. This implies a strategy that relates specific vocational training to other necessary changes in the institutional framework.[23] Maximum effort can be undertaken with individuals already involved in specific forms of economic activity. The chances of gross aggregate distortions are minimized while the moderate size of a large number of specific projects permits continuous feedback correction of errors. Failure in a number of small activities is counterbalanced by small successes that point the way to broader programs. There is an important place for planning, but planning to provide the institutional framework for small-scale operative decision-making, not the wholesale making of such decisions. Perhaps we can examine the application of this approach first with respect to technical and commercial training, and second in the context of agriculture.

22. For a discussion of similar problems in planning outputs of skilled personnel in another area, see Arcadius Kahan, 'The economics of vocational training in the U.S.S.R.', *Comparative Education Review*, vol. 4, (1960), no. 2, pp. 75–83.

23. For a specific application of this approach, see discussion of education, pages 210–37 in The World Bank Survey Mission on Kenya and the much fuller analysis in the initial report prepared by C. A. Anderson for the Mission (mimeo). The Mission's report, entitled *The economic development of Kenya*, was published in 1963 by Johns Hopkins Press, Baltimore.

IV. Training Technical Manpower

Initially, the production of really high-level technical manpower is perhaps the easiest problem. There is no question here that formal educational institutions at the university level (locally or overseas) must take the general responsibility for training professional workers, though there is a need to make sure that curricula are suitably modified to meet the needs and actualities of the local environment. There is no doubt that certain portions of prevailing instruction can be adapted more closely to actual work situations. There is perhaps also a need to ensure that study, even at this level, is combined with periods of field-experience for the high-level specialists concerned. Nonetheless, we contend that, at present, African needs for the uppermost levels in trained manpower are not so great as supposed. The issue here is to see that limited numbers of individuals possessing high-level skills are used effectively and economically. It is frequently evident, for example, that highly trained engineers in some areas are heavily involved in routine administration and paperwork which could be effectively performed by individuals possessing no professional skills.

It should also be noted that at this level there may be no shortage of numbers of applicants for high-level training but an acute shortage of applicants who have had the basic education that is essential if they are either to complete a regular schooling sequence or to qualify for technical post-secondary training programs at high levels within industry. This points to the need for more adequate general education at the secondary level and a more thorough preparation in basic subjects on the part of aspirants. Indeed, we suggest that this is the really effective thing that the schools can do at every level. Rather than attempting to load them with vocational subjects, providing a sound general education with a bias toward general science and English or French, essential at all levels, can provide the basis for later effective specialist training. Here, indeed, is the area in which imaginative and constructive curriculum work can be undertaken.

However, it is at the intermediate levels of technical and vocational training that the greatest difficulties arise. Many observers acquainted with the development of intermediate technical institutes and vocational schools in underdeveloped areas are only too aware that many institutions built at considerable cost remain partially empty or are filled with students who are for the most part composed of 'rejects' from selective academic-type institutions. This is a situation that the technical schools are likely to face for some time. In itself, this is not disastrous since it implies that intermediate technical schools must reconcile themselves to being unable to choose freely the most able students. But there is also a subtle pressure developed which tends to transform these schools progressively into academic institutions. Students at entry frequently do not regard their courses as terminal, leading directly to artisan work; instead they regard them as 'stepping stones' to enable them to enter professional-type courses. In some areas disturbances have resulted when students were not allowed to take pre-university examinations. It must be recognized that wherever technical education is given largely in institutions which are part of the formal educational structure, the expectations of the students may pervert the intentions of the planners.

Furthermore, there is a need to examine most carefully the actual courses given in such institutions. To a considerable degree in colonial and former colonial territories the pressure to emulate the standards of the metropole has led to a remarkably generous investment in institutions that provide lengthy and elaborate instruction. In practice, certain specific forms of vocational education may in consequence become quite dysfunctional in terms of the later work experience of trainees. To be sure, skilled artisans are produced, but in some cases they may be trained on technical equipment that simply cannot be matched outside the schools. Training which is closely related to work situations is very desirable; yet it is strange that although marked criticisms are often made of the 'deadwood' and inappropriate content of academic curricula, there is little realization that technical curricula may also be ossified and irrelevant. This argues not only for a careful examination of what the schools teach, but also for the provision of 'sandwich' courses in technical schools alternating with on-the-job experience. Such an approach narrows the gap between formal vocational instruction and actual work situations. Some African territories must be commended for initiating developments in this direction.

When all is said and done, however, vocational and technical training must be carried on mainly outside formal institutions. There is ample precedent for this in the West, whose early expansion was facilitated by a host of informal educational and training programs outside the schools. Some readers may rejoin that such alternative institutions as apprenticeship do not exist in Africa and that this necessarily throws the burden of training on the schools. This is not altogether true. For example, a considerable amount of road transport in West Africa is serviced and maintained not by highly trained operators but by 'bush mechanics' who themselves have very little formal instruction. Upon this basis has developed a burgeoning system of informal apprenticeship; though most of the instruction is extremely rudimentary, here is an expanding base which can be built upon. The provision of short courses and up-grading instruction for this sector of workers would provide an opportunity to develop on the basis of a going concern. The plain fact of the matter is that there are more opportunities for this kind of training than most of the large-scale planners are prepared to admit.

Second, there is opportunity to capitalize upon the labor needs of existing industrial and commercial firms. It is not infrequent to hear the schools criticized by some of the larger concerns for not producing the kind of people needed in their activities. Most of these complaints rest upon a totally unrealistic notion of what schools can do. What these complaints do show, rather, is the need for stimulating these employers to undertake their own training programs, since they have a clearer definition of their requirements. It is heartening to observe that some of the larger companies are moving in this direction. Such activities are clearly advantageous to both employer and government, and there is no reason why training of this type should not be aided through tax remissions or partial government subsidy. It is important for the governments of these areas to appreciate that the best kind of vocational education is that which is partially paid for by those who participate in the market for the skills to which the training is directed.

Furthermore, the direct role of government as the largest single employer of skilled labor cannot be ignored. In most areas the public service has been obliged to develop its own vocational training schemes connected with railways and harbors, roads, and a number of other activities. These training schemes are not directly part of the formal educational system, but they have the great advantage of being adjusted closely to the quantitative and qualitative requirements of employment. Interestingly enough, these programs are often not included in official enumerations of students undergoing vocational training. Such activities constitute another existing base upon which vocational training can be developed and expanded without complicating the task of already overloaded schools. The expansion of ongoing programs is likely to be more economical and the wastage of trainees is almost certainly likely to be less than it has been from vocational training schools which are part of the formal educational system.

Particular importance must be attached, in the context of the new African nations, to one group who are of immense strategic importance for the growth of local economies – the local small-scale entrepreneurs who are to be found in increasing numbers in trade, commerce, transport, and small-scale manufacturing. To a great extent these are the 'forgotten men' in development plans. Yet it may be suggested that the quickening in the rate of economic growth will be largely dependent upon their activities. However, the majority of these businessmen possess limited education and lack knowledge of elementary business procedures that would enable them to survive and expand their activities. There is no shortage of business acumen in many parts of Africa, but there is a deficient mastery of routine procedures of stock-taking, simple accounting, and management; many small-scale enterprises fail for lack of these skills. There is a good case to be made for providing instruction in simple business procedures to this class of person through the development of extension courses, both residential and nonresidential. This aspect of adult education is particularly valuable in the urban areas, and it has the advantage that there is no lack of direct incentive to acquire useful techniques on the part of businessmen themselves. In this context it should be noted that the provision of short courses for small-scale traders has met with some success in some parts of East

Africa, an area in which development is at a far lower level than in West Africa.

Finally, it should be noted that one of the major failures of colonialism was not an overall lack of development. The primary shortcoming lay in the fact that colonial personnel did not perceive that a large part of their activities should have been directed toward the training of African artisans and technicians as part of ongoing projects – that these should have been in part 'educational' projects. There was an understandable conflict between the need to complete particular developments as rapidly and economically as possible and a competing requirement to create a reservoir of trained individuals. It was assumed that the schools should undertake this latter function. As a result, the completion of individual enterprises produced too few Africans who had benefited from specific on-the-job training. It would seem desirable in the future that a large number of enterprises (public and private) have built into them some provision for training of middle-range personnel, often in association with alternate short courses in technical institutions. It must be admitted that this requirement may slacken the speed with which enterprises are completed and it may initially increase costs. But these disadvantages would seem to be outweighed by the possibility of creating an additional force of skilled and semiskilled workers; thereby the costs of future projects would be reduced and the potentials of both private and public enterprises for the future would be increased.

This policy would seem especially appropriate where large-scale projects are undertaken on contract by overseas companies or agencies; governments might well insist that provision for on-the-job training of Africans be made part of any contractual agreement with an overseas enterprise. It may be necessary to give additional financial inducements to such agencies in order to enlist their cooperation but it should be clear that it presents another chance to shift the responsibility for particular types of vocational training onto the shoulders of those particularly qualified to undertake it. It seems especially crucial here that such training have specific reference to maintenance and upkeep of newly developed physical capital; in the past, lack of specific training of this nature has frequently resulted in the rapid deterioration of plant and facilities because of a lack of adequate personnel with the 'know-how' that can be learned only in close association with ongoing projects.

In summary, these limited examples drawn from various fields of activity point to the possibility of inaugurating various types of vocational training without, at the same time, forcing vocational education into the formal school structure or providing massive developments in the forms of specific technical and vocational schools for full-time pupils. To be sure, such institutions must play a role in development but their number should be expanded carefully; they should be associated closely with actual developments in the economy through the provision of 'sandwich' and short courses, and their clientele should be largely individuals who are actually employed. So far as possible, the burdens of vocational training should be shifted to those groups who are actually demanding skilled labor of various types.

In this context, the role of the formal schools becomes clearer. At present, their most marked inadequacy at the lower and intermediate levels is that they perform relatively ineffectively the basic functions of general education upon which further vocational training can be given with profit. At present a number of vocational schemes are hamstrung by trainees' lack of basic skills in literacy, English, computation, and general background. If at present the schools perform these basic functions ineffectively, it is patently absurd to expect them to incorporate a range of auxiliary vocational activities – quite apart from the relative absence of staff either competent or willing to undertake such activities. Given more limited objectives the schools can make a significant contribution to development of technical competence by turning out pupils able to absorb and utilize effectively specific forms of vocational training. Lack of auxiliary vocational training does not support the argument that the schools should or can provide a good substitute; the main problem is to stimulate the growth of informal ancillaries without which no self-reinforcing economic growth is likely to emerge.

V. Problems of Agricultural Training and Development

Agriculture remains, however, the most crucial area for development; here also it seems that the most intractable problems of resistance to change exist. We have asserted that scientific training in agriculture by itself is unlikely to have any marked impact on agricultural output. Any attempt at vocational training in agriculture presupposes that a meaningful structure of incentive exists for the individual farmer to increase his output, improve his techniques, and expand his range of activities. Without such incentives and opportunities, agricultural education can have little impact. Instruction must go hand in hand with changes in those institutional factors that militate against innovation Clearly, an important area for investigation is the functional impact of traditional systems of land tenure in retarding development. It might be argued that the emergence of the concept of land as an individually owned resource, freed from traditional restrictions upon alienation and transfer, could do more than anything else to facilitate the emergence of progressive farming.

It must not be supposed that African farmers are uniformly apathetic to innovation and change when new opportunities present themselves. No one acquainted with the spread of cocoa farming in West Africa, largely the result of African initiative and enterprise, could assume that all traditional cultivators are inherently 'conservative'. Furthermore, in Ghana, in particular, there are encouraging signs of innovation: the development of commercial poultry farming, the production of foodstuffs for sale to the larger urban centers, and the gradual utilization of new techniques such as crop spraying in the cocoa areas.

Agricultural education of farmers must include not only instruction in new techniques but also information on new and profitable cash crops and potential local markets. Such agricultural education must be directed toward the farmer himself and not toward school pupils. No one acquainted with agricultural teaching in West African schools can fail to be impressed by the apathy of the students, which is matched only by that of the teacher. Indeed, the cynic can observe with some truth that the best way to ensure that students acquire a lifelong distaste for anything savoring of agricultural activity is to see that they are

419

obliged to have courses in agriculture during their school careers. So long as one of the primary motivations for entering school remains the desire to escape from traditional agriculture, no amount of exhortation to remain on the land and take up farming is likely to have any effect.

Returning to some of our opening remarks, we may now ask what effective role *can* formal educational institutions perform in agricultural change? In this paper their task has been conceived to be two-fold in nature. First, higher institutions, whether university departments or specialist agricultural institutes, can undertake significant research in the development of new agricultural techniques and new crops suited to particular environments. It has already been pointed out that the absence of suitable crops in some areas holds back agricultural growth; in such a region as the Accra Plain, for example, much experimental research is necessary before agriculture can become profitable. There is need also for veterinary and livestock research and investigation into the nature and extent of plant and animal diseases.

The second function of higher institutions lies in the effective dissemination of research findings. Here, indeed, the example of the American land-grant colleges can be utilized, although their primary contribution was not to train farmers.[24] These institutions failed their early founders in this respect; relatively few graduates became practicing farmers although many became agricultural specialists. But the land-grant colleges have made unique contributions in the field of research; they developed effective extension work in rural communities to disseminate information for farmers and their wives. This kind of activity needs to be expanded in Africa.

No doubt the objection will be raised that much of the agricultural extension work undertaken in Africa, particularly by the agricultural departments of governments, has not been very striking in its results. There is substance to this contention, indicating the need to examine carefully the content and nature of many existing techniques of extension work and to integrate instruction with other much needed change in order to promote conditions in which new techniques can be utilized. Thus there is

24. See Mary Jean Bowman, 'The Land Grant Colleges and Universities in human resource development', *Journal of Economic History*, vol. 22, (December 1962), pp. 523–46.

evidence from Kenya that such efforts are effective when accompanied by programs of land consolidation and land tenure change. In the last resort, extension work will be utilized where farmers perceive it to be to their advantage to change. Recent developments in both West and East Africa show that agriculturalists can effectively utilize new techniques of agricultural production when given meaningful incentives to do so. Even the emergence of a relatively small group of 'progressive' farmers can operate as a catalyst for the agricultural sector as a whole.

The lower schools, however, must be given a more limited role in these developments. Reciting rote formulas about new curricula which will not detach children from the rural environment is merely an excuse for lack of reflection. The schools will detach children from the rural environment largely irrespective of what they teach. Middle and especially secondary schools can produce individuals with a sound general education and some knowledge of science, some of whom can undertake further training to become either rural agricultural technicians advising farmers or research workers on agricultural problems. It is not likely that the schools will ever be able to do much more than this, but this could be quite a lot.

In the last resort, it must be confessed that we know very little about the factors that really promote large-scale agricultural development among peasant farmers in Africa. There is no doubt that agricultural education outside the schools is a necessary if not a sufficient factor in growth, but at present there is no simple formula for application. After thirty years of agricultural experiment and a vast technological revolution in agricultural methods, the Soviet Union is still faced with a chronic problem of raising agricultural output. It is therefore not likely that overnight growth will be achieved in Africa by the naïve application of new technology. The farmer himself remains the greatest unknown variable in the equations of large-scale agricultural planning.

VI. Educational Strategies for Development

Throughout the previous pages I have argued against total mobilization of the formal educational system in the direction of specific vocational training. Schools, in general, tend to be rather monolithic institutions not easily susceptible to manipulation; no amount of curriculum juggling is likely to produce the kinds of mass results anticipated by the proponents of technical, vocational, and agricultural education. I have advanced the thesis that a great deal of training must be developed outside the schools through the use of auxiliary institutions, with special vocational institutes being created in particular cases where their endeavors can be closely meshed with on-the-job training and with the actual manpower requirements indicated by the market for skills. Rather than massive reforms in the whole educational system I have suggested a multiplicity of small-scale experiments which may meet with some success and enable development to proceed from the roots of the economy. The alternative is to involve the schools in broad development schemes only to discover that results fall far short of objectives. Those who favor such broad schemes expect far too much from the schools, and certainly anticipate far more from them than has ever been possible in even the most economically advanced nations. Indeed, it may well be that future research will indicate that the most marked impact of education on economic development in these areas will come not from the vocational implications of formal education at all, but rather through the indirect effect that schooling has on consumption aspirations. Formal education of whatever type is likely to lead to personal dissatisfaction with current living standards and opportunities. If such dissatisfaction provides personal incentives and if at the same time institutionalized means exist to meet new aspirations, then the schools will have contributed indirectly to economic growth.

In this sense, formal schooling is valuable in terms of its 'detachment' effect from the traditional environment as well as in terms of the specific skills it inculcates. However, anthropologists have not been slow to point out that anomic phenomena may frequently be the consequence of levels of aspiration that cannot be met by the occupational structure. This is precisely the kind of risk that must be offset against the apparent advantages stemming from formal education.[25]

25. See M. G. Smith, 'Educational and Occupational Choice in Rural Jamaica', *Social and Economic Studies*, University College of the West Indies, Jamaica, vol. 9 (1960), pp. 353–4.

Some of the observations made here are not likely to commend themselves to those who automatically assume that overall massive economic planning into which the schools must be fitted is the *sine qua non* for African development.[26] There are, of course, multiple strategies that can be employed in economic development programs. These range from compulsion and forced labor to making existing opportunities more visible to individuals or manipulating salary differentials to stimulate variations in the supply of different types of labor. Such methods, whether effective or not, do not necessarily involve the direct mobilization of the schools in the planning process but rather influence them through indirect pressures.

'Thinking big' is, of course, sometimes an excuse for not thinking at all. Paradoxically enough, it is one of the legacies of 'capitalist' colonialism, where it was generally assumed that most economic advance was necessarily the result of governmental planning and centralized direction. The real problem is not the issue of planning *versus* non-planning. Rather, it is (1) to ascertain where government activity in the field of education can make a contribution and where it cannot; (2) to identify potential situations in which other agencies can with adequate inducements take over a large number of educational functions; and (3) above all, to indicate what are the comparative advantages and limitations of various types of educational programs, in the schools and outside of them, in economic growth.

26. It is not entirely unjust to suggest that the mediocre success of large-scale economic planning in Britain itself has led certain individuals to consider it worth while trying in far less developed areas. How this can be possible in regions which lack even the rudimentary data essential for large-scale decision making is not very clear.

Further Reading

General surveys of the subject

BENSON, C. S. (1961) *The economics of public education*, New York, Houghton Mifflin.
Deals only with American educational problems and teaches the economic concepts that are needed as it goes.

BOWMAN, M. J. (1966) 'The new economics of education', *International Journal of the Educational Sciences*, vol. 1, no. 1, pp. 29–46.

BOWMAN, M. J., DEBEAVAIS, M., KOMAROV, V. E., VAIZEY, J. (eds.), *Readings in the economics of education*, Paris, U.N.E.S.C.O., 1968.

CORREA, H. (1963) *The economics of human resources*, Amsterdam, North-Holland Publishing Co.
A suggestive but erratic book. Includes an early version of the so-called Correa–Tinbergen model.

HARRIS, S. (ed.) (1964), *Economic aspects of higher education*, Paris, O.E.C.D.
A pot-pourri of articles of varying quality.

MUSHKIN, S. (ed.) (1962) *Economics of higher education*, Washington, D.C., Government Printing Office.
A comprehensive collection of outstanding papers, including essays on the demand for higher education, the contribution of higher education to economic growth, and the costs and finance of higher education.

ROBINSON, E. A. G. and VAIZEY, J. (eds.) (1966) *The economics of education. International Economic Association Conference*, London, Macmillan, 1966; New York, St Martin's Press.
A collection of papers which, far from covering the field comprehensively, does succeed in conveying the flavour of the subject.

SCHULTZ, T. W. (1963) *The economic value of education*, Columbia University Press.
Stresses cost–benefit analysis of education. Includes a comprehensive bibliography.

VAIZEY, J. (1962) *The economics of education*, Faber and Faber.
A brief book with a wider canvass than any other. Rejects almost all recent work in the subject and seems to defeat its own purpose.

History of the economics of education

JOHNSON, E. A. J. (1964) 'The place of learning, science, vocational training, and "Art" in pre-Smithian economic thought', *Journal of Economic History*, vol. 24, no. 4, pp. 129–44.

KIKER, B. F. (1966) 'The historical roots of the concept of human capital', *Journal of Political Economy*, vol. 74, no. 5, pp. 481–500.

Further Reading

WEST, E. G. (1964) 'Private *versus* public education: A classical economic dispute', *Journal of Political Economy*, vol. 72, no. 5, pp. 465–75.

Measurement of the contribution of education to economic growth

BOWMAN, M. J. (1964) 'Schultz, Denison, and the contribution of "Eds" to national income growth', *Journal of Political Economy*, vol. 72, no. 5, pp. 450–64.

This fundamental paper examines the bridge between the production-function and the rate-of-return approaches to educational investment.

DENISON, E. F. (1962) *The sources of economic growth in the United States and the alternatives before us.* Committee for Economic Development, Supplementary Paper No. 13. New York, Committee for Economic Development, ch. 7, pp. 67–80.

The reader will find it useful to consult M. Abramovitz's review-article of this famous book in *American Economic Review*, vol. 52 (1962), no. 4, pp. 762–82.

MCCLELLAND, D. C. (1966) 'Does education accelerate economic growth?', *Economic Development and Cultural Change*, vol. 14, no. 3, pp. 257–78.

An important article that relates secondary school enrolments and the stock of educated adults to measures of electricity consumption in different countries around the world.

NELSON, R. R. (1964) 'Aggregate production functions and medium-range growth projections', *American Economic Review*, vol. 54, no. 4, pp. 575–606.

An outstanding critique of growth models based on aggregate production functions that allow for improvements in the quality of labour and capital.

VAIZEY, J. (ed.) (1964) *The residual factor and economic growth*, Paris, O.E.C.D.

Contains, among other important papers, a defence by Denison of his aggregate-production-function model of the American economy, and a discussion of the Correa–Tinbergen model of the relationship between the economy and the educational system.

Cost–benefit analysis

BECKER, G. S. (1964) *Human capital, A theoretical and empirical analysis, with special reference to education*, Princeton University Press.

Develops a general theory of human capital formation and applies it to such diverse phenomena as interpersonal, interracial and interregional differences in earnings in the United States, the shape of age-earnings profiles, and the rates of return on high school and college education in 1939 and 1949.

HANSEN, W. LEE (1965) ' "Shortages" and investment in health manpower', *The economics of medical care, Proceedings of a Conference, May 1962*, Ann Arbor, The University of Michigan, pp. 75–92.

Estimates rates of return to doctors and dentists in the U.S.A.

HANSEN, W. LEE (ed.) (1967) 'Symposium on the rate of return to investment in education', *Journal of Human Resources*, vol. 2, no. 3, pp. 291–374.

Rate-of-return calculations by T. W. Schultz, G. Hanoch, M. Blaug, A. M. Nalla Gounden and M. Carnoy for the U.S.A., the U.K., India and four Latin American countries.

MACHLUP, F. (1962) *The production and distribution of knowledge in the United States*, Princeton, N.J., Princeton University Press.

New estimates of the total costs of formal and all types of informal education in the U.S.A.

MILLER, H. P. (1960) 'Annual and lifetime income in relation to education: 1939–59', *American Economic Review*, vol. 50, no. 5, pp. 962–86.

MINCER, J. (1962) 'On the job training: Costs, returns and some implications', *Journal of Political Economy*, vol. 70, no. 5, part 2 (supplement), pp. 50–80.

Estimates the amounts of resources invested in on-the-job training and the rates of return on such investment in the U.S.A.

SCHULTZ, T. W. (1960) 'Capital formation by education', *Journal of Political Economy*, vol. 68, no. 5, pp. 571–83.

Estimates of human capital formation in the U.S.A. since 1900.

SOMERS, G. S. (1965) 'Retraining: An evaluation of gains and costs', *Employment policy and the labour market*, A. M. Ross (ed.), California University Press, pp. 271–98.

WALSH, J. R. (1935) 'Capital concept applied to man', *Quarterly Journal of Economics*, vol. 49, no. 1, pp. 255–85.

A pioneering article, still worth consulting.

WEISBROD, B. A. (1961) 'The valuation of human capital', *Journal of Political Economy*, vol. 69, no. 4, pp. 425–36.

An estimate of human capital in the U.S.A. in 1960.

WEISBROD, B. A. (1964) *External benefits of public education. An economic analysis*, Industrial Relations Section, Princeton University.

Deals with geographical spillovers among school districts in the U.S.A.

WEISBROD, B. A. (1965) 'Preventing high school dropouts', *Measuring benefits of government investment*, R. Dorfman (Ed.), Washington, D.C., The Brookings Institution, pp. 117–49.

WILKINSON, B. W. (1966) 'Present values of lifetime earnings for different occupations', *Journal of Political Economy*, vol. 74, no. 6, pp. 556–72.

Manpower-forecasting approach

BLANK, D. M., and STIGLER, G. J. (1957) *The demand and supply of scientific personnel*. New York, National Bureau of Economic Research.

Further Reading

An attempt to test the hypothesis of a shortage of scientific personnel in the United States.

BOWMAN, M. J. (1963) 'Educational shortage and excess', *Canadian Journal of Economics and Political Science*, vol. 29, no. 4, pp. 446–61.

BOMBACH, G. (1965) 'Manpower forecasting and educational policy', *Sociology of education*, vol. 38, no. 5, pp. 343–74.

A powerful defence of the manpower-forecasting approach to educational planning.

DEWITT, N. (1961) *Educational and professional employment in the U.S.S.R.*, National Science Foundation, Washington, D.C., Government Printing Office.

HARBISON, F., and MYERS, C. A. (1964) *Education, manpower and economic growth. Strategies of human resource development*, McGraw-Hill.

A book full of practical wisdom but based on a dubious theoretical framework.

HARBISON, F., and MYERS, C. A. (eds.) (1965) *Manpower and education. Country studies in economic development*, McGraw-Hill.

Essays on eleven developing countries whose educational plans are based on manpower forecasts.

HOLLISTER, R. G. (1966) *A technical evaluation of the first stage of the Mediterranean regional project*, Paris, O.E.C.D.

LAYARD, P. R. G., and SAIGAL, J. C. (1966) 'Educational and occupational characteristics of manpower: An international comparison', *British Journal of Industrial Relations*, vol. 4, no. 3, pp. 222–66.

O.E.C.D. (1963) *Employment forecasting. International seminar on forecasting techniques, Brussels, 4–7 June 1962. Final report*, Paris, O.E.C.D.

Influential papers by experts from various European countries.

PARNES, H. S. (1962) *Forecasting educational needs for social and economic development*, O.E.C.D.

This volume sets forth the rationale underlying O.E.C.D.'s Mediterranean Regional Project.

O.E.C.D., *Human resources and development in Argentina*, Paris, 1967.

PARNES, H. S. (ed.) (1964) *Planning education for economic and social development*, Paris, O.E.C.D.

A valuable collection of twenty-one lectures.

SINHA, M. R. (ed.) (1965) *The economics of manpower planning*, Bombay: Asian Studies Press.

All the seven essays in this volume are reprinted from the *International Labour Review*.

WOLFLE, D. (1954) *America's resources of specialized talent. A current appraisal and a look ahead*, The Report of the Commission on Human Resources and Advanced Training, New York, Harper and Bros.

A path-breaking book on manpower projections for specialized professional occupations.

Education and income distribution

BECKER, G. S., and CHISWICK, B. R. (1966) 'Education and the distribution of earnings', *American Economic Review*, vol. 56, no. 2, pp. 385–69.

MINCER, J. (1958) 'Investment in human capital and personal income distribution', *Journal of Political Economy*, vol. 66, no. 3, pp. 281–302.

MORGAN, J. N., DAVID, M. H., COHEN, W. J., and BRAZER, H. E. (1962) *Income and welfare in the U.S.A.*, McGraw-Hill.

An ambitious study of family-income determination in the United States, emphasizing the effect of formal education.

Issues in educational planning

ADAMS, D. (ed.) (1964) *Educational planning*, Syracuse University Press.

A valuable collection of papers.

BLAUG, M. (1967) 'Approaches to educational planning', *Economic Journal*, vol. 77, no. 306, pp. 262–87.

An attempt to combine the rate-of-return, manpower-forecasting, and social-demand approaches to educational planning.

HARRIS, S. E., DEITCH, K. M., and LEVENSOHN, A. (eds.) (1965) *Challenge and change in American education*, Berkeley, California, McCutchan Publishing Corp.

HARRIS, S. E., and LEVENSOHN, A. (eds.) (1965) *Education and public policy*, Berkeley, California, McCutchan Publishing Corp.

An uneven series of papers. Worth perusing.

Higher education. Report of the committee under the chairmanship of Lord Robbins 1961–63, H.M.S.O., 1963, Cmnd 2154.

Not only the basic report, but also the five statistical appendices and the seven volumes of oral and documentary evidence contain materials relevant to the economics of higher education.

LAUWERYS, J. A., BEREDAY, G. Z., and BLAUG, M. (eds.) (1967) *World Yearbook of Education 1967. Educational planning*, London, Evans Bros. and New York, Harcourt and Brace.

A collection of articles, dealing with educational planning in both the developed and underdeveloped world.

O.E.C.D. (1962) *Policy conference on economic growth and investment in education, Vol. II. Targets for education in Europe in 1970*, Paris, O.E.C.D.

O.E.C.D. (1966), *Organisational problems in planning educational development*, Paris, O.E.C.D.

O.E.C.D., *Methods and statistical needs for educational planning*, Paris 1967.

UNESCO (1964) *Economic and social aspects of educational planning*, Paris.

A valuable anthology covering all aspects of the subject.

Further Reading

Bibliographies

ALEXANDER-FRUTSCHI, M. C. (ed.) (1963) *Human resources and economic growth. An international annotated bibliography on the role of education and training in economic and social development*, Menlo Park, California, Stanford Research Institute.

BLAUG, M. (1966) *Economics of education: A selected annotated bibliography*, Pergamon Press.

DEITCH, K. M., and McLOONE, E. P. (1966) *The economics of American education: A bibliography, including selected major references for other nations*, Bloomington, Inc., Phi Delta Kappa.

WHEELER, A. (ed.) (1964) *Educational planning: a bibliography*, International Institute for Educational Planning.

Acknowledgements

Permission to reprint the papers published in this volume is acknowledged from the following sources:

Reading 1   T. W. Schultz and the American Economic Association

Reading 2   The Organization for Economic Co-operation and Development

Readings 3 and 4   Harry G. Shaffer, T. W. Schultz and the American Economic Association

Reading 5   Her Majesty's Stationery Office

Reading 6   Mary J. Bowman and the American Sociological Association

Reading 7   The University of Chicago Press and the *Journal of Political Economy*

Reading 8   The University of Chicago Press and the *Journal of Political Economy*

Reading 9   Columbia University Press, The University of Chicago Press and the *Journal of Political Economy*

Reading 10 The University of Chicago Press and the *Journal of Political Economy*

Reading 11 *The Manchester School* and Kraus Reprint Ltd

Readings 12 and 13 The Organization for Economic Co-operation and Development

Reading 14 C. A. Moser, P. R. G. Layard and the Royal Statistical Society

Reading 15 The *Quarterly Journal of Economics* and Harvard University Press

Reading 16 Evans Brothers Ltd

Reading 17 Evans Brothers Ltd

Reading 18 Basil Blackwell

Reading 19 Philip J. Foster and the Aldine Publishing Company

Author Index

Author Index

Subject Index

Subject Index

Penguin Modern Economics Readings

Economics of Education 2
Edited by M. Blaug

This second volume of Readings in *Economics of Education* concentrates on the implications of the cost of education. Part One explores the international comparisons approach to planning, with particular relevance to the needs of developing countries. Part Two stresses the growing importance of mathematical models in planning and includes the 1964 Tinbergen and Bos development of the Correa–Tinbergen–Bos model. Professor Blaug includes in Part Three, 'International Migration of Human Skills', the leading article by Grubel and Scott (1966) that 'put the cat among the pigeons and altered the entire nature of the debate on "brain drain"'. Part Four deals with the problem of measuring the output of educational systems and 'educational vouchers' – a contentious issue that, Professor Blaug concludes, 'virtually forces every reader to clarify his own values'.

Penguin Modern Economics Readings

Other titles available in the series:

Public Enterprise
Edited by R. Turvey

Public Finance
Edited by R. W. Houghton

Regional Analysis
Edited by L. Needleman

Transport
Edited by Denys Munby

Penguin Modern Economics Texts

A new series of short, original unit texts on various aspects of thought and research in important areas of economics. The series is under the general editorship of B. J. McCormick, Senior Lecturer in Economics, University of Sheffield.

Balance-of-Payments Policy
B. J. Cohen

The Control of the Money Supply
A. D. Bain

The Economics of Agriculture
David Metcalf

The Economics of the Common Market
D. Swann

Elements of Regional Economics
Harry W. Richardson

Industrial Concentration
M. A. Utton

The International Monetary System
Herbert G. Grubel

Nationalized Industries
Graham L. Reid and Kevin Allen

The Principles of Development Aid
E. K. Hawkins

The Theory of Taxation
Charles M. Allan

Trade and Specialization
Ronald Findlay

Wages
B. J. McCormick